AN AUGUST DERLETH READER

An August Derleth Reader

EDITED WITH AN INTRODUCTION BY
Jim Stephens

Prairie Classics No. 3

Prairie Oak Press
MADISON, WISCONSIN

First edition, first printing

Prairie Oak Press
2577 University Avenue
Madison, Wisconsin 53705

Typeset by KC Graphics, Inc., Madison, Wisconsin
Printed in the United States of America by BookCrafters, Chelsea, Michigan

Library of Congress Cataloging-in-Publication Data

Derleth, August William, 1909–1971
An August Derleth reader / edited with an introduction by Jim Stephens. — 1st ed.
p. cm.
Includes bibliographical references.
ISBN 1-879483-11-4 (pbk.) : $16.95
I. Stephens, Jim. II. Title.
PS3507.E69A6 1992
818'.5209—dc20
92-24433
CIP

CONTENTS

SAC PRAIRIE SAGA

WISCONSIN SAGA

POETRY

INTRODUCTION

"... cerise and magenta and old rose in the diminishing day ..."

The time is certainly ripe for the appearance of an August Derleth Reader. Today, more than twenty years after his passing, we are suddenly finding ourselves in the midst of a shattering American culture, a babble of valueless tongues. Derleth, within his homeplace of Sauk City, Wisconsin, was acutely aware of the knots our now thoroughly confused society was tying into itself. It is within the nature of his discipline as a regionalist thinker that he could see this.

Even though he was very much a man of his own time, this morel-gatherer and student of Thoreau, chronicler of the human drama within his own community, this often brilliant Americanist, saw through his work the dharma of tribal spirituality at the heart of our hemisphere, traditionally called Turtle Island, but more recently America.

What Derleth accomplished, as his contemporary Frank Waters is still doing in his own southwestern homeplace, was to gather a Wisconsin mythos which gave respect to the ancient fundament of our contemporary life. These two writers knew how to keep balance by remaining connected to the endless circle of life, and in this way know a future within the community of Earth.

What manner of man was this in the heartland of North America?

People close to Derleth tell this story, of the occurence several days after his passing in 1971, during the graveside services at St. Aloysius cemetery across the road from his home, Place of Hawks. That several moments into the ceremony, rolling thunder like drums began coming off the Baraboo Hills to the north and west. People began looking at each other and wondering if this was God talking, or Augie. And then three hawks appeared, just circling overhead.

Other people have their own tales of August Derleth, also in awe of his legend in Wisconsin. How he loved playing mind games with those he had just met and was attracted to, how a person gained his greatest respect if

Augie was bested in his little conundrum. How he could drive people to tears through his unyielding behavior during classes at Rhinelander School of the Arts. Or how Derleth would favor a protege in his first reading at Frei Gemeinde Hall by sitting directly in front of the podium, arms folded in major expectation across his barrel chest.

And for the man who loved best walking the byways of his own community, always with a good word for the people with whom he shared life, for he knew them all, all of these stories told with the same expansive relish, in memory of the man who came to be known as "The Dean of Wisconsin Writers."

August Derleth, born early in 1909 in Sauk City, the fourth generation of his people come from Germany. This robust kid grew up running the streets, backwoods and river sloughs of Sac Prairie. He was so close to the place, less than one-hundred years before, of one of the largest of the Native Sauk towns. Thus were the old embedded Earth-Spirits truly strong in his bearing.

Derleth wrote his first piece of fiction at the age of thirteen, while recovering from the mumps. Forty rejected stories and three years later, he sold his first, "Bat's Belfry," to *Weird Tales*. It was then he knew he could write, that he had it all down pat, that he could indeed, as he would later recount, "turn out the tripe."

After receiving his Bachelor of Arts degree from University of Wisconsin–Madison in 1930, he worked as associate editor for the Minneapolis-based Fawcett Publications' *Mystic Magazine*. The magazine was discontinued after four months of his work there and Derleth returned to Sauk City for good.

That summer of 1931, he collaborated with childhood friend Mark Schorer in writing one story a day in a shack they rented as both worked at the local canning factory. Many of these tales were collected years after as *Colonel Markesan and Less Pleasant People*.

The four novellas of *Place of Hawks* (which were the first entries of the Sac Prairie Saga) were published by Loring & Mussey in 1935.

Two years later, while beginning his long-standing relationship with famed Scribners' editor MaxwellPerkins, his first "serious" and extended novel, *Still is the Summer Night*, was published. (He would continue his prolific schedule over the next thirty or so years, while writing 750,000 to one million words a year. He did so, as he noted, out of sheer economic necessity. The hawk he was riding had been purchased at considerable mortgage to his being.)

The following year he was awarded a Guggenheim; sponsors were Sinclair Lewis, Edgar Lee Masters and Helen C. White. Years later, he would recall with some glee how he used his stipend in binding his world-class comic collection.

In 1939 he founded Arkham House with Donald Wandrei. Their idea, at the very beginning, was to publish the works of the legendary super-naturalist H.P. Lovecraft, since Derleth's teens his special correspondent. Arkham House continues to this day to be family-owned and the backbone of the hemisphere's industry in fantasy and gothic horror writing.

The same year Derleth began teaching his course in American Regional Literature at University of Wisconsin. This course, as so many other things connected with Derleth, was not for the weak of heart and constitution; he would startle students during the first class (making them rue the day they shelled out their $16) by handing out his tome of a reading list, and he would announce that he expected them to read each item on the list.

And in 1939 he purchased the ten-acre estate of famed botanist Edward Lueders. Here he was to build his homestead, Place of Hawks.

In 1941, he took up the position of Literary Editor at the Madison *Capital-Times*, beginning a sometimes stormy relationship which was to continue the rest of his life.

He married in 1953 his young sweetheart Sandra Winters. His two children, April Rose and Walden William, were born 1954 and 1956. Derleth and his wife divorced in 1959.

In 1960, he began editing the poetry magazine *Hawk and Whipporwill*, and he discontinued its publication four years later. In 1967, notwithstanding what he knew to be the precariousness of maintaining a journal devoted to literary interests, he instituted *The Arkham Collector*.

This he continued until his passing on July 4, 1971, after a several-year illness which had gradually taken his vigor. His life on earth had spanned 62 years, his literary output more than 150 book titles, comprising his Sac Prairie and Wisconsin Sagas, his journals, his poetry, his work in detective, science-fiction and super-natural modes, the juveniles as well as incidental work and anthologies. This in addition to his weekly newspaper columns, all work filtered through the sensibility of one man.

Certainly an extraordinarily single-minded feat, but how was all of this accomplished? Edward Wagenknecht, in *Cavalcade of the American Novel*, wrote that

> What Mr. Derleth has that is lacking . . . in modern novelists generally—is a country. He belongs. He writes of a land and a people that are bone of his bone and flesh of his flesh. In his fictional world, there is a unity much deeper and more fundamental than anything that can be conferred by an ideology. It is clear, too, that he did not get the best, and most fictionally useful, part of his background material from research in the library; like Scott, in his

> Border novels, he gives rather the impression of having drunk it in with his mother's milk.[1]

What Wagenknecht can not have realized is the earth-oriented aura surrounding so much of Wisconsin's literature. Here, there is placed the value in simply *being*. In this place where John Muir and Aldo Leopold had their first visions of good life, where Zona Gale and Lorine Niedecker remained, that is the mother's milk. For writers like Derleth, existing very much within a tradition in their home place, the Earth and her community *is* the idealogy.

This wholeness was present in the maturing Derleth. But he was also fortunate to assume a number of teachers whose words would encourage him to see within a wider stream than a narrowly provincial Wisconsin. Here is how he was supported by Lovecraft, that imaginator of monstrous retribution in our modern world:

> A man belongs where he has roots—where the landscape and milieu have some relation to his thoughts and feelings, by virtue of having formed them. A real civilization recognizes this fact—and the circumstance that America is beginning to forget it, does far more than does the mere matter of commonplace thought and bourgeois inhibitions to convince me that the general American fabric is becoming less and less a true civilization and more and more a vast, mechanical, and emotionally immature barbarism de luxe. . . . I cannot think of any individual as existing except as part of a pattern—and the pattern's most visible and tangible areas are of course the individual's immediate environment; the soil and culture-stream from which he springs, and the milieu of ideas, impressions, traditions, landscapes, and architecture, through which he must necessarily peer in order to reach the "outside."[2]

This is a truly radical perception, and seemingly all the more so from our vantage of sixty years later. But it reached Derleth because he was already imbued with it.

I don't know if his enthrallment with Thoreau started before or after, but in his discovery of the Concord holy man, he would have found our great prophet of a life centered within an ego-less self. What a value Thoreau has become to a global twentieth-century American life! By 1940, Derleth was thoroughly his student. This is what he wrote in "Rendezvous in a Landscape"[3], about learning to *be*:

> . . . listener, to hear
> what was in the wind, and in the wind, to hear
> and carry it express. . . .
> This is a silence to be accomplished
> . . . at a place where

he could root himself most firmly into earth
to rise at last into the upper air
of heaven in the same proportion, a rebirth
quietly desired. . . .

It is the path to the inner ocean, in the process to become "track-repairer of the planetary orbit."

In these words, I am close to the view already expressed by Evelyn Schroth, who has written the one extended Derleth study. It is a wonderfully insightful book.[4] His hero, she points out, is Moral Man. "Derleth," she writes, "in addition to being a champion of regionalism, a historian, an epic poet singing the beauties of the land, is also a prophet as he warns that man by destroying humanism and sentiment and human dignity may produce a world completely mechanized, the latter fate no better than the barbarian world from which we have sprung."

My thought is that Derleth, by the nature of the historical thread he recreates, often represents values which are called pagan in this Christian-centered world. While he is thoroughly grounded in a Christian Europeanism, Derleth is in the process of recognizing within his culture something else, something deeply earth-centered. He is a European-American, one of the "boat-people," struggling toward acceptance of a traditionalist ethic quite indigenous to Turtle Island. His protagonist is on the path to becoming, as the Anishnabeg say, *Ashke Biimadizhig*, one of the "New People."

Derleth and Frank Waters, as I've pointed out, assay very similar ways of looking at the world. Both writers recognize the mystic sensibility at work on this continent, its often sub rosa nature, that it can for the moment *seemingly* be overwhelmed. But if its nature is not followed, this neglect to do so becomes at great peril to the individual soul.

These two writers had, of course, very different life experiences. Waters was born of mixed-blood origin. He had the great fortune to have lived among the uncomprising Hopi, traditionally People of Peace. Waters, among his ramblings, has become heir to the great sciences of Time given expression in ancient Middle America. So there are often more insistently cerebral and immediately political qualities within his writing.

Derleth, on the other hand, lived within the chthonic temple which Wisconsin remains. He possessed a sensitivity for the energies welling up around him. He knew the power the Earthen structures carry in Wisconsin and realized how they work toward an actualization of the self. So do his works wear the pure dress of sensuous experientiality. Wisconsin's spirit is that of the cauldron, he is continually pointing out through his fictions and songs. By looking into her eyes, the person can turn one's life.

In his historical novels, there are always present the Native messengers to warn that the newcomer is not proceeding upon a fruitful path. This will often be a fictional bearer of the tidings, but in works such as *Bright Journey* and *Wind Over Wisconsin*, the teachers are the historic personages Red Bird of the Winnebago and Black Sparrow Hawk of the Sauk.

Here is that center resonating within *Bright Journey*:

> "But I starve," answered Red Bird in a voice terrible for its sudden strength and the imprisoned violence of it. All his fierce longing came tearing out of him now, and his voice made tangible the poignance of his imprisonment, the shutting away of this primitive child of the wilderness, whose kinship had always been to tree and bird, to flower and cloud, who knew the pungence of the massasauga and the voice of the wind in the trees, who read the message of turned blade and leaf, who knew the portents of the seasons in their majestic passage and responded to them, spoke to them in his spirit without word or sign beyond the intangible oneness of himself with nature.[5]

It is this thinking which remains traditional upon Turtle Island to recognize and carry the thought-forms of nature, to live with awareness, totally and holistically or perish. "It is not of the body," enjoins Red Bird, cut off from the sights and smells necessary to him. "It is my spirit that starves."

In *The Wind Leans West*, noble Chalfonte Pierneau discovers for himself the alive moral strength of the defeated Black Sparrow Hawk. Pierneau recognizes the true quality of enslavement: "But his land was vital, alive, final; nothing in his time could change it very much; the face of it was eternal, whether grass waved there in the wind, or grain. . . ."

This thought is part and parcel within the very wind, Derleth continually says to us. Of the Lakota holy man *Tasunke Witko*, Crazy Horse, Derleth perceives this vision:[6] "His the proud, fearless turning upon the centuries; his the turning alone. . . ." For Derleth did understand the true loneliness of life, the continual grieving which was necessary on the mystic path.

This was something of what attracted him within the great example of Henry David Thoreau. Be anchored within this New World, Derleth is insisting. Do not live desperately, in confusion, fear and greed. For the soul to live in dignity, *du musst dein leben andern*, as Rilke wrote, "you must change your life."

Of course, the polar opposite energy was illustrated within Derleth's horror fiction. He wrote a good many of these macabre pieces. At the center of their production were the stories which described the monster Cthulhu and his cosmic minions.

It was a pastime he played with a number of writers across the country. They were inspired by the work of H.P. Lovecraft, and the group included

Clark Ashton Smith, Robert Howard (best known for his Conan the Barbarian tales), J. Ramsey Campbell and others. Later, Stephen King would get his start writing these stories. It was a huge serious game for them, and Derleth described this mythology-building in an essay he wrote around 1948, "A Note on the Cthulhu Mythos."

> The deities of Lovecraft's Cthulhu Mythos consisted first of the Elder Gods, which, though beyond mundane morality, beyond "good" and "evil," were nevertheless proponents of order and thus represented the forces of enlightenment as against the forces of evil, represented by the Ancient Ones or the Great Old Ones, who rebelled against the Elder Gods, and were thrust—like Satan—into outer darkness. The Elder Gods (only one of whom, Nodens, Lord of the Great Abyss, is given a name) existed at or near Betelgueze in the constellation Orion, very rarely stirring forth to intervene in the incessant struggle between the powers of darkness, seeking to gain control, and the races of Earth. The Ancient ones, who make terrifying appearances in Lovecraft's tales, were led by the blind idiot god Azathoth—an "amorphous blight of nethermost confusion which blasphemes and bubbles at the center of all infinity"—and included Yog-Sothoth, sharer of Azathoth's dominion, a being not subject to the laws of time and space, but co-existent with all time and conterminous with all space. Nyarlathotep, the Messenger—Great Cthulhu, banished to hidden R'lyeh in the depths of the sea—Hastur the Unspeakable, exiled to the Hyades—Shub-Niggurath, "the black goat of the woods with a thousand young"—suggesting parallels to the elementals of air, earth, water, etc.[7]

The congregation is reminiscent of so much which occurs throughout world literature. The spectres resonate well in human consciousness.

As a mythological construction, it probably owes a lot to the envisioning of Madame Blavatsky as much as to occult legends in general. The Classic Greek descriptions of the overthrow of the first gods, the Titans, are present within the Mythos. But also present are so many other cultural imaginations, including those of the primal Americas. The stories recall universal machinations hidden deep in our subconscious, such as the Iroquois or Mayan legends of the Twins, who contain on the one hand the positive energies of Light, on the other hand the impositive energies of Darkness. The Twins themselves represent the binary forces inherent in human emotional chemistry, energies which lead to either growth or destruction.

But even more precisely, the stories can be related to the legends of actual events embedded deep in our human psyche. As in the grisly ritual described in "The Dweller in Darkness," they are actualizations mirroring the great cataclysms in our past. In the Lovecraftian stories are human recognitions, and, as such they are a pulp literature playing with our fear.

Within all of this, I am saying that for a full understanding of what Derleth was able to perceive from his place in Sauk City, it is necessary to keep in mind the total body of his work. August Derleth carried with him a vision of the world representing the complete circle of life and death. He just happened to "parcel out" the products of his imaging due to the demands of the literary marketplace of his time. This could be the reason his reputation continues to suffer today. Of course, the public misunderstanding of his work as it was represented by friends such as Sinclair Lewis probably did not help Derleth's cause much either. I would suggest that within the much-discussed 1945 Esquire piece "Sac of Fortune,"[8] Lewis was as confused by Augie's persona as much as he was with the ways Derleth constructed his Saga stories.

Lewis' feature was a belittling attack on Wallace Stegner, Derleth and James T. Farrell, three of the younger Midwestern writers of the period. Lewis focuses his sights on Derleth, in one of the most quotable of his descriptions, remarkable for its overweening cuteness. Derleth was a ". . . burly, bounding, bustling, self-confident, opinionated, and highly-sweatered young man."

Lewis goes on to criticize him for the unmolded character of his work, for the great volume of his claimed reading and writing, for the dull words, stamped by a machine. Lewis dislikes the high use of the regionalist's notebook in Derleth's work, for the long letters in French which occur in some of the novels. Lewis would like to see the appearance of more ordinary people as characters, less noble gentry.

I can understand how Derleth would have felt betrayed by this, coming from a writer he considered an ally. For it is journalism, meant to entertain and keep the upstart in his place, whatever the legitimacy of the criticism. There is a small value here, but what comes through for me is the lack of centeredness on Lewis' part, in his attempt to score points with Eastern literary interests.

For I think that it is more truthful to realize that Derleth's work carries the full sights, sounds and smells, visible and invisible, as they occur within his community of Sac Prairie and Wisconsin. He is presenting all that he sees to the reader within clear prose, constructed in a manner which is very circular.

In this way, he will often detour within a story line into the descriptions of flora and fauna. Or he will continually be describing cosmic and stellar events peculiar to the moment. In this way he is connecting the human drama occuring on the ground to the grand procession of non-human time as it plays itself out in the heavens. Within both these stylistic peculiarities, the relationship between Mother Earth and Father Sky is very much in his mind.

Even the non-human beings of Earth are represented in his work as influencing human behavior, and in his way they are characters in their own right. The hills will stand watch, the wind lean west.

Or, in the novella "Place of Hawks," Derleth introduces a hill which is part of the landscape near his home, carrying it into his fiction. I'm referring to the summit which stands so magnificiently west of Sauk City, called Lodde's Mill Bluff. It was here he placed the Pierneau mansion. In the story, Grandfather and Steve Grendon are driving up the hill to the towers and they go along the spiral road to the top. Thus Derleth is representing his attraction for the traditional High Place of legend; he gives to this hill the natural metaphor which carries the process of the cosmos.

Within all of these natural enclosures, Derleth is recreating the human drama as it occured around his awareness. And as he carries his many observations into his fictions, he is expanding our awareness of all the phenomena which can influence us.

It was in *The House Above Cuzco*, one of his later stories, that Derleth expressed the true attribute of his environment in Wisconsin. Here, the Derlethian character, then living in Peru, describes the province of his homeplace. He calls her Wilderness. As he does so, he expresses the awe which so many native Wisconsin people feel for the powerful energies in this land.

And in a reciprocal way in Wisconsin, the memory of Derleth still remains, twenty years after his passing. He was viewed as a figure somewhat larger than life during his tenure on Earth, and today this has turned into legend. His good friend Edna Meudt, who has herself since passed to the other world, wrote in 1971 of the literary partner she esteemed so greatly.

> *A Simple, Honorable Man*. This was the warp of him, the loom or frame composed of those natural virtues of prudence, justice, temperance, and fortitude. And behind the tapestry-mask of an exaggerated ego were his quick responses to the human drama, his intense loyalties and opinions, his generosity with self as well as with goods.[9]

Likewise Norbert Blei, who, in his ability to turn out volume after volume, still carries the Derleth spirit, as well as the community-based consciousness which Derleth worked so hard to keep alive. Blei travelled to Place of Hawks just before his friend's death, writing this account for Chicago Tribune:

> And there is an August Derleth, the man who was still at home here in the 70's, retreating to the source that always made more sense to him than men: the earth, the water, the air—mumbling a solitary hymn to the magic of

watercress, the silence of mushrooms, the language of birds; leaving giant footsteps alongside the brook, and then disappearing forever into the upper meadow.[10]

Except it should be known that August Derleth, old Augie, did not disappear. He is still here, the presence of his spirit open like bloodroot to those who proceed in quietude and in receptivity, within the land that was of his own. I hope you are able to find him for yourself, as he is, within the following pages.

* * * *

I would like to express appreciation to a number of people whose ideas and work made my editing of this reader possible. There are, first of all, a few appraisals which are valuable as one reads Derleth. A survey of his regional work which I've found very helpful was done by John Stark and appeared in the *1977 Wisconsin Blue Book.* That would still be available in every library in Wisconsin. Evelyn M. Schroth has written *The Derleth Saga* and this was published in 1979 by Quintain Press of Appleton, Wisconsin. Alison Wilson's *August Derleth: A Bibliography* appeared in 1983 from Scarecrow Press. Both of these are readily available in libraries or bookstores, or should be. *Remembering Derleth,* a collection of appreciations edited by Bill Dyke, can be obtained from The August Derleth Society, c/o 100 Jefferson Street, Sauk City, Wis. 53583. Through the years, the Society Newsletter edited by Richard Fawcett has published a number of critical appraisals which are notable, among them the continuing work by T.V. Olsen and John Stark. The newsletter is available from Fawcett at 61 Tecomwas Drive, Uncasville, Conn. 06382.

In addition, I wish to thank the following people, whose active support has made this Reader possible. They are: Rod Clark; April Derleth; Walden Derleth; Tim Hirsch; Mark Lefebvre; Harry Miller and the staff of the Archives Room, State Historical Society of Wisconsin; Jerry Minnich and Kristin Visser of Prairie Oak Press; Kay Price and the members of August Derleth Society; the staff of the Sauk City Public Library; James Turner, Editor of Arkham House; John Stark; George Vukelich; and Mildred Westburg, who with her husband, the late John Westburg, edited North American Mentor magazine and were so supportive of August Derleth's memory.

Jim Stephens
Taycoderah
June 6, 1992

1. Edward Wagenknecht, *Cavalcade of the AmericanNovel* (New York, 1952). Pages 435–6.
2. Derleth, *Walden West* (New York, 1961). Page 65. Reissued in 1992 by University of Wisconsin Press.
3. *Collected Poems 1937–1967* (New York, 1967). Pages 284–296.
4. Evelyn M. Schroth, *The Derleth Saga* (Appleton, Wis., 1979). Page 17.
5. Derleth, *Bright Journey*. (New York, 1940). Pages 215–6.
6. "American Portrait: 1877. *Collected Poems*. Pages 163–4.
7. *The Trail of Cthulhu* (Sauk City, 1962). Pages 245–248.
8. Lewis, "Sac of Fortune," *Esquire*, XLIV (Nov. 1945), Page 79.
9. In *Remembering Derleth* (Sauk City, 1988). Pages 54–56.
10. Norbert Blei, "August Derleth: Storyteller of SaukCity." *Chicago Tribune Magazine*, August 15, 1971.

ACKNOWLEDGEMENTS

The Wind (1929)

from *Place of Hawks*
(Loring & Mussey, 1935)
I, II (pp. 175-214)

from *Country Growth* (Scribner, 1940)
Holiday For Three (pp. 136-155)

from *Evening In Spring* (Scribner, 1941)
But Soft — The Morning Air (pp. 3-34)

from *Wisconsin In Their Bones*
(Duell, Sloan & Pierce, 1961)
The House of Moonlight (pp. 207-254)

from *Walden West*
(Duell, Sloan & Pierce, 1961)
Of Mornings...the musk of the Wisconsin (pp. 36-39)
The Harness Shop (pp. 39-44)
The Process of Renewal (pp. 53-56)
Frieda Schroeder, Thoreau and Emerson (pp. 56-59)
Sometimes of evenings (pp. 259-262)

from *Return to Walden West*
(Candlelight, 1970)
A Host of Sounds (pp. 128-9)
Every spring I went in search of morels (pp. 167-170)
The Breunig Hill (pp. 190-194)
A Post in the Country (pp. 222-227)

from *Wind Over Wisconsin* (Scribner, 1938)
(pp. 3-5, 9-16, 115-121, 131-134, 136-148, 152-167, 191-198, 275-278, 352-368, 391)

The House On The Mound (Duell, Sloan & Pierce, 1958)
from Leave To Ponder (pp. 93-99; 132-141)

The Hills Stand Watch
(Duell, Sloan & Pierce, 1960)
from Tranquility, Farewell (pp. 3-21)

The Wind Leans West (Candlelight, 1969)
from New Country (pp. 16-31)

from *Collected Poems* 1937-1967
(Candlelight, 1967)
Deer in Snow (pp. 10-11)
American Portrait: 1877 (pp. 187-189)
Man Track Here (p. 5)
Little Elegy: Herons at Dusk (pp. 17-18)
Elegy on a Flake of Snow (pp. 187-189)
Brush Fire (pp. 25-26)
The Solitary (p. 102)
The Hawk as Time (pp. 104-105)
Elegy: Autumn (pp. 107-108)
Rendezvous in a Landscape (pp. 284-296)
Sirius: Midnight (pp. 43-44)
On a Locomotive Heard in the Forest (p. 44)
Windy Trees and Evening Star (p. 56)
Old Turtle (pp. 60-61)
Eine Kleine Nachtmusik (pp. 77-78)
In the End Was His Beginning (pp. 301–302)
Morel Morning (p. 145)
A Little Elegy for my Father (pp. 246-247)
Apologia (pp. vii-viii)

from *The Moon Tenders*
(Duell, Sloan & Pierce, 1958)
Bogus Bluff (pp. 65–75)

from *The Beast in Holger's Woods*
(Crowell, 1968)
2–3 (pp. 18–50)

From *Something Near*
(Arkham House, 1944)
The Dweller in Darkness (pp. 232-274)

from *Dwellers in Darkness*
(Arkham House, 1976)
Fool Proof (pp. 196-203)
The Night Road (pp. 106-115)

from *Lonesome Places*
(Arkham House, 1962)
The Extra Child (pp. 130-139)
The Place in the Woods (pp. 140-151)

from *Still Small Voice*
(Appleton-Century, 1940)
The Early Years (pp. 3-21)

from *The Wisconsin: River of a Thousand Isles*
(Farrar & Rinehart, 1942)
Hungarian Count (pp. 117-126)

Sac Prairie Saga

The Wind

IT HAPPENED TWICE. Once when I came into Sauk City on a special train, and once when I went out. Both times it was night. I was sitting on the observation platform, looking southward over the marshes on the left bank of the Wisconsin River. The conductor was sitting behind me, and near him a brakeman. We passed into a clump of bushes and out again. Pussy willows, I thought, but I knew with a shade of regret that it was too late to see them out in little furry blossoms. As we came out, we turned slightly to cross the river.

"There he is again," said the conductor to the brakeman.

"Uh-huh," said the brakeman, and both of them lapsed into silence.

I strained my eyes and saw on the edge of the clump of bushes a hunched, inert black shadow. The train turned, and he was lost to my sight. It was curious that a man should sit here on the marsh alone under the starlit sky; I gathered that he had often been seen there. We crossed the bridge with a great clatter; both the conductor and the brakeman got up and went down front. Then we passed a solitary arc light. Beside it, the weather-beaten side of a house showed dimly. Then in the sky loomed the swinging tentacles of a scraper. That, too, flashed by, and now we passed the canning factory; they were working that night; and I looked up at the windows where I myself had laboured not so many years ago. The engineer blew his whistle twice shrilly, and there was a sudden chorus of yells and in a patch of light on the second floor I could see a hand waving. I waved back; I don't think anybody saw me. I remembered when I, too, had waved from that door. Then, unconsciously, I found myself thinking about that solitary figure on the marsh. I hoped the conductor would come out again, so that I could question him. But he did not come out.

We rumbled into the station, where a group of idlers stared curiously at me. I got off and hurried over to my car. Then, in a minute, I was crossing the river again, farther up this time, and swinging upward along the left

---

1929

bank. There was the house, dark and sombre, rearing itself upon the bluff looking at Sauk City across the water. In a moment now the lights were on, and I was home again, and I knew that if the editor of the weekly paper at Sauk City saw them he would write up his usual paragraph about my coming home, and would wind up with asking when I was coming home for good. And to that he would add for good measure a few words of praise for my book, without understanding what it was about, but saying nice things because he felt it was his duty to say them. Now I was in my library, searching for the book I had come to find. From there, it was but a step outside, and then I found myself on the south terrace, looking down over the marshes, where I knew that curious solitary to be sitting. I was half-minded to order out the car and go in search of him. There is a story there, I said to myself, and resolved that I would hunt it up. And all that night my fitful slumber was haunted by visions of that dark, solitary figure. Two nights later I went back to Chicago. He was there on the marsh again, and this time I asked the conductor.

"Oh! he's nuts," said the conductor, and nothing more.

"Oh!" I said, and wondered. I did not ask again.

I anticipated seeing the solitary figure again when I returned to Sauk City; I knew I should have to come in three weeks again. But it was sooner than that, and the return was more urgent, so that I had to go by air to Madison, and have the car meet me there. I lost the sight of him, but the chauffeur had found out his name—if I wished, I could now communicate with him. I felt rather awkward, and wondered what I should write to him.

But it was simpler than I had imagined. It was he who wrote me first. There was a letter that same evening. It was a bare two lines, scrawled in a scarcely legible hand; it asked permission to wander unmolested over the hills on my estate. It was signed "David Stone". I returned the note, and wrote on the back "Will you come and see me tomorrow?"

He came.

All day I waited for him, but it was not until that hour when people have supper in Sauk City that he came. I saw him first on the bridge, that same bridge on which I had spent so many night hours in my youth, and which was still warm from the heat of the sun that July day. I fixed my glasses on him, and saw him turn and regard the glow of the setting sun, and stare southward toward the marshes, and occasionally over toward the hill on which my house stood. I think it took him an hour to come from the bridge to me—it was only half a mile. Often he stopped on the rough path—he walked the path, not the paved road—and bent over a flower or a twig. Pick it, I thought; pick it if you like. But he picked nothing.

Then suddenly he was before me. My first impression was one of sombre black eyes and full red, cherry lips. His face was white and unnaturally coloured beneath the eyes. His hair, I noticed, was a wavy black. The rest of him I didn't seem to see at all.

"You wanted to see me?" he asked in a low soft voice.

I nodded. "If you are David Stone, I do."

"I am David Stone, yes. I wrote you and asked whether I could roam your woodland and hills."

"I know," I replied. "You may feel free to wander about my estate whenever you like. And at such times when I am home," I continued, "I should be glad to have you come in for lunch at any time."

He nodded as if he had not heard. But he had heard, despite the faraway look in his eyes, for he answered. "That is very kind of you, certainly. I want to thank you. But I eat very little."

I looked at him oddly. "You are not well?"

He smiled, and reminded me of someone I had known so long ago in those fast dimming days of my youth. He saddened me strangely.

"The doctor says I am sick, but he does not know what it is."

"And do you?" I asked.

"Oh! I know little of medical science. I do not feel unwell—but I dream often." He laughed softly. "The doctor says I have illusions."

What a strange boy, I thought. One would certainly not take him for twenty. But I knew that he was twenty—almost a year more.

"Shall we go inside?" I asked. "It's getting dark out here."

He followed me in silence into the library and stood waiting soundlessly until I bade him sit down. Then he sank into the chair so light that I marveled at his grace. His face seemed to glow in the half-light, and his eyes flamed.

"I saw you some weeks ago," I began suddenly, "down on the marsh at night. If I am not too curious, may I ask what you were doing?"

He stiffened perceptibly; I felt suddenly that I should not have asked him. But he was speaking. "I did not think you were like the others," he said in a cold voice, clipping his words shortly. "You ask, and if I should tell you—then you, too, will smile. Discreetly, perhaps, yes, but you will smile."

"My boy, when you have gone through as much as I have, you will have learned to smile at nothing," I answered. He smiled. "You judge me before you have heard."

He regarded me in silence for a moment. In the half-light of the library I saw that his eyebrows had a mephistophelian curve. Then suddenly he got up and turned out the light. There remained a patch of moonlight on the floor. He reseated himself; now his black hair was lost, but his white face looked over at me in the darkness.

"I was listening for the wind down there."

"Oh?" I said, "and you heard?"

He nodded—at least I believe that he did. "And all those sounds from outside."

I caught my breath. "Outside?" I repeated.

"Beyond," he said in a voice so low that I could scarcely hear. "Beyond us—far out in the sky, and in the earth. Wherever there is life."

"Oh."

He was silent. Then, after a moment, he spoke again. "You do not believe me. Will you come with me now, to let me show you?"

The boy startled me. "I will," I said, and stood up at once.

We trudged down the road away from Sauk City, and finally entered the marsh at a spot, parallel to the clump of willows where David made his seat. From there he led the way over the treacherous ground; more than once my foot slipped from the clods of ground into water. But how firmly David trod them!

There were thousands of fireflies, all about us, and directly ahead, from the low trees at the very edge of the river, came the weird cry of the whip-poorwills. Then suddenly we crossed the tracks, and in a moment, came to a dryer spot afforded by the willow bushes growing there. There we sat down. How eerie it was! Neither of us spoke after David's one brief caution—"Listen!"

The minutes passed. The marsh grew, and grew, and assumed gigantic proportions in the night. The fireflies and whippoorwills seemed myriad. In the distance dimly was the hum of motor cars. Then a sudden rumble to the south of us, and at last the night train went by.

Without somehow my being aware of it, the night sounds faded away, and I heard faintly, as if at a great distance, a curious flutelike singing. In front of me, David swayed slightly from side to side. There was music, certainly, and there came now a freshness, and a sense of spring, and of light winds blowing, and at the same time a great sweetness of growing things. I could feel it now, this wind, on my face, my hands. It seemed to grow here, and to die here. It bathed us in its freshness, and it brought with it faint and weirdly beautiful music. David was looking upward, far out into the sky. He was looking past the glow in the sky where Sauk City was; I looked, too, up at the stars, but I saw nothing. Yet always came that sweet distant music, and the wind, the spring wind that arose from nowhere and swept upon us through the night from the infinite. The willows were still and calm; no leaf stirred. The long marsh grass was quiet and smooth as far as I could see. But the wind was there.

I made the journey home in somewhat of a dream. I frankly cannot remember leaving the marsh, but I have a faint recollection of walking up the road. At the bridge I left David, but I asked him to write to me occasionally if he found time.

The next day I left Sauk City. In a week I sailed for Europe.

Almost a year to the day I came back from Europe. Again the car met me at Madison and drove me to Sauk City by the lower, longer road which led past the marshes. It was night, a warm summer night, and I felt certain that David would be at his old place on the marsh. I thought of him out there, and then, suddenly, without quite knowing why, I said "stop the car" into the speaking tube. I got out at the spot where David had struck into the marsh a year ago. I followed the path to where it was lost in the soggy land farther away from the road. Then I made my way more carefully, and at last, with many slips into the mire, I reached the clump of willows.

David was there.

"David," I said, and he turned.

"I knew you were coming—sometime."

It was a pleasure to hear that low, soft voice again.

"I got back only tonight," I answered. "Left the car on the road and sent it on ahead. How are you? And what are you doing?"

"Listening," he said, and his voice dropped. "Listening."

I said no more but dropped readily into an attitude of eager lassitude. And once more I heard the cries of the birds die away in the darkness after the train had gone by, and again I found myself listening intently to sweet music carried on the wind that passed and repassed without so much as bending a leaf of the willows above us. Whence did it come?—the wind with its sweet music of growing things. It led me across the bridge of years, and I thought of those early summer days when I had been alone and wandered so often over the hills. I remembered how often I had sought gray pussy willows, how many times I had found the first passion flower, and how only I knew where the small drowsy-scented white violets grew. And I thought of the bees singing in the apple blossoms in May, and of purple lilacs in full bloom, and of great white moonflowers like dead eyes in the moonlight. I saw myself watching the fireflies, glowing green in the night, and drinking deep of the smell of new mown hay. And I heard again the cry of the whip-poorwill as it had come to me in my youth—a faint, sad cry.

I looked over at David. How could he be so much of me? I felt as though he were a part of me—a part long dead. He was crooning softly now, as if he had forgotten me.

At last I reached out and touched him; how cold he was! I knew this marsh would in the end ruin his health, but I feared to tell him so, lest he should think suddenly less of me.

"It's very late, David. Don't you think we had better go?"

He turned shining eyes upon me. "Yes," he said. "I suppose we had better go."

We walked out over the marsh and up along the road toward the bridge. I left him there, and watched him recede into the distance. There was something strange about this boy—even more strange than when I first saw him. There was something about him, too, that did not seem strange—something closer to myself than I was. I could not know how spiritually alike to me he was, and yet, as I saw him vanishing in the darkness of Sauk City at the other end of the bridge, I felt a vague feeling of unutterable loss.

At home again, I set myself to the task of going through my mail, late as the hour already was. I read letter after letter, and at last scanned the Sauk City weekly paper, which the editor had neglected to forward to me in London.

I remember that I looked through papers as if I sought some specific thing. And then I found it. An obituary notice stared me in the face—"David Stone, 21, Died, 27, December." I felt that there must be some mistake, but I knew at the same moment that there was none. And the notice was certainly clear enough.

I remembered then what had seemed so strange about him that night—when he had gone under the arc light, he had left no shadow!

If the boy was dead, I could not have seen him on the marsh that night.

I certainly did see him on the marsh!

And, after all, the boy was dead!

from Place of Hawks

I

I STILL THINK of the deserted old Pierneau house as I have always thought of it since my first visit—the place of hawks. Hawks have nested year after year in the wall of ancient pines and oaks that almost hides the house, and sometimes, too, great bald eagles have been known to hide there.

The house is almost lost in the trees towering aloft from the flat top of Pierneau's Hill on the river's edge just southeast of Sac Prairie. For two centuries it has stood there, preceding by over ninety years the founding of Sac Prairie itself, a house alone, hard of access, one with the hawks. It has been forsaken only for the past decade, since the death of Letty Pierneau. Its chimneys are still red through the trees, but its roof is indistinguishable except on a very clear day, for it has taken the colour of the encroaching trees, so old it is. Age has yellowed and worn the stones of the house, and about its secluded self hangs the subdued softness of old things, no less subdued upthrust against the sky on this peak higher even than the remotest hills against the enclosing horizon, though the peak itself, fronting the prairie and the broad Wisconsin curving northward, is cold against the world, cold and fiercely alone, like the hawks.

I think of the Pierneaus as figures from a group of painted panels that came at long intervals to startled life, figures still and calm, to whom movement came, and many-faceted grace, yet endowed with a certain timelessness, perhaps deriving from the harsh reality of the malign fate which had marked them for destruction. The three who were in the house at first—Miss Julie and Miss Virginie, the old ladies, and their nephew, the idiot boy Sevyer—come a little clearer. They stand more to the foreground, and yet not too far from Noel, who came later, nor yet away from the shadowy long-lost Michel, and the parents of the three boys, Auguste Pierneau and his wife, Markanna, both long dead, one by an unknown murderer's hand, the other by her own. Letty Pierneau, who came last to live in the old house, stands in a mnemonic haze together with Will Ransom, the man of all work, old, too, like the sisters who employed him. And in the far background, too, hovered the veiled shadows of the old Baron, Pierre, and his wife, Madeline, parents of Auguste and his unmarried sisters, who lent an air of half-

---

Place of Hawks, 1934

truth to village legends of haunted rooms by their constant talk of those who had gone before.

My first visit to the house with my grandfather was an unpremeditated one, though the Pierneaus, like the Grells, the Farways, the Ortells, and a few others, were old patients who preferred to have my grandfather as family doctor despite his having given over active practise into my father's hands. My grandfather had picked me up after school one false spring day in February to take me for a short drive. The horse jogged southward out of the village and into the marshland, then turned east toward the river. Twice my grandfather halted the horse, once to point out flocks of winter birds feeding on the low cedar bushes on a little knoll, and again to indicate an early robin, whose burnt orange breast flashing against the grey-white of thin snow had caught his eye.

He had said something about the robin when, looking around him, he saw that we had passed beyond Harber's farm and had come to the foot of Pierneau's Hill. He had not been watching the progress of the horse particularly, and it was with some surprise that he said, more to himself than to me, "Why, here we are at Pierneau's!"

He looked up toward the shrouded peak, stroked his moustache thoughtfully for an interval, and then suddenly announced, "I think I'll pay them a little visit." Turning to me, he warned, "Be on your manners, and don't gawk of they bring Sevyer in. He's an imbecile, not extreme, but worse than Josef Grell, whom you remember."

With these words he turned the horse into the stony road that led in a long upward spiral against the side of the hill to the house of one of the few French families remaining in the region of the Wisconsin River valley at Sac Prairie. The road was heavily arboured by trees, whose low-hanging branches my grandfather had frequently to dodge, which, coupled with occasional patches of ice along the way, made going slow.

The house at first view had the appearance of an old tavern, with its low stone porch and its large, inviting door, which stood open against the somnolent sunlight on our arrival. It was quiet and mellow in the afternoon, and gave off an air of sombre peace. Though it was for the most part a one-story building of numerous small gables occupying a considerable portion of the hill-top, the eastern face of the house had a second story which seemed to have built itself gradually up and away from the lower gables. This second story faced the river, and was surmounted on one end by a small tower, half a story higher.

For several feet before the porch, large flat stones had been sunk into the ground, and a path of them led outward to the huge rock which served as a hitching post. My grandfather drew up before this hitching rock, and getting down from the buggy, tied the horse to one of the old-fashioned steel rings fastened into the stone. Then he led his casual way toward the house, indicating with a pleasant smile a few snowdrops lifting their white blossoms between the stones near the porch.

My grandfather caught hold of the knocker on the opened door and struck it several times against the iron square surmounting the wood of the centre panel. Immediately the sounds of movement came from within the house; feet tapped lightly somewhere, a door opened and closed, and a figure emerged into the hall which we were facing from the porch.

It was that of an old lady, dressed in a long white gown of an old-fashioned design, though at the moment it was partly concealed by an apron. She carried in one hand a feather-duster, which, with the apron, suggested that she had been cleaning. She was short in stature, though her white hair, piled high upon her head, lent her height. She had remarkably black eyes beneath long, curving eyebrows, which, at the moment of her approach, were raised inquiringly. Her high cheeks were flushed and smooth, contrasting the lines about her eyes and her small, slightly open mouth.

"Oh, it's Doctor Grendon," she said in a precise little voice as she came up.

"Yes," replied my grandfather. "I thought I'd drop in, Miss Julie. I was just taking my grandson for a drive, and the horse found his way here."

The old lady smiled and nodded at me, touching my hair lightly with the fingers of her free hand. "You're going to look like your grandpapa," she said. "Tell me how old you are."

I answered that I was fourteen.

She widened her eyes and smiled again, then transferred her attention to my grandfather, saying, "But I'm forgetting myself. You're coming in, surely?" Without waiting for a reply, she went on into the house, my grandfather and I following.

As she went down the hall she put out one arm and indicated that my grandfather and I should go into a room opening away from the dusk-filled corridor, while she continued toward one of the doors farther along. While we went into a spacious room which seemed to be a combination of sitting-room and library, she could be heard going through the house toward a stairway in the rear, and presently her voice sounded.

"O, Virginie Petite—voici Monsieur le docteur Grendon."

There was an indistinct answer from above, and in a few moments the old lady came back and entered the room where my grandfather and I were sitting. I had taken a seat near the window from which I could look down upon the river, which seemed to be almost directly below, despite the encircling trees, though the appearance of a sheer descent was false, for the bluff was cut away only for a short distance and then sloped into hillside. As the old lady entered the room, I turned my attention away from the river to her, and was surprised to see that instead of coming directly across the room, she veered suddenly away in the middle of the floor, described a small half-circle about an open place on the floor, and came on to a low, comfortable chair, obviously home-made many decades before, just between my grandfather and me.

"Ginny will be down in a few moments," she said to us. "She's up in the tower with Sevyer, watching the hawks; he likes to see them."

"There was no need to disturb her," protested my grandfather.

The old lady smiled. "Perhaps not," she said. "But Ginny wouldn't have liked it if I hadn't told her you were here and had let you go away without seeing her."

My grandfather made no direct replay, but, after a momentary silence, inquired, "How have you been? I haven't been up here for some weeks now, and I confess I never thought to use the telephone."

"We're well," said Miss Julie precisely. "But surely, Doctor Grendon, we don't have to get sick to bring you here?"

My grandfather smiled. "Am I being taken down?" he asked.

Miss Julie gave a little laugh and said, *"Ah, non!"*

At this moment footsteps sounded in the hall, and in the expectant silence that fell, Miss Virginie Pierneau entered the room, bowing and addressing my grandfather in rapid French, to which he replied in the same language, though the interchange was too rapid for me to understand what was being said, since my grandfather had begun teaching me French not very long before. She was slightly taller than her sister, and more youthful, for her hair was not quite so grey, and her face was more smooth. Yet not many years stood between them. Miss Virginie was dressed in an old-fashioned gown with puffed sleeves and a suggestion of a bustle; the gown was made of some dark material, and relieved only by a white brooch at her throat.

Miss Julie, catching her sister's eye, indicated me with a gracious smile and said, *"M. le docteur a amene son gran'fils, vois-tu."*

Miss Virginie looked at me, her eyes sweeping me from head to foot, smiled, and murmured something about my resemblance to my grandfather. Then she gave her attention with her sister's to him, leaving me to turn back to the river, which showed blue between the trees. The hawks, too, engaged my interest. Occasionally one of the handsome birds drifted down from the sky and was lost in the trees, and sometimes I could see a soaring hawk circle slowly and majestically for what seemed a long time high above, then suddenly drop away and vanish toward the river and the prairie below.

I had been watching the birds for some time when something that Miss Julie was saying caught my attention. I turned and listened.

"... There he lay, stretched out on the floor, his own knife through him—our Auguste, murdered!"

"Et le sang, Julie, comme c'etait sur le tapis," interjected Miss Virginie quickly.

Miss Julie nodded. "All over the carpet, all over—and we never knew, we'll never know." As she spoke, she gesticulated with one hand, marking the spot on the floor before her. Following the direction of her outflung arm, I saw that the indicated space on the floor was the same as that which she had so oddly circled when entering the room.

Despite the startling strangeness of her words, my grandfather only nodded impatiently, he having apparently already heard them previously. He turned to Virginie almost rudely and asked casually, "How is Sevyer? Julie tells me you've been with him in the tower watching the hawks."

Miss Virginie nodded uncertainly and, after a hesitant glance at her sister, replied, "He is as usual. He's particularly taken up with the birds, it seems. He watches them through Auguste's old glasses."

Miss Julie, yielding to my grandfather's very evident desire to change a subject which for some reason was distasteful to him, put in, "He seems to have identified himself with the birds, for the other day he came down to say that he was a hawk."

"Yes," interpolated Miss Virginie. "He said, 'I'm a hawk!' like that. It was very disturbing, Doctor."

My grandfather smiled. "I can imagine it was," he said. "However, such temporary delusions are natural enough, and, as you know by this time, always give way to others."

Miss Julie nodded, her gold earrings striking against her neck. Miss Virginie, who had been looking for a few moments at me, said suddenly, *"L'enfant se tait beaucoup."*

"Mais il entend bien clair," replied my grandfather at once, with a broad smile for me.

The two old ladies laughed delightedly. Seeing that he had amused them, my grandfather made an additional remark about my attentiveness to the conversation of others which caused a fresh outburst of laughter. The old ladies, delicately flushed with pleasure, were happy with child-like naivete.

But a sudden shrill grunting sound coming from somewhere at the rear of the house cut into the gaiety in the room, and instantly the sisters Pierneau stopped laughing. For a moment there was complete silence, the only sound being the broken grunting from beyond the room, now apparently moving closer.

Miss Julie, looking very grave, presently shot a questioning glance at my grandfather and with a slight nod in my direction, said, "It's Sevyer. He has come down from the tower."

My grandfather pursed his lips and half-smiled. For an instant I thought he would rise to go before Sevyer reached the room, but he relaxed his lips and said, "It's all right. Let him come."

Miss Virginie had risen to intercept Sevyer in the hall, but at my grandfather's words she sat down again, clasping and unclasping her hands nervously.

The three of them turned toward the door. The sound of shuffling footsteps came now, and presently the shrill grunting was supplanted by a thick voice saying something that sounded like, "Hawk, eagle, hawk, eagle, hawk, hawk, hawk . . ."

Then Sevyer Pierneau stood in the doorway, and a stunned silence, broken only by harsh cries of hawks beyond the house, descended upon the five of us. Sevyer was no longer a boy, as I had thought, having instinctively stood him up alongside the mnemonic image of Josef Grell at my grandfather's coupling of the two names, but a man either in his late twenties or early thirties. Yet his face was that of a boy's, so smooth it was, and the longish hair on his chin was as soft as down, apparent even from the distance of the width of the room. But what was most singular about him was the enormity of his head, which lolled absurdly to the left. It was startlingly abnormal and yet not horrible, for the deformity of it was considerably alleviated by Sevyer's large, black eyes, which looked from one to the other of us with a depth of melancholy almost inconceivable, and by his long flowing black hair, which hung in curls about his shoulders. Save for their deformed exaggeration, his features were not unlike those of his aunts, the family resemblance being marked in the high cheeks, the small mouth, and the long curving black eyebrows.

He was dressed in absurdly old-fashioned clothes which had evidently at one time belonged to someone of a much older generation. These clothes fitted him not badly, though it was obvious that they were by no means meant to be his best, for the ruffs at the wrists were frayed and torn and dust-stained. His hands were soft, and his fingers slim, like a woman's rather than a man's.

He stood there in silence, looking at each of us in turn, and finally he fixed his sad eyes on me. That he knew he had not seen me before was evident in the perplexed expression which crept over his face. After a few moments' scrutiny, he turned toward Miss Virginie, thrust forth a hand in my direction, and said in his guttural voice, "Boy?", the inflection of the word making it a question.

"This is Doctor Grendon's little grandson, Sevyer," said the old lady.

Whether he understood this or not, Sevyer did not indicate. The expression of perplexity gradually smoothed away from his face, and presently he turned to my grandfather, and with a broad smile of recognition, said, "Doc'r," slurring the word.

"Well, Sevyer," said my grandfather, nodding, "your Aunt Ginny tells me you've been watching the hawks. You like to see them?"

Sevyer nodded, the largeness of his head making this act grotesque. "I like 'um," he said, his voice taking on a quality of eagerness. "I'm a hawk. Fly."

A momentary gleam of alarm shot through my grandfather's eyes. "Not fly, Sevyer," he said gently. "You can't fly. You must be a hawk that stays below—not one that flies."

For an instant it seemed as if Sevyer had not understood my grandfather, but presently an expression of pleasure grew in his features. "Not fly," he repeated, and nodded vigorously to show that he understood. Then he grinned widely, stepped backward into the hall, and vanished, the sound of his retreating footsteps marking his passage back to the tower.

The two old ladies seemed to breathe relief at his going, yet their eyes were tender with regard for him. My grandfather, observing their concern and knowing that Sevyer was a delicate subject for them, turned the conversation into another channel.

"What do you hear from Noel?" he asked.

Both the old ladies seemed to come freshly alive at his question. Smiles took possession of their lips, and their eyes gleamed eagerly. They sat expectantly forward.

"Noel," breathed Miss Julie. "Doctor, I haven't told you—but we think Noel is coming home, to stay."

Though the attitude of the old ladies clearly indicated that they expected my grandfather to be pleased at this information, and though he manifested superficial pleasure, it was evident to me that he was anything but pleased.

"How did you learn?" he asked presently, having expressed a pleasure he obviously did not feel.

"To tell the truth," put in Miss Virginie, "we don't know for certain, but his last letter, about ten days ago, hinted that he might soon be with us—for good."

My grandfather winced unaccountably at her words, but recovered his composure at once, though not quickly enough to prevent Miss Julie from noticing. To keep her from giving voice to her surprise, he assumed as casual a voice as he could and asked, "You've had no further word from him, then?"

"None," replied Miss Virginie. "But we have come to expect him. It will be lovely to have him here. You remember, Doctor, Julie and I have never seen him—he wasn't brought back from France for his parents' burial, he was so young then."

"Of course, I remember," said my grandfather. Then he cleared his throat uneasily and said something that seemed very difficult for him to say, "But surely you know what he looks like? Surely he's sent you pictures, perhaps in this last letter?" He seemed anxious for them to answer in the affirmative.

Miss Julie put in, "Oh, yes, but most of them are in makeup, in the roles he takes at the opera, and he is always clothed so voluminously. His face, though, is clear."

My grandfather seemed relieved at Miss Julie's yes, but as she continued, his face clouded again. I was unable to account for the agitation which seemed to possess him. He made a hasty remark in French, intended to be quaintly humorous, but it did not come off very well. Then he fidgetted with his hat and advanced his cane along the floor, indicating his readiness to leave.

Miss Virginie, however, not noticing his agitation, said, "Now, if we only had some news of Michel, if only we knew that he still lived somewhere—then our happiness would be complete. We could look forward perhaps to another generation to take our place—and others beyond."

Miss Julie sighed happily. Then, suddenly seeing my grandfather's readiness to rise, she said, "But we're keeping you, Doctor, with our small talk. Come, let me go to the door with you."

My grandfather went through the act of pulling out his watch and saying, "Yes, it's getting late, and the boy's mother will be wondering about us if we don't be on our way."

Then he rose, and with Miss Julie walking at his side, one hand resting laxly on his sleeve, he pushed out of the room, through the hall, and on to the porch beyond. While I ran ahead to unhitch the horse, he stood speaking to Miss Julie in French. Then, briefly patting the old lady's hand, he clapped his hat on his head and came on out to the buggy.

It was indeed late when we arrived home, and my mother jocularly demanded an explanation from her place at the supper table. But her jesting attitude vanished as my grandfather took his place across from her and she saw the gravity of his expression.

He began to talk almost at once. "I took the boy for a ride," he said, "and we landed at Pierneau's."

"Oh, something happened," she guessed quickly.

"No, nothing happened," he replied, shaking his head.

"But something disturbed you, I can see," she persisted.

At that he nodded. "Yes," he admitted, "something did disturb me. It's Miss Julie and Miss Virginie. Apparently their nephew, Noel—the opera singer, you know—is to come home. So at least he has hinted to them."

"But surely there's nothing to worry about," protested my mother.

"Ah, well," continued my grandfather, leaning back from the table, "it is, though. You see, those two old ladies are living just for the hope that the family will live in future generations. The Pierneau family is one of the oldest in Wisconsin, certainly the oldest for miles and miles around Sac Prairie. Then, there's something for them in knowing that the family dates back many noble generations; the brother of the old ladies, Auguste, could have called himself Baron, as his father did. He didn't, however. But that's neither here nor there. It helps, though, to create an attitude.

"At the time of Auguste's strange murder thirty-two years ago, his sisters, after over a decade in Europe, were on their way home. The murder, and the suicide of his wife, Markanna, took place within a few hours of each other, in the year that Sevyer was born. At that time the older boys, Michel, then about twelve, and Noel, ten, were en route to Europe for study. The sisters, who had already arrived in Chicago at the time of the tragedy, returned at once to Wisconsin. It was manifestly impossible to call the children back for the funeral. They went on to Europe and began their studies there. Not long after, Michel disappeared from a cousin's place near Cambrai, and he has not been heard from since that time. Noel, however, has become the fairly famous singer he now is, but has never returned home. Thus it is that the sisters, though remembering Michel as a baby, have never set eyes on Noel."

"But then Noel's coming ought to be more a matter of rejoicing, I'd say," my mother put in.

"Yes, on the face of it, surely," said my grandfather with a harsh little laugh. "But there's more to it than that. Those two old ladies live in a world of phantoms more real to them than this village or the people of the surrounding countryside. They have their parents, Baron Pierre and his wife, Madeline, Auguste and Markanna, and they've got the romantic figures they've made out of the lost Michel and the unknown Noel. And there are others—Captain Marryatt, who, when he made his way down the Wisconsin, stopped at the house and copied a few lines from his diary describing the valley for them; Father Inama, who built the first church nearby; the Sac Indian Chieftain, Black Hawk, whom their father knew well; and others. Of course, the sisters themselves never knew these people; they brought them to life from the page of a manuscript, a crucifix, a few trinkets, but they're alive for the old ladies. That's their world.

"I don't like to think of what effect it will have on them to introduce into their world a figure so different from what they've imagined Noel to be."

"Oh, what do you mean?" asked my mother.

At that moment the telephone rang and my father, who had been listening with interest to the conversation, rose to answer it. My grandfather remained silent until my father returned.

"For you, Dad," said my father.

My grandfather rose and went to the telephone. "Hello," he said, and a moment later added, "Oh, Miss Julie—I recognized your voice." Then he listened for an interval, interjecting only a sudden, startled, "Oh!" and presently he concluded what was largely a one-sided conversation by saying, "Yes, I'll be glad to do that. If I'm somewhat late getting up there, don't worry. The train may be delayed."

He turned away from the instrument and came slowly and thoughtfully back to the table, where he faced his plate with a very grave expression on his face. "That was Miss Julie," he said suddenly. "They've just had a telegram from Noel. He arrives some time to-night. I'm to meet him."

For a moment there was silence at the table.

Then my grandfather turned to my mother and said, "Your question just before the telephone rang—what I meant. This. When I was in Europe seven years ago, I met Noel Pierneau in Vienna. He's a hunchback, and apparently a confirmed misogynist. The old ladies have only to see him to know that they can hope for no future generations from him."

A cry of dismay escaped my mother. "And they think of him as a strong, handsome man," she said. "I understand."

My grandfather nodded. Then, without touching food, he rose from the table and went into his office, closing the door behind him.

That night the whistle of the late train drawing out of the village woke me from sleep, and though I must have fallen almost instantly asleep again, it was a light sleep, from which I was awakened not long after by the sound of voices from the first story. Listening, I could determine that someone was standing in the hall, evidently waiting for my grandfather to return from one of the inner rooms, and was answering my grandfather's remarks from there.

". . . understand the situation," came in my grandfather's voice.

"Yes, Doctor," said a soft, clear voice in reply.

"Whatever happens, you must spare your aunts as much as possible. They've gone through a lot with Sevyer."

"I can believe that, yes."

At this moment my grandfather evidently came into the hall, for his voice came more clearly, and together the two of them went toward the front of the house.

"Finally," continued my grandfather after a momentary silence, "you must in no circumstances reveal your proof of Michel's death to them, or even hint at it."

Then the outer door opened, the replying words were whipped away by the wind, and the door closed.

II

My next visit to the Pierneau house took place some weeks later. It was the day of the spring equinox, and though it was very warm, a high wind was blowing. As in the case of the previous visit, my grandfather had not intended to call upon the Pierneaus, for he had seen them only a few days previously, but the wind, which he enjoyed keenly, led him up the hill toward the house, where it blew with the fury of a gale.

My grandfather did not immediately descend from the buggy upon his arrival at the hitching rock, but sat watching the hawks. High above the hill they hung, seven of them, flecked darkly against the fresh blue of the March sky. So still they hung, so slowly they spiralled, that it was as if they were suspended by invisible cords from the limitless blue itself, moving in accord with the movement of the earth, of the universe, strength in their height, and a matchless beauty in the grace of their slightly tilted wings. Peregrine falcons, my grandfather called them, though the farmers knew them only as chicken-hawks, raiders of the poultry yard.

Suddenly my grandfather caught sight of Miss Julie advancing from the house down the stone path, she having undoubtedly caught sight of us as he sat watching the birds. "Good afternoon," he called to her.

"I saw you from the hall," she said as she came on. "I'm glad to see you again."

She sounded wistful. She did not seem to be so gay as she had been on my previous visit, though this might have been due to the fact that she was now dressed in a sombre, yet handsome grey dress of some heavy material and wore a gold lorgnette on a long chain which was hooked to her dress just above the waist. She came down the path to the hitching rock, put one hand easily into my grandfather's, and the other taking mine, turned with us to the house.

"Tell me," said my grandfather as we walked with her, "has Noel told you of his illness?"

The old lady nodded wordlessly.

My grandfather smiled tightly, and presently said in a careless voice, "I like this wind to-day."

She gave no indication of having heard, but suddenly she said, "It's somewhat hard to think of him just coming home—to die. It sounds unreal to say it because we've waited so long. You know, Doctor, we had so hoped he'd bring a wife along, or if not a wife, perhaps at least a child." Her voice sank into silence.

"I know," said my grandfather gently.

As we reached the porch and mounted it, Miss Julie said, "Our hope now lies in Michel." She closed her eyes and allowed a faint smile to cross her lips.

Remembering what I had heard at home on the night of Noel's return, I looked quickly at my grandfather. He was regarding the old lady without moving a muscle of his face, which was fixed in a quizzical half-smile.

A lull in the wind occurred at that moment, and the sound of singing came to us from in the house: Miss Julie immediately flashed open her eyes, and turning to my grandfather, said, "Listen—isn't that beautiful? It's Noel." As she spoke, she advanced upon the door, threw it open, and led the way into the hall, halting just beyond the door to listen.

Again the voice sounded, the words dropping with bell-like clearness into the stillness within the house, the liquid and subdued notes of a piano falling gently into the background. From outside came the muffled roar of the wind, and once the shrill, piercing cry of a hawk sounded, but inside the song welled out and occupied the house, the notes enclosing the house in an almost supernatural bowl of sound. As the song went on, it became apparent that Noel was singing both parts of a duet, which was identified the following moment by a whisper from Miss Julie, *"Pelleas et Melisande,* the second act," at which my grandfather nodded to indicate that he had already recognized the song.

"He sings almost all the time," she went on. "It makes things different here."

"I'm sure it does," replied my grandfather, smiling.

But almost immediately Miss Julie's face clouded. "It will make it all the more difficult when he's gone," she added.

"Don't contemplate that," said my grandfather, tinging his voice with severity. "Wait until it happens."

Even as he spoke, the song from above was rudely broken by the sound of sudden, violent coughing. It was Noel. Miss Julie started forward, evidently to go to him, but my grandfather caught hold of her arm and restrained her.

"Wait," he said, "it will pass."

As my grandfather had predicted, the spell of coughing passed in a few moments, and presently the piano sounded again, though Noel did not immediately begin to sing.

Miss Julie now led us into the sitting-room, where as before she went around the unmarked place on the floor and took her seat between us. As we sat down, Miss Virginie appeared in the doorway. She, too, looked different from the first time I had seen her. She was wearing an apron over a dress of dark red, and in one hand she held a long-handled spoon which she had obviously been using in the kitchen.

"I heard your voice," she said, addressing herself to my grandfather, "and I thought I'd come in right away to ask whether you and the boy wouldn't stay for supper. We'll be serving quite soon. I think Noel would like to have you."

Miss Julie added her voice to her sister's, saying, "He isn't used to being so isolated, Doctor. Do stay."

My grandfather smiled at them and agreed to stay without hesitation. Since my mother would have to be notified, he said, "Ginny, take the boy to the telephone so that he can call his mother and let her know we're staying."

Miss Virginie beckoned to me. I rose and went toward her, unconsciously respecting the avoided place on the floor, an action which caused a curious restraint to fall upon my grandfather and the two old ladies. For a moment Miss Virginie hesitated in the doorway, looking across at her sister with an odd expression in her eyes. Then she moved slowly away down the hall.

The telephone was in the hall, midway between the sitting-room and a group of doors at the far end. It was attached to the wall next to a high-backed chair, which was evidently placed there to accommodate anyone using the instrument. Miss Virginie left me at the telephone and disappeared through one of the far doors.

After calling my mother and telling her of my grandfather's decision, I made my way back toward the sitting-room. Just before entering, I heard my grandfather saying somewhat impatiently, "Nothing supernatural about it, Miss Julie. The boy simply saw you doing it, and did it unconsciously. Perhaps he heard you, too, the other day."

Then there was a little sigh from the old lady.

I went into the room and this time deliberately went around the avoided place on the floor. My grandfather looked as if he might say something to me, but evidently thought better of it and did not.

Miss Julie somewhat nervously said, "If you'll excuse me, Doctor, I'll go out and help Ginny."

"Go ahead," said my grandfather. "We'll go up and visit with Noel."

"That will please him," said Miss Julie, smiling.

Then she rose, anticipating my grandfather, and accompanied him down the hall toward the doors at its end, where they parted, she going toward the kitchen, and he making his way with me at his heels into a shorter hallway which terminated in a rather steep staircase. Up this my grandfather went.

The stairs opened directly into a small box-like room, from which another spiral of stairs led upward. A door in the east wall led into a larger room, handsomely furnished, though in keeping with the atmosphere of age that enveloped the house. In one corner stood the piano whose notes still sounded, and at it sat Noel, who, hearing us as we advanced across the room, turned, rose, and came slowly toward us.

He was by no means an unhandsome man, and at first glance the deformity of his back was not noticeable, though whenever he turned slightly, the hump stuck out with ugly sharpness. His face, however, was clean-shaven and aquiline, with a sharp nose and clear eyes, though there were signs of ill health evident in his flushed cheeks and circled eyes. His hair was dark. He was clad in a black dressing-gown so long that it swept the floor behind him; it was obviously meant to be belted, but he had not tightened the belt, letting its end fall at his sides, so that his white silk shirt, open at the neck, could be seen to the waist.

"I'm glad to see you, Doctor Grendon," he said in a jerky voice, which I instantly recognized as the one I had heard on the night I had been awakened from sleep. "And this," he continued, not giving my grandfather an opportunity to speak, "is no doubt your grandson, of whom my aunts have spoken." He took my hand in his, which was soft and somewhat clammy, and shook it lightly.

My grandfather nodded. "Don't let us disturb you," he said. "Your aunts are getting supper, for which they have kindly invited us to stay, and we thought we'd come up and keep you company until they finished below."

Noel nodded jerkily. "I was singing the duet from the first scene of the second act of *Pelleas et Melisande.* I can sing both parts, you know."

"And very well, too," put in my grandfather.

Noel disregarded this, continuing, "It's an opera in which I've always wanted to act, but of course—of course, it has no part for me, the cloaking isn't quite adequate, not quite—I think I always made too good a villain."

My grandfather regarded him with poorly concealed compassion and with a faint twitching of the lips. "I understand," he said gently. Then, abruptly changing the subject, he said, "You've made this old room into something like a studio, I see."

"Yes, it lends itself well. There's a good view over the countryside, and it's quiet here when the wind does not blow, and when the hawks are not too loud. I've never seen so many hawks. It seems they nest all over, and apparently they've been here for ages. Julie and Virginie like them very much. Two days ago I saw an eagle, and watched it for a time. I think it's nesting in the tall pine at the far edge of the cemetery."

We had moved to one of the broad windows cut into the eastern wall as he spoke. When he mentioned the cemetery, I was considerably surprised, for I immediately assumed that he had reference to the village cemetery west of Sac Prairie, halfway between the village and Grell's mill. I looked with some perplexity at Noel, and saw that his gaze was fixed upon something beyond the window. He was looking to the southwest and, following the line of his eyes, I saw through the trees to the far side of the peak on which the house rested. The pine that Noel had mentioned was obviously the focus of his gaze. Then, dropping my eyes, I saw at its base patches of yellowed stones, and I realized that he had reference to the Pierneau family cemetery, of which my grandfather had once or twice spoken in my hearing.

At that moment Noel moved again away from the window, and as my grandfather turned also, I did likewise. Noel sat down near the piano, though my grandfather paused to leaf through some of Noel's music, which lay on both ends of the piano bench and stood upright on the instrument as well. Then he sat down on the piano bench facing Noel.

"Tell me how your aunts have recovered," he said slowly.

Noel made a nervous and irritable gesture with one hand. "They go on endlessly about Michel," he said. "It's difficult for me to keep from betraying myself. Time and again I've thought I ought to tell them."

My grandfather shook his head. "No, never do that. They've been keeping themselves alive for years on hope, and that's been taken away from them little by little. Leave them this bit—at least as long as it's possible."

An expression of dissatisfaction grew into Noel's face. After a momentary hesitation, he said, "I can't help feeling bitter at proving such a disappointment to them."

"Nonsense," said my grandfather sharply. "Don't look at it that way. Neither you nor your aunts can change things."

"No, I suppose not," said Noel softly. But he was insincere, and my grandfather frowned, recognizing his attitude. Yet my grandfather was also puzzled by it.

Leaning slightly forward, he fixed Noel with his eyes. He opened his lips to speak, but at that instant he was interrupted by a loud shout from above, followed immediately by a rush of footsteps across the floor of the tower and down the stairs beyond the room in which we sat.

Noel looked jerkily upward, his lips parted in alarm, and my grandfather made as if to rise to his feet, but did not.

Then Sevyer burst into the room and, seeing us, halted just within the door. "Hawk!" he shouted gleefully, teetering absurdly back and forth. "Hawk! Fly!" and extended his arms rigidly above his head to bring them swiftly down to his sides, raising and lowering them with increasing rapidity.

"No, Sevyer," said my grandfather sharply. "Not fly, remember. Not fly."

Sevyer fixed his melancholy eyes on my grandfather, and for a brief interval recognition showed in them. "Not fly," he repeated dully, an element of disbelief sounding in his voice.

"No," repeated my grandfather firmly, "not fly."

For a moment Sevyer's face was alternately vapid and baffling. Then he thrust his arms frenziedly upward again, shouting, "I'm a hawk. I fly. I fly!" and flapped his arms vigorously up and down, his grotesque head lolling jerkily about on his breast.

My grandfather draw a sharp breath of alarm, came to his feet and strode to Sevyer's side. He grasped one of the imbecile's arms firmly, then the other, holding the two tightly. "No, Sevyer," he said gently, "not fly. You can't fly."

The imbecile began to cry suddenly, and my grandfather released his arms. Sevyer knuckled his eyes. My grandfather waited until his crying spell had ceased, which it did as abruptly as it began, then repeated, "Not fly, Sevyer."

This time Sevyer only looked at my grandfather, saying nothing, he evidently feeling kindness in his words, yet being unable to embrace or accept his meaning. His eyes, still gleaming with tears, were inconceivably sad, and his mouth was outthrust and petulant. Finally he said, "Not fly," in a melancholy voice, nodded his head awkwardly, and, turning with a sharp cry, ran from the room.

My grandfather stood listening until he had assured himself that the imbecile was going down stairs and not back up into the tower. Then he turned to Noel, saying curtly, "I must confess I don't like the persistence of that fancy of his, and yet I suppose it's natural, in view of his daily sight of the birds."

Noel nodded. "Yes, Aunt Julie said something about it just the other day, but, of course, I didn't realize the delusion was a recent one. However, such delusions are common enough, aren't they? And they lack any real intensity."

My grandfather agreed with a curt inclination of his head. "But usually one gives place to another with some degree of speed," he supplemented.

Shrugging his shoulders, he concluded, "However, to-morrow it may be gone, and there are other things we could better talk about."

The two of them now launched into a discussion of opera stars and contemporary operas, and, since their conversation did not interest me, I went over to a low couch near one of the windows to the east and sat looking out.

The sun had set, and the afterglow reflected pink upon high banks of clouds in the eastern sky. In the northeast, two peaks of cumulus clouds reared white and beautiful boulders against the dying blue, and from above, dark purple strata moved down. The aspect of the sky, however, was impermanent, for the high wind which still rushed past Pierneau's Hill was not confined to Sac Prairie, but extended also to the clouds on the far horizon, with the result that for a considerable time there was a constant shifting of clouds within my range of vision, and during this interval I was taken up with constructing figures from the clouds driven so rapidly across the sky—horses, ships, heads, sometimes emerging with startling clarity. For a brief minute the sky appeared to be clearing, and in the southeast stars gleamed brightly forth.

Then, so rapidly that it seemed as if a cosmic hand had drawn them curtain-like across the heavens, clouds in a solid bank of grey and black descended from the zenith to the eastern horizon. The abrupt darkness that came into the room caused Noel to rise and light a lamp, which he placed on the piano. For a moment his face seemed to hang in space, a serenely beautiful face crowned by its dark curly hair; then the outlines of his shoulders and the deformity of his back were limned against the twilit background of a far corner.

I turned back to the window. Presently I saw that the wind, which had been blowing steadily from the south all day, had suddenly shifted to the southwest, and its velocity had increased instead of decreased, as was usual with winds at sundown.

During a lull in the conversation at this moment, my grandfather, too, noticed that the wind had shifted, and he came over to the window and bent to look out. Turning, he said over his shoulder to Noel, "The wind's shifted to the southwest. Likely we'll have a storm to-night." He looked again at the sky, and then he pulled out his watch and consulted it, an anxious line crossing his brow. As he turned back to Noel, he said, "If it weren't for disappointing your aunts, I'd drive back right now instead of waiting for supper."

Noel laughed. "And let a storm scare you out, Doctor?" he chided.

"Only because it's likely to be an exceptionally severe one," retorted my grandfather. "You forget, to-day's the spring equinox—and equinoctial storms are always pretty strong."

"Oh," said Noel. "Well, if you want to go, I'll explain to my aunts. They'll understand."

"But they'll still be disappointed," replied my grandfather. "No, we'll stay. But we must go immediately after supper."

The sound of the stair door below opening broke into the conversation, and Miss Julie's voice rose into the room. "Supper's ready—come on. Sevyer's down already, Noel."

Noel rose leisurely, bent and blew out the lamp. Coincidentally with the blackness that fell upon us, a flare of sheet lightning swept across the eastern sky and sent weird shadows dancing momentarily across the floor and walls of the room.

"It's coming," said my grandfather. "That wind'll hurry it along, I'm afraid."

We descended to the first story, where we were met by Miss Julie, who stood at the foot of the stairs holding aloft a lamp to light us down.

"There's a storm coming up," she said briefly over her shoulder as she turned to accompany us down the hall.

The dining-room was situated across and a little farther back down the hall from the sitting-room. Its size did not compare so favourably with that of the sitting-room, but it seemed somehow cosier, an impression fostered largely by the bright yellow wall paper, now subdued by the lamp-light, and the deep dark shadows mottling its surface. The room was sparsely furnished with old-fashioned but extremely homely things.

At a table almost in the centre of the room Sevyer was already seated, a large napkin tucked into his collar, knife and fork held upright in clenched hands resting upon the white cloth. He did not look up at our entrance, his eyes being fixed hungrily upon a browned chicken occupying the plate before which Miss Virginie sat down as we arrived at table. It was evidently her task to carve the chicken, for this she proceeded to do as the four of us took seats, Miss Julie and Noel on one side of the table, my grandfather and I on the other, so that I sat between my grandfather and Miss Virginie, with Noel directly across from me. There were candles on the table, but apparently this illumination did not serve, for hardly had she sat down before Miss Julie rose again and brought to the table the lamp she had been carrying and which she had put down on a sideboard against the north wall.

Noel said a prayer so short that it seemed but a breath between two crosses, and Miss Julie frowned disapprovingly, thought she made no protest. Sevyer began to eat immediately, which he did without the noisiness I had suspected I might hear; apparently his aunts had influenced him not in vain. A desultory conversation sprang up also, but it did not make progress, for my grandfather was obviously ill at ease, and glanced from time to time toward the windows, where, though the curtains had been almost fully drawn, the lightning flashed vividly, dimming the lights on the table. That the storm was approaching with great rapidity was evident, for thunder began to roll before the meal was at an end.

Sevyer provided a brief diversion when, upon pushing away from the table, he made his way to the windows, raised a curtain, and stood there looking out at the stormy sky. He seemed to take delight in the lightning flashes, crowing softly under his breath, and occasionally capering wildly about before the window, an action which drew immediate reprimands from his aunts. His enjoyment, however, was short-lived. Looking suddenly up into the sky with his face pressed to the window-pane, and pretending to notice a hawk hurrying to its nest, he pointed excitedly and shouted, "Hawk!" Then he wheeled and, with an expression of frenzied joy on his features, he flung up his arms, extending them tensely from his shoulders, and, casting behind him a grotesque and ominous shadow, wavered upon the wall by the lights at the table, he cried out, "Hawk! Fly! Fly! Fly!"

My grandfather was at his side almost instantly. He pulled down the curtain at once and drew Sevyer back to his chair at the table. "No, Sevyer, not fly," he said harshly.

Then he returned to his own seat, quieting the momentary alarm of the two old ladies with a gesture of his hands. He observed Sevyer for a few moments and then, seeing that the imbecile was quiet, glanced at the old ladies and asked, "Have you any sleeping powders in the house?"

For a moment they looked startled. Then Miss Julie answered, "I don't know. I don't think we have, but I'll see." However, she made no move to leave the table, regarding my grandfather instead with disturbed eyes.

"Yes," he said, nodding, "I want something for Sevyer. Don't be alarmed. The storm upsets him, and I don't like that in conjunction with this fixed idea of hawks occupying his mind. Minor violence may possibly result."

My grandfather looked vaguely annoyed, evidently regretting that his retirement from active practise save for his few old patients in and about Sac Prairie made it unnecessary for him to carry his bag with him on these casual visits. He gave voice to this thought in the next moment when he said, "I'm sorry I haven't got my bag with me. I used to carry sedatives all the time, but of course now that I'm no longer very busy, I don't carry anything at all unless I'm called out. I'm afraid I'm getting too much out of harness."

"Well, perhaps we have something here," said Noel calmly. "I think, too, that a sedative might help Sevyer."

His calm attitude seemed to relieve the tension between the two old ladies, and Miss Julie rose and put her napkin next to her plate. With a hurried, nervous glance at Sevyer, she said, "Very well, I'll see," and left the room.

At the same moment a terrific detonation sounded from outside, and a wall of sound advanced across the valley, the steadiness of its oncoming apparent in the stillness of the room. Immediately after, torrential rain thundered on the roof above our heads. The full furry of the storm had reached the hill.

My grandfather listened for a moment in nervous silence; then he rose and moved over to the windows, where he lifted a curtain slightly and looked out. Noel and Miss Virginie followed him with questioning eyes, and Sevyer watched eagerly for the lightning to flash.

My grandfather turned back toward the table just as Miss Julie re-entered the room.

"I'm afraid there's nothing, Doctor," she said, an apprehensive expression on her face.

My grandfather shrugged as if to dismiss the matter. "Then we'll do without it," he said. "But if the storm keeps up all night, as I think it will, he's apt to become more excited. However, we'll see."

Sevyer apparently neither heard nor understood my grandfather, for he kept his eyes fixed upon the curtains, from behind which the lightning still flashed and played over the window-jambs where the curtains did not fit tightly.

Miss Julie resumed her seat at the table as my grandfather did likewise. For a moment all eyes were fixed on Sevyer, but since his attitude did not indicate anything of an alarming nature, conversation was presently taken up again, my grandfather leading off by saying, "I'm afraid the boy and I will have to impose on you to-night by staying here until morning. That wall of rain will make the road down the hill just about impassable, and I don't want to undertake it in the dark. If I were alone, I wouldn't mind particularly, but I don't like to jeopardize the boy."

Both the old ladies responded at once. "There's plenty of room, and we'll be glad to have you." Miss Julie said, while her sister said, "Of course you'll stay."

"Good," said my grandfather. "I imagine the boy's mother will expect us to stay, but I'll have to call her presently and explain."

Silence fell again, during which Miss Julie again manifested some uneasiness on Sevyer's account. This she attempted to cover by saying suddenly to my grandfather, "I'm particularly glad you're staying, because of Sevyer."

My grandfather smiled but did not reply.

Noel, who had maintained silence for a considerable time, abruptly changed the subject. "If I'm not mistaken," he murmured, "it will be thirty-three years ago next week that my father was murdered and my mother killed herself."

My grandfather nodded. "That's right," he said. "I suppose your aunts have told you as much as they know about it."

"I think so, yes," replied Noel, turning to the old ladies with a wan smile.

Noel's words had dropped silence upon the old ladies, and for a few moments their faces were masked. Then presently their features seemed to soften, to set in a gentler mould, and their eyes fixed in space as if upon some far object, and it was evident that they were going back into the past.

"Yes, thirty-three years," said Miss Julie reminiscently. "And of all of us, only Sevyer and you, Doctor, were here then. If I remember it rightly, it was Judge Holm who was in charge—at least it was he who sent the telegram that got to us in Chicago. Just as we were boarding the train, it was. We got there so soon that Auguste still lay where they found him."

My grandfather, too, returned in memory to the year of the tragedy. As Miss Julie paused, he nodded, saying, "Yes, Judge Holm was in charge. I saw him only two weeks ago in Portage, and he happened to mention the case. No doubt he could tell more about it than anyone else."

Noel fingered the stem of a tall wine glass thoughtfully. "It has always seemed odd to me that no clue—nothing—was ever discovered about either my father's murder or my mother's suicide," he said.

My grandfather shrugged. "The case was not given up until every possible inquiry had been looked into," he replied. "I remember very well that Judge Holm pressed the sheriff on several times when he wished to file the case as unsolved."

"It was Auguste's lawyer who met us at the train that night," Miss Julie continued. "Such a stern man. I've forgotten his name, but I remember he wanted to keep us out of Auguste's library. He failed—I've often wished he hadn't. I can't go into that room but what I see Auguste there, how he lay, so stretched out and fallen together, and the blood all over the carpet."

She paused, and in the silence that fell, Miss Virginie said in a soft voice, "The window to the left was open and a wind was blowing the curtains. Do you remember, Julie?"

Miss Julie nodded. "Yes, I remember. The wind was damp, too. It had rained not long before. Everything is so clear, everything just as it was in that room."

"And in the next room they had put Markanna, all wet from the river," continued Miss Virginie, sitting with clasped hands and veiled eyes, "with her hair undone and spread out on the floor around her head."

"Why did it happen?" asked Noel suddenly. "Why was he killed? Why did mother kill herself?"

"There was no reason," said Miss Julie.

"None at all that we could find," added Miss Virginie. "We have thought about it so often that nothing can help us to understand any more."

My grandfather coughed suddenly and changed the subject. I had noticed him growing uneasy during the conversation, and had seen what seemed to be an air of knowing more than he wished to say. He was somewhat worried, too, his worry showing in the lines of his mouth.

All of them at the table welcomed the change of subject, and after a quarter of an hour of more casual conversation, the old ladies began to clear the table, with my grandfather and Noel helping to carry the dishes from the room. After the table had been cleared, my grandfather went to the telephone and called my mother to explain to her that we were staying the night at Pierneaus'. It was still raining steadily, a tremendous volume of water dropping on the prairie and its enclosing hills.

Not long after, Miss Julie at my grandfather's request showed me to a bedroom on the lower floor, between the dining-room and the kitchen, which my grandfather and I were to occupy. My grandfather did not come immediately to bed, and though I lay awake long enough to hear the old ladies retire from the sitting-room, Sevyer having been sent to bed shortly after I had gone, I did not hear him come in. Sevyer's room was just across the hall from that in which we were to sleep, while Miss Julie and Miss Virginie occupied a large room between Sevyer's and the rear hall from which the stairway to the second floor led upward. Noel apparently slept in his studio.

My grandfather and Noel remained in the sitting-room for some time after the old ladies had retired, and the sound of their low voices reached me in the bedroom, though their words were indistinguishable. Presently, however, despite my attempts to await my grandfather, I fell asleep to the sound of a gentler rain pattering on the curtained windows and the distant roll of thunder along the rim of the prairie.

I was awakened some hours later by the restless tossing of my grandfather and by the sound of broken whispering. For a moment I could not understand from where the whispering came, but presently I found that my grandfather was talking in his sleep. Fully awake, I rose on one elbow and listened.

". . . but Markanna? What reason? . . . No, Judge, it must not get out. Mark it unsolved before breathing a word of it. . . . Good God, Markanna! I still can't believe it. . . . Yes, yes, I saw the cut on her hand. I didn't think of it. . . . Yes, I see now that it was a knife. I thought of a rock in the river.

. . . Careless, yes. But Judge, I knew the two of them. It's a mad puzzle, a ghastly dream. I can't believe . . ."

His voice droned away into vague murmurings, and after several short uneasy exclamations, he became silent. His words had brought me far from sleep, and I sat up in bed, being careful not to disturb him. Presently I slipped out of bed and went to the window, where for a few minutes I stood watching the storm, which had subsided considerably, its "tail end," as my mother would have said, passing over with occasional flashes of lightning and distant rumblings of thunder. Rain fell in a fine drizzle, and through the slightly opened window came a rich odour of spring mist rising from the soaked ground.

Just as I turned away from the window, the sound of a door creaking open somewhere in the house reached my ears. Curiously, I went over, and, opening the door of our room, looked into the hall. My glance fell upon Sevyer Pierneau, who stood in the hall just beyond his door, a candle held in one hand, the other shielding the flame, so that a weird and frightening shadow danced grotesquely on the wall.

He observed the open door at once and fixed his melancholy eyes on me. For an interval I was afraid lest he should advance across the hall, but he only stood and looked at me, his head on one side, his features, except for the occasional slow blinking of his eyelids, motionless. He stood like a figure fixed to the floor until I moved to close the door and retreat into the room. Then he bent his head slightly forward and in a low, harsh whisper said, "Hawk. Fly." Then he smiled rapturously, and I withdrew.

I stood for a moment against the door, listening for any sound from the hall, but since none came to my ears, I assumed that Sevyer had retired again, and presently I went back to bed. In a semi-conscious haze of sleep I heard a window slide up from the upper floor where Noel slept, and for a moment the house seemed to hold its breath; then I fell asleep again.

When I awoke in the morning a babble of words greeted my ears. The bed at my side was empty, and my grandfather's clothes were gone. For a few moments I lay listening in growing amazement, for voices other than those of the Pierneaus and my grandfather came to my ears.

Suddenly among the garble of voices I heard someone say, "Please, I want to know who saw him last, and when."

There was a confused silence, ended in a moment by Miss Julie, who said, "I did—when he went to bed. It was about nine o'clock last night." Then her voice seemed to crack and she lapsed into French, *"Ah, mon dieu, mon dieu, pourquoi est-ce que personne ne l'a garde?"*

My grandfather made himself heard at this point, his voice gentle and soothing, yet firm. "The fault isn't yours," he said. "If anyone is at fault, I am. Come, Miss Julie, please be calm."

There was a moment of silence, after which my grandfather, apparently addressing someone else, said, "This delusion of being a hawk had been growing for some time. The storm last night heightened it. I noticed it at supper, and regretted my inability to do something then to quiet him."

Miss Virginie, like her sister upset, as I could tell be the hysteria in her voice, interrupted my grandfather to say, *"C'est possible qu'une potion calmante l'ait sauve."*

"Non, non," said my grandfather with a touch of impatience. "Likely it would only have prevented it for a short time—no more."

Noel's voice sounded clearly, cutting into my grandfather's impatience. *"Le ciel l'a predit, tante Virginie."*

Apprehensively I dressed myself, the excited conversation beyond the room continuing during the few moments it took for me to get into my clothes. Then I opened the door and stepped outside. Beside my grandfather, the old ladies, and Noel, there were in the hall two men, one of whom I recognized immediately as Sac Prairie's undertaker; the other, I later learned, was the county coroner, who had been visiting in Sac Prairie, and like my grandfather and me, had been prevented by the storm from returning home.

Miss Julie, whose eyes I saw were red with weeping, as were Virginie's also, saw me at once, and with a quick exclamation turned to my grandfather and gripped his arm in her long, slender fingers. *"O, voila l'enfant!"* she exclaimed warningly.

The others turned to look at me, and my grandfather stepped forward and took my arm, saying, "He must be taken home immediately." Addressing the coroner, he said, "You go on with it, Hawley. I'll be back as soon as I can."

With that, he strode from the house into the bright sunshine of the morning, doubly alight with the gleaming drops of water which still clung to every twig and stone. His haste was such that his grip on my arm almost pulled me from my feet. He did not pause, but went immediately around the large Pierneau house to the stables in the rear, once or twice looking grimly down the short steep incline walled off from the flagstone path along which we had to walk to reach the stables.

Will Ransom, a heavy-set man beyond middle age, chiefly characterized by a pair of spectacles evidently several sizes too large for him, so that they were constantly perched on the end of his somewhat thick nose, met us at the stables. He helped my grandfather get the horse and buggy ready for the homeward trip, once or twice pausing in his work to shake his head, look at my grandfather lugubriously over his spectacles, and murmur, "Turrible, turrible thing, Doctor. Turrible thing t' happen." To these remarks my grandfather made no reply. Indeed, during all the time that it took him to help make ready the horse and buggy, my grandfather said nothing, nor did he enlighten me on the way home regarding the events which had brought the undertaker and the coroner to the house that morning.

Not until evening did I learn that in the night Sevyer Pierneau, following to its logical end his delusion of being a hawk, had attempted to fly from the lone window of the tower, and had fallen to his death on the rocks at the river's edge.

Holiday for Three

I DIDN'T WANT the bicycle in the first place, but mother was bound I should have one, especially since all the other boys had bicycles; so they got it for me and that summer I had my mind all fixed to go somewhere. I said I was going for a long trip through Wisconsin on that bicycle, and if anybody tried to stop me it would be just too bad, I'd run away, and what would they do about that?

Mother said, "You can't go alone, and that's all there is to it."

I said I could take Sim Jones. Sim had a bicycle and was a better rider than I. He never fell off. I fell off first one side and then the other and the only time I really stayed on the way I should was when I was going like the dickens, and then Mother said it was dangerous and reckless and did I want to break my neck? Father said, "That's right."

"Simoleon Jones!" exclaimed my mother. "He's younger than you are. And no more responsible, either. No."

I said maybe I could take Paul, but he always went so fast, and Carly didn't have a bicycle and then there was Fidel, but you could never depend

Country Growth, 1940

on him, one day he might be there and the next day he might be in the lock-up for stealing something, with his restless hands.

"No," she said. "If your father weren't so busy, he might go with you himself."

"Pa!" I hollered. "I don't see why I can't take me another kid along. Anyway, Pa wouldn't want to go."

"Your father is a man of parts," my mother said.

"You talk like Great-uncle Joe," I said. "Parts."

Mother looked at me and put her head a little to one side and stroked her cheek with her fingertips. She looked thoughtful. She walked over to the window and stood there in the July sunlight with her eyes on the hollyhocks and the basswood trees beyond.

"Joe used to be a great bicycle rider," she said. "I don't doubt he's still good at it. You could take Uncle Joe along."

That was a little better. It was better than taking Father along. Father was all right, but he never did crazy things like Great-uncle Joe. I could depend on my great-uncle to go out of his way to do something that would set Great-aunt Lou to talking for a week straight, complaining about that man of hers and how could a body stand living with him!

I said I didn't like the idea. It wouldn't do to seem eager about having him; so I grumbled. I said the first thing you'd know he'd take Gus Elker along, and then you couldn't tell whether I was in Wisconsin or in Missouri, not that I'd mind going to Missouri where I could call on Lena Meyers' girls, who usually came up to Sac Prairie every summer. You could have a swell time with them, just doing nothing.

Mother said, "The more I think of it, the better I like the idea. I think he ought to go along with you. I can bring Aunt Lou around to the idea."

"What about the farm?" I asked. "It's harvest time, almost, and he can't leave the farm."

"I don't look for you to be gone more than a day or two," she said.

I thought the main thing was to be gone; after that the bicycle trip would take care of itself. I didn't say anything.

"And if he does take Gus, so much the better. There'll be two of them to keep an eye on you."

That was the way she figured—keep an eye on me. I thought I could depend on Great-uncle Joe to keep his eyes somewhere else.

"Besides," Mother went on, "I don't believe you could pry Simoleon away from town for that long a time."

"Listen," I said, "he goes camping with Pete now and then; he'd go with me if I wanted him to."

"And he's so young, too; his mother would never let him go, you know that."

"He's only about a year younger than I am," I said.

Mother shook her head. "It's settled now."

Great-uncle Joe fixed it so that we could start out from his place and bike down to Spring Green. We could always figure out where to go from there. He wasn't as heavy then as he was later, but he was still a big man with thick moustache and eyebrows. His face was heavy and his cheeks redder than they were later, with the thin-skinned redness all the Stolls had in early and middle-age, as if their skin were very delicate and sensitive.

Great-aunt Lou saw us off from the front porch. She stood there with her hands folded in her apron and her spectacles slid down her nose, her eyes fixed on us above them, her head cocked a little and a worried look on her face. Her thin lips were working while she watched us get ready.

"I don't know what your ma was thinkin' of," she said at last, "lettin' you go off with that man a mine. He ain't fit to take care of a horse, let alone a child. Heavens to Betsy!—a bicycle trip. What you don't all think of!"

"I took care a *you* all these years," said great-uncle, grinning. "You ain't got cause to complain."

My great-aunt kept on talking to me. "I mind me that time you come out here lookin' for birds' eggs," she said. "And that time you got up out of bed and set out after that whippoorwill singin' on the porch. You got over birds' eggs soon enough."

I said I was finished collecting birds' eggs, yes, and I was thinking of making a collection of butterflies or insects. Sim Jones had a collection like that. It looked very nice in a case with a glass cover, the butterflies and bugs with pins stuck through them.

"Your poor mother," said my great-aunt, shaking her head.

"You talk too much, Old Timer," said great-uncle. "We better get a move on."

He got on his bicycle a little unsteadily, and started away, waving and shouting to my great-aunt. She waved back, but she kept looking at me.

"You're mighty young for takin' on like this," she said, "but there ain't no one else. You keep an eye on that man a mine, boy."

I didn't promise. I got to going and shouted good-bye to her from the road.

She stood there waving her handkerchief until the bend in the road cut her from sight.

I caught up with great-uncle. He was riding his bicycle as foxy as you please, his hat pushed down on the back of his head, and his seat-length coat flying out behind him. He looked so contented it made my uneasy, glancing around only once to see if I was coming or not; the rest of the time he kept his eyes on the side of the road.

That road from Grell's Mill to the Fair Valley store, where you turn to go to Spring Green if you don't want to go on to Logtown, twists and winds around among the hills. It follows the hills along the marshes to the south, and in the summer sun it lies there with hill-shadows on it as inviting as you like. That day the basswood trees were blooming, yellow with flowers and clouded with bees, and in the marshes the kaiser-kronen were scraping the tall grasses, like oranges riding the wide green lake. The heat stood over it, shimmering and waving, and the low clouds banked up along the Ferry Bluff range beyond the marshes.

We got around a few turns, and sure enough, there was Gus Elker. He was standing there with an old bicycle that looked as if it might fall to pieces the moment he got on it. Gus Elker is a small man, though to look at his clothes, you'd think his smallness was a recent thing; he always wore things too large for him, his overalls turned up a foot at the ankles and the rest of them so baggy that anybody taking a good hold of Gus could shake him right out of them. The shirt he had on was big, too, but he had cut the arms of it as a concession to the heat. He had on a straw hat, though he usually wore a felt one with holes in it and his hair sticking out. His moustache was about the color of his hat, and it curved sadly down around his lugubrious mouth. The way he stood there and looked up with his melancholy eyes you'd have thought we were going to a funeral, and you would never believe he had in him all the life he did. He would have denied it, too, if you had put it up to him.

"I thought you was never comin'," said Gus.

"My ol' woman gave us a talk," great-uncle explained. "Are you ready?"

Gus got on his bicycle and swung into the road. He had hardly got out when Hank Bloom's bloodhound bitch Sally came crashing out of the underbrush and set out after him.

"What in hell's that dog Sally doin' here?" asked great-uncle.

"I brung her," said Gus. "I figgered we might git t' do some huntin'."

Great-uncle stopped his bicycle and stood there half straddling it, with one leg on the ground and the bicycle supporting him a little on the other side.

"I be dog if you ain't a born idjit, Gus," said great-uncle. "We ain't no need for a hound."

"I reckon we might use her," said Gus stubbornly.

Great-uncle looked at him in disgust, his face gleaning with sweat in the hot July sun. "Gus," he said, "you ain't aimin' t' take that hound dog along?"

"I got her," said Gus. "I reckon I'll take her."

I mounted my bicycle and went down the road. It was too hot to stand there arguing about the dog, and they were likely to keep at it for an hour and not notice that any time had passed. My great-uncle shouted at me to wait, and got on his bicycle again to take out after me. I looked back and saw Gus getting ready to follow. Sally stood in the road wagging her tail, waiting for him to get started.

Great-uncle caught up with me at the Fair Valley store. He was still grumbling about Gus and the dog. Just past the turn, Gus caught up.

Don't let that old pot-belly be tellin' you anything, boy," he said. "That Sally's a good dog. You like t' died t' seen her workin'."

"Huntin' with a bloodhound," said great-uncle to the July air. "The man's a plain dumb fool."

"Hoh!" shouted Gus, "who's talkin'!"

I didn't listen. We were going along the Spring Green road through rolling country where corn stood in the fields better than knee-high, all deep green and with a shine to it like sunlight there even after the sun had gone under a cloud, and the cut grain was stacked in the fields, buff and yellow, and clover cut, and the smell of it in the air, deeper here where the dew had not yet gone from the pockets. All around us were the hills, and the woods dark as night, so thick the trees were. It was good land, and held the rain and the dew in it, so that the grain grew well there. And what a day! with the flycatchers and the thrashers and the peewees and phoebes singing along the roadside, and once in a while the call of a thrush from the woods, and all along the way the smell of linden trees, and alfalfa and clover hay, and the rich smell of barnyards from the farms we passed.

We got down to Cassell before Gus thought to look for the dog. She was nowhere in sight, and the road went back a piece before being lost in the hills we had left.

"I might a knowed it," said great-uncle. "We'll have t' wait for her t' catch up with us, that's all."

Gus said, "I reckon we will."

We sat down at the roadside and waited. Nobody said anything. Pretty soon the dog came along, tongue out but still looking as happy as a hound dog can ever get to looking. I was ready to go again.

"We can't go yet," Gus protested. "We got t' give Sally her chance t' rest."

We rested that dog for half an hour, and by that time I was beginning to feel like going back home and getting Sim Jones and starting out all over again. But we got to going after a while, and came down off the Cassell prairie into marshland, where there were trees on both sides of the road and sometimes a glimpse of the sloughs with golden water-lilies on the green water. The air was cool and there were different bird sounds here, and sometimes snakes along the road.

I saw a blue racer and got off to try to catch it. It got away, but Gus almost fell off his bicycle from shock.

"Ain't you knowin' that's a poisonous critter, Old Timer?" he demanded. "W'y, that snake's so poisonous one drop a his poison is like t' make the flesh crawl of'n your body."

I said that my grandfather Adams had assured me that blue racers were not poisonous snakes and that it was all right to pick them up, providing you ran fast enough to catch them.

Gus said, "I don't hold with your grandfather there, Old Timer. I mind me that time Herk Butler got bit by one a them things in his hayfield. W'y, he like t' thrown conniption fits before he died."

"Did he die?" I asked.

"He sure did," said Gus solemnly, with a cautious glance at the place along the roadside where the snake had vanished.

The dog caught up with us again, and we went on, a little more slowly now, because it was cool here, and nice travelling. After a while we came out of the hills again and missed Sally. We had to wait for her once more, and great-uncle was likely to burst with things to say to Gus, but he didn't say them. Gus enjoyed resting. I began to feel bad about the whole thing. If Gus wanted to bring the dog, it was all right, but great-uncle should have known he'd do a thing like that. The only fun I got out of it then was the thought of what my mother would think when she heard about it. Keep an eye on me like so much! They had all to do to watch that hound dog.

We go to Spring Green at last that afternoon, after waiting for the dog three times. The sun was high now and the clouds gone; it was hotter than ever, and my great-uncle was not liking it at all.

"I reckon maybe we could go back the Logtown road and stop for a time at your Aunt Jessie's place," he said. "And might be we could see your Great-uncle Arnold the other side a Logtown."

"Go back!" I hollered. "I don't figure on going back. I figure on going down the river road a way. Maybe down to Prairie du Chien."

"That's a two-day trip," Gus said, awed.

"I don't think we'd ought t' do it on these here bicycles," said great-uncle, after a thoughtful interval. "How about riding' it on the train?"

If there was anything I liked better than biking, it was riding on a train. I said that would do. Gus was agreeable, too; he said it would give that dog of Hank's time to rest a good spell. So great-uncle bought the tickets and arranged for the bicycles to be stored in the baggage car with the dog. We sat down to wait for the train.

It was a long wait, but we had lunch to eat. Afterward, great-uncle and I walked around a little; Gus stayed behind with the dog and the bicycles. The train whistle caught us a couple of blocks away from the station, and we made it on the run. We got to the train just in time.

"Where's Gus?" I asked.

"In the baggage car," said great-uncle. "Likely he's watchin' over that hound dog a Hank's."

I watched the town slide away from the train. The conductor came in, took our tickets, and talked a while with Great-uncle Joe, whom he knew. The window stood open, and the country around was baking in the heat, but it was comforting to see grain being cut and stacked, men in the cornfields, and horses and men along the sky on the hill-slopes.

"Funny Gus don't show up," said great-uncle after a while.

I said maybe they couldn't find a crate for the dog and Gus had to sit back there and hold him, and great-uncle agreed that this was probably what had happened.

Great-uncle went to sleep with his hat over his face. He had just began to snore when the conductor came into the car at Boscobel and woke him up.

"We got one whistle on this train, Joe," he said grinning. "Here's a telegram come for you to Boscobel."

"'Y God, somebody died," said great-uncle, his eyes widening.

I said nobody knew we were on this train; so it was nothing like that.

He tore open the telegram and read it. In a minute his face got red and his mouth began to work the way it does when he gets angry.

"What's the matter?" I asked.

"It's from Gus," he said. "That damn' fool fell asleep in the depot at Spring Green and he's jest now come to. Says for us t' meet him in Prairie du Chien."

I laughed until I remembered that he had all three bicycles and the dog to look after. It would be a miracle if everything got to Prairie du Chien all right with Gus to look after it. Still, it was funny, it was to laugh, and after a while I laughed again. I could see Gus's face when he heard the train had gone out. Like as not he blamed the station agent at Spring Green for not waking him.

"That means we got to spend the night in Prairie du Chien," great-uncle said. "There ain't another train this way for hours."

"We got all night to figure out where to go next," I said.

Great-uncle looked at me sideways, a little distrustful.

Staying in Prairie du Chien overnight wasn't as bad as I thought it might be, by the way Great-uncle Joe carried on. It was an old town with a good many things to see in it, Fort Crawford, the old French Cemetery and the Villa Louis, and best of all, that night there was a show boat on the river and we took it in. Gus got there all right, bicycles, dog and all, around midnight; he had three different stories about how he came to go to sleep, but they were useless as far as great-uncle was concerned. He wouldn't believe any one of them, and each was more outlandish than the next.

"Well, where to now?" asked great-uncle the morning.

I said I had seen a bridge over the Mississippi and I was set on crossing the river. "It's the Father of Waters," I said. "I read about it in geography. I can go home and tell Sim I crossed it. And I want to see if it's muddy."

Great-uncle spread out his hands and looked up at the ceiling of his hotel room. I could tell he was beginning to think this was not as much of a holiday as he had thought it might be. But I was bound to have a good time, whether it took two days or a week. It was all the same to me. Come September, I'd be cooped up in school long enough.

"And then where?" asked Gus.

I said likely we could travel a piece in the country around on the other side.

"It's hill country," Gus said dubiously. "I don't peddle so good in hill country."

I said he could wait for us here.

"We ain't gone yet," said great-uncle.

I said I was going whether he was or not, and he had better make up his mind. The sun was getting higher in the sky, and even if it was a cooler day, it looked a little like rain, and I didn't feel like getting caught in it, not that it would make much difference to my clothes. They were old anyway; Mother had had sense enough to see to that even if I wouldn't have had.

We set out right after breakfast. It was a toll bridge, and all the way across my great-uncle grumbled about paying. His grumbling was like something in the distance; I didn't hear much of it because I was too interested in seeing the river below and the train crawling up along the opposite shore, along the Iowa bluffs, a freight train like a red-brown centipede with a black head winding down the river.

It was a west wind blowing, cool and sweet, and we were riding into it, strung out in a line across the bridge, with me in the lead and that hound dog of Hank Bloom's in the rear. The sun was inching toward the clouds, and already there was a fresher smell on the air, as if it had rained in the west.

We got over the river into Iowa. We passed through McGregor, and pretty soon the trouble about the dog started all over again. We had to wait for her to catch up. I began to think of how many times we would have to wait for Sally, and I didn't like to look forward to it. If we went any distance at all, it would be pretty tiresome going at that rate, even if we all rested waiting.

But the worst was yet to come. I wanted to see the Indian mounds north of McGregor. I said Sim had seen them, he had often come down by train to McGregor where he had an aunt or an uncle or some one living, and he had seen those mounds in the shapes of animals, and I meant to see them, too. That was how we came to go north. Great-uncle was all for going back now, but he was beginning to want to go back every time we stopped. He carried on as if he had to look after Gus and the dog and me, all three.

After the Indian mounds, we kept on going north, and by nightfall we got to Lansing, a nice town on the river. We would have made New Albin, but for that dog and waiting for her to catch up. It was enough to make me wish I'd run off after all, even though I couldn't help laughing about it. I told Gus he ought to buy a basket and set it on his bicycle and put the dog in it, but he said it wouldn't work, the dog wouldn't stay, and there was no use trying. Great-uncle said nothing, but he kept grumbling about going home.

"This county's strange t' me," he said. "I don't reckon none of us know where we're goin'. Do you, Old Timer?"

"No, but I'm having as much fun as I can," I said.

"My old woman'll be worryin'."

I said, "Think of how Ma'll carry on."

"I been thinkin'," said great-uncle.

That was the second day, the day my great-aunt Lou had thought we would be home. Gus was completely satisfied. He had a man or two to run his farm, and the housekeeper he had wouldn't miss him to speak of. Great-uncle was worrying more about what Great-aunt Lou and my mother would have to say than about anything else.

The next day we crossed over into Minnesota, and by noon we rode into Caledonia. We went into a restaurant for dinner, and when we came out the dog was gone. It was as simple as that. All the other times she had stayed close to our bicycles, and now she was gone. There was nothing for it but to find her. By this time great-uncle was complaining bitterly about his legs, how they couldn't stand much more. Gus kept making remarks about how old men hadn't any business on bicycles anyway, and got great-uncle so red-faced and ornery, he wouldn't help hunt for Sally. I said I'd go up and down the streets looking for her, but Gus was all for going from house to house asking for that hound dog. If anybody wanted her that bad, I figured they could have her.

"Ain't they enough paper salesmen around the way it is?" hollered great-uncle. "Without you goin' askin' for that dog!

You hadn't ought a brung her."

Gus looked at him mildly and said, "It was you asked me t' come along."

"But I didn't ask that dog," protested great-uncle.

"Well, she's come this far, and I don't aim t' leave her, I be dog if I do," said Gus.

He set out looking for her. I peddled up and down the streets and the alleys, but that dog was nowhere in sight. Every once in a while I saw Gus going from house to house, and when I got back down town and stopped for a sundae in one of the restaurants I heard some men talking about "a nut out looking for a dog." They were calling Gus *Whiskers*. I laughed over my sundae and listened. They had the color of the dog down pat. One of them had got it from his wife and was telling the others. A lean, tired-looking man with a scar along his jaw said the last time he had seen that dog she was heading for the woods with half the dogs in town after her. To hear them talk, Caledonia was no town to bring a bitch dog to.

I went back to where great-uncle was waiting, but not until I saw Gus heading in the same direction. Great-uncle was looking for us. He was all excited, his eyes bright, and his big body almost shaking with eagerness. He was all combed up, he had got most of the dust off his clothes, and looked about ready to go somewhere, but not on the bicycle. He had forgotten all about the dog, for he never even asked about her.

"I jest heard they's a bicycle race comin' off in this town this afternoon. We jest got time t' make it," he said. "We c'n see some real bicycle riding."

"You ain't seen that dog come back this way?" asked Gus.

"We c'n look some more for that dog after that race," said great-uncle. "That race won't wait, but the dog will."

We rode a little way out of town and came to a crude track. It looked as if it had been used before. The bicycle race was something out of the ordinary, judging by the crowd standing around. There was a fifty-dollar prize posted for the winner, nothing barred. There were a couple of women, a girl, about a dozen young men, some older, and a score of kids all set to go. We came riding up just before the gun cracked. The crowd thought we had come to take part in the race, and got aside to let us pass. I slid off my bicycle at the edge of the crowd just as the gun cracked. Half a second later I heard Gus Elker let out a whoop.

I climbed up on a fence-post and looked around. There was Gus going hell for leather down that race track hollering to beat the band, and way up ahead of him and all the other riders was a dog. I could tell right away what had happened. Gus saw that dog and took it for Sally; maybe it was, but it would have taken a better pair of eyes than I had to be sure of it. There he was, going down the track, and great-uncle after him. My great-uncle was swearing; I could hear him over all the shouting, and I could tell by what I could see of his face that he was madder than a hornet.

I wouldn't have believed it if I hadn't seen it myself.

I sat there laughing fit to kill, and everybody looking at me as if I wasn't all there. They didn't see anything funny in it at all. After a while, I wasn't so sure that it was funny, either. I figured that by the time they got out of that race, they'd be so tired they wouldn't want to go on, and I had my mind set on making La Crosse that night. It was a way to go, but I had studied it out on the road map and I knew we could make it.

That dog came down the track and loped off up the road. Gus tried to get out of the race, but he couldn't do it. He kept on coming and coming and trying at the same time to get somewhere and by the time they were on the last lap, he was out ahead. He won that race but he never stopped; he went right on through to the road, and lit out after that dog. Great-uncle stopped to get the money.

I didn't wait. I set out after Gus; I didn't even look to see whether great-uncle was coming. I took it for granted that he was. About a mile away from the race track, I caught up with Gus. He had the dog. The first time I looked at her, she looked like Sally. The next time I knew there was something wrong. Sally had a big spot under her left ear on the neck; this dog had only a little worm of black. But she *did* look like Sally. I opened my mouth to say something about it, but caught myself in time. Gus hadn't noticed anything. I reasoned that if I said something, he'd be all for going back after Sally. That would be holding us up all the more, and by this time I was getting pretty tired of waiting around for a dog. That dog had more or less balled up the whole trip so far. So I kept still, hoping great-uncle wouldn't notice anything.

He didn't. He was so excited about Gus winning the fifty dollars that he forgot everything else. He even forgot about how tired he was, and kept right on along the road to Hokah with us.

That dog was an improvement over Sally. She hopped up on the little rack behind great-uncle's bicycle and rode there as content as you please. I thought for a while Gus and great-uncle would notice the difference at that, but Gus said right off that she was tired of walking, and talked for a while about how smart that dog was. I knew Hank Bloom would know it wasn't Sally, but that was Gus's worry. She looked to me like just as good a dog as Hank's, a little trimmer in the shape of her, and quicker. We had trouble with her only once before we got to Hokah, but that lost us half an hour. My mind was made up by that time. I was tired of waiting for dogs, and the way I had it figured out I could fox them all yet, Mother included. That was after great-uncle talked about taking a train at La Crosse and going home that way.

"I be dog if I c'n stand it one more day," he said. "My legs is ailin' fit t' kill."

My own legs hurt, but no one heard me say a word about it. I was bound to get to La Crosse that night. We had supper in Hokah but I wouldn't listen to staying there. Not for me, I said. I meant to get back into Wisconsin that night, even if I had to ride all night. They could come after me, I said, but I was going on. Gus took his fifty dollars and went for some beer. After a couple of bottles each, great-uncle and Gus were ready to go on. I was a little less eager, especially since Gus wanted to sing. But it wasn't far to go, and I figured we could do it, unless Gus took to acting up.

Great-uncle began to talk more and more about taking the train at La Crosse.

"It ain't as if we didn't have our bicycle ride," he kept urging insistently. "We did. We had more'n our share a bicycle ridin'. And you like train ridin' all right."

I said I had my share of train riding. I said that time it had lost us almost half a day, and there was no telling what Gus would do this time.

Great-uncle said, "I'll see t' him."

"Who'll see to the bicycles and the dog?" I asked.

That held great-uncle for only a minute. "You," he said.

"I reckon you're able."

I thought about this, and the more I thought, the more it came to me that I couldn't do any better.

So we fixed it that way. I said I'd go back in the baggage car with the dog and the bicycles, and they could ride up front.

"Unless we ride with you," great-uncle said, dubiously.

"No," I said. "I'll do it alone."

I was sure about it by that time.

When we got to La Crosse, we had a little lunch, and Gus bought the tickets. I was sorry to see that money spent for my ticket, but I figured Gus had come by it easy enough. I got into the baggage car on one side and out on the other. I left a note for my great-uncle on his bicycle; I had written it out during the while I left the table at lunch. I had the road map with me, and night or no, I was off across country through West Salem and Sparta for the highway leading down to Sac Prairie. It was a night with a moon, and all the coolness that stood in the air after rain was there, and the smell of grain in the fields and the still dark cows and horses at night grazing. It was good to be riding along all alone in the soft moonlight with only my shadow on the road and not the worry about great-uncle and Gus Elker and that hound dog.

It took me three days to make that trip. I took my time, I stopped when I wanted to, and fooled around at the Dells and at Devil's Lake. I came into Sac Prairie late in the afternoon six days after we had left. Coming down the bluffs from Baraboo I got to thinking about Great-Uncle Joe and Gus. The more I thought about them, the less I could believe they'd go home without me. I could imagine what Great-aunt Lou would have to say to that, and there'd be no end to the way Mother would carry on.

But I had to make sure. I stopped in the drug store and asked someone to call up Stolls and ask for Joe. He wasn't there; my great-aunt said he was on a trip.

I began to feel a little bad about it, but I knew what I had to do. I couldn't show my face at home without Great-uncle Joe or Gus, either. One way was as bad as the other. Like as not they just went somewhere and stayed put. No two ways about it: that place would be Mazomanie. It was the last stop before the train came to Sac Prairie.

They were there. Gus only looked at me and looked around for the dog; he was ready to go without any further explanation.

Great-uncle said, "You fixin' t' go home at last?"

I said I'd been home and come to find him.

"Hoh!" he snorted savagely.

They had waited two days and two nights, alternating between the hotel and the railroad station.

On the way home Gus said, "That old pot-belly sure did some swearin' when we found that note."

Half an hour later we lost the dog, and I heard Great-uncle Joe swear myself. After that I couldn't stop laughing; the fit just took me and held on until we got to Sac Prairie, and not even my mother's grim face could put a damper on it.

But Soft—The Morning Air

"THERE GOES THE bell," said Sim. "I told you we should a gone."

"All right," I said. "You told me."

The angelus rang into the April twilight, its mellow sound drifting from Sac Prairie eastward among the islands in the Wisconsin where it curved around the paw of land upon which the village lay. From the hills across the broad blue river echoed thinly bells swung from cows going home in a long line athwart the slopes, along the winding path near the wing dam, almost directly opposite from the river's edge where we were. Overhead a killdeer flew and cried, leaning eastward toward the sandy strand in an uneven line south from the old timbers of the dam.

Sim was gathering up the poles, winding the lines around with elaborate care, cleaning off the hooks. But his eyes were on the tall clouds piled above the hills, magenta now in light from the west.

"I won't catch it," he said with some satisfaction, rolling the words on his tongue.

"I will," I said, "But I don't care. And I'll get out of it if Grandpa Adams is there."

"He smells trouble for you," said Sim, his long, lean face alight suddenly with appreciation. "Both my grandpas died before I was born," he added reflectively. I could feel him wondering behind his eyes what they might have been like. "One of them was a cabinetmaker. He made good cabinets. we got some."

I pulled up the fish and counted them again. Six bluegills, a black bass, two sheepshead.

"You take three bluegills and the bass," I said. "I'll keep the sheepshead. They've got stones over their eyes—good luck stones. I've got eleven already."

Sim grinned, his even teeth flashing whitely. "You need luck," he said. "But you don't seem to be gettin' it. Come on."

Footsteps made a curious soft sound, an intimate sound in the sand. All over lay the fragrant pungence of the willows. In the west, the new-leafed trees stood dark upon the afterglow, and the church steeple with its great brass ball and cross rose above the trees, sunlight still flashing brilliantly

---

Evening in Spring, 1941

from the brass. Vesper sparrows made their dulcet song in the underbrush, and robins carolled with the soft sad agony of the mourning doves. The air was wonderful—the smell of trees, of new leaves and old, of sap flowing; smell of river and sand, of moldering wood, secret flowers blooming where daylong the sun shone and brought the summer near.

Sim walked lithely ahead, thin and growing tall now at fourteen; he went through the brush like a deer, and hardly a leaf stirred. The rabbits never fled at his approach as they did at mine. If I had been capable of it, I would have envied him this, as I would have envied him the sanctuary of the old harness shop and his "office" in the shed behind the shop, and his post card and stamp collections.

Through the brush to Ehl's Slough, where three pintails flew up complaining at our intrusion. Out from under a mass of pondweed in the water at the slough's edge, a wave furled where sunfish scattered, disturbed by the tremor of earth under our feet. We walked slowly, watchfully around the north end of the pond, looking as always for lizards, and went up the disused road to Water Street, looking back to wave at the old rugweaver among his bees.

"I'll cut through the park," I said.

"You didn't bring an extra stringer," said Sim, glancing at the fish.

"No. You take 'em. I'll come down after supper."

I took my pole and went up the road into the park, dark now upon the west. Home was just beyond the park, across the railroad tracks; from the far edge of the park I could see the kitchen light burning. I walked slower now. Already I could hear Mother saying: *First it was Carlie you went fishing with and now it's Sim, and you still don't come home on time!* That was harking back to the time Carlie and I went fishing in Dickerson's Slough and the sunfish were biting so fast we got a pailful each and didn't come home until after dark, and then met his mother and mine coming down the *Rheinpreussenstrasse* looking for us, sure we had fallen into the river and were drowned, and so glad we hadn't that they had bawled us out all the way home from there—ten blocks. I could still feel disgust at the memory of it. But there it was; I was still coming home too late. Give me a watch then! I could hear myself saying that.

The street lights came on, flowering softly into the spring night, like great moths among the trees and along the lanes. The afterglow was crimson now beneath a wash of amethyst and lemon deepening to copper, and trees were darker still, thickened buds and new leaves swollen with spring. Robins with their breasts turned toward the west carolled bright song against the gathering dark.

Some one was in the park going down the cross path, wheeling a buggy. It was Margery Estabrook, Margery, whose long braids I pulled in school. I was bound to meet her. I might as well be an hour later now, I thought. I stood behind one of the old bur oaks near the bandstand and waited until she came along. The buggy creaked. I wondered whether a buggy could be oiled. When she came abreast of me, I shouted and jumped out at her. She kept right on going with her head in the air; even in this dusk you could see the color in her cheeks. But the baby began to howl.

"Now see what you did, Steve Grendon!" she said angrily, looking back over her shoulder.

"All right. I didn't mean to scare the kid."

"Well, you did."

"Well, I didn't set out to."

"You wouldn't scare me and you know it."

She went on past, trying to hush her baby sister. I stood looking after her. There was something different about her. She looked fresh and more grown up somehow. The braids that were usually down her back were coiled around her crown. She looked all of three years older.

"Margery, wait a minute," I called.

She turned around and stood waiting, moving the buggy back and forth on the path. There were still uncertain snufflings coming from the buggy's depths. I came up to her and looked into the buggy. Now that she had waited for me, I did not know what to say, I did not understand why I had wanted her to wait. But something there was about her this night that made her different, more than the way she had put up her hair, something I did not understand: an indefinable wanting suddenly to be near her, to say something to her.

"Did you have supper?" I asked.

"Sure. We ate early."

"Listen, I said, "maybe, after you take the baby home—maybe we could go for a little walk." I could feel my pulse pounding, and I half hoped she might saw no, she couldn't go. Sim would never let me hear the last of this, I thought.

"I don't know," she said dubiously. "I'd like to—but if Mother thinks I went out anywhere, I don't think she'd like it." She smiled shyly, warmly.

"Aw, come on," I said. "Your mother needn't find out."

"I could go over to Norma's and you could meet me somewhere—maybe down beside the Park Hall at eight o'clock."

"All right, Margery. It's a date."

I met her eyes for a moment before she turned away; in the dusk of the park they were as if separately alive, something that lived independently of the rest of her, something that belonged to the growing dark, to the last robins' carolling and the keening of the screech owl in the old hollow oak in the park's northeast corner. Her eyes spoke to me just as surely as her lips could have done. I knew she would get over to Norma's somehow, no matter what her mother said. And I knew I would get to Park Hall, no matter what anybody at home tired to do to stop me.

I ran through the rest of the park, among the trees, across the railroad tracks and the field beyond, dropped my pole beside the house and ran inside.

"Am I late?" I asked, and sat down to the table, not daring to look at the clock.

"Late!" hollered my mother. "Late? 'Am I late?' Where were you this time?"

"I was fishing with Sim," I said. "We got some bluegills, and a bass, and some sheepshead."

"Where'd you catch 'em?" asked Father, looking at me over the flame of the match he was using to light his pipe.

"Right there at that fallen tree across from the wing dam. Where we caught that whole school of sunfish that Sunday last year."

"Wasn't the day long enough?" demanded Mother. Her warm eyes grew suddenly sharp, fixed on my hands. "You haven't washed your hands. How often have I told you?"

I got up and washed my hands as fast as I could.

"First it was Carlie and now it's Sim," said Mother. "I don't know what's to come of that boy. Now don't eat so fast."

I said I had to hurry and get down to get those fish from Sim.

"You're going down to Grandpa Grendon's after supper with your father," said Mother.

I knew from the way she said it that there was no use arguing about it. I could still get to Sim's place from there, but I knew I would miss Margery then, and tonight I would not miss meeting Margery. I ate faster.

"Don't eat so fast," said Mother again. "I don't know what we'll have to do to teach you how to get home on time. I should think you'd know better. It's no fun sitting here waiting for you to come home before I can clear the table."

I said that the fish were biting so good and all, it was a shame to leave the river, and I had had no idea that it was so late, I wasn't watching the sun; first thing I knew the six o'clock bell was ringing and it was supper time. Then we came straight home, both of us. It was a long way across the sand from the river to Water Street, and it was over three blocks from there, even through the park.

Father observed that the tree at which we were fishing was practically in a straight line from the back door.

"There!" said Mother, with the air of having received the last possible ounce of proof of my irresponsibility.

I dunked the last piece of bread and swallowed it practically without chewing it at all, not before first carefully removing the crust.

"Eat the crust!" hollered Mother. "It's good for you."

I pretended I hadn't heard her.

"Now we'll have to come to an understanding," she said then. "You'll have to learn to come in on time. When?"

What can you say to that? Grandfather Adams lowered the paper and resettled his hat on his head; he had been sitting there all the time ready to go back to his own house, his hat shoved back on his head, reading the headlines and discounting them by ninety percent, as he always said. He had a broad face filled with good humor; his dark-blue eyes were sly, so that I always thought he had done his share of hell-raising when he was a kid. Now he fingered his moustache and looked at me quizzically, a smile on his wide, firm-lipped mouth; he was waiting to hear what I had to say for myself.

"Well, I always try to get here," I said. "I can't try any harder."

My mother was a handsome woman; people always said she looked more like my older sister. A handsome woman angry is twice as emphatic, and Mother was getting angry. It was time for somebody to take the situation in hand. I looked over at Grandfather Adams with my left eyebrow up.

"Try!" exclaimed Mother in a withering voice. "You don't know the meaning of the word—unless it's something you *want* to do. Then just try to make you do anything else."

"I know what I want to do," I said.

It was the wrong thing to say. "I should say you do. And I know what I want you to do. And I don't want you coming home late to supper. We'll come to an understanding right now. I stood for your tin cans, and for your funny papers, but I'm not going to stand for your coming in late to supper night after night."

I said quietly that I meant to collect funny papers for a long time yet.

"Don't try to change the subject," said Mother.

Time was passing. I looked at the clock and thought of Margery. I had to go down to Grandfather Grendon's yet. I looked over at Dad, but he might have been somewhere else; he wasn't listening.

Grandfather Adams erupted suddenly with a big laugh. "Great God in Heaven, Woman!" he shouted, "A man'd think the boy was in the dock.

There's only one way to look at it—if he gets home in time, he gets supper; if not, he doesn't."

"It's not good for him to do without his food," replied Mother.

"Come, come—do you think your sermons do his digestion any good? Look at him—watching the clock, itching to get away—God damn it! you'll give the boy stomach ulcers if you're not careful."

She did not know whether he was joking or not and looked at him a little apprehensively. He pressed his advantage; his voice softened, grew jocular, persuasive.

"Besides, it seems to me the issue isn't worth it—you sit around the table anyway a good forty-five minutes; so what difference does it make if he comes at six or half-past? It's *his* food that's no longer warm." He shook his head, coming to his feet. "The trouble with women beggars description! Stand clear, my boy." He went to the door and looked back at my mother. "Any word for Ma?"

"Tell her to come over tomorrow."

He went out.

Father took out his watch and said, "If we're going down, we'd better go now."

Father was thick-set and strong. He was taciturn and did not talk much, either to my sister or me. I knew he liked my sister better than he did me, but that was only natural became my mother liked me better, or else she would never have hollered at me so much. I had to hurry to keep in step with him, and all the time had the smoke from his pipe coming into my face, a sweet, not unpleasant aroma that was already diluted by the smell of April by the time it reached my nostrils. We went past Norma's house, and I looked in, but Margery was not there yet. Father took long certain strides. It was only two blocks beyond Norma's house that Grandfather Grendon lived.

"Why do I have to go down?" I asked. "I ought to see Sim."

"You saw Sim all afternoon. It's good for you to sit still a little. Grandpa likes you. You can go after while; you don't have to wait for me."

"Then I won't be late anyway," I said.

I looked down Margery's street, the way she would have to come to get to Norma's, but she was not in sight. What's the matter with me? I thought. I never looked at her twice in school. Now there was that curious kind of tingling, a trembling in the flesh whenever I thought of her, the quickened pulse, and I traced her features in my mind's eye, saw them as clearly as if she were there before me.

Grandfather Grendon was reading *The Times*, with the paper flat on the kitchen table, and the green-shaded light pulled down so that it hung between the paper and his eyes, and made a bright pool glowing before him. His knotted hands lay at the paper's edges, and his heavy, square-jawed face was softened by the reflection of light striking upward, his moustache silvered by that same light, his eyes made to gleam. Beyond him, in the half-light, sat Grandmother Grendon, a short, almost dumpy figure, whose dark-brown eyes were as birdlike as her movements could be; she was shucking dry beans from a store kept in the room above the kitchen.

I greeted both of them and went over to Grandmother, offering to help.

She laughed. "They'd be all over the floor," she said. "It's nothing. You just let me do it."

I sat there on the chair between her and Grandpa. Dad sat across the table. They were talking about the day's activities, the little things that had gone on in Sac Prairie that day. Ferdinand Bremer had had a stroke, said Grandpa phlegmatically; he would not recover. The young Lerner widow had had her baby; it was bad business. Father told him how I had come home late for supper again. Fishing.

"Fishing?" said Grandpa, looking at me askance.

I nodded.

"All the joys of life are ended by overdoing," he said. "You should learn to come home on time."

"I know what I want to do," I said.

His eyes seemed to mellow as he looked at me. Was he really thinking of me? I wondered; it did not seem so; it seemed as if he were looking through me, past me, into the darkness of the room's farthermost corner.

"We all know what we want to do," he said. "But there are some things we must do. You'll have to learn which trifles are important, and which are not." Without changing the direction of his eyes, he said to Dad, "Does he give you a lot of trouble, then?"

"Oh, no—but it's true, he knows what he wants. He's stubborn—well, stubborn as all the Grendons are. You know what that means."

"Yes, yes," he said, fingering his bristly jaw. "He has my chin. You missed that, Will. Yes, I see now, he has that look in his eyes, he'll fight, maybe not with his fists, but he'll fight to have his way. I don't know that it would be wise to break him. I would say no, don't do it. Let Rose worry about that; it will keep her from thinking of more serious troubles." He shook his head slowly, thoughtfully. "So he will be like all the rest of us. He will be a rational man, but perhaps never happy."

I did not know what that meant.

Grandma got up and went into the pantry. She came out with a piece of coffee cake, smiling shyly in her confidence that I would understand this.

I sat eating it and watching Father, to whom Grandpa had turned once more. Every little while Father would look in my direction, but he made no sign to release me. Behind Grandpa on the wall the clock's hands crept close to eight. I finished the coffee cake and shifted around a little uneasily, trying not to think of Margery by repeating to myself what Grandpa had said: *He will be a rational man, but perhaps never happy.* Then abruptly, I caught Father's offhand, casual little nod, and I got up, made my excuses, and hurried out, not forgetting to replace my chair, since that would suit both Grandma and Grandpa.

A small wind had come up, blowing from the south, swaying the street lights a little. The shadows danced at every street corner. I ran up one street, across to another, and came into the park from the east, lost at once in the darkness there. I made my way noiselessly, unseen, around the great old Park Hall to the southwest corner, just out of reach of the street light's glow fingering into the park, standing close to the wall where the shadows were deepest. Would she come? I wondered.

My first date—and hers, too, maybe.

I stood in the shadows there against the west wall of the Park Hall, secure in the darkness coming swiftly, swiftly now, with afterglow now only a faint vermilion line along the western rim, and the day only a ghost of amethyst above. The stars shown, great Sirius brilliant in the southwest, Orion angling earthward, and in the northeast, somewhere behind me, the amber eye of Arcturus was looking down. A door opened and closed down the street, and the shrillness of Norma's voice saying good night rose on the wind. Two houses down from the park—a hundred steps away, scarcely that. Now—if she were coming, she would come now. My pulse beat faster, faster; I almost held my breath.

I saw her coming along the fence at Mrs. Carliner's; she made no sound walking there. She came under the street light, walking quickly, almost spectral in her passage, and soon she was among the shadows, where no one could see her. She was uncertain now, and came more slowly, hesitantly.

I came out cautiously and called, my voice little more than a whisper.

She heard.

"Mother thinks I'm over at Norma's," she said. "If she found out, I'd catch it. Where can we go?"

It did not seem that I had thought of this at all, and yet I had. I knew at once where we would go. "We'll go up the back way to Upper Sac Prairie; we'll go up through the park here and the park there, and to the high school there, and then we can come down that road past the old wine-cellar. No one ever goes that way; no one'll see us."

She put one hand gently on my arm. "Come on, then," she said urgently, a little afraid, lest her mother materialize from the shadows and work her vengeance upon her. I liked the touch of her hand.

We went through the park, secret and alone, for no eye to see. There were long minutes then. I did not know what to say to her, feeling a kind of satisfaction just to be with her. We were well out of the park before I said anything.

"I like your hair that way," I said.

She laughed shyly. "Well, you can't pull it so easy now.

I don't know whether I ought to keep it up. Mother says it makes me look so old."

"Heck, no—keep it that way. I like it," I repeated earnestly.

"I'm glad you do, Steve."

Faster than I thought it possible, we were in Upper Sac Prairie, we were walking through the dark park there to the deeper darkness of the high school. We walked more cautiously now, lest someone be there before us; but no one was there, no one sat on the steps beneath the new-leafed lilac bush, whose fragrance was almost as of blossoms, strong in the April air of evening.

I cleaned the step with my handkerchief and Margery sat down; I stood for a moment looking into her upturned face before I sat down beside her.

I felt a little foolish now, I didn't know what to say, I didn't know what to do. I thought perhaps she expected something of me now, but I was content to be near her, just to sit there without talking, just touching her a little from time to time. It was the first time I had ever been alone with a girl I liked. I was beginning to understand that I had liked Margery before this, I had liked her even in high school where I pulled her hair; I was coming to know that the only reason I pulled her hair was to attract her attention. It was still a little confused in my mind, but I knew I didn't want to pull her hair again; there was something more I wanted now. But I didn't know what it was, I didn't know what the quickened pulse, the fluttering as birds' wings inside me meant, except that I was happy, I was glad to be here with Margery and to think that there would be other evenings like this, evenings without end, in a time without end.

The lilac fragrance held us as in a cloud, so that even the sounds of life in Sac Prairie seemed muted—of cars going up and down Water Street, the voices of children still at last play before bedtime, music, where some one played *My Wild Irish Rose* on a mouth-organ, the steady *clop-clop-clop* of horses' hoofs receding westward into the country along one of the lanes leading out of Sac Prairie. All around us was stillness, save for the high nasal cry of nighthawks, and the zooming of the air in their wings. Margery scuffed her feet a little.

"Mother'll be wild if she finds out," she said.

"What's the matter with her?"

"She hates all Catholics, and if she found out I was with you, I'd catch it."

"I guess the Catholics aren't any worse than anybody else," I said, feeling a little uncomfortable, remembering how some of the priests had said all the non-Catholics were sure to go to hell, and Grandfather Adams had answered that as far as he was concerned all priests with such ideas ought to spend the rest of eternity in some especially well-heated section.

"I guess so, too," said Margery.

I looked at her, meeting her eyes once more. A change had come over them, something indefinable, mysterious, remote, and yet they were intense and warm; I could almost see the blue of them, despite the darkness, the clear bluelike water in the brook in May. But now suddenly she was invested with a deep mystery, an elusive magic that diffused itself over everything; I could not take my eyes away.

"Steve, I've go to go."

"Oh, not yet!"

"I promised I'd be home by nine o'clock—it'll take us half an hour to walk back; we can just make it."

There was an eternal moment of waiting, a hushed instant. I bent toward her, touched her soft cheek with my lips, put my arms around her and found her mouth; in that moment time ceased; an ecstasy of purest happiness flowered within me. I kissed her again and drew away, abashed now.

But she was not angry; her eyes looked down, her lips smiled a little, though my own mouth burned.

"Do you like me, Steve?" she asked.

"You know I do."

"I like you, too." Her voice was low, infinitely sweet.

I felt choked up. I stood up and said a little roughly that we had better start, or else we'd be late, we wouldn't be able to see each other tomorrow night.

"Tomorrow night?"

Yes, I said, tomorrow night. Same time, same place.

"If I can, Steve."

"Margery—you've got to!"

We slipped away, back through the park, down past the wine-cellar whose mouth yawned blackly into the night. All too soon we were back in Lower Sac Prairie, back near the Park Hall.

"I can walk farther than this with you," I said.

"Just to the corner, then," she answered nervously.

She really was afraid. If she thought that much of me that she would come out, afraid like this, she must have felt that way a long time. I thought of the way she had held to me when I had kissed her, the way her mouth came alive against mine, and the warmth of that moment came back, took possession of me once more.

She would let me go no farther than the corner where old Mrs. Stillman lived. She touched my hand nervously, hurriedly. "Good night, Steve," she said, and was gone. I stood there watching her go down the street and around the corner to her house, across from the high school in Lower Sac Prairie. Only when the light went on in her house did I turn away.

Nine o'clock.

It was not too late to go down to see Sim. If he had not gone fishing again, he would still be in his office. I began to think of the fish we had caught. Perhaps Sim had better keep them all; then I wouldn't have to clean them before I went to bed. I walked quickly down the street to where the old harness shop stood. I looked into the shop and saw Sim's father sitting at the long bench against the north wall, his head wreathed in the green smoke rising from his asmodor; he had asthma, and had to inhale this smoke from time to time so that his breathing might be eased. The shadows were grotesque all around him on the old walls of the shop: of collars, harnesses, hames hung to dry, of old Fred himself, sitting on the stitching-horse, with his elbows on his work-bench, and his head bent, his spectacles slid down on his nose, his eyes closed against the smoke. He was alone.

I went around the shop to the office; a thin sliver of light came from behind a carefully drawn curtain. I tried the door; it was locked. I tugged impatiently. "Come on Sim; it's me. Open up."

Sim opened the door and backed to sit down in the old rocking-chair from which he had got up. "You come late to everything," he said. "I cleaned those fish."

"You can have 'em all if you want."

"Did you catch it?"

"Oh, not much. Grandpa Adams was there."

"Where were you?"

"Down to Grandpa Grendon's place and around."

I sat back. The single light globe threw a pale, sickly yellow glow over the room; the light was shadeless, and depended from the center of the roof on a long cord so that Sim always had to duck to avoid hitting it. Magazines were piled against the walls; a home-made table held cuttings, tearsheets, funny papers, Sim's postcard collection. Fishing rods leaned into a corner, and tacked onto one wall was a glassed-in case containing Sim's collection of butterflies.

"Do we go fishing again tomorrow after school?" asked Sim.

"I don't know," I said. "It depends."

Sim went on to talk about the possibilities of fishing off Third Island instead of Second. The water was deeper there at Bare-Ass Beach then at the fallen tree where we had fished today, he said. There were pike and pickerel lying in the eddy there, and probably bigger bass than the one we caught this afternoon.

But I was restless, I was not thinking of fishing, I was thinking of Margery. Even this old familiar room seemed to take on an added magic now with the memory of Margery so strong that she became a part of it. I did not want to sit still and talk; I wanted to get out and walk around. I got up.

"I've got to get home," I said. "It's going on ten."

Sim looked over at me curiously. "What's the matter. You got orders?"

No, I said, I hadn't had any orders. It was just that I wanted to get home, I had to get to bed; there was no point in getting mother too riled up. "Walk along," I suggested. "You got time."

"All right," he said.

He turned off the light, carefully locked his office, and carried the key on a big ring into the harness shop, hanging it on a nail there. Then he came out and joined me where I stood beyond the window waiting. He had said nothing to his father and I thought, He doesn't have to tell him where he goes. Old Fred hadn't even noticed him, for that matter; he had been putting the asmodor away and never turned around, knowing Sim's step.

We went out on Water Street and looked down the half block to the business section, where the new white-way lights were now half up, making half the street bright and the other dark. A few cars came along the street, a wagon which was Karl Sansey's, Mr. Elpy, the pants-presser, carrying a pair of pants on his arm, and the widow Halgenau with her daughter wheeling a wagon of wash up the street: that was the life on Water Street at nine-thirty.

"Karl Sansey's some place taking a snifter," said Sim laconically, looking at the wagon. "And which speakeasy he's gone to ain't hard to figure out."

We walked slowly up Water Street to the old Brogmar house where the public library was, and there turned toward the park, now dark with the deep darkness of trees pressing close upon Park Hall from all sides.

"You got something on your mind," said Sim.

I wanted to tell him, but I could not.

"You must a got hell all right," he went on phlegmatically. "You don't act natural for somebody who talks as much as you usually."

I grinned and said I was thinking.

Sim laughed gently, but said nothing more, and when he turned off down his own street, I did not urge him to go on through the park, as sometimes I did. I wanted to be alone now. I wanted to walk with the spectre of Margery at my side, through the park where before we had walked together, renewing briefly that too short time. I did not know how I could wait until tomorrow evening and we could be together again.

I went home and went straight upstairs to bed, lying there in the dark with my arms around a pillow and thinking of Margery while the April wind flowed into the room, soft, fragrant, the same wind invading Margery's room down the street a little way, not far at all, and in this darkness, we were not apart, and the promise of tomorrow and tomorrow after loomed close.

I went to school earlier than usual the next morning, just so as to get to talk to Margery before classes began. There she was, the same as always, with her braids down her back, and nobody so much as looked at her. All the Freshman girls were ignored anyway by everybody except the boys in their own class and a few Sophomores. There was nothing about her to make me think of last night, except what I could see in her eyes and her mouth when she looked at me, and I could tell she was thinking about last night, too.

Sim came over and said that there would be no fishing tonight.

"Why not?" I asked.

"Storm coming," he answered laconically.

I had not looked at the sky at all, but it was true; there was a great bank of dark clouds all along the western sky, and it was darkest in the southwest, which was the direction most of our bad storms came from.

"It's going to be a corker," said Sim. "You can feel the air waiting for it."

"That'll be over by the time school's out. And the fish will bite so much better."

Sim shook his head. "Cloud's been there just like that for an hour. It'll take its time. Maybe we'll go tomorrow."

Sim was usually right about the weather. But I hoped this time he was wrong. If we had a storm tonight, I could not see Margery. I sat and watched the clouds, but they did not seem to move, growing darker when the sun came out from behind other clouds in the east and shone on them, and lighter again when the sun was gone. There was no breath of air; the wind stirred not a leaf, and it grew hot as summer in the assembly room. Even before classes started, the janitor lumbered around opening one window after the other.

All day I watched Margery slyly, so that no one might see, and once I passed her a note when Mr. Slatterfield was not looking. Mr. Slatterfield was the principal, and he was in charge of the only assembly period throughout the day when Margery and I were both in the room. He was a short, nervous man, with pop-eyes and one of those come-now smiles, and twice a year he gave all the boys misty lectures on sex, and one on spitting, making a great to-do about "those juicy yellow oysters" which had no place on the sidewalk. He made all of us think of a somewhat overgrown banty rooster, and he was all right as long as everybody permitted him to believe that he was running things. He was mild-tempered and lenient, and his only fault was not knowing much about what he was supposed to teach.

So I kept Margery on my mind all day, even in manual training, which was a mistake. I was working on a board, squaring it, getting ready to make a book-rack, and I was thinking about Margery, not a straight line, so that by the time Mr. Nichol got around to looking at my work, one side of that board was like the ski-slope in midwinter. Nick just grabbed the board, hollered, "What in hell's that, Grendon?" and sailed it out the window.

When I went home after school, the clouds were still low in the west. The sun was touching their upper edge now, and soon it would have gone down behind. There was still no wind, still that summer heat, and there was something in the air that made the dogs uneasy; you could hear them whining from time to time, and scuffing restlessly from place to place. But at home the supper table was set for an early meal, since Grandfather Adams and Grandma were coming over to play cards, and they always came about five-thirty or so. Mother was sitting at the piano playing *On Moonlight Bay.*

I got right to work and got done as much of my home work as I could before supper, so that I could get out of the house as soon as possible. The clock's hands crawled toward five, and the three hours before eight seemed like a day to come. Father came home from work, and right after supper, Grandfather Adams came with Grandma.

"Storm coming," he said.

"That's been coming all day," I said, hoping he was wrong. But I knew he wasn't; if Sim was usually always right, Grandfather Adams was never wrong.

"That cloud-bank's moving up," he said, sitting down and tipping his hat back on his head. He sat there with his arms a little akimbo, both palms flat on his knees. "It's going to be a real one. Feel this heat. Been that way all day," he went on, as if we had been out of town and just got back in time to hear the news. "I remember one time in the seventies we had a day like this. Got kind of a cyclone out of it."

"A cyclone!" exclaimed Mother, shooting a fear-struck glance at Father.

"Wind anyway," said Grandfather.

"Oh, Pa!"

"Great God, girl—don't lose your head. You've got a big cellar."

I went over to the window and looked out. Sure enough, the cloud bank had moved up. Already it was dark enough for two hours later; the clouds were boiling out of the west like smoke from the locomotive's stack. Grandpa was right; we were in for it. I still hoped it would be over by eight o'clock. When the angelus rang out, you could tell by the wildness of the bells that a wind had come up.

The table was cleared, and they were playing cards: Mother and Dad. Grandpa and Grandma. Grandpa kept talking about storms, as if there was nothing doing outside and the creaking of limbs and the smack of the wind against the loose windows were something remembered from another day. Grandma Adams, who was heavy-set and good-natured, was as uneasy as Mother; she looked from time to time at the window of the living room, as if she expected the storm to announce itself, her gentle blue eyes high with alarm.

Someone knocked on the door and my sister opened it.

It was Mrs. Mulrooney. Mrs. Mulrooney was one of our neighbors, a good-hearted Irishwoman who had an almost indecent reverence for anything which had to do with religion. Grandfather Adams was as Catholic as the rest of us, but people like Mrs. Mulrooney tried his patience, and it wasn't the thing to do, to try Grandfather Adams' patience. Of course, Mrs. Mulrooney was a fine woman compared to my Aunt May, who spent far too much of her time saving some one from hell fire and embarking on one crusade after another, usually at a considerable expense to any one on the receiving end. Mrs. Mulrooney would come over day after day and praise her husband, whom she called to supper—"Den-nis! Den-NIS!"—in a voice you could hear downtown, five blocks away. And she praised her children, one by one, from the smallest one, who was a pretty, curly-headed baby, to her oldest daughter, Essa, and it was hard to hear Essa praised, because every time I heard her name mentioned in such a praiseful way, I got to thinking of how Rayme Gend took her out one time and what he told me about her, putting his hand up under her dress. So every time I heard Essa praised I thought of that, I thought of Essa with her hot eyes and her cozy smile, and I was filled with a kind of irritation because there was something wrong, something not as it should be—not about Essa, perhaps, but just wrong about her mother never suspecting anything, not knowing at all.

But this time Mrs. Mulrooney had not come to praise Dennis or their children. She was alarmed, and she sat there, with her deep brown eyes opened wide, and spoke in a hurry, her wide, friendly mouth snapping shut occasionally as if to give some one else time to talk. She was alone at home; the kids had gone to see their grandmother some miles out of town; Dennis was in Upper Sac Prairie, and there was such a storm coming up. "I tell you, I've been praying for the last half hour, but it's coming right on," said Mrs. Mulrooney.

Grandfather kind of shook himself, but he said nothing.

"I'm afraid it may be a severe storm," said Mother. If she had been alarmed before, Mrs. Mulrooney had done a good job of really frightening her.

"Oh, I know it will be! We'll be punished by the wrath of God."

"God!" exclaimed Grandfather. "What has God got to do with it?"

Mrs. Mulrooney was a little taken aback, but rallied. "God knows all and His ways are mysterious," she said.

Grandfather met Grandmother's glance and swallowed hard.

Mrs. Mulrooney got nervously to her feet again. "I can't leave the house alone. Just see how it's lightning!"

If the night had come a little early, the lightning was making up for it, and no mistake about it. It gashed down the sky and revealed the trees bent before the wind so that any moment now they might break off. And thunder was rumbling closer, driving in from the southwest across the prairie, rolling down from the Baraboo Bluffs and over the little prairie into the village, coming back from the hills across the river in a shaking echo. I thought only fleetingly now of Margery; the imminence of the storm coming at last drove everything from my mind.

Mrs. Mulrooney gazed fearfully from the window and made for the door. She could hardly shut it against the wind.

"The force of Mrs. Mulrooney's prayer doesn't seem so strong against the wind," observed Grandfather dryly.

"Father, you shouldn't talk like that. It's disrespectful."

"Pshaw! the Lord has a sense of humor." He grinned. "He's got to have or he couldn't have stood the human race this long."

"That's some wind," said Father a little uncertainly.

"Cyclone," said Grandfather quietly, as if he were talking about weather in China.

"Maybe we'd better go into the cellar," suggested Mother.

"Oh, I don't think it's as strong as all that. I may be wrong." Nevertheless, it was reassuring to hear Grandfather Adams express an opinion like that. "But it's more than just a wind, all the same."

At this instant there was a blinding flash from outside, and simultaneously a clap of thunder so loud that the house shook. A ripping, tearing sound was followed by a loud crash.

"Oh, Pa!," cried Grandmother. "It's come."

"That was a tree," said Grandfather.

"The old maple," answered Father, from the window. "She's down, all right. Out by the roots."

"That tree was over a hundred years old," said Grandfather Adams. "It seems a shame. Sound, too."

I looked out the window. The tree was down, all right; the great mass of it athwart the lawn. When the lightning flashed, I could see the yellow ropes of the swing still handing from one of the thick branches. I began to feel badly about the tree, because it was so low it was one of the few I could climb without difficulty.

The fire-bell began to ring, a terror-striking sound astride the wind. Often of night its harsh, strident clanging had awakened me, my pulse pounding with terror at this voice of alarm making its high crying in the close-pressing dark.

"It's struck somewhere," said Grandfather.

"In this wind, too!" cried Mother.

The sound of the fire-bell had hardly died away before the door was assaulted, and a wild crying arose outside.

"Maybe it's our house!" exclaimed Mother, getting to her feet.

Grandfather Adams grinned.

It was Mrs. Mulrooney again. She stood there wringing her hands and talking almost incoherently. She was distraught; her hair was coming down, her mouth trembled. Behind her against the southwest sky rose a great glowing where the fire was.

"For God's sake, come in," said Grandmother.

Mrs. Mulrooney came in and stood there trembling. "Lightning's struck Witwen's barn! Just look at that fire. It's right in the wind's direction! Oh, it's God's punishment on us! We'll all be burned out!"

"That will save the Devil some work," observed Grandfather tranquilly.

She looked at him, her hot eyes hollow with fear. "God wouldn't want you to say that, Mr. Adams."

"I've not asked Him," said Grandfather.

"Pa, keep still," cried Mother. "You only make things worse."

"Hoh!" shouted Grandfather. "I couldn't. Sit down, Mrs. Mulrooney." This last was literally roared forth, so that Mrs. Mulrooney dropped into a chair as if she had been knocked into it.

Grandfather subsided into grumbling, which was scarcely audible over the wind's tearing at trees and houses, the thunder's ceaseless rumbling outside. Mrs. Mulrooney's lips began to move; it was clear that she was praying. Grandfather got up and went over to the window and stood there.

"You shouldn't stand at the window when it lightens, Mr. Adams," said Mrs. Mulrooney. "It might see you and strike."

"Great God in Heaven!" exclaimed Grandfather Adams. "Superstition rides high!"

"You don't have to believe it if you don't want to," replied Mrs. Mulrooney with some heat, recovering a little now from her fear, "but I had a cousin whose wife's brother stood at the window like that during a storm and lightning struck him. Killed him right away."

Grandfather glared at her for a moment in dead silence; then he shrugged and, turning back to the window, said, "Woman, this round is yours." In a moment he added, "They've got that fire under control, which is probably due more to the rain than the efforts of the fire department. More likely the barn's burned down."

In a little while too, the storm had subsided.

"I wonder if it's safe to go home, now," said Mrs. Mulrooney.

"I think you could just make it between an Our Father and a Hail Mary," said Grandfather.

"Mr. Adams, you wretched man," said Grandmother.

"Live and let live!" shouted Grandfather, beaming on Mrs. Mulrooney with the tenderness of a cat examining a mouse slated for its dinner.

When we got outside after the storm there was, apart from the old maple in front of our house, only one other sign of the storm's passage in our block; this was plainly visible in the glow of the street lights, now on once again—Mrs. Mulrooney's house had been moved two feet off its foundations.

"Praise be!" cried Grandfather. "The Lord heard Mrs. Mulrooney, and moved her two feet closer to the church!"

The air was fresh and cool now, almost cold. In the west a great wedge of blue was opening up among the clouds, and the wind was rising, going higher, away from the earth; the evening star shown. As the wind died away, there rose from all around us the hum of inquiring voices, the voice of the village coming once more into being, the ceaseless murmur of life in Sac Prairie. And I thought once more of Margery.

"There'll be some damage done," said Grandfather.

"What time is it?" I asked.

"Eight o'clock, a little after," answered Father.

"I'm going," I said.

"Hold on!" hollered Pa. "Where do you think you're going now?"

I said I was just going down to Sim's place, and then likely we were going around to see what damage had been done.

"What with loose wires and all—you'd better stay home," said Mother.

"Go on, go on," said Grandfather. "Just keep away from any wires hanging down. Now then."

But no one argued with him.

I ran down the street, hardly with eyes for any of the trees lying down, until I got to Margery's house. She was safe. She was there inside; I could see her walking around in the living room, and I knew she was not coming to meet me at the Park Hall. I stood there for a while, and then went down to Sim's. Everywhere trees were down, and big limbs blocked the roads; I had to crawl over and among them in places. But there was not much damage to the houses: a few broken windows, a chimney or so, in one place a barn collapsed and in another the edge of a roof torn off. It was not a bad storm after all. People were all over, shouting to each other, pointing out one thing and another, and talking across alleys and streets, saying it was a good thing it had come early in the evening and not later, saying if the fire-bell rang now, the machine would never be able to get to the place with all these limbs in the way, talking about how fresh the air was now, how hot it had been, saying all those important little things that come out at such times.

Sim was not in his office; he was in the harness shop. Old Fred had gone home at the first sign of the wind, leaving Sim there alone. He was sitting on the stitching-horse sewing up two pieces of leather.

"Ma can't stand to be alone in a storm," he said.

I told him what had happened to Mrs. Mulrooney's house and our old maple tree.

"Oh, there was a window pane out in the office, too, but I get her put back already," he said.

He didn't seem excited at all by the storm. In the middle of it he had gone up to see the Witwen barn burn down. He liked fires, but that barn burned too quickly. The wind had all but picked him up on his way back; so how could he get stirred up about a window or two and a few trees down? I could see the point of that and said nothing more, watching him bent at his work, thinking how he would probably be just like old Fred, just the same in time to come, the light from the green-shaded workbench globe pushed back up into his face and soft there.

Without looking at me, he said, "Heard you went out walking with Margery Estabrook."

I admitted it.

He turned and grinned at me over his shoulder. "You just invite trouble," he said. "Her ma's got a temper you can't beat, and she hates Catholics. I used to go to Sunday School with her."

"Who? Her ma?"

"No, Margery."

"Oh." I did not want to talk about her. I pushed my hands into my pockets and leaned up against the workbench, looking toward the darkness of the south wall. If I looked long enough, I could see Margery's face there, like something brought out from the mind's eye.

"Well, they can't say she ain't pretty," he said.

"No," I agreed. "They sure can't. She's pretty enough."

I wanted to ask what he meant about inviting trouble, but I could not. I thought he might say something against Margery, and I would have minded that, coming from Sim. I asked him whether he had to keep on fixing that leather piece.

"Heck, no! I'm just trying to see how good I am," he said, pulling it from the vise. "Why?"

I said I thought we could walk around town a little and look at the damage done. There might be things to see. After all, I had gone down only about ten blocks and there was a good deal more of Sac Prairie than that.

"Well, the way I look at it," he said, "after I came all the way back from Witwen's place, it won't be any fun; it's too much work for just the looking. And I guess I better stay here until Pa comes back."

"All right," I said. "It's all the same to me."

Nevertheless, I wanted to go. I sat there a while longer, not saying much, wishing old Fred would come back; so Sim would have less excuse not to go; but he didn't come. I kept thinking about myself inviting trouble, as Sim had said. I wouldn't ask about it, but pretty soon Sim began to talk about it just as if I had asked.

"You take it now the first time a feller gets to going with a girl," he said, "what's the first thing that happens?"

"He falls in love."

"Gosh, you sure looked sick when you said that," he came back, grinning again. "I guess you got hit, all right. But I didn't mean it that way. I meant it different—what happens to him outside of that?"

"Why," I said, "that's easy. He's got a new interest in life."

Sim laughed. "Now, I observe it different. The first thing, it seems to me, is the way everybody else takes it. The whole high school teases them about it, but they can take it, and sometimes they even like it. Then pretty soon, if it looks like a steady thing, everybody else says, They're too young to be going together like that! It ain't healthy! and such stuff."

"Hold on! I'm fifteen!" I exclaimed. "I'm old enough to know what I'm doing."

"Sure, but not old enough to prove it," said Sim.

"Well, it's my business."

"Maybe your grandpa'll agree with you on that. But nobody else. You wait and see."

I said I would be able to handle that all right, never fear. I had had to handle a lot of opposition in my life, I said. "Look at that time they tried to keep me from collecting tin cans," I said. "I didn't stop till I got good and ready. Look at that time they tried to take the sandpile away from me and never bring back a fresh one. I just took and piled all that sand in my tin cans and hid them in the oven of that old stove that used to stand just inside the shed out in back, and they just gave up the idea. Look what a time they had with those funny papers. Why, even my aunts in the cities send 'em to me now. No sir, I guess I can take care of that all right."

I didn't like the way Sim just sat and ginned. You would have thought he was older than I was, and he wasn't. He didn't know half the things I knew—not that he wasn't smart. He was. He was much smarter than I was in algebra and geometry, even if I beat him in history and English.

"Well," I demanded. "Don't say it's not so."

"I don't have to say anything," he said. "But I hope you're right. You take that time Ma and Pa thought I was sweet on Norma—why, they just about locked me in the attic for the rest of my life!"

"Oh, well, your ma and pa are kind of old-fashioned."

"Maybe so," agreed Sim. He turned the light up toward the clock's face; it was after nine. "I guess Pa's not coming down again. I can lock up then."

"One thing you can make up your mind on," I said, when I stood waiting for him to clean up a little. "There's nothing going to separate Margery and me unless it's so that I'm ready for it. You can just bet on that."

"It'll sure be hard on you."

He put out the light over the workbench and stood there a minute looking toward the front of the harness shop where the street light's glow came in and lay in long parallelograms across the floor and the counters of harness straps and horse-blankets, currycombs and cans of Neatsfoot. Then he followed me out of the back door and locked it.

The wind had gone down entirely now, and the night was fragrant beyond words with the freshness of rain, the rich aroma of earth riding the wind from over the newly plowed fields on the prairie west of the village. We walked along, saying nothing, just breathing in the sweet air, and parted at Sim's house, from which I hurried over the street through the park and home, still thinking about myself inviting trouble and a little irritated now because Sim had said all that, and because Sim knew I had been out with her and I hadn't thought to ask how he knew it.

The House of Moonlight

THE HOUSE IS still there, its stone walls aged in the sunlight of the years, yellowed where it stands on top of the highest of the moraine hills across the blue Wisconsin, east of Sac Prairie. It is closed now; it has been closed for a long time; its sightless windows are like a wall separating past time from this, and, looking at it when of an evening the late sunlight, or at night, the moonlight gives a deceptive luminousness to its remaining panes, I can still see in mind's eye strange old Mrs. Merrihew, and the way she customarily sat listening to voices on another plane, from another world, that proud woman with her arresting blue eyes and her white hair; I can see the two young women, Rikki and Hester, dimly and, more spectral still, the illusion of Peter, who was never there except as he was conjured into existence in the troubled brain of Joel Merrihew, who was, too, a being of night and moonlight. People still speak of him as a local genius whose great future was cut so tragically short; but from this perspective it is possible to say that even as there is a time to be born, there is a time to die. Perhaps Joel Merrihew knew. Whatever it was that lay in those years he was away from Sac Prairie, no one discovered—not my Grandfather Grendon, who wanted most of all to know, not old Mrs. Merrihew who set out on her strange quest in the year he died, and died herself far away, in Prague, searching in vain for a young man who may not have lived, who was even in the flesh evanescent and ghost-like.

Under the moon, the house has even yet a kind of tangible inner life, as were it about to spring to animate existence at any moment, as were those who once walked there to appear again and declaim once more the lines of the tragedy in which they took part. A house of moonlight, belonging to past time, existing for me in that indeterminate age between childhood and adolescence, as it were, in a place where the moon shines forever, and nothing changes or grows old, those halcyon years when Grandfather Grendon had retired from his practise but still saw, on occasion, those old patients who demanded his services, when life in Sac Prairie was not harried by time and circumstances, and all the world seemed young. . . .

Wisconsin in Their Bones, 1953

II

I do not remember how old I was when I first met Joel Merrihew; I might have been thirteen; I could not have been much older. He had spent most of his early years at schools of music all over the world, and because he was often talked about at home, his very absence from Sac Prairie had made him into a figure looming large on the horizon, however intangibly. Our first meeting took place one summer day in a train out of Chicago on the way to Madison. He did not know me, of course, but he did know my Grandfather Grendon. I saw him some time before he noticed us, without recognizing him, since I had never seen him before. He was extremely handsome, and caught my eye almost immediately; he had a rather long face, as I remember it now, a very straight nose, dark brown hair which was longer than customary, and dark luminous eyes; but the most attractive part of him seemed to be his wide, sensuous mouth when he smiled. He was lithe without being thin, and carried himself with a peculiar grace that gave him a faintly apologetic attitude. He was in every way as I had imagined he might be from comments dropped by my grandfather or my parents, except that his fingers were not as long and slender as I thought they might be, and he was much more nervous. Despite having seen him several times after that, before the tragedy that ended his career, I remembered him perhaps most definably as he was that day, pacing the length of the car, back and forth, preoccupied and troubled.

His back was toward us when we entered, and we had taken seats before he turned. He passed us twice without noticing us, for his eyes were fixed on the carpet in the aisle, and his slight frown showed his preoccupation. He sat down only after the train had started, and then for some time he stared out of the window at the fleeting landscape. Presently, however, he looked casually from one occupant of the car to another, and thus his eyes came to us. There was an uncertain and, for me, surprising recognition at once. My grandfather's quick smile convinced him, and he rose to come over.

"Dr. Grendon," he said in a soft, yet firm voice.

My grandfather's smile broadened and he said, "I hardly thought you'd know me, Joel. It's been a long time since you've seen me, and I've not been growing any younger."

"I've a pretty good memory for faces," he said in an offhand way. Then his eyes turned from grandfather to me.

"My grandson, Steve," said my grandfather at once and, turning to me, added, "this is Joel Merrihew." Without giving us time to more than acknowledge this casual introduction, my grandfather said, "You're twenty-seven now, aren't you, Joel?" He asked this, but he knew that Joel's acknowledgment must come, for my grandfather could give at any time almost the precise age of every living person he had helped bring into the world, and Joel Merrihew was one of them.

"Now tell me, my boy," my grandfather continued, "how is the music coming? We hear things now and then from your mother, of course, and we see clippings. Seems you're keeping yourself pretty much out of the limelight."

"I don't feel I'm good enough yet," Joel replied with some reluctance. Then he looked abruptly away, and once more a slight frown appeared on his forehead. "And besides," he added in a low voice, more to himself than us, "Mother doesn't think so either, even if Rikki does."

My grandfather looked at him with narrowed eyes and increased interest. Apparently he did not know who Rikki was. Joel Merrihew's face cleared after a few moments, but not before his expression had conveyed evidence of some inner struggle, subdued perhaps, but not entirely hidden.

"I'll want to hear you play," my grandfather said. "And I want Steve to hear you." To me he said, "When Joel was twelve he could play far better than anyone else in town—except perhaps Linda Grell."

Joel Merrihew's position in the aisle was becoming awkward for him; so he reversed the seat before us and sat down facing us. He sat for some minutes in silence, and in the meantime we entered Wisconsin. Noticing this suddenly, he said, "It feels good to be home again."

"You didn't like Paris?" asked my grandfather quickly.

He shrugged. "Not very much. I got tired of the arty people in the Quarter—all talk, no work."

My grandfather's smile indicated that he thought well of Joel Merrihew's frank disapproval. "You traveled, of course?"

"Oh, yes. I liked Vienna—Weimar—Rome. Liszt country, you know." He said this half-apologetically, half-defiantly, his mouth oddly petulant at that moment, as if he were aware of speaking controversially.

My grandfather chuckled. "Liszt—the God-man," he murmured.

"Without him, none of the moderns from Wagner could have come when they did," Joel replied, looking away in faint annoyance.

My grandfather wisely dropped the subject. "Did you go into Spain at all?"

Joel nodded. "Yes. I visited de Falla."

"A modernist?"

"Partly, I suppose. You ought to hear his splendid *Concerto for Harpsichord,* as well as his *El Amor Brujo* in its entirety—not just the popular *Ritual Fire Dance.* I'll play some de Falla for you some time."

"Do you plan to continue your work at home, boy?"

"I think so, yes. Perhaps I'll go on a tour after a while—when I'm sure." He stopped talking and made a curt gesture with his hands, as if to signify that he did not want to say more. He looked at me. "And you," he said, "what do you think of doing?"

My grandfather answered for me. "He wants to write. Can you discourage him?"

"Perhaps," Joel answered. "But why? I suppose you want him to become a doctor like his father and grandfather—you want to make a family tradition out of the practise."

My grandfather smiled but made no replay. Joel looked at me carefully—"sizing me up," as my grandfather would have said. "And how do you think you ought to start your career?" he asked.

"I want to go places and see people," I answered.

He shook his head with almost irritated impatience. "Don't do it. Don't go anywhere before you've absorbed everything there is to know about your home town and the people in it. After that, perhaps travel will help."

He turned to my grandfather and began to talk of people he had known at home before he left for Europe. He had been gone more than ten years. Part of this time his widowed mother had been with him, part of the time she had been in the States; but he had never come home. She had made three or four trips to Europe and back in those years, sometimes staying with him as much as a year at a time. But not he. Now he was coming back to Sac Prairie which, inevitably, he would find changed—not in little changes which had taken place one at a time, but in the accumulation of those changes. The Sac Prairie to which he was returning was not the village he had left a decade ago. But the Merrihew house was not in the village, precisely speaking; the hill on which it stood was just across the Wisconsin from town, a low hill, certainly, but still dominant over the village on its lip of flatland jutting out into the river there where the Wisconsin made its great bend below Portage to reach out toward the Mississippi. He mentioned people I knew, vaguely. He expressed regret at Linda Grell's suicide; I remembered later that he had said, several times, "But I could understand it; I could understand her doing a thing like that."

Shortly after we passed Beloit, the conductor came on through the coach with a telegram for him. It struck me that he had been waiting for something like this, for he was not surprised. He ripped open the envelope eagerly and withdrew the sheet of yellow paper. There was evidently not much to the message, but what there was brought an expression of worry to his face. He crumpled the telegram in his hand and threw it to the floor in such a manner that the name of the sender plainly showed. I read it unconsciously: "Rikki." At the same time, he turned to the conductor and asked about sending a wire at the next station.

The conductor produced a pad and pencil, and Joel wrote hastily with the pad across his knee. I read the name of the addressee—Mlle. Frederique Janoux—but by the time I had deciphered this much, he had finished the message and handed it over to the conductor, who immediately read it over.

"What's this?" he asked. "'Come next Friday not before'—is that right?"

"Right," said Joel, nodding.

The conductor computed the cost of the message as from Janesville, the next stop, and Joel paid him. Then the conductor went off down the coach and Joel turned once more to my grandfather.

"There's something more I want to see you about," he said with that abruptness which was characteristic of him. "I want you to meet Rikki, for one. Look, why don't you come over to dinner Sunday evening? And the boy, too?"

"Perhaps we can," said my grandfather. "I'll let you know."

They sat talking about many things, to which I listened with but half an understanding; then the train reached Madison, and Joel went to collect his baggage and make his separate way to Sac Prairie, twenty-five miles away.

That night, not long after I had gone to bed, and within ten minutes after mother had passed through and put out the light on *The Adventures of Sherlock Holmes*, I heard my grandfather go to the connecting door between the house and my father's office and start talking. His voice came more clearly than my father's.

"I had the impression today that something was troubling Joel Merrihew," he said slowly. "Something deeper than just a passing worry."

"Probably you saw him in a period of self-doubt," my father replied. "Creative people are apt to become depressed from time to time, particularly after the expending of effort."

"Is he creative? I wonder."

"Oh, in any case—artistic people—temperament."

"No, no," answered my grandfather impatiently. "I don't mean that."

"But Dad, you know that most artistic people aren't normal."

"Oh, fiddlesticks! When you're a little older you'll think twice about dividing people up into those who are 'normal' and those who aren't. Son, the only certainties in this world are the mathematical ones, and the entire science of mathematics is founded on a premise incapable of proof if your audience is unable to comprehend or rejects the premise. Normality as you understand it doesn't enter into it. Self-doubt, perhaps, yes. If so, profound."

"In short, Dad, he's sick."

"Yes."

He went into the office then, closing the door behind him, and I heard no more. I lay for a long time trying to understand. Joel Merrihew had not looked sick to me; I thought of someone pale and listless, and he was certainly not that; I thought my grandfather had read a lot in his frown and his restlessness.

III

That Sunday we went over to the Merrihew house for dinner.

Grandfather got out his horse and the riding buggy, waving aside my father's offer to drive us over in the car, and away we rode down the street to the old wooden bridge across the Wisconsin. Grandfather stopped to talk to the bridge-keeper, who took the toll—a short, hunched-over man with a straggly white beard who was always afraid that a new bridge would be built and take away his only means of making a living—and then we drove on over the bridge.

It was late in the afternoon, and already the ridge east of the Wisconsin shone bright in the sunlight falling on it from the western heaven. The house was right at the edge of the highest hill; it shown white in the sunlight, white as snow, almost, though it had a dark red roof, which was uncommon in those days. It stood there as if it grew naturally out of that hill; the slope came up on both sides, and the bluff sharp up the front; the house crowned it, bright in the sun, with its green shutters and its maroon roof, and the lawns that stretched away under the trees behind to the east along the top of that hill. And down along the bottom, far down, flashing among the rocks of an old wing dam there, the river went by, bluer than the sky, a deep blue that was cobalt.

Grandfather drove along Lovers' Lane and down the road which lay at the bottom of the hills there. Then he went into one of the ravines and made his way up around the drive there to the back of the house, where stood a carriage-house as old-fashioned as the house seemed new. There were sheds here, too, a summer-kitchen, and certain other buildings, one of which, said grandfather, used to be Joel's studio.

An old man with a white stubble on his chin came out of one of the sheds to take care of the horse and buggy.

"Evenin', Doc," he said. "Ain't seen you for a while."

"How are you, Dan?" asked my grandfather.

"Oh, I git it in the back now an' then, but I can't complain. I'm doin' all right on one kidney."

I jumped out of the buggy; grandfather followed.

Mrs. Merrihew saw us and came out.

"You are almost a stranger, Jasper," she said.

"You're looking good, Celia."

Mrs. Merrihew was a slender woman with white hair and very blue eyes. She was old, as old as my grandfather, perhaps older. She wore skirts that reached down to her ankles and habitually dressed in black, brown, or grey, with a cameo brooch at her neck-line. She seemed glad to see grandfather, and she always, as she did today, made some remark about his bringing "the boy," as if this were a special treat for her, but after that she hardly ever noticed me. I used to watch her, and I thought of her as two different people because once in a while she would be gay and animated and quick, and she would have a good time talking with my grandfather, and then again she would be dark and moody and strange, she would sit saying very little and always leaning over a little to one side with her head tilted and her eyes far away, just as if she listened to someone nobody else could see or hear.

"It's always so nice to see you, Jasper," she said as we walked into the house. "The two of you. You know, it's like meeting one's past . . ."

"Ah, yes, I *am* getting old, I know," said my grandfather.

"And one's future." She gestured in my direction, looking toward me but not at me.

My grandfather flashed a quick, quizzical glance at me but said nothing.

"Joel will be so glad to see you. He's been looking forward to your coming. He told me the first day how he ran into you on the train. How lucky for him! He did need someone to talk to—all these years not being back to Sac Prairie, as if there weren't anything for him to see here or do here or no one to talk to."

"And there is, of course, said my grandfather.

"Yes, yes, of course there is."

Their eyes met, held together for a moment, and then hers dropped. She pursed her lips and her lids lowered over her eyes. Then she took a grasping breath and went on.

"I should tell you—there is a young woman with him. I know nothing about her, except that he seems fond of her. French, I think. A strange, dark creature. Please don't mind, Jasper."

"My dear Celia!" protested my grandfather laughing. "Should I mind a young—and presumably attractive—woman?"

"Oh, you!" she said, and a smile fluttered around her mouth, her thin, pale skin colored a little, and with one hand she swept her full black skirt out of the way as she opened the door to the conservatory, which was a large room looking out on a narrow balcony which ran its length beyond French doors, and past the balcony, to Sac Prairie and the low rolling fields and pastures and oak groves falling away into the west, where the hills lay dark blue on the rim of sky.

Ahead of us was a wide expanse of room in which there seemed to be nothing but the grand piano at the far end, and Joel Merrihew standing beside it; then you saw the low chairs along the walls on both sides, and the woman sitting on the far side of the piano, just away from the French doors, of which there were three pairs.

It was a tableau. For a moment nobody moved. The late sunlight flooded the room with a kind of old rose haze, and Joel stood in it like a statue, like somebody posed for the photographer, with one hand resting lightly on the piano, and the other in the pocket of his trousers. Behind us Mrs. Merrihew still held on to the door's knob. Only my grandfather moved leisurely into the room. Then Joel came forward to meet him, one hand languidly outstretched.

"Dr. Grendon—and Steve." And then, having included both of us, he turned and included the woman, too. "Rikki, come and meet my friends."

He introduced Mlle. Frederique Janoux. She was dark, with an olive skin, and a full red mouth like something angry in her face. Her eyes were grey-green, and they seemed to burn when she looked at anyone or anything. She spoke with an accent, and she was smoking a cigarette; I saw it when she got up; she had made a kind of gesture as if she meant to put it out, but then she thought that it didn't matter; so she came up with it still in her hand and said something about she hoped we would not mind if she smoked, she was addicted to cigarettes.

"You are Dr. Grendon," she said to my grandfather. "I have heard much of you."

It was plain to see that she had not heard much at all about my grandfather, but was just saying so to seem polite. I could tell that my grandfather knew it, too, because his dry chuckle gave him away, a kind of rasping sound that meant he did not like something.

Mrs. Merrihew had come in after us, and now she said quickly, "Joel, dinner will be ready in just a little while. I know Jasper would like to hear you play, and perhaps it would be better now than after dinner?"

"Would you, Dr. Grendon?" asked Joel, turning to him.

"You know I would, Joel."

He turned, strode over and sat down before the piano. "And what would you like to hear?"

"Just anything. Let me feel your taste, my boy."

Joel looked thoughtfully out of the open French doors toward the western heaven, all copper and gold now with the setting sun. Then he looked at his mother, briefly, and then at Rikki. As soon as her eyes met his, she spoke.

"You might play something from *El Amor Brujo*, Joel," she said softly. "You know—the *Ritual Fire Dance*."

"But a transcription . . ." he began hesitantly.

"Oh, do, please, for me."

He played it. It was exciting; it shattered something in the room and the house; it made me think of something wild and fierce flung out into that fire of sunset. It was good and very well played. But Joel apologized.

"I'm sorry," he said to my grandfather. "That really doesn't give you a sampling of de Falla. It's not my mood, not just now."

"Why don't you play something in your mood?" asked my grandfather.

"Schumann," whispered Mrs. Merrihew.

"Play just what you like, Joel," said grandfather then, quite persuasively. "We'll all be still for as long as you play. I want to feel your music without interruption."

He began then, lovingly, with Schumann's *Vogel als Prophet.* I knew it; I had heard it often. I had heard Linda Grell play it long ago. But the way Joel Merrihew played it made it sound like a question that came to life and haunted the room; it was something in the tonal quality of the music, something in the way he lingered over certain notes, something that seemed like a question lying far back in his mind, a question he could ask only in music. Then he played something to make a transition in his mood—Liszt's *Valse Oubliee*, after which he went on to a very melodic piece I did not know, but which grandfather later told me was the romanza from Mozart's piano *Concerto in D Minor.* This he played very contemplatively; he lingered with it, and, as I learned long after, when I had heard it on records and in concerts, he improvised steadily throughout, he played variations on the theme which were not written into the score, and perhaps he composed these variations as he played, though it was more likely that he had committed them to memory from previous experimentation. And then he ended up with Chopin's *Nocturne in D Flat Major*, which was pensive and melancholy and deeply moving as he played it.

During the while he played the room reflected the hour of the day. The sun went down, the afterglow flamed a lambent crimson at the prairie's edge, the brightness went out of the room and a kind of twilight took possession of it, softening it, and creating stranger shadows which drew in from the walls toward the spacious center of the room. When he had finished, he sat for a moment flexing his fingers before he turned around.

"That was very fine, Joel," said my grandfather.

"Have I improved then? Grown?"

"Can you doubt it, my boy? You should know here,"—my grandfather struck his chest—"and you must."

Mrs. Merrihew got up, rustling. "Rikki, will you help me?" she called across the room. "I know the table will be too much for Emma alone."

"Of course," said Rikki, and passed around us.

"But there was a question in your voice, Dr. Grendon," said Joel, after they had left the room.

"Did you think so?" asked my grandfather. "Or was it the echo of the question inside you, Joel?" he continued in a gentler voice. "Why that uncertainty?"

"I don't know that I'm uncertain," replied Joel.

My grandfather had got up. Now he lit a cigar. For a moment he did not say anything. "I'm not a musician, you know," he said presently. "I am just—an audience. I know what I like and what I don't like; sometimes I know why. Not always. The direction of the heart or the direction of the mind—it does not matter how you see it or say it—is determined by many factors other than the specific criteria or criticism."

"And you felt—a question?" asked Joel.

"Yes. You asked it."

"Did I?" asked Joel quietly.

"You asked it in Schumann. You tried to forget it in Liszt. You explored it in Mozart. You despaired of an answer in Chopin." My grandfather chuckled quietly. "Or would you prefer to believe I'm romancing, my boy?"

"I know you, Dr. Grendon."

"Do you? But that's an ambiguous answer, surely."

"In every artist—or, no, let us not say 'artist'—let us say in everyone who is in any way creative, there is of necessity that question: Am I or not? Do I exist on my own terms for others, or not?"

"Yes," said my grandfather thoughtfully. "Yes. But that isn't the question you asked."

"No?"

"No."

The door opened and Mrs. Merrihew stood there.

"Oh, Jasper, you exasperating man," she cried, "you've gone and lit a cigar and you knew we'd left to put the table on."

"The cigar can be put out at any moment, Celia."

"Well, come then, we're ready."

"After you."

She walked so swiftly to the dining room that she seemed, in the dusk of the corridor, to be floating there. I walked after her. Behind me came Joel and my grandfather. I could just hear them say a little more before I was out of hearing.

"I sometimes forget, Dr. Grendon, it must be inescapable for men in your profession to be in that frame of mind conducive to looking upon people first as patients, and secondly as people."

"I have no patients, Joel," said my grandfather gently. "I never have had. What you call patients are just people, like you and me, who are in trouble."

I could not hear what Joel Merrihew replied, for I had followed Mrs. Merrihew into the dining-room, which was long and narrow, with a long table in the middle of it, and a woman to serve us standing off to one side next to the door that led into the kitchen. Rikki was there, at one side of the table, leaving Joel to go to the head of it, and my grandfather and me around to the other side.

The table was lit by candles, which shed a subdued glow over everything. The twilight which still shone outside did not invade the room to any marked degree, but the candles cast enough light. The dining-room was a kind of connecting room, between the conservatory and Joel's bedroom to the south, and the kitchen and other rooms on the north, and it looked out to both east and west, so that where I sat I could watch the moon come up over the sheds and among the trees east of the house.

The dinner conversation was about Joel—what he had done in Europe, whom he had seen, where he had played and studied. I did not listen at first; I was hungry and I was intent on watching the moon come up and thinking about something else. But after a while I began to be aware of a pattern in the conversation. Joel would begin quite animatedly to tell about some event in his European sojourn; then Rikki would take up the story and carry on with it; and, as soon as possible thereafter, Mrs. Merrihew would change the subject. Then it would happen in the same way, and each time Joel would seem to lose interest as soon as he had ceased to talk. Perhaps it was because each story he began took on a subtly different meaning or color or tone when Rikki had finished with it.

It did not matter what the subject was. Always there was Rikki. Though he had gone quite alone to spend a week with Richard Strauss, and Rikki had never been there, yet it was Rikki who completed his story with one of her own, which she had heard from Joel. When he had played with Beecham at Covent Garden, she had been in Deauville, yet she finished his account of the concert. Somewhere in each of his stories, she inevitably interrupted with, "And don't you remember, Joel—" and from that moment it was her story, and as she unfolded it, Joel's interest and animation declined, not of resentment, but almost of relief or something akin to it; and at the same time his mother turned to another subject, until at last, she retreated into silence and sat quietly in her place in that familiar attitude of listening, always listening, not to any of us, but to someone or something no one else could hear, leaving everyone else to feel as if she were someone in a distant place, a strange woman living in a world apart from these enclosing walls.

"And what are you planning to do now, Joel?" my grandfather asked at last.

"Joel is going to concertize," said Rikki.

Mrs. Merrihew looked once more into the present. "Not for a while, I hope," she said.

Joel shrugged and grimaced. "You see, Dr. Grendon?" I am between two fires. For my part I want to compose. I am at work on a piano transcription of Franck's *D Minor Symphony*, with variations. I must confess the destiny motif fascinates me. But perhaps it will be too much for me; a season on the concert stage here in America might do me good. It ought to be stabilizing in a way."

"That's madness," said Mrs. Merrihew quietly. "Constantly uprooting one's self from one place to another—meeting people—the papers—everything. Stabilizing?"

"But it's fun to meet people," cried Rikki passionately.

"For you," said Mrs. Merrihew, bowing toward her. "But what is it for Joel?"

"Oh, he loves to play. It's his life!"

"Yes, indeed," replied the older woman. "But he can play here as well. With more peace of mind, perhaps, than on tour."

Joel looked over to my grandfather and asked, "Shall we go to the conservatory, Dr. Grendon? I want to play you some records I brought from Vienna—some new work of Richard Strauss."

My grandfather got up and drew away from the table; I followed him.

In the conservatory Joel turned up two very pale lights near the phonograph, but before he could put a record on the turntable, my grandfather laid a restraining hand on his arm.

"Tell me, Joel, do you want to concertize?"

"I don't know. I don't suppose it matters very much." He bent to take a record from the album he had selected.

"One more question, which may be none of my business. If so you can say as much. Do you love this woman, Joel?"

"Rikki?"

"Yes."

Joel stood for a moment without replying. He did not resent my grandfather's question. "I suppose I do," he added at last. "As far as people like me are capable of love. Mother has often said that people with strong creative egos have a narcissistic tendency, and I suppose it's true in a way."

"Love is no respecter of egos," said my grandfather.

Joel smiled. "Do you like her, Dr. Grendon?"

"People always interest me."

At this Joel laughed outright. "Now who is being ambiguous?" he asked.

"Touché," said my grandfather, smiling.

Joel put a record on the turntable and the music of *Der Rosenkavalier* flowed out and took possession of the room. As soon as it began, Joel walked leisurely across to the open French doors and stood looking out over the river and the prairie, with the village caught in a maze of moonlight there, light so bright that it cast a mist about the yellow eyes of streetlights and windows in Sac Prairie.

He was still standing there when Mrs. Merrihew and Rikki came in, but he turned at their entrance and came back to the phonograph, which he tended thereafter for an hour or more, playing not only Strauss, but Sibelius and Stravinsky and Rachmaninoff in foreign recordings which were new to my grandfather. When at last he was tired of selecting and playing records and turned the phonograph off, my grandfather came to his feet.

"You're not going yet, Jasper?" said Mrs. Merrihew.

"I'm afraid I must," he said. "It's past ten o'clock."

Joel made no effort to delay our departure. He was tired now, a little withdrawn; he wanted to be alone. He bade us goodbye and asked us to call again, and he was especially at pains to tell me that if I liked music I should feel welcome to come over whenever I wished, although he could not promise to entertain me.

Mrs. Merrihew walked outside on my grandfather's arm.

"It's a beautiful night, Jasper," she said. "So calm, so peaceful . . ."

"Yes. And is it calm within, Celia?"

"I wonder." She did not explain this apprehension. "Goodnight Jasper. Do come again. You shouldn't wait just to be invited."

On the way down around the hill, one of the reins got caught and was twisted. My grandfather had to stop to unfasten it, and it took him almost five minutes to do so. By the time we reached the road that led away over to the highway and cross the bridge into Sac Prairie, we could hear music coming down the hill from the house on its crown, and grandfather stopped the horse a few minutes to listen. It was the phonograph, not the piano; I had thought Joel tired of playing records. Perhaps Rikki had persuaded him to begin again. He was playing the Franck *D Minor Symphony*; he was playing it with the volume way up; the magnificent chords rolled out over that moonlit landscape like thunder.

My grandfather pursed his lips and drove on. He was very thoughtful and said nothing all the way home.

IV

It was about ten days later that I came home from school one afternoon and found my father and grandfather playing the phonograph. Or perhaps my grandfather played it, and my father listened, for he had that attitude—a kind of hurried attitude, sitting on the arm of a chair, listening to music and the voice of my grandfather. I did not know the piece that was on the phonograph, and I went on through the room to my own room to change clothes. I could hear very well there, without trying.

My grandfather was talking. "The opening theme suggests various other pieces, you see, Will. Not only this one. This, too, is Franck—the third of the *Beatitudes.* It suggests Liszt's *Les Preludes,* too, but there is not actually so close a resemblance to that initial subject of the symphony as there is to this. Listen now."

He stopped the phonograph and altered records. Another piece I did not know was being played; chamber music of some kind.

"What is that?" asked my father.

"The Beethoven *Quartet, Opus 135*—I've put it on at the end. However unrelated they may actually be, the opening subject of the *D Minor*—d, c-sharp, f, I think—suggests a parallel to the end of this quartet, that final interrogation—g, e, b-flat. He spoke of being fascinated by the 'destiny motif'; I don't know whether this question of Beethoven's qualifies. *Musz es sein?*—it's not the same as the 'fate knocking at the door' theme of Beethoven's *Fifth Symphony.* But, of course, the provocative question may yet be a question of destiny."

"It would be whatever he wishes it to be, Dad."

"Would it now? Perhaps. Let us play just part of it again.

My grandfather next played three records of the Franck *D Minor Symphony*—the opening and the ending of the symphony.

When he had finished, he played no more.

"Now, then," he said to my father. "What do you feel in that symphony?"

"Doubt, perhaps—but also affirmation," replied my father.

"Sadness, resignation, and that eternal question which haunts the entire symphony," said my grandfather.

"But also faith and triumph," said my father.

"Restlessness and melancholy—and everywhere that mysticism which characterizes so much of Franck's work. Yes, there are faith and affirmation, there is even some tranquility, but the dominant motif is determined by the restlessness and provocative question in the symphony's initial subject."

"Let me interrupt you, Dad—what is it you're trying to prove?"

"I'm not trying to prove anything," said my grandfather patiently. "I'm trying to find out something. I want to know why Joel Merrihew is identifying himself with this symphony. Why particularly this one? I ask because it poses a contradiction if so—because Joel is chaotic, and this symphony is wonderfully unified."

"The attraction of the opposite, perhaps?"

"Mmn. Could be."

"What makes you think there is that identification, Dad?"

"Listen—out of the last ten nights, he played this symphony on eight of them. He's preparing a transcription for the piano. Now, I'm not a creative person at all, but it would seem to me rudimentary that transcriptions such as he projects can be done by anyone; the composer is far more likely to take a theme and prepare variations on it, perhaps at some length. He's transcribing the whole thing, with variations. Moreover, he would work from a score, not repeated playings of the recordings. And he has literally thousands of recordings, so that there's no necessity for him to play the Franck night after night."

"He likes it. It may be that simple. The desire for a subject to diagnose might well supply one, Dad."

"I know you think I'm chasing hares, son. But I don't think so and that's more important to me."

I came from my room just as my father was returning to his office. Seeing me, grandfather called to me not to go far, because he meant to go over to Merrihew's; he had telephoned them that he was coming; he wanted me to go along. So, instead of leaving the house, I found the book I had begun to read two days before, took it out to the porch, and lay there on the couch reading it.

We were not to go to Merrihew's that night, however, for scarcely twenty minutes later Mrs. Merrihew drove up in her car. Grandfather, who had come out to the porch, too, took her into the house. It was a warm day, and the windows were all open. Mrs. Merrihew was agitated and she walked back and forth in the room.

"It sounds dreadful, Jasper, but you must forgive us," she began. "You must not come over tonight. Joel is in a dark mood—he's not fit for company, truly he isn't. Tomorrow, thank goodness, Miss Janoux is going away."

"You dislike her, Celia?"

"No, no—I don't dislike anyone, I hope, Jasper. But she doesn't love him—she wants to own him; it isn't the same thing. I know how that happens, how they can make themselves indispensable—I am a woman, too."

"But you're still glad she's going?"

"Yes, for his sake. I can endure, if I must. But he is subject to her every whim—if he wishes to play Debussy, no, it must be Delius; if he wants to listen to Sibelius, then it must be Brahms. Sometimes I think she is the very imp of perversity. But can I say so to him? No, never. I am his mother. I am the last one who could say anything, because she could say I am the possessive one, I am the jealous one."

"Are you jealous, Celia?"

"No—how can you ask, Jasper!"

"I asked because jealousy need not be anything more than possessiveness; often it isn't. What do you want him to do?"

"Whatever he wants. That is important. Let him develop along the directions which have come into being inside him. Not according to her wishes or whims—for they're never more than that, actually."

"He'll miss her, then."

"Very much, I'm afraid. I thought of this—someone who could be there, but who would not disturb him. Do you think Steve might come?"

"I'm sure he would like to," said my grandfather with some caution. "But I should have to ask him."

"Of course. And you could not say anything to Joel?"

"No."

There was a little silence then, before my grandfather spoke again. He had evidently arrested her pacing.

"Sit down, Celia. Don't give such rein to your nerves. Now tell me—you've had time enough to see him. What about Joel?"

"Oh, he isn't the same boy I left last time I was in Paris, Jasper. Something has happened to him. Now he is uncertain, sometimes lackadaisical, moody—I would expect that; his father, too—but he throws himself into this Franck transcription, and I tell you, Jasper, that is nothing—nothing!"

"I disagree."

"Don't," she said with sudden, impatient imperiousness. "I know music. I know it is nothing."

"I am not speaking musically, my dear Celia. I disagree because I think it may be necessary and wholesome for him to complete this task."

"Oh, never fear, I shan't stop him," she cried. "But it is such a waste. He could better occupy his time by spending two hours every day on the Chopin mazurkas or the Brahms rhapsodies. Or Bach—why, he once played Bach almost flawlessly, and now I have yet to hear him play Bach since his return. Oh, a *bourree* or a *gigue*, yes. But Bach is lost to him. His Mozart is beautiful, true; but there is melody, melody, melody, and the contrast is all the greater. But he is no child; I cannot say to him to practise Bach, to play Haydn, as I would go to a child and command him to do his scales. No. I can only sit and listen and wonder. What happened to him? What disturbed him? What filled him with doubt? Because he is filled with doubt—not that he has reason to be doubtful of his talent, but doubt of something personal which has been communicated into his playing."

My grandfather did not say anything for a long minute.

"You asked, and I've told you," said Mrs. Merrihew almost defensively.

"Yes, of course," said grandfather. "If something troubles him, though, it may work itself out, given time. He seemed to me to eat well when I was over."

"Oh, yes, he eats."

"And how does he sleep?"

"I don't know. I know only he's up at all hours of the night. She has been with him sometimes, but most always he is alone. I see him. I never interrupt him. He may be at work, and that is never subject to the strictures of any clock."

My father came out on the porch at this time and sent me to get a prescription filled and to deliver it. When I returned, Mrs. Merrihew had gone, and my grandfather had retired to his own office, where he remained until summoned to the supper table.

V

Within that week I went over to the Merrihew house for the first time alone. My grandfather had told me he wanted me to be his "eyes and ears" in that house. The prospect of hearing Joel Merrihew play was an attractive one. I set out not long after supper and walked over, dawdling on the bridge to examine the catches of the fishermen there, and in the bottoms along the river so that it was dusk when I reached the house.

Mrs. Merrihew was waiting for me. She gave me an enigmatic smile and a reassuring pat.

"Just go right into the conservatory and sit down, Steve. You needn't disturb Joel. If you go in and sit down, it won't disturb him at all. He's playing."

I could hear him. The music was sombre, but very lovely. Though I did not know it then, it was the *Sonate pathetique* by Beethoven. He was in the middle of it when I slipped into the room. He did not see me, for the room was lit only by the wan light of the waxing moon low in the western heaven. The moonlight gave a strange luminous quality to the room; it reflected from bowls and the chandelier, from the shiny top of the piano itself, and it lay in strange places because of this reflection. Joel himself looked unreal; he wore a long black dressing gown, so that only his hands and face showed; he looked like a ghost at the piano.

When he had finished the sonata, he was about to begin another piece when he was aware of someone else in the room. He did not see me; he did not even look in my direction; he just raised his head a little and said, "Is that you, *Maman?*"

"No, I said, "it's me."

"And who is 'me'?" he asked, looking in my direction. "Oh, it's Dr. Grendon's grandson."

"Yes," I said. "I like to listen if it won't disturb you."

"Listen as long as you like."

He turned back to his music and began to play once more.

He played a wonderfully melodic number, something enchanting that wove a kind of spell in the room. I thought it required great skill to play something which sounded so difficult and was so beautiful. The music cascaded forth, sometimes lyrical, sometimes challenging and triumphant; the walls and darkness and the night fell away. Oh, he could play, he could bring melodies to life as no one else I ever heard could do. It was Franck's *Variations Symphoniques* that he played. For a long time after he had finished, it seemed as if the music still kept on, echoing and re-echoing in the inner ear.

"Do you like that?" he asked out of the darkness.

"Oh, yes," I answered. "I liked that very much."

He touched a few keys tentatively, exploratively. Then he played a little rondo of his own composition; it was quiet and good to listen to, but it did not stir and excite and move like its predecessor. I did not want him to ask me how I liked it, and he did not. Next he played a long selection evocative of disturbing sombreness. I did not know it then; I heard it years later—the Mozart *Fantasia and Sonata in C Minor*—and I realized then that the interpretation Joel gave it was a profoundly moving and beautiful one. He played himself into it. Having finished it at last, he began it over, but did not proceed very far beyond the opening statement of the pensive and almost un-Mozartianly grave theme. Then he turned to other music in a similar vein. He went on playing until he was tired; then he got up, still in darkness, which was all the more dark now for the moon was low and large and deep yellow, touching the haze at the rim of the earth, and no longer shedding much light into the room.

"I'm going to play records," he announced.

I said nothing.

He turned on a soft light at the phonograph and assembled records which he put on the arm of the player. Then he put out the light again and turned on the mechanism. The music began with *The Swan of Tuonela.* When he was satisfied that the tone was right, he sat down to listen.

At first he seemed to enjoy the music very much, but toward the end of the Sibelius recording he grew restless; he got up again and began to walk around; I could see his dark figure moving toward the French doors and back again; beyond, the yellow lights of the village were obliterated when he walked against them. When Sibelius had finished, Liszt's *Les Preludes* came on, followed by Franck's *Psyche,* both strange, haunting works, the latter especially productive of a mood—a dark, almost eerie mood, one of withheld exaltation—with always the eternal question in its lovely theme, the question Joel heard and for the answer to which he sought ever in vain. It was disturbing music that made itself felt in the room in something that communicated to Joel Merrihew and from him in turn in a distortion of its melody. I could not explain it. The music seemed to be part of him, or he seemed to be part of the music. Sometimes he paused to listen to it; once he struck a few notes on the piano in harmony with it; but most of the time he just walked to and fro, saying nothing, until at last his restlessness cast a pall over the music, which had now changed to Strauss's *Also Sprach Zarathustra.*

He stopped at the phonograph and shut it off.

"I'm sorry," he said out of the darkness. "I don't feel like any more of it tonight."

I got up instantly and said that I must go.

"Shall I drive you home, Steve?"

No, I said, I could walk. I wanted quite suddenly to get away, to go out into the night and away from the conflict in that room.

Mrs. Merrihew was in the hall when I came out.

"I want you to come again, Steve," she said. "I want you to come just as often as you like. I feel that Joel needs someone besides me to play to."

"Yes," I said. "Thank you."

I went out of the house and started down the flagstones set into the slope of the hill. When I looked back I could see her still standing in the doorway, one hand on the door-knob, the other resting lightly against her cheek; her head was titled to one side, and it was just as if she had been arrested there by the sound of that voice no one else could ever hear, and she stood listening, listening. There was no sound from the house; it was still, and the conservatory was dark.

Outside, I felt free. I ran down the hill toward the road and the bridge leading to the lights that were Sac Prairie and home, hoping I would not have to come here again for days and weeks.

In the morning, which was Saturday, Grandfather Grendon was just setting out to drive to Grells' place west of town when Mrs. Merrihew's car drew up beside the buggy. Grandfather pulled the horse to a stop and leaned forward.

"What is it, Celia? You look very tired."

"I'm driven, that's all, Jasper. I'm on my way to send some telegrams. I thought you might like to know that Joel's gone."

"Gone?" echoed grandfather.

She nodded, her mouth a little bitter. "Entirely without his permission or even his knowledge, Rikki arranged a series of concerts for him. She telephoned him in the night and told him. He felt he had to go. So he went."

"Certainly he was under no obligation."

"No, it was Rikki, that's all. I couldn't stop him," she cried. "I couldn't even try. She would know that. Now what can I do but see to it that some of Jolauriet's friends know he is coming to play."

A glance passed between my grandfather and Mrs. Merrihew, and quite suddenly Mrs. Merrihew bit her lip and looked away.

"My dear Celia," said my grandfather gently, "I've known ever since he was born."

"Have you, Jasper?"

"There was never anything of Henry Merrihew in him. How could you hope to deceive anyone who had even some rudimentary knowledge?"

"I must say this is an unconventional place to speak of such a matter," she said with some spirit.

Grandfather chuckled. "The subject is unconventional, too."

"And with him beside you." She waved toward me.

Grandfather shrugged.

"If I had any shame, I would resent that, Jasper," said Mrs. Merrihew. "But I haven't. I never had. You know what Jolauriet meant to me, and you know all about Henry—alive and dead." She started her car again. "I hope you won't forget that I live just across the river, now that Joel is gone again."

"He won't be gone forever."

"I wonder."

She drove off, raising a cloud of dust. Grandfather shook the reins and old Ben set out once more.

"Acedia, perhaps," said grandfather as we rolled into the lower road leading to Grells' Mill.

"What's that?" I asked.

"That's a diagnosis," he answered. "Acedia is a kind of malaise—let us say a sickness characterized by an inability to make up one's own mind."

"Is it fatal?"

My grandfather pursed his lips and narrowed his eyes. "I suppose in a way you might say it is. Fatal for many things. Mortal—not necessarily." He looked at me quizzically. "Did you bring a fishpole? I'll likely be with Grells for a while, and the pond's filled with sunfish."

VI

It was seven months before Joel Merrihew returned. He came back at the far edge of winter, after the thaws had taken away most of the snow, and the pussywillows and alder catkins were blossoming. My grandfather had not known he was on his way home; he had followed his concerts with interest, whenever opportunity allowed, and from time to time he discussed Joel with my father in a casual manner. He had discussed, too, the criticisms of Joel's concerts; however favorable many of them were, there was always some dissatisfaction manifest, and my grandfather could not doubt that these criticisms must have upset Joel very much. Nor did he know immediately of Joel's return.

It was not until almost two weeks after Joel had come back to the house on the hill that my grandfather knew he had returned. Nothing had been given to the local newspaper, nothing of Joel had been seen in Sac Prairie. But one Sunday morning the Merrihew car stopped before the house. Grandfather and I had just come from church, and I was in the kitchen arguing with my mother about changing clothes, when the car drove up.

"There's Mrs. Merrihew," I said to grandfather.

"You will not wear your good Sunday suit, and that's all there is to it," said my mother with finality. "Go and change."

"I'll just see what she wants," said grandfather.

On my way to my room I flashed a glance toward the woman coming up the walk. It was not Mrs. Merrihew; it was a young woman, rather pretty, carrying a parasol and wearing a wide-brimmed, floppy hat. She was dressed more for summer than for spring. As she came up the walk, she looked a little uncertainly at the house. It was the Merrihew car, all right; I could tell that. I stood where I could see her pause at the bottom of the steps; grandfather had reached the porch.

She looked up and smiled. "I'm looking for Dr. Grendon."

"There are two of us," said grandfather.

"I'm sure you're the one. Dr. Jasper Grendon. Mrs. Merrihew asked me to stop. I'm Hester McClane."

My grandfather acknowledged the introduction and invited her up to the porch.

"No, thank you. I have just a moment. Mrs. Merrihew would like you and your grandson to come to dinner tonight. You know Joel is back, Doctor."

"I didn't know."

She laughed pleasantly. "I should have thought everyone knew everything that went on in so small a town."

"You might be surprised at how little people really know," replied grandfather. "How is Joel?"

Immediately her face sobered. She looked at him challengingly. "I hope you may be able to help him, Doctor. I've tried. I know his mother's tried. But sometimes I think he's somewhere else, apart from us, apart from everyone—even, yes, even himself. But I'm sorry; perhaps I shouldn't talk so."

"Do," urged my grandfather. "Tell me about yourself. Have you taken Rikki's place?" he asked bluntly.

She looked somewhat startled; her lips parted as if to speak, but she did not immediately say anything. She twirled her umbrella and half-smiled. "I don't quite know how to answer that question. You see, Doctor, I'm puzzled as to what 'place' Rikki had, and what 'place' Peter had before her."

"How long have you known Joel?"

"I met him in St. Louis when he played there. My father knew Jolauriet very well. Joel and Rikki were at our home that weekend." She paused abruptly and said, "You haven't told me you could come."

"Of course we'll come."

"At seven then, Doctor."

Grandfather stood looking after her, as she went down toward the car. He was still standing there when I came out.

"Changed clothes, eh?" he said, looking at me. "You'll have to change back again; we're going to Merrihew's."

I complained.

"Don't carry on so, boy. Tell me, did he ever mention Peter to you?"

"Who?"

"Why, Joel Merrihew, of course," he answered impatiently. "You were over there that night."

I said he had not. Perhaps Peter was someone he had met on his recent tour.

My grandfather shook his head emphatically, and sat down with the Sunday paper to chuckle over *The Katzenjammer Kids* and *Happy Hooligan.*

We did not go that night until almost the hour Hester McClane had set; it was already late twilight, and it promised to be a dark night. The sky was overcast, but a mellow south wind blew steadily, heavy with the musk of the thaw-swollen river. My grandfather did no more than hail the bridge-tender and toss him the toll, going by, leaving the old man peering curiously after us from the place where he stood under the thick-budded soft-maple tree at the corner beside his little house.

Once again, as before, Mrs. Merrihew came out to meet us, but this time it was clearly to have the advantage of speaking to my grandfather before he saw Joel. Because of the coolness of the early spring night, she wore a long cape with a hood on it to protect her head; she looked very diminutive in it and, perhaps because it was black, very pale. She showed some anxiety to get out of the wind, apparently feeling its chill edge more readily than either of us.

"What did you think of Hester, Jasper?" she asked, once the customary greetings had been passed.

"I didn't see enough of her to make a decision. But you seem to like her, or you'd have never sent her with your invitation."

"She's much better than the French one. Not so selfish. Of course," she said with an attempt to counterbalance any lingering malice she may have felt, "we are all of us determined upon our own courses set in life, and everyone else looks selfish to us—probably in proportion to our own selfishness."

"How does she come to be here?" asked my grandfather.

"Rikki quarrelled with him, and they parted. But now—I'm not sure—he can't seem to forget her, for all that he's fond of Hester. He telephoned about Hester from St. Louis; of course, I knew her father. I hoped he would bring her. When he finished in Pasadena, he came back by way of St. Louis and persuaded her to come here with him. I think she's fond of him. In any case, she knows something is wrong—just as I do."

"And what is it?"

"I wish I could lead you to it and say, there it is. But I can't, Jasper. I wonder so often about it. Has he lost faith in himself? Or what? You know the notices were not too favorable—or, I should have said they were satisfactory enough, but not he. Concertizing did not help; I knew it wouldn't. I think down underneath he felt it, too. By why, then, did he go? I can think only it must have been because of Rikki, and if that is so—if it means he considered her before he thought of his music and his reputation, then I'm afraid Joel has suffered a profound disturbance."

The light that streamed out of the house and lay against her features emphasized the degree of her concern, shadowing the lines of her face, darkening her eyes.

"Is he fond of this woman?" asked my grandfather.

"Fond? What do you mean, 'fond'? I suppose he is; he wanted her to come along."

"To be at his side, to listen to him? Or is he in love with her?"

"Oh, Jasper," she exclaimed in a hushed voice, "how can you speak of 'love' as if it were a label to be pinned on? Does any one of us ever really know what love is? Can you believe that I loved Henry Merrihew before and after and yes, during, Jolauriet? Perhaps not. It doesn't matter. Joel matters now, and we shall have to do something about him."

She opened the door and we went in.

As grandfather took off his overcoat, he said, "Why 'we,' Celia? You should realize that if your own fears are justified, there's nothing we can do—either you or I, or both of us together. It must work itself out in him or destroy him."

"I don't believe it, Jasper."

"You don't want to."

Under her cape, Mrs. Merrihew wore a long grey dress which enclosed her neck way up under her chin. She had blue stones around one wrist and blue pendants in her ears, but wore no other color; she looked very pale, and her thin lips, pressed firmly together, seemed almost bloodless.

"Go right in, Jasper."

My grandfather went down the little hallway to the conservatory.

Joel was talking when we went in. He was speaking of music which, though built on classic patterns, was yet modern in many harmonies and in the essential freedom of its structure. Seeing us, he interrupted his monologue.

"Dr. Grendon and Steve. We were just talking about Franck's music."

Hester McClane got up and came over to be introduced to me. I saw her now close up for the first time. She was not beautiful, but she was handsome. She was taller than most women, but she was well proportioned. She had eyes of a very strong brown; they were warm and, it seemed to me, expressively kind. She had a kind of sympathy about her, unlike the other woman he had had there, the French woman, and she shook hands just as if I were grown up. I liked her voice, too; it was soft and smooth. She was not brunette, but she was not blonde, either; her hair was kind of a rich brown.

"Don't let me interrupt you," said grandfather, sitting down. "I'll just light a cigar and listen. If no one minds."

"Please do," said Hester. "Go on, Joel."

He shrugged nervously. "Oh, well, there's nothing much more to say. I've always liked the ruminative, mystic quality of Franck's music—particularly in the *D Minor* and in the *Variations*. Yes, and the *Beatitudes*. And I find myself fond of his polyphonic style. I've said all that before."

"But do you like it because it's ruminative and mystic?" asked Hester.

He shook his head. "No. It has form, it has unity."

She hesitated for a moment before she said, "Joel, it's almost as if you said that feeling nothing else had form or unity—not even you."

He looked at her, it seemed, for a long time, his eyes unwavering. In the light that shown on him, his face had a look of surprise and wariness, a combination of the two, as of someone caught at mischief. Then he turned away almost rudely and looked from one to the other of us, after which he sat down at his piano and, without a word, without more than a brief pause where it was signified in the score, he played the *Sonata Appassionata* of Beethoven. Though I did not understand it then, I understood later that this was his defiance, this was his answer.

My grandfather never once took his eyes from Joel Merrihew, though the blue smoke of his cigar concealed the keenness of his interest.

When Joel finished, his mother, who had come to the threshold, joined in the applause.

He came to his feet, just as if he were on the concert stage, bowed, held up one had for silence, and said without a flicker of emotion, "As an encore I will play Debussy's prelude, *Les sons et les parfums tournent dans l'air du soir.*" Then he sat down and played it, with just as much delicacy and restraint as the force and technical mastery he had demonstrated in the sonata. Its notes lay in the air with a quality that was almost a reluctance to die away.

When he had finished, Mrs. Merrihew said, "Come now. That is enough. None of us wants his dinner cold."

We all went in to dinner then, Joel coming last with my grandfather, as before, and again, as before, we were seated in the same manner around the table, with the shadowy Emma, a women in middle-age who, it seemed, never spoke, to wait on us. Only this time there was something else at the table with us. Before, it had been the newness, the strangeness of the adjustment to this young man who had become famous in a modest way, and in turn his adjustment to the home he had left as a boy; now it was something less tangible and yet more to be sensed, something that lay like an invisible web over the table.

There was not that silent dueling which had gone on among Joel and his mother and Rikki; now it was as if everyone waited upon Joel, expecting him to begin each conversation, to open each subject; but he said nothing, he ate in brooding silence unless spoken to; and by their very acquiescence, Mrs. Merrihew and Hester made it necessary for my grandfather to carry the conversation during dinner. Despite this, it was still as if the two women expected Joel to begin at any moment; there was an air of waiting so noticeable as to create a tension about the table, so that several times what my grandfather said might not have been said at all, except for Hester, who made every attempt to keep up with him.

Mrs. Merrihew, eating little, soon was once again lost in her private world, sitting with her eyes fixed on her son, but not really seeing him, and listening, one felt sure, listening to the conversation of someone not on this plane, beyond the auditory grasp of anyone sharing her table. It was fascinating to glance at her from time to time, to see that distant alertness, that seeming perception of something no other ear could hear, no other eye could see.

The only subjects in which Joel seemed to show any interest were those pertaining to music, and even then he showed no particular animation. When my grandfather asked about Rachmaninoff, who was on tour that year, he gave little better than monosyllabic replies, though he did speak about certain little-appreciated nuances in the seldom-played first concerto. When my grandfather mentioned Prokofieff, Joel spoke about technical virtuosity and said that he was left cold by much of the work of that composer. But when my grandfather repeated the rumor that Senator La Follette might run independently for the presidency at the next presidential election, he might well have been speaking in a void, for no one answered him.

Perhaps because of this difficulty in conversation, the dinner seemed endless. Yet it proceeded without any noticeable delay. Hester ate nervously, Mrs. Merrihew with a deliberation matched by my grandfather's, Joel mechanically. When dinner was done, it was grandfather who, somewhat abruptly, rose and excused himself.

This in turn roused Mrs. Merrihew, who, without passing through any kind of transition from the world of her preoccupation and this, instantly once again assumed her role as hostess, rose herself, and said, as usual, that Hester would help her briefly, and they would join us presently in the conservatory.

In the conservatory Joel turned at once to my grandfather and asked, "Did you see the criticisms of my concerts, Dr. Grendon?"

Grandfather nodded casually.

"Terrible, weren't they?"

"Were they just?" asked grandfather.

"I think so."

"Then they weren't terrible. And then, also, they have no importance whatsoever since they weren't telling you something you didn't already know."

"But I knew they would be that way," answered Joel. "I knew it before I went. I knew I never should have gone on that tour."

"Why did you?"

"Because I couldn't help it. Believe me, Dr. Grendon, I couldn't prevent myself from going."

"Why not?"

"It will seem absurd to you; I can hardly believe it in words myself."

"Because you thought you were in love with Rikki, is that it?"

Joel sighed and walked over to the French doors, looking out toward the lights of the village. Without turning toward my grandfather, he began to speak in a low voice, "It isn't as simple as that. Because love has always seemed terribly necessary to me. I don't think I mean physical love. Perhaps it was because I never knew it when I was small. Even at four, I knew my father didn't love me; he didn't care whether I existed or not; I was just something in his way. My mother loved me in her fashion; but then I understood that she loved me not for me alone but because I represented something or someone else to her; even today, you know, she lives in her own world quite as much as I live in mine, but she is adjusted to her way of life, she has found moorings."

"And you have not?"

"In music alone."

"Every mooring a man has, whether he plays the piano or whether he counts shingles in a lumber-yard, is inside himself. If his moorings are secure, he doesn't need tangible evidence of them before his eyes. If you find security in music alone, then be resigned to it and resolve the conflict."

"Yes, yes, I know. All that is true. But even as a child, I felt the need to be necessary to someone. It never seemed to me that anyone cared whether I lived or died. It was only when I played the piano that I was happy. But even that, later on, when I began to play in public, brought me a kind of specious attention—it was not real, it rested on the music, not on me apart from music. Each time I have thought to find genuine affection, I have been disillusioned. Yet it is necessary, vitally necessary to me."

Grandfather sat for a moment in silence. Yet Joel did not turn. "A man approaching thirty must have realized long ago that life is a sense of progression from one disillusionment to another," said my grandfather then. "A man who at that age feels insecure has no genuine faith in himself. And if he is lonely, it is because he has not realized that everyone is lonely, that creative people are so most of all by the very solitary nature of their calling, and that each of us, in final analysis, lives and dies alone."

"I know all that, Dr. Grendon."

"But do you believe it? I wonder."

"The women are coming," said Joel in warning accents, and turned to walk toward the piano.

Though I had not heard a sound, he had evidently apprehended their approach; the door was flung open and the women came into the room. Mrs. Merrihew had put on a colorful shawl, explaining that she felt chilled and was tired.

"Play me one number," said Mrs. Merrihew. "I'm ready for bed."

"I'll play Ravel's *Gaspard de la nuit*," said Joel.

When the women were settled, he began to play. It seemed to be a very difficult number, for in the middle of it he faltered, collected himself, and began the passage anew. But this faltering was fatal for his performance, and he abandoned Ravel for the Mozart *Fantasia*, which he made the introspective, self-searching music of a man deeply aware of inner conflict. But in this, too, he faltered, and this second faltering violated the imaginative evocativeness of the work; for quite abruptly he stopped playing and stood up, a strange, baffled expression lying in his dark eyes and the twist of his sensuous mouth, half defiance, half fear.

My grandfather got up, applauding, and said, "You must forgive us, Joel—we must go."

Mrs. Merrihew, taking her cue from him, said, "And I must get to bed. I don't know why these dinners of ours always take so long."

They went out together, myself after them, leaving Hester, who had not moved, alone with Joel Merrihew. At the doorway I looked back fleetingly. He was sinking to the piano bench, one hand, fingers wide-spread, covering his sensitive face, and Hester was walking noiselessly toward him.

"You see, you see," whispered Mrs. Merrihew huskily, as soon as the door had closed. "This is what I mean."

"Yes, I understand," answered my grandfather.

"What is to be done?" implored Mrs. Merrihew anxiously.

My grandfather shook his head gently. "Please, Celia—what must come must rise from within. There's very little anyone else can do."

"We can't just sit here."

My grandfather shrugged, but his mouth was grim. "Of course, you could treat him as if he were ill. You might take him to a psychoanalyst."

"Oh, no."

"The psychological effect would be bad, I think. But there's nothing else."

"No, Jasper, he wouldn't go."

"And if he did, he might begin to think of himself as ill. That would be unfortunate." He paused and put a firm hand on her shoulder. "My dear Celia, simply wait and hope that Hester may be able to do something with him. He needs a regeneration of some kind. I do not know everything in his background; I wish I could find out what went on in his Paris years. Perhaps you could tell me?"

"I know so little. I believed in leaving him be, in not interfering . . ."

"Except at a safe distance?"

"Yes, that. I didn't interfere with his active life."

"No," said my grandfather musingly. "And you didn't think he might need you—as any growing boy needs maternal love and understanding."

"Joel was always an artist," she said proudly.

"Oh, yes, yes, Celia," said grandfather wearily, "but a boy, too. Did you think it could be otherwise? Tell me, do you know—who was Peter?"

"Peter, who?"

My grandfather shrugged. "Just Peter. I should say someone he knew in Paris."

"Oh, *that* one. He was an English boy of Joel's own age; they studied and lived together for most of the time Joel was in Paris."

"What became of him?"

"Oh, I don't know. Joel used to write about him, but in the last two years or so, there were very few references to Peter. Perhaps he died or went away—I don't know. Is it important?"

"I don't know. I wanted to ask, that's all."

We were at the door now. Mrs. Merrihew would have walked outside with us, but grandfather forbade her to do so.

"You're tired, you look rundown, and the air is chilly. Stay inside, Celia. Good-night."

"I want you to come soon again, Jasper."

"I will. I want to keep Joel under my eye. In a day or two, then."

As we were driving home through the damp night, which was thick with the musk of thawing snow and ice showing white in the black water of the river under that clouded March sky, my grandfather turned to me and asked, "How are you coming with that girl of yours, Steve?"

"Oh, all right," I said.

He chuckled. "Isn't love wonderful!" he mocked good-naturedly.

"Sure, it is. I love her, all right."

He sobered again instantly. "You don't know what love is," he said. "But the chances are you'll find out before he does."

VII

As March wore away and April, too, my grandfather visited Merrihews' two or three times a week. He never said very much about his visits, though occasionally I overheard him discussing Joel Merrihew with my father; but as the weeks wore on, their discussions were too technical for me to understand. I did realize, though, that Joel was not altering very much; they talked about him as if he were ill, yet sometimes I could hear him playing when I walked up along the river opposite the house. Or I could hear the phonograph, which amounted to almost the same thing, since Mrs. Merrihew seldom played it. Hester was still there, though she was supposed to have gone a month ago; she could not put off going much longer, however, for her family was growing anxious.

One Saturday morning before I got up, Hester McClane stopped in to see grandfather. They sat in the living-room, and I could hear them talking. Hester had come to tell him that she was returning to St. Louis the following day.

"I'm sorry to see you go, Hester," said grandfather.

"Oh," I understand. But, believe me, Dr. Grendon, I know there's no good in my staying any longer. I'm very fond of Joel, true, but he doesn't feel the same way about me. Perhaps he's afraid to trust his emotions any longer; perhaps he's too emotionally bound up with those influences before me—with his mother and Peter and Rikki—and theirs is an influence he seems incapable of shedding or combatting. In itself that wouldn't be so bad; but somehow they've got all tangled up in his music, and there's a raging torment inside him that affects his work. He seems to know this, too, but he still appears to be helpless in the face of it."

"I had hoped you could help him regain his self-confidence."

"I know. I thought I could. I wanted to. But it's too late, I'm afraid. My father has telephoned twice; I have my own life to live, you know. If there were any reason to hope that by staying I could help, I promise you I would stay. But there isn't. Can you honestly believe, Doctor, that there is?"

"I don't know, but I'm inclined to agree with you," said grandfather after a few moments' silence.

"Doctor, what is to become of him?"

"I wish I could say. There's still a chance that he may adjust himself—if it is an adjustment that's wanting. I'm not a psychoanalyst. Even if I were, I don't think his status would be appreciably altered, until the root of the trouble were uncovered. He will not co-operate."

"I'm terribly worried about him, and I know Mrs. Merrihew is, too."

"Yes, but that won't help."

"But, Doctor, there must be some way back to the beginning of this trouble or state of mind or whatever it is."

"There is. We must find it. Some profound psychological disturbance, perhaps. Who is to say? I thought at first it might be the simple inability to make up his own mind, but it's more than that. Far more. The need for affection of which he speaks is affection on his own terms, clearly, and if that's so, it must be explained why he is apparently at the behest of those who offer him affection only on their terms."

He walked from the house to the porch, and from there to the curb with her then, and I heard nothing more.

What happened after that took place very quickly.

The next day Mrs. Merrihew telephoned to find out whether I would come over that evening. She asked me to come for dinner but, remembering that last long-drawn-out meal there, I made excuses not to come. I went over after dinner instead, and, as before, Mrs. Merrihew was waiting for me.

"Go right in, please."

She was so agitated that, quite unconsciously, she pushed me a little, as if to hurry me. Yet even in the midst of her agitation, she seemed to be only partly aware of me, she seemed, as I came to remember her most especially later, to be *en rapport* with another dimension, as if waiting upon some communication from a world beyond perception, with a kind of almost eerie distance in her eyes. I left her standing in the hall beside a shaded lamp, standing with her head tilted a little to one side, that familiar posture of listening soundlessly to something soundless to all other ears but hers alone.

I opened the door of the conservatory quietly and lost sight of Mrs. Merrihew.

Joel Merrihew sat with his back to the door and did not hear me when I slipped in. He sat before the phonograph, which was just beginning to play the Franck *Symphony in D Minor.* He had turned up the volume to such an extent that the measures of the symphony were almost unbearably loud. But, because he did not see me slip in and sit down, he did not stir, and I noticed how he reacted to the symphony.

As the first record developed, his face began slowly to light up in an almost supernatural manner, a glow as of intense fever coming into his eyes, a slow flush mounting from his delicate lips over his thin cheeks. His eyes were fixed unseeingly upon the phonograph; his hands lay clasped unmovingly in his lap; not by a flicker was the immobility of his features disturbed. Yet an ecstasy seemed to shudder occasionally through his entire body; it was as if some deeply hidden wellspring of power within him had been touched, as if the Franck symphony released the deepest creative urge in him, for, though he made no move, he was as if transported in spirit far beyond this room, far beyond even the valley which flowed away to the west, its white, moon-haunted expanse quiet beneath the stars, and seemed close to the eye from the confines of the dusk-filled room.

As the record turned over, he shifted his position and suddenly saw me. He stared at me with an almost terrifying fixity, his eyes unusually wide, so that if I could have done so I would have shrunk down and disappeared.

"God!" he exclaimed in a muffled voice, "I thought—just for a moment—I thought you were Peter!"

He shuddered and an expression of pain crossed his face. He turned his back to me. Though the music was too loud for me to hear anything but its notes, I thought that he had begun to weep; but whether he had done so or not I could not discover, for he walked out to the balcony presently and there he stood in silence looking out over the village and the prairie to the western hills and the late winter stars now lowering earthward with the waxing moon. He did not come into the room again until the second movement of the symphony had begun, and when he did come, he came in a strange and unemotional quiet, during which the flush slowly died out of his cheeks. While his eyes continued to shine, their glow now seemed more feverish than before. He stood quietly beside the machine, like someone graven there in stone, and was brought alive again only when the crescendos carried by the reeds and strings swept into him an emotion which was somehow akin to his startled surprise at seeing me and the mistake in identity to which it had brought him.

Throughout the third movement he paced the floor with nervous energy, his pace varying with the tempo of the music—now slow, now fast. When the symphony was finished, he stood for a while in silence. Records still moved about mechanically in the machine, and when presently Liszt's *Concerto in A Minor* began to play, he turned down the volume. Then he looked at me once more, somewhat more animated.

"I sometimes think I'm not responsible for what I do or say," he said. "I hope you don't mind."

I shook my head, not trusting myself to speak.

The music was now as soft as before it had been thunderous. Joel stood there with his head cocked a little to one side, as if trying to determine whether the volume was right; evidently it satisfied him, for he looked around him then at the lights, and moved to turn them off, saying that he hoped I would not object to sitting in the dark, for the room would not really be dark, since the moonlight was now invading much of it. Though I did not say so, I welcomed the darkness; I sensed that something was wrong with Joel Merrihew, though but a few years before I had accepted Josef Grell's derangement and Rella Farway's madness with the grave acceptance of any child before whom all things are strange, and, being strange, belong to childhood's world.

The Liszt concerto was somehow soothing; its adventurous melody took possession of the room, I thought, with more ease than the over-loud symphony had done. Having put out the lights, Joel drew a chair up to the French doors and sat down where he could look out over the prairie to where the moon sank toward the western rim. He was thus almost the width of the room away from me, and from that place he began to talk.

"Did your grandfather send you?" he asked.

"No," I said.

"Then mother sent for you."

"Yes."

"Why?"

I did not know what to say.

"You may tell me, Steve. I won't say anything."

"So you'd have someone beside her to talk to if you felt like talking."

He laughed harshly. Then he was silent for a long time. "To talk to!" he exclaimed bitterly at last. "And what would I say? Would I tell you that I am a failure, I am finished as a pianist, as a composer? Would they expect me to say that?"

"No," I said naively. "I suppose they expected you to tell me about the trouble."

"What trouble?"

"The trouble that makes you act this way. The beginning of it. Grandfather says that if he could find the root of it, perhaps it could be cured."

He got up then and walked back to where I sat. He crouched down so as to bring his face almost level with mine. In the moonlit darkness his eyes were soft and luminous, his mouth too was soft as a woman's, but there was an inexpressible sadness in his face. He touched my cheek with his fingers; his fingers were as delicate as thistle-down.

"Oh, you are young, Steve. And it's wonderful to be young, to be loved for yourself alone," he said. "It's only afterwards, when one discovers that youth is the least breath of time, only when it's done. . . ."

He rose abruptly and walked back to the seat he had left. Since it was a barrel-backed chair, he was almost completely hidden in its recesses. He sat for a while in complete silence, while the concerto made its magic in the room, and the moonlight gave a kind of spectral existence to everything within the enclosing walls. Then he began to talk in a voice so low that there were times when I could not hear him at all.

"It was not a root, but a lack of it," he began "It isn't like picking up a trail—a fox and hounds chase—and following it back. A beginning may have many beginnings. I know that sounds . . ." Here his voice was lost to the music, but in a few moments it picked up again. "When I was very young, younger than you, I went away from here to study. My father was dead many years then, my mother was forever somewhere else, I lived in a world consisting of a piano and various teachers. Then I went to Paris to continue . . ." Once again the music interrupted the sound of his voice, drowned it in a burst of flamboyant melody. ". . . Peter was a boy like myself studying music. Piano, too. He came from a little village in Cornwall, just as I came from a little village in Wisconsin. After a while we lived together. We became very attached to each other. Neither of us had ever had . . ." The music broke in once more, a crescendo of sound sweeping over his voice. ". . . to Rome together. Everywhere. I think in more ways than I know I lived for Peter." He was silent, and in that interval the records on the arm of the phonograph had reached full circle, and the Franck *D Minor* began once more. "A long time after, it seems, there was Rikki. She came between us. At first it was Peter, and then it was I. Was that, too, love? Or was that only another kind of possession, of being owned? The possession which robs the possessed of the will to do at last, which leaves him a husk, a shell . . ." The music welled forth.

He came out of his chair with lithe grace and, reaching the phonograph, turned up the volume once more. Then he came swiftly over to where I sat and bent above me, offering me his hand.

"Go home now, Steve. Good-bye," he said in a low, hushed voice.

Outside the house I could hear the Franck *D Minor* once more rising to thunderous heights of glorious melody, a surging tumult of powerful, joyous, musical triumph.

VIII

Looking back over the years now, I can only guess what Grandfather Grendon made of what I told him. For I did tell him as exactly I could remember what Joel Merrihew had said, and he made more of it than I did at that time.

"Peter is the key," he said ruminatively. "Did he mention his last name?"

"No."

"We must try to find him," he said thoughtfully, and with that he left my room and bade me go to sleep, for it approached midnight when I reached home that night.

But it was too late to find Peter. Hester McClane had been apprehensive; perhaps some intuition forewarned her. Mrs. Merrihew, too, had feared for

Joel. Only my grandfather, perhaps because he tended always to look toward hope, to take faith in tomorrow, was not fully prepared for what happened.

Disturbed by what I had seen and heard, I slept restlessly and lightly that night. I do not remember whether I heard the telephone ring; but in any case, the telephone's nocturnal ringing was not unusual in that house. But just before dawn, I heard my father's car drive up, and, waking, I heard also the hurried approach of Ben's hoofbeats, and I knew that both father and grandfather had been called out. They met in the driveway.

"Why, Dad—where've you been at this hour?" I heard my father ask.

"Over there," said grandfather in a weary voice.

"Merrihew's! What's wrong?"

"Joel's dead."

"What happened, Dad?"

"Mrs. Merrihew found him on the rocks below the balcony. There was a break in the railing there. It might have been an accident."

"I see," said my father reflectively.

"It wasn't much of a break," said grandfather then. "I saw it before she did. I thought best to enlarge it a little to diminish her doubt. She's been told it was an accident."

"What do you think, Dad?"

"What I think isn't important. I know nothing, except that yesterday he was alive, and today he isn't. Yesterday his spirit was broken, and today his body is broken, too. Great God! but I'm tired."

Both of them came into the house then.

Dad went into his office, and Grandfather Grendon went to his room. When he passed my room he paused at the door, as if listening for any sound from inside.

But I did not stir, I lay there trying to think of Joel Merrihew dead, trying to imagine how he could have fallen from that familiar balcony, and in the channels of my memory I could still hear the music of that symphony rolling out into that moonlit room, and the distant receding echo of Joel Merrihew's voice saying, "a husk, a shell . . ."

from Walden West

OF MORNINGS, NO matter what the season, the musk of the Wisconsin pervaded the village, in frosty fog or warm vapors, the smell of thaw or in the freshness of water, strongest on summer days, when people were accustomed to speak of it as were it an ichthyic odor, something unpleasant, instead of the diffused pungence rising from the uncovered stones and sandbars, a rich, spreading musk which moved far back from the river's edge and lent to the early hours of the day a kind of perfume which was primal on the earth before the advent of mankind, the exhalation of the river itself, sometimes invisible, sometimes caught in spectral mists, as if the very river-bed were breathing, giving off a distillation in which was inherent the smell of earth and water and air, out of which the wild nostalgic crying of killdeers, the plaintive calls of the solitary sandpipers, the cree-ee of wood ducks, the phoebe's cry and pewee's song came like essential integers, all together speaking as with one voice of many tones of the same primal sentience as the river's musk, with the first sunlight slanting to the water, and the shadows along the eastern shore inviting the angler and the contemplative oarsman in the very unawareness of man and his handiwork which remains so much a part of any running stream.

With day's advance, the musk was dissipated. The river rose, the almost soundless lowered stream gave place to another which spoke in many voices—laughing in the shadows, rushing and murmuring around the piers of the bridges, singing among the rushes and the willows along the shore, lapping at the bars, making a sibilance of whispering where it flowed among the grasses, the stream deepening, broadening, reclaiming the early uncovered bottoms, and spreading inland, exhaling a freshness, the damp, cooling fragrance of running water; and the birds of the early hours were silent before the keening of mourning doves and the screaming of gulls, the harsh triumph of bald eagles, and the pleasant threnodies of song and vesper sparrows. The Wisconsin's voices swelled and grew into the afternoon, in late winter mornings carrying abroad still the smell of thaw, and bearing southward to the Mississippi the cakes of ice broken away from winter's persisting masses along shore, in summer inviting the swimmers and the anglers and the river-lovers, old men who came to sit on its banks, or walk

---

1961

across its bridges, and dream of yesterdays beyond some receding corner gone by out of reach, even as the ceaselessly flowing water went past, heedless of man and all his work, as it flowed before the advent of man, and would flow when earth had reclaimed the very spoor of man.

It swelled and grew throughout the day, becoming a broad impressive river, and into the evening, when the water began once more to recede, the bars and the stones of the river bottom came out again, and once more gave off that musk, breathing into the dusk, where the killdeers still cried and the owls hooted, nighthawks foraged low over the water with swallows and chimney swifts, whippoorwills cried out of the riverside groves, and the water gave back the face of heaven, the stars, the moon, the planetary wanderers. A sense of mystery came upon the murmuring waters, the pulsing susurrus of the stream, the exhaling musk invading cell and bone, with the multiple sounds of water-dwellers strange and unknown to most listeners—of muskrats, beavers, minks, of frogs, toads, fishes leaping from the water and falling back in an ecstasy of living, of coot and heron foraging in the shallows, the river given over to twilight and evening star, its voices slowly, slowly falling away, receding with the level of the water.

And all night the Wisconsin, given to darkness, moved in the dark like a great sentient being, breathing its disturbing musk into the night, making man to think of earth and of man's existence on earth, the river lying in the darkness unseen save for the glint of starlight and the mirror of heaven, giving back in their seasons Arcturus and Antares, Orion and Aldebaran and Vega and Sirius, and the moon in all her phases, and the planets in their courses, while the river filled the village and covered the countryside along its valley with exhalation, the musk which seemed always the very essence of earth and running water, making itself known unseen in the darkness, the broad stream which was always in my youth the mecca of boys, and remained for innumerable adults a halcyon country of escape from today and tomorrow, a country changeless forever.

THE SCHWENKER HARNESS shop was the natural magnet which drew me when I was forbidden the Derleth blacksmith shop. The Schwenkers and the Derleths were among the earliest settlers in Sac Prairie, and had been friendly for generations. Once or twice a week Grandmother Derleth went to call on Paulina Schwenker, and once or twice a week Mrs. Schwenker repaid the call; and when he was down town, Grandfather Derleth stopped in at the harness shop now and then to pass the time of day with Bill Schwenker—or Willi, as Paulina called him; and it was only natural that I should find in Hugo, their only son, born to them late in their lives, when other parents of that age were thinking of becoming grandparents, an amiable companion who shared my own delight in nature and was as "handy" with his hands at one kind of work or another as I was in getting out of work.

The harness shop was an old building when I first walked into it. It stood two stories high on Water Street, Sac Prairie's Main Street, a block and a half north of the bridge, which opened out across the Wisconsin to Madison, twenty-five miles away. Its false front looked across the street to a row of worn buildings, equally as old, and beyond them to the river, and beyond the Wisconsin to the moraine along the river's east shore. Outside, it was unprepossessing, though not without a certain warmth inherent in the old siding.

I usually came to it from the rear, setting out across the railroad tracks from home, through the Freethinkers' Park, across lots to a little walk behind the shop, framed by Hugo's "office" on the one side—a little shed in which he kept his fish-poles, magazines, and the like—and the harness shop two-holer on the other. Not far away a snow apple tree leaned over the walk, and a flowering currant bush, both aromatic in season, and a little bed of lilies-of-the-valley. The walk went along the north wall of a storage shed, in which we used to undress and dress again when we went to swim off Karberg's bar, a block or so to the north. The shop itself was framed on the south by the old Naffz office, another frame building of one storey, and on the north, immediately adjacent to it, by the snug little house occupied by the Burleigh Fuchs family, to the roof of which and the flourishing grape arbor carrying away from the corner of the building over a kind of patio the only north wall window of the harness shop opened.

The harness shop was mellow with age; its inner walls were literally stained with years. It had once been a general store, but there was nothing, save for an old fountain recipe or two scrawled on the walls, to thin the atmosphere of the harness business. A long workbench was attached to the north wall all the way from the northwest corner of the building to the chimney about half way up toward the front; in evenings and dark days it was lit by two green-shaded lamps which shed warm pools of yellow light on the bench and the dark panes of the window looking out to the sloping roof and vaulting elms to the north. Beyond this bench and the chimney, the north wall was filled with hooks on which hung hame-straps, collars, and the like; so too the east end of the south wall. Between them were two large counters filled with more collars, collar-pads, Neatsfoot Oil, and other paraphernalia. Along the west end of the south wall stood an old-fashioned secretary, reaching almost to the ceiling, a small stepladder, and another workbench. Between the two workbenches were an oil dip, some wooden horses on which in the season harnesses were put together, and two stoves, one of which was kept burning, and the other of which was used more or less as a dummy, for Bill Schwenker's wry sense of humor was always stirred by the spectacle of farming clientele coming in and stretching their hands over this cold stove to be warmed on winter days. In the season the harness shop was dark on the sunniest days because harnesses repaired and oiled and waiting to be picked up by their owners hung from hooks in the ceiling over half the shop. And, like as not, the shop was filled with steam brought in from the shed out back, where the harnesses were washed, and this moisture always accentuated the smell of leather and oil which predominated in the shop.

Hugo was seldom at home in that gracious house where his bird-like mother reigned, a house of horsehair furniture, period paintings, whatnots and various antiques; he preferred to be at the shop, not alone because he helped his father, but simply because he liked the setting better. Hugo was taciturn and tended to be uncommunicative, which, of course, suited me very well, since I was always very communicative and highly vocal, and I had thus nothing much to content with, unless it were the occasional sly comments which Bill Schwenker, whom we had nicknamed Eli, Alias the Night Wind, interjected into our conversation from time to time. Mr. Schwenker was in reality of my grandfather's generation, and he was thus already a middle-aged man when I first knew him, a thick-set, broad-shouldered man who wore spectacles and a moustache in his rather broad face, and suffered from asthma, to ease which he constantly sought the relief of the green smoke of Asthmador, which he burned and inhaled from a little tin on the north-wall workbench, a palliative to which Hugo later resorted also, perpetuating the not unpleasant pungence of the smoke in the old shop.

Mr. Schwenker had a highly tolerant view of young people. I do not recall that he was ever impatient with Hugo, not nearly as much as Hugo might be with the clientele; he was much given to casual comments by means of which he hailed me whenever I walked into the shop—"Look who's here—the lost Charley Ross! Where you been?"—"Look what the wind blew in!"—"Ain't seen you in a coon's age!"—and similar comments, always delivered with a good-natured smile. Once in a great while he grew inpatient with our arguments, which were usually about whether or not Hugo would join me in a hike, and at such times he exploded with, "Oh, go on—get out and walk!" which customarily ended any argument.

There is no question but that the harness shop took the place of the blacksmith shop in my esteem. Blacksmithing declined a little faster than harness-making and harness-repair. The shelves above the north-wall workbench were still host to countless boxes of snaps, pins, and other appurtenances of the trade; the repaired harnesses still hung from the ceiling hooks; the farmers came in during the season—the winter months—and stood making the small talk which is the fabric of life in such an establishment for almost twenty years after the blacksmith shop had closed its doors, and thereafter it became for a time a place for Hugo to tie flies and make fly-rods, and then, finally, a woodworking establishment, once more filling the old building with life and warmth, substituting the fragrance of cedar, birch, oak, black walnut and other woods, of resin and fillers and stains for the oil and leather of the earlier days, for Hugo, like myself, had inherited one trait above all others from his father—a need and love for work, for Bill Schwenker, like my father, was devoted to work, and was not happy for very long apart from work, and even as my father was constantly at work in his garden or at some repair in the house, whistling heartily while he worked, so Bill Schwenker could be found all week long, well into the evenings—and sometimes on Sunday, clad in his Sunday best—at the north-wall workbench, sewing on the stitching-horse or simply sitting, contemplating the view from the window, smoking a cigar, or standing at the old secretary, in which he kept a little brandy for an occasional nip.

The harness shop was soon an integral part of my daily routine. If I went down town of a morning, I took the harness shop route, and returned by way of Grandfather Derleth's; if I went down for the evening paper, I always went early, so that Hugo and I could sit on the little shelves along the front windows of the shop and peer down the street toward the post office to determine the right moment to set out for the mail—the right moment being when the windows went up after the mail had been distributed to box-holders. At the harness shop—or in Hugo's "office" out in back—he and I poured over stamp approvals for possible purchase from our meagre funds for our collections. And it was from the harness shop that we set out on our hikes into the hills or the marshes, year after year, from childhood through youth into middle age.

It was an altogether enchanting place. I used to like to sit on the top of the little stepladder against the south wall, hidden by the secretary, and absorb the shop's atmosphere, listening to the small talk of the farmers and to their excuses when they were late with a harness and demanded that it be repaired forthwith, and to their complaints, which was testimony to the occupational flaws they could not escape, for the Schwenker prices were uniformly low and remained unchanged to matter what the nature of the complaint. Mr. Schwenker's personal friends soon became our personal friends, too, and for the most part they were a highly individual lot who came in to "let off steam," as it were, much to our delight.

These friends included Mr. Karberg, an amiable old man who was confused about knowledge and belief, and orated constantly on this and allied religious subjects with the same magnificent confusion which ruled his thoughts, a hearty, hale man who used to come troubled to the harness shop, and after a monologue directed at Mr. Schwenker or Hugo and me, departed happily, with a load lifted from mind and heart, and happy he would remain until the confusion gathered again and he needed the patient ears of an audience to relieve himself once more. They included Gus Naffz, a retired druggist who was spending his declining years at fishing and caring for his two spinster sisters in the proud Naffz house of red brick at one corner of the Freethinkers' Park, and liked to come in to reminisce about the golden years of *Gemuthlichkeit* at the turn of the century until he began to fret about his health and gradually went into a mental decline. They included old man Pauli, who appeared at least once a year for one of the calendars which were always to be had on the counters in December and January—and Otto Gross, a short, myopic man who talked vaguely with a tittering laugh about "blowing up" somebody or something, which he never did—and John Ganzer, who roomed above the harness shop, and was always filled with slightly risque tales to tell—and John Baer, with his glittering golden teeth, who lived next door and carried on a constant war with his car which he drove in second gear all over town and which he swore was worthless, "Damn' car, no go!"—and L. P. Bach, known as Mr. Elpy, who had a haberdashery across the street, which, like its owner, was sinking into the slough of despond.

No matter what changes came about in the life of Sac Prairie, the harness shop was never known as anything other than the harness shop. The blacksmith shop closed and was turned finally into apartments; Bill Schwenker fell on the ice one winter day and broke his hip, and mended a little, but in the end faded from the harness shop and died; nervous, birdlike Paulina Schwenker suffered a paralyzing stroke, recovered, and suffered another and died, all in the space of one year; Gus Naffz and Mr. Elky and L. P. Bach died; old Paulie defied his doctor who told him not to split wood with his cold hanging on, took pneumonia, and shuffled off this mortal coil; Grandfather Derleth, Grandmother Derleth, and all their generation passed into the shadows; Hugo sold the fine old Schwenker home and refurbished the apartment above the harness shop—and the old shop endured.

THE PROCESS OF renewal which is inherent in many things we do every spring is nowhere more apparent than in the long afternoons spent "over the hills"—on the moraine east of Sac Prairie on the far side of the Wisconsin. The afternoons are long only in the sense of clocked hours, for none is ever too long, time spent here has no limits. I suspect I go there so often not alone to inspect familiar paths and corners, long-known slopes and valleys, but also to take pleasure in a renewal of acquaintance with places with which some of my earliest memories are associated. The hills are not alone a vantage point from the eminence of which I can view all Sac Prairie—the village on its paw of land, the encircling hills, the undulating prairie between, the broad cobalt Wisconsin winding by—nor a source of nature lore—for an observant man can find something new at each walk along a familiar path—but also a wealth of memories which bind me to these slopes so firmly that I mourn the loss of every tree felled by the woodsmen, each invasion of every turn of the hillside path by the encroaching river, and the alteration of every portion of the landscape there.

Discounting that part of my attachment which rises from sentiment, for these hills are bound up inextricably with first love, it seems patent that here in this place which changes very little from year to year there is something of that illusion of permanence which we all seek so diligently in one form or another throughout life. The hills are an assurance that some aspects of individual existence are immutable, and briefly the flaw in the crystal is not apparent—for these are the same paths walked decades ago with Margery and only yesterday with Cassandra, these are the same vistas, the same horizons, even the same trees, flowers, fruits, so that on some days it is as probable that is was Cassandra who walked here beside me decades ago and Margery who was here but yesterday. The conviction of continuity is strong in such places where physical change is as slight as on the hills. I return to them year after year to be renewed by their seeming immutability. though I know the illusion, I know the infinite erosions and decayings which go on ceaselessly from moment to moment, and to which the mind adjusts to imperceptibly as to obviate them, so that it seems that they have not taken place at all.

I exist in such places on several planes; the eyes that perceive the fox sparrow busily foraging in old leaves do not blind the mind's eye from acknowledging that this leaning tree was once a trysting place for Margery and me, that only a little way apart a hidden hollow sheltered Cassandra and me when, in communion with the sun and earth and air, we lay unclothed in that ecstasy which is at once brother to birth and death, with the wind's whisper in the sheltering leaves and the sun warm on skin, the river's murmur and the hawk's scream ringing overhead, integral. Every aspect of the hills has its significance—the pasque flowers and hepaticas, the flowering birch and wild honeysuckle, the bird-foot violets and the delicate, aromatic white violets deep in a pocket of the hills, the soaring hawk and pensive song sparrow, the mulberry tree and the old cottonwoods, the wing dam down along the river and the slopes where once, as boys, we shouted and cried at play—all signify an act, a state of mind, an experience, a mood which, taken together, make up the texture of life. I come to a kind of spiritual rebirth on these hills every spring, and I renew it each year despite increasing awareness of death inherent in that rebirth, an awareness which exists independent of volition or conscious act.

It is significant, I sometimes think, that the facets of nature which quicken my pulse with that awareness of both life and death are inextricably associated with the loneliness of man's mote-like existence in the cosmos—and acceptance of man's essential solitude on earth, or by love, or both together, for they are only different aspects of the same face. Hawk, whippoorwill, lilacs in bloom, the shy white violets, hepaticas starring the slopes with their pastel colors, streetlights and trees at night, new moon and evening star, the manifold aspects of familiar houses and streets—all are symbols, all occur and recur without much alteration from one year to the next, as do the hills, of my going to which it has often said that I had better travel in new places, as if it were not true that some men learn more out of one book than others do from thousands.

MY HIGH SCHOOL years in Sac Prairie were enlivened not only by an early romance—that brief, poignant first love affair with Margery—but also by the presence on the faculty of Miss Frieda Schroeder. Miss Schroeder taught English with all the freshness of twenty-one or twenty-two years, and she was simply too attractive to be stood up in front of a class of adolescent boys. Miss Schroeder's appeal was almost entirely on a physical plane, and I often wondered how significant it is that a majority of the girls and young ladies who subsequently caught my eye wore one or more aspects of Miss Schroeder and were, most of them, of what would be called her "general type," save that they were, none of them, as blonde as she. I have no doubt that more than one of us profoundly regretted the presence in the Statues of Wisconsin of laws about contributing to juvenile delinquency designed to protect us, but in this case certainly frustrating a wholly natural instinct. I did.

But Miss Schroeder's appeal was not, fortunately for me, entirely on a physical plane. I came to her class fresh from Sister Isabelle's, and Miss

Schroeder continued Sister Isabelle's encouragement of my writing. More than this, she encouraged me to read even more than I might naturally have done by the simple expedient of promising any of us who read more than the required number of books extra credit in our English courses. We thus had the triple incentive of pleasing Miss Schroeder, gaining extra credit, and adding to our store of knowledge, and some of us forthwith plunged into the world of books with renewed energy and dedication.

I read everything I could lay my hands on. I began with *Mosses from an Old Manse* and *The Scarlet Letter* and went through book after book to *Dracula* and *In the Midst of Life.* And, because it was evident soon that Miss Schroeder was particularly pleased when any of us read in American literature, I took up Emerson's *Essays*, and what I read there and in *Walden* profoundly influenced the course of my life. The ideas that unfolded before my youthful eyes found fertile soil in which to take root and grow. Perhaps it was that I was already then conditioned to accept without question what I read in Emerson and Thoreau. I do not know that I would have come upon Emerson and Thoreau had it not been for Miss Schroeder. There is in every life the right time for enlightenment, for exposure to the life of the mind, for a door to be opened into that wider world that unfolds from one's own doorstep, a moment all too soon lost in time, and I had come to it, and the door had been opened for the light to flow in—not such a light as would open to me all the secrets of life and death, but only such a light as to illumine my own path through the years ahead. Miss Schroeder was, however unwittingly, the impulse which drove me to the door.

I was ready to believe *There is a time in every man's education when . . . he must take himself for better or worse as his portion; that though the wide universe is full of good, no kernel of nourishing corn came come to him but through his toil bestowed on that plot of ground which is given to him to till.* I knew beyond cavil that *No law can be sacred to me but that of my nature. Good and bad are but names very readily transferable to that or this; the only right is what is after my constitution; the only wrong is what is against it . . . Nothing is at last sacred but the integrity of your own mind.* I was open to the conviction that *Nothing can bring you peace but yourself. Nothing can bring you peace but the triumph of principle.*

And certainly I have advanced far enough into my life to recognize that *For every thing you have missed, you have gained something else; and for every thing you gain, you lose something . . . You cannot do wrong, without suffering wrong . . . There can be no excess to love, none to knowledge, none to beauty . . . In the nature of the soul is the compensation for the inequalities of condition.* And surely, in *Nature* I could not do other but greet with deep agreement such words as these—*The incommunicable trees begin to persuade us to live with them, and quit our life of solemn trifles. Here no history, or church, or state, is interpolated on the divine sky and immortal year.*

And what I found profoundly true in Emerson, I found even more true to my nature in Thoreau's *Walden*, which became a sort of Bible—not one to be preached from, but one to be kept in the recesses of my mind, not so much thought of as lived. When I read *What a man thinks of himself, that it is which determines, or rather indicates, his fate,* I found support for confidence in myself. My ambitions were given even greater direction when I read *I learned . . . that if one advances confidently in the direction of his dreams and endeavours to live the life which he has imagined, he will meet with a success unexpected in common hours.* And I too, preferred truth to fame or money, I had already at fourteen begun to find my occasions in myself, I was also a fisher in time, I appreciated simplicity, and I already knew *It is life near the bone where it is the sweetest.* It was as if I found in this book justification for my dawning belief that, without confusing the microcosm with the macrocosm, Sac Prairie was the microcosm which reflected the macrocosm of the world.

It is not thought to be that everything in Emerson and Thoreau took hold of me at once; it is never thus; but, little by little, the ideas thus taken in begin to trickle into my awareness and took hold of me, with roots that grew firmer with each passing year. Moreover, Emerson and Thoreau were shortly fortified by Walt Whitman and the delightful and pointed irreverence of H. L. Mencken and *The American Mercury*, and the wise counsel of H. P. Lovecraft, a middle-aged writer, who was a correspondent, together with the guidance of the village librarian. Nothing thereafter was to alter the course upon which these mentors had so firmly set me. Nothing was to shake these foundations.

Perhaps it is folly to put the onus of it all on Miss Frieda Schroeder. But I think not. If she had not been so attractive as to draw upon herself all our libidinous desires, it is doubtful that I would have exerted myself so much to demonstrate my admiration for her in the only way open to me at fourteen—by reading the books I thought it would please her to have her students read.

Seldom have the first stirrings of desire been so fruitful!

SOMETIMES OF EVENINGS there is in the air a quality which makes for the temporary illusion of timelessness. A subtle transference is effected by a fragrance, a scene, a familiar face, a pattern of light and shade, so that the present falls away and seems to merge into those aspects of the past first associated with awareness. Usually it is a fragrance related to change which effects this reversion—the smoke of burning leaves marking the turn of autumn to winter, the indescribable musk of thawing snow, presaging the spring, on which turns the experience of walking into the past.

I have known this illusion many times—who has not? It is one which is perhaps peculiar to long familiar places—of walking down toward Water Street on a night of thaw and of suddenly seeming to be once more an adolescent on the way to the Electric Theatre where I was sure to meet the object of my first affections beyond the home circle; the trees, houses, walk, road, the lights in the windows, the pervasive smell of thawing snow, all are the same, and for a few moments the illusion is the reality—but then today intrudes in the absence of the outside lights of the long-abandoned theatre, the illusion falls away, yesterday returns to its proper perspective;—of walking through a smoky October evening homewards, and seeming briefly once again on the way to Grandfather Derleth's home with the evening paper, the mind's eye recreating that familiar scene of two old people sitting together at the table under the green-shaded light in that long-known kitchen—once again trees, houses, even the voices of passersby, the cries of children on bicycles, the sweep pungence of burning leaves, all are the same, and time is not a dimension but a state of mind.

One expects at such times the very physical presence of those who have peopled the past—that first girl in all her shy loveliness; the grandparents who were once thought to be the fount of wisdom—that first girl who became a tired, complaining housewife, forever lost to the girl she had been; the grandparents who divided into a lonely, ill woman, and a weakening old man, betraying himself by his fear of loneliness. One expects even more—the recreation of the exact scene, a projection of the mind's eye from the near past or the remote years; the ill-lit post office becoming once again that magic place from which one might receive, after the evening mail was in, a treasured letter from that first girl; the depot where the evening train came in, with old Mike and Beau Wardler waiting at the station platform, and the mischievous boys, as always, troubling them, with the angular agent himself pushing and pulling expresswagons and carts around, shouting at the boys before the locomotive's whistle sounded at the bridge; the supper table at home, under the yellow lamplight's glow, with father and mother and sister restored as at first the child's groping awareness recognized them for his haven and his security from the cold, physical and spiritual, outside.

Perhaps these moments are integral in an existence close to the familiar scenes of childhood and youth, wherever there is a continuity of living. They do not occur with nostalgia, they come without warning; suddenly the chance of the moment, the place, the scene, the familiar sensual experience combine, and the present becomes fleetingly once more the past—time, in effect, ceases to exist, despite the unalterable clock. It is a kind of meeting with one's self, a meeting and passing by, the man meeting the boy he once was, meeting once more the scenes and the people of that boyhood, an experience that is an essential part of life in any long known place. The owl that keens softly in the summer evening park is the owl of childhood and youth; the arc-light swinging at the corner is the light of adolescent years; the children playing in the park are the companions of one's own childhood; the long street of arc-lights yellow on the western afterglow of April evenings still opens on the promise of adventurous expectancy; and every corner, every turning, offers still the same adventure, the identical expectancy of something beyond the commonplace, something waiting to be created in the country of the mind and translated, however inarticulately, into the familiar face, the long-known tree, the ancient house, into the eternal afterglow, new moon and evening star.

Perhaps it is the subconscious yearning for past time, for a time of irresponsibility, which lays traps for the unwary, the longing for a return to the dark, enclosing place, the intimacy of being lost to alien eyes, of being secret and alone, which may be another expression of the desire to be merged with all things, with earth itself, an awareness not of timelessness as such, but of the obliteration which is both death and the merging into time, the moment behind is the moment that has died, as were it knowledge that death always lurks behind, and before, the unknown, and beyond the unknown somewhere death at full circle, life and death being one.

from Return to Walden West

A HOST OF sounds, scarcely audible or so seldom repeated as to go all too often unheard, companion the well-known voices of the night—the low, cooing hoot of a long-eared swamp owl, the muted conversation of teal, the bell-like song of the saw-whet owl—existing on the very rim of

---

1970

awareness. Who, among the most solitary of night-walkers, commonly hears the quirting of whippoorwills, the mewing talk of muskrats, the voices of voles and meadow mice? Yet these sounds are everywhere in the spring and summer evenings, lost among the more commanding songs of birds and frogs, or so subdued as to be audible only to the waiting ear.

There are, too, the occasional unidentifiable sounds, the strange voices of uncommon birds or animals—of a migrant bird not native to the Sac Prairie country, stopping briefly overnight, or an animal long alien to this place passing through under cover of darkness, or the infinite small variations in the songs of little known warblers or frogs which lend a tantalizing strangeness to evening and night, rising out of the dusk and darkness of the woods and announcing that briefly an unknown visitor has paused in this familiar milieu, and will be gone again ere the inquiring eye can find him—a bird little given to voice, like the black-crowned night heron whose barbaric cry rises now and then out of the slopes near the river. Such voices invest the night with something alien, but are not apart from the dark wood itself, for was not a dark wood forever the heart of mystery, the source of the unknown from the beginning of man's consciousness?—since it stood for the tangible foe of man as he conceived it; earth itself arrayed against his small fire and the multitude of his fears.

The night speaks with many voices in the thousand tongues of earth, not all known to the listening ear; each shouts its triumph in life into the enclosing womb of darkness, under the moons and stars and suns of this one infinitesimal galaxy in the cosmos; each throbs in harmony with the pulse of the night-walker passing by, of whom inhabitants of the dark and darkening woods are often less aware than he of them. He may not know whence these voices come; he might be astonished to discover that the fluted piping making a choir of an April night in the meadows rises from a creature so small as to take three or four of them to cover the face of his watch; that the last breath of sound may come from the sleek, magnificent otter, a creature of size and power; that the ventriloquial voice of a screech owl rises not from many yards away but almost at his elbow; that the wild, sobbing scream from the high hills is the voice of the now rare wildcat.

The night is filled with voices—the sounds of gnawing, the songs of mating, the scuttering of passage, the screams of death, constantly, forever, the step of the night-walking solitary marking off another moment of his allotted time before he returns to dust which he will share in common with all the known and unknown habitants of the wood around him, all in due, inexorable time; the hyla choir no less than the whippoorwill's song, the jacksnipe's weird winnowing no less than the wild duck's whistling, the rabbit's death scream no less than the beaver's insatiable gnawing, the rustling of mice passing by no less than the weasel's remorseless pursuit, the love song of the woodcock no less than the proud high cry of the hunting hawk are all integral to the pattern of life and death.

EVERY SPRING I went in search of morels, sometimes day-long, whenever the weather permitted—and occasionally when it did not, hunting hills and woods, pastures and byways, from the time of the first *Morchella angusticeps* in late April to the fading of the last *Morchella crassipes* in early June, setting out early, when the grasses still hung with dew, and coming back often with the setting sun. I came to the hunting of these mushrooms by chance; not long after my return from an editorial position in Minneapolis, where I had spent such free time as I had at the Wandrei home, Donald Wandrei and his mother paid a visit to Sac Prairie, in the course of which I took them down to Ferry Bluff to unfold for them the pleasant scenery of the riverside, and there the Wandries, ardent mushroom gatherers, discovered growing within sight of the landing a score of prime *Morchella esculentas.* This introduction to the morel—followed by the tasting, confirmed me in the hunting, which soon became a pleasure I allowed nothing to diminish.

Perhaps it was as much the season of the year as it was the succulent quarry that took me from my desk into the woods, for it was the time of wild plum and cherry bloom, of violets and the first pungence of bergamotte that rose from underfoot where the hardy young plants were thrusting into May, of wild apples that stood like random clouds of pink and white in the middle of the green woods, of hawthorn blossoms with their cloying sweetness, of oak leaf pungence spilling into the south wind, of the last pasque flowers and the first yellow-orange puccoon, of mandrake and trillium and shooting stars, of the brook's voice singing through the vernal forest, the time of the height of odors and perfumes rising from the earth, from the musk of new-turned soil to the fragrance of opening leaves, of the spring glory of the trees, with the myriad shades of green that held in them the colors of autumn; and it was the time of migration for many birds, when I could be certain of seeing and hearing scarlet tanagers, prothonotary warblers and others of that family, rare least bitterns and seldom seen black-crowned night herons. And many an hour afield was spent watching the flight of hawks, in solitary majesty, or in mating play—observing the antics of kangaroo mice—satisfying the irrepressible curiosity of a bemused woodchuck—building a waterfall in a brook to increase and vary its voices—and in other such pastimes that enriched my spring days at the same time they added to my larder, for the morels, which I gathered by the thousands each spring, were taken home to be strung up and dried, giving off at first a semenal musk that startled visitors, and at last a nut-like pungence very pleasant to come upon in the house.

Morels in numbers were not easy to find, though one memorable afternoon, while hunting with Donald Wandrei, I came upon an elm stump from the dying roots of which we collected almost a thousand morels; but for the most part morels grew sparely—two and three and perhaps a half dozen or twice that number around the base of diseased oaks, aspen, prickly ash, apple trees, and butternuts, where they could be found year after year until the host tree had either died or recovered its health, after which they were seen no more; and I walked many days as much as ten miles to return home with but a few hundred of these flavorful fungi. The search led me over high hills and through deep valleys, through open woods and slopes covered with brambles and underbrush, along fence-lines through cut-over land, into the marshes and thickets of blackberries and poison ivy. It was not until the Dutch elm disease struck down the elm trees that morels were easy to find, but this very easiness lessened a little the challenge of the hunt, for all that it did not diminish the pleasure of the season. I carried the morels in a creel and a basket, scattering spores everywhere I went, though few of them found a viable host.

What a sense of freedom was integral to those days! The earth never seemed more beautiful, with the wild plum and cherry trees making a lace of white along the wood's edge and marking out the fences dividing the black fields, while their perfume rode every wind; and the grasses in open places were yellow with dandelions, star-grass, and buttercups, and blue with the large bird-foot violets that grew profusely in many places; and in some hidden spots the tiny true white violet flowered and from its blossoms rose an ineffably delicate fragrance, though in time these beds vanished together with the wild crabapple that also gave forth a perfume that had no counterpart in the wild. It was still possible to see, when I began hunting morels forty years ago, farmers afield behind horses, making a kind of bucolic poem seen from a hillside, the dark field framed by pale green leaves and often white blossoms, and the farmer and his team moving steadily back and forth across, in silence broken only by the songs of birds or the alarm cries of chipmunks and blue jays and the occasional jeering of crows flying over.

These long walks into the countryside around Sac Prairie disclosed it as nothing else could have done. I learned where the whippoorwills nested, I chanced upon woodcocks and their young, I found where lady's slippers grew, and Indian pipes spectral in the dark woods, and showy orchids; I discovered badger digs, no longer common in south central Wisconsin, and knew where the redtails nested; I saw blue racers in the ecstasy of mating, unmindful of me, and now and then a gyrfalcon floating high in the blue or hunting the woods, rare birds and, rarer still, a great grey owl down from the far north. I knew where the brook was at its most amiable, from what heights the countryside was most gracious to the eye in its sweep over fields and mounds, past farms and hamlets, to the hills along the horizon.

I never tired of carrying the fruit of my labor, though my body protested on occasion at the unwonted exertion to which I put it, despite the manifest rewards offered by the countryside at every hand. These rewards were harvested, too, with the greater pleasure, and carried forever deep inside, a reserve of beauty to draw upon in darker hours.

THE HIGH ROUNDED crown of Breunig Hill—the central and largest part of which belonged to George Breunig and later to his son, Carl—lay tall against the horizon east of Sac Prairie. Though a pastured hill, it was—save for an abandoned hilltop field that eventually became pasture too—still well wooded, in some part, on the western or Ganser slope, almost too thickly for easy passage. It was a large, sprawling hill, stretching more than a mile from its northern base to its southern extension along the brook that flowed from behind the hamlet of Roxbury through the marshes into the Wisconsin; and a hill, moreover, that was home not only to the more common animals to be found in the Sac Prairie country, but also to a family of badgers, at least two of redtails, and one of black-crowned night herons, while its wild fruit—raspberries, elderberries, blackberries, wild plums, cherries, and apples, hazel nuts, black haws, hickory nuts—fed countless thousands of birds and animals as well as that casual walker who passed by in the season.

The hill drew me early in my peregrinations through the countryside. From the open pasture on its crown it was possible to view the landscape to the north and west, the great prairie of the Sacs and the Wisconsin winding along it unrolled before the eye against the ancient range of Baraboo Bluffs that edged the northern horizon; from the promontory on the south, framed by birch and aspen trees, a low morain swept westward to the river, and revealed the vista beyond to the Ferry Bluff range, seen in May over a greensward made blue by violets, while to the south the Wisconsin Heights, where once a battle of the Black Hawk war had been fought, rose into the heavens; and from the high crown on the east I could look down upon the Roxbury country, with the old cemetery under the pines, the hamlet itself, and the yellow stone church steepling into the blue like a scene from Gray's *Elegy in a Country Churchyard* seen in October from under a spreading wild apple tree red with succulent fruit that tasted like none other to be had in country or town.

I usually went up along the Breunig-Ganser line-fence, following a cow-path for part of the way to the hilltop pasture, now slowly being taken over again by birch and aspen trees, crossed the crown of the hill to the east, and sat down under the wild apple above the valley, under blossom or fruit in their seasons, to read and write and contemplate the serene scene unfolded before me. It was a place for meditation, with the wind's rune and cowbell sound for music. Far below, the roads ribboned past, too far away to allow the hum of cars save distantly; high overhead, redtails screamed at my invasion of their domain; and all around, mice and voles and chipmunks rustled in the grass, and birds called and sang; and deep in the woods down the slope to the south, on the way to the brook, pewees and ovenbirds called pensively all afternoon in the spring and summer and early autumn. The scene below—perhaps because of the church and the pine-grown cemetery that were central to it—always seemed to me one of ineffable peace and contentment; while that seen from the promontory to westward was more intimate, framed as it was by the white birch boles and the new green leaves and pendant yellow blossoms, and with wild plums in riotous blossom along the fences all the way to the Wisconsin.

Now and then I gathered wild apples there, and hazelnuts, and fairy ring mushrooms (*Marismius oreades*). Puffballs grew in some profusion in the hilltop pasture from early summer to mid-autumn, and the diligent hunter could find boletes and collybias and other edible mushrooms—as well as the deadly destroying angel and dubious russulas widely scattered on the slopes and in the pastures. It was a place little visited by others; privacy was assured there; now and then Carl Breunig came along checking his line-fences, but no one else passed by except during the hunting season. In their time I brought Myra, Marcia, and Caitlin there, and spent many a pleasant hour reading with Rikki, taking the sun in the hilltop pasture, untroubled by any intruder and discovered only by chipmunks and blue jays and hawks and saluted in turn by one after another of them. In March and April the pasque-flowers and buttercups grew there, in May the anemones, the shooting stars, the columbines and puccoons, and the hawthorns and black haws flowered; the seasons unfolded as in wilderness, with seldom an invasion by any human being other than myself and the owners of the land, who came less often.

Sometimes I crossed the hill and went over to the brook, to sit there among the Indian mounds above a bend in the brook, where a great thunderbird mound crowned the slope that rose from the water's edge, sat listening to the lulling talk of the water flowing among the stones in the brook-bed, which would be dry by summer unless the rains were heavy and frequent; though once the brook flowed through several vernal months until the areas of its source were drained and the springs stopped up by farmers who turned the meadows and marshes there into fields; and then presently walked back again, having written such lines as I meant to write and read what I intended to read, and fed my soul out of solitude and tranquility—a long walk, every foot of which opened up to such views that each walk up and across the Breunig Hill enriched me beyond measure.

Often, too, I went down the craggy south promontory to the base of the hill facing southwest, crossing to the Ganser land. A fence divided the hill pasture from fields there, and a cowpath ran parallel to the fence, past a long row of ancient elms and maples through patches of prickly ash, wild plum trees, may-apples, dutchman's breeches, and anemones. I took the path and walked it leisurely, pausing frequently to look out across the black fields so often found in May framed by wild plum trees in full bloom—so many of them that their perfume pervaded the woods, over a gently undulating landscape, across the highway to the hills beyond; and, followed it along the western extension of the hill, past the old yellow limestone Ganser house and the adjacent barnyard, and out to the road that led along the northern base of the hill, though as the years wore away and the hillside was no longer used for pasture, nature rapidly reclaimed her own, the prickly ash grew over the path and had to be cut away every spring if I meant to walk the path under the arboring elms, and the way along the western base was finally overgrown by blackberry canes and young honey locust trees, the thorns of which were too formidable to make that part of the path any longer pleasant; so I began to go back the way I had come, climbing the hill once more to cross the crown near the middle of the hill, and thus passing near the badger dig—where once a family of four badgers came running up the slope to vanish into their dig—and arousing again the redtails what nested not far from the place where I walked, so that they followed me, dark crosses on the blue dome overhead, their warning screams harrying me up and over the hill.

The Breunig Hill was an oasis of intimate enchantment. Though the evidence of man's industry was visible from every elevation, no sound of it fell to ear; once on the hill I was lost in nature, and thus as well in myself.

AT THIRTY I became a man of property. I bought for a thousand dollars—the sole capital I had managed to save from the scant earnings of my pen—

the ten acres of the old Lueders homestead just over the western line of the village and across the road from the tree-naved cemetery. The two spinster Lueders sisters, Miss Augusta and Miss Carlotta, were its sole owners, and parted with it reluctantly, though they had a little house in the village and now lived there. Their father, who had bought the property almost a century before, had been a member of the Academy of Natural Sciences of Hamburg, and had brought from Germany many plants and cuttings, and had put them in on his acres, so that now the property was singularly attractive, for on it one could find a great variety among its hundreds of trees, from European larch and hemlock to Scotch pine, sycamore, hackberry, linden, cedars—both white and red, box-elder, red birch, aspen, maple and oak—a great, centuries-old white oak dominated the center of the acres on the edge of the wood-lot that made its western half, and the woodlot itself walled off the western rim with groves of cedar, hickory, and oak.

Flowers flourished there in noteworthy profusion—English violets, bloodroots, Dutchman's breeches, wild ginger, anemones, spikenard, spiderwort, prairie penstemon, columbine, sweet rocket, roses, lilies-of-the-valley, lilacs, nightshade, day-lilies, wild bergamotte, milkweed, toadflax, goldenrods, and periwinkle—which covered a large area north of the cedar-arbored path that led in from the front gate on the east, and in the spring months there was in the air a constant flower fragrance that reached its peak when the hundreds of thousands of lilies-of-the-valley were in blossom, for these plants, their growth unchecked, had spread not only along the path that led up from the front gate, but in all directions from it, even to the line fences at the front and south edge of the property, and into the woodlot, where they vied tenaciously with ivy in covering the ground, and mingled with their wilder cousins, the Solomon's seals.

Though a field of two acres on the north had produced corn for many years, and though the woodlot had been used sporadically for pasture by neighboring farmers, there were many wild tenants on the ten acres—at least two families of skunks, which, though infrequently seen, now and then announced their presence with their mephitic musk, one of opossums, two of woodchucks, an occasional red fox—which remained on the grounds long enough from time to time to raise three or four kits, a family of raccoons, many dozens of red and grey squirrels, a handsome bullsnake and some garter snakes, gophers, and thousands of field mice and their relatives. Deer came up from the Wisconsin River bottoms a quarter of a mile to the south to browse during the winter months.

The avian population was even greater; no less than five dozen quail came single file out of the woodlot to forage around the old Lueders house, and to serenade the summer silences with their *bob-whites* ringing around the small, T-shaped building of wood and bricks, moulded and baked from the blue clay found under the surface of that land, a building now somewhat fallen together at one elevation after decades of sheltering that remarkable family of German immigrants who had built it—seven pairs of screech owls came out of the dusk to tumble in play over the gables of the old building and to fill the evening air and the dawn with their bell-like notes and their keening song—hermit thrushes lived under the ivy in the woodlot and saluted each day with their lyricism—crows passed over the grounds, resting occasionally in the oaks, to challenge all its inhabitants—a redtail hawk occupied one of the hemlocks throughout the winter—and a host of lesser birds—wrens, pewees, brown thrashers, redwinged blackbirds, Western meadowlarks, bronze grackles—which came by the hundreds every autumn to conduct pleasant conversations in the pines, phoebes, nighthawks, killdeers, mourning doves, bluebirds, robins, catbirds, brown creepers, nuthatches, woodpeckers of various kinds, juncos, kingbirds, cuckoos, cardinals, chickadees, and, in winter, evening grossbeaks, pine siskins, and that rose-colored finch so ineptly called "purple"—and in season, many kinds of warblers, and rarer visitors, like barn owls, long-eared marsh owls, whippoorwills, peregrine falcons, gyrfalcons, buzzards, and, on one memorable occasion, a great grey owl, down from the far north. Brown bats and pipistrelles foraged with swallows among the trees, and in the summer months nighthawks skycoasted down the buttes of air all around the grounds. Moreover, the house was close enough to the bottoms of the river to be within range of hyla choirs and the lulling song of toads during the spring months.

The property afforded me a retreat, a place of my own for contemplation and meditation. Though the highway was not far north of it, the trees shut it away, so that the sound of the traffic always seemed more remote than it actually was. On the land, not quite in its center, my father, the dour Wilfred Cork, and Chris Anderson, a Norwegian who was extremely loquacious and much given to telling tall tales of his adventures, with the aid of Paul Schara and his crew of masons, put up a solid, thick-walled house of limestone from the quarry behind the Ferry Bluff range along the Wisconsin, a house of oak, butternut, and knotty pine under a thatched roof; it rose on the site of the old house and had a similar shape, though its expanse was greater; and for a while the sounds of hammer and saw vied with the matins and vespers of the birds and excited the curiosity of the animals which, as Miss Augusta had explained, had indisputable proprietary rights to the property, and were not to be dislodged. Nor were they, for they pursued their own affairs as I mine, and there was no conflict among us; the quail came out to feed on the food I scattered around the house; the screech owls tumbled over the gables of the new house as they had of the old; each skunk recognized my path and got out of my way when I came along, as I did out of his when I was on his run.

Much of the land had been reclaimed by nature during the years the Lueders sisters were too old and enfeebled to work more than a small garden plot, though the ancient apple trees and grape arbors flourished and fed the wilderness children, and the new house fitted into the pattern of the old. For a while, of winter nights, there were ghostly footsteps to be heard in the snow outside—and never a footprint to be seen, as if the phantom of old Federick Lueders were still on his wearying round of labors, coming home from the village at a late hour, as he had so often done, or as if the shade of the lost son who had run away from home had come back to view the change that had come upon the homestead, but in time these faded and were heard no more.

The house was no pond-side cabin, no Walden; Sac Prairie was that, in its entirety; and it had no more solitude than the solitudes within me, solitudes that never faded and were never wholly plumbed. It was as much an economic experiment as Thoreau's, but a relative one, for mine was a house of many thousands of books, and what simplicity there was was less visible; and there impended always the war between owning and being owned, which never troubled Thoreau, for the land at Walden was not his but Emerson's. I never waited upon men and women and young people to come to me, but rather went to them, though they came to visit the house and in some ways to make it their own, to serve their amusements and pleasures.

My necessaries were more numerous and multi-faceted, though my mode of living remained as common, however impractical it must have seemed to others. "Who will take care of such a big place?" wondered Mary Cork, when she came to look at the house and the grounds, knowing that I would not plant beans or keep the rows of irises free of weeds, that I would do little more than mow the lawn and pick the wild strawberries and black-capped raspberries that ripened there. I expected what was enclosed by the rail fences stretching from the red cedar gate my father hung at the end of the path to take care of itself, to grow and spread as nature intended, the wild grapes and bittersweet, the roses and Virginia creeper to entwine the rails, while I continued my observation of the ways in which the men and women who were my neighbors in the village and at its perimeter came to terms with life.

When the house was built and enclosed, I had little more means than Thoreau; but I had more varied ambitions, wider horizons, and many debts and obligations. My foundations were as solid; I had been building them in Sac Prairie for three decades; like Thoreau I had been for as many years walking forest paths, cross-lots routes, rail-beds, and woodland lanes; marking the comings and goings of hawks, terns, wild geese, owls and whippoorwills—and here, at this new post, once heard one persistent whippoorwill cry his name 1,507 consecutive times; keeping a record of wilderness talk as well as of the multifarious concerns of my fellowmen; listening to what was in the wind; and keeping my presence at the rising of the sun each morning and its setting in the evening; playing calf to the moon; and observing the morning and evening stars.

I sought this house in the country to transact some private business, too, but with all the more obstacles a century of time and human experience could bring about; all my occasions were not within, but almost as much outward, and here in the open country I was closer to the stars. I did not intend to live meanly here, but to live within my limitations, and to pursue a modest career with my pen at a suitable distance from my neighbors, and toward this goal I advanced with as much confidence as Thoreau had toward his, living a life perhaps not quite as I had imagined, and meeting a modest success which was hardly more than I expected or sought, knowing that such goals as fame and wealth and social status were altogether too shabby to be held up on the same plane as peace and love and truth, all as implicit in the gentian's blue and the song sparrow's threnody as in the drone of the bee, the cricket's churr, the pewee's invitation to come into his woods, in trees, blossoms, grasses, in the thunderheads forever on every horizon, the tints of the dawn and the afterglow, as in the higher laws that govern the universe. I knew that the universe was wider than my view of it, and would always be, and I learned that if the mass of men lived lives of quiet desperation, too often they were, for want of confidence or courage, the authors of that desperation.

At this house in the country, surrounded by my kindred of the wild, I went about putting the foundations under the castles I had built in the air during my childhood—none very high, or many-turretted, or any more imposing than this dwelling within easy reach of my fellowmen at one elevation, and bounding on the opposite not only the fields, but the wind and the new moon and evening star and all their promise of adventurous expectancy, and the wider sky that marked the rim of the infinite universe.

from Wind Over Wisconsin

SOFT-WALKER, THE QUIET one, paused on the trail and smelled the air. The east wind blew gently, not enough to dispel the cloying odor of locust blooms and the thick sweet fragrance of wild crab-apple that grew in the lowlands like pink clouds over all the prairie. There was something more, and the Sac's nostrils isolated it from the fragrance all around him: it was the smell of smoke. He stood for a moment in the early June dawn and marked its direction on the wind. It came from the east, along the river there; having ascertained this to his satisfaction, he set out silently through the underbrush toward an eminence not far to westward, and, mounting this, looked out upon the expanse of green that rolled away to the broad river's edge and the hills beyond.

All about him rose the growing sounds of breaking day: incessant warbling and crying of birds, insect stridulations deep in undergrowth, furtive flutterings and rustlings, the cries of animals: but from among them came the sound of human voices, faint and far. And he saw the thin curls of smoke rising from the river's shore. He could not understand who might be there, whether friend or foe, but in a moment had begun to move in that direction to settle his doubts. He went soundlessly among the trees, going so effortlessly that even a fox, lying in wait for grouse but three feet from his path, did not move, the water thrush and redstarts along the sloughs were not disturbed, and a prothonotary warbler's golden yellow throat did not cease trembling to its song at the passing of his near-naked red-brown body. In this manner he approached the place where the fire was, and at last, with the caution of his race, he found himself looking upon seven men, white and strangely clad, and he watched in curious amazement.

Some of them were making ready their canoe; one was putting out the fire whose smoke had spoken to Soft-Walker's nostrils in the wind. Another sat making signs upon a paper on his knees, but, not satisfied with what he had done, crumpled it and threw it into the wind, and wrote anew. The last of them had fixed to a tree there a crude board, upon which were other markings carved with a knife. There were in the legends of the Sacs white men in black habits, similar to those worn by two of these men; but of the others, who were differently garbed, there was nothing. Soft-Walker listened to the strange language they spoke, seeking vainly for some familiar word, some sound he might come upon to know; but he heard none.

1938

Alarmed at their number, he took care not to show himself, but waited until they had gone in their canoes down the river. After they had passed from sight of the prairie at that place, he came out of the underbrush and took up the paper crushed and thrown away, flattened it out, and looked upon it with suspicion, his eyes held by the strange markings there . . .

Ce Meskousing et tres-large, son lit est sablonneux avec grand' nombre d'ecueils qui entravent la navigation. On recontre partout des ilots couverts de lianes et de vignes, et le long de ses rives on voit des terres fertiles semees de bois, de savanes, de coteaux. On y trouve des chenes, des noyers, des tulipers, et une autre espece d'arbre aux branches armees de longues epines. Point de petit gibier ni de poisson, mais des cerfs et des elans en grand' nombre . . .

He turned from it to the board fixed to the tree, and with one quick motion, tore it away. But the markings it bore likewise meant nothing to him.

Jolliet—Marquette: juin 1673

He felt a faint disappointment, but knowing these for trophies, he had no hesitation about taking them with him. He turned and vanished into the undergrowth again; and travelled for many days along the trail to the Sac village in the north whence he had come.

In time, the things he brought became legend to the tribe, and the adventure of Soft-Walker, the quiet one, was spoken from father to son from generation to generation, told in the lodges and wigwams of the Sacs, and the legend became one with the tales of men from the south, who were the Spaniards, and men from the north, who were the French. And, after a century, the tribe came to the place of Soft-Walker's tale and there among the oak groves built a great village.

To them came one autumn morning, much in the manner of Soft-Walker's legend, another man, without fear of them. He was a comely traveller who made signs of friendship and sat down among them and wrote. The Indians crowded around him, examining him and watching, from the youngest of them to the Chief Pyesa and his wife, who carried within her now the son who would be named Black Sparrow Hawk. They could not understand his name, no matter how often he traced it on the earth for them: Johathan Carver: *and were aware only of his friendship and his questions. Like that other man of Soft-Walker's tale, he wrote upon a paper what they told him, and they pressed close to watch the marks he made, though they were mystified and baffled by these signs. . . .*

There is here a great village of Indians calling themselves Sacs or Saukies, and they say this place is a word, which, as nearly as I can make out, means the Great Prairie of the Sacs. And as for the river, though I had difficulty understanding them, I believe it was Ouisconsin they called it. . . .

The old house was restless in the wine-yellow sunlight of mid-afternoon: the sienna limestone of its walls, the long wooden verandah and receding second story, the conical turret with the deeply inset windows: about it an inexplicably vital air of waiting, as if watching in the soft sunlight for the night to wheel over. As far as the eye could see, there was no movement in the wilderness; all was still, no leaf stirred, no blade of grass waved on the prairie; from its eminence there on the hill at the bend in the Wisconsin, the house held close to it the muted sound of human voices. All about it, stillness and the horizonless quiet of wilderness. At the foot of the hill, an Indian sat motionless on the river bank near the landing; immediately beyond him, two canoes, one laden with furs, were drawn up on the sandy shore. The river swung away to the southwest, a wide, slow stream, in its channel many wooded islands, now hazy with autumn sunlight. A large bluebottle circling about the Sac did not disturb him, though he saw presently how it fell prey to a swift-winged dragon-fly.

From the hilltop the tawny prairie, open in many places, stretched away in a long proud sweep to the bluffs rising out of the northern sky. So, too, to westward, this prairie. Beyond the river lay a low ridge of hills, past them a higher chain lying upon the eastern sky, and in the south, wooded marshes held both shores of the Wisconsin. The river came out of the ridge in the north and wound halfway around the high hill where the house and its outbuildings stood, its broad stream half circling the hill's base from the north to the southwest. Close to the river, the trees were rich with October color, and up the long slope of the hill, aspen and birch were yellow and gold, oak trees claret, maroon, sepia and garnet.

Sunlight lay in pools before the house, in the midst of it a growth of blue and purple asters crowding orris and thyme and sweet basil along the stone walk. The heavy walls of the house forbade the sun, though its roof welcomed the glow, from the low porch and the body of it to the turret at the far end. Two children played in the sun behind the house: a small girl with golden hair and intense black eyes, and a dark-skinned boy with fair, curly hair and soft blue eyes, who gazed from time to time at his companion with frank adoration. From the open doorway of a large stable beyond them, a middle-aged man stood watching them out of eyes drowsy with sunlight. Behind him stretched a row of sheds: for the chickens, for storage, an ice house, a building for furs—these two of stone—a few lesser buildings for the animals dwindling in the direction of the hill's northeast brow, where among the trees at the end of a well-worn path passing an orchard where now apples hung red and yellow opposite the sheds, stood the low stones of a small cemetery.

Beyond Fonda and the children on the western edge of the hilltop stood a compact summer house of stone.

In the kitchen, two young women worked preparing food for the evening meal, laboring in silence before a ham roast on the spit and a kettle on the trammel over the hearth fire: the younger of them, mistress of the house, save for dark hair, the adult double of the girl who played in the yard: the other dark-skinned as her son, but plain-featured, with hair drawn severely back from her forehead. Their movements were effortless and without haste, for the supper hour was still comfortably in the future. The kitchen door stood open to the day's warmth, and the sounds the women made drifted into the yard and were lost before the children's cries falling sharply into the room from time to time.

Presently an older woman, firm-featured, with a long, aristocratic face that held away the aspect of age more surely than her greying hair, came from the heart of the house to the threshold of the kitchen, her tranquil eyes fixed upon her daughter-in-law, the younger of the two, who turned at her approach to let her own dark eyes and warm smile encompass her husband's mother.

"Are the men staying, maman?"

The older woman shook her head. "Chalfonte didn't say. But he never knows, he never thinks to ask; he thinks only of his furs and now he is upset about other things." She shrugged. "Besides, these men will want to reach the Post before midnight."

In the large front room at the southeast corner of the house, the young Baron Pierre Chalfonte Pierneau stood with hands clasped behind him, his eyes fixed upon the eastern hills. Sometime, he had told himself often, someone will come over them and see the prairie. His moustache and beard were carefully trimmed, but the soft hair on his head was touseled from passing hands through it many times. He was a handsome man, with something powerful about his lithe figure, and the strength of him easily apparent in his long fingers. Despite the isolation of his home in the wilderness, he was well dressed, though at the moment his waistcoat was half open, and his clothing generally a little disheveled.

If he lowered his eyes, he might see the traders sitting there. But he had already assimilated them: Lapiage, fat and too short, with hard eyes and a mouth so firm that it might always have been so: Souligne, bird-like, with an eagerness about his watery blue eyes and his uncertain lips, and a habit of laying a finger cautiously against his fine nose before venturing an opinion.

They had measured him as easily, finding his strength not only in his hands but in his eyes, sometimes grey, but capable of a quick transition from gentleness to firmness, and darkening, purpling in that change. Afterward, one would say to the other, as always, that he was much like his father, the "old Baron," with whom they had traded in years past—and yet perhaps somehow a little softer.

Though they had spoken together for the past hour, they had arrived at nothing; yet they understood each other, Pierneau knowing he must decide now, since they must be on their way to Prairie du Chien with what furs they had, in order to have the daylight for most of their passage.

He dropped his eyes, bending forward a little on the balls of his feet. "It's always been my habit to call upon either M. Brisbois or Mr. Lockwood when I came to the post, but if Mr. Dousman . . ."

"Mr. Dousman has nothing to do with it," interrupted Lapiage in a precise, dry voice.

Chalfonte looked at him thoughtfully, choosing to believe otherwise. "You misunderstood me. I understand that M. Rolette is buying for Mr. Astor. I'm content to deal with him."

The fat man nodded and waited, his eyes taking on an expression of craftiness. Dousman buys for Astor, too, he said in his thoughts, but no word passed his lips.

"I dislike to feel that I must trade with one man and no other, said Chalfonte as an afterthought. "I've found it a pleasure to deal with Lockwood and Brisbois . . ."

"And Mr. Dousman?" asked Souligne abruptly, finger against nose.

"From what I hear of Dousman's handling of the Indians, I don't think I'd care to deal with him," Chalfonte answered shortly.

Lapiage flashed a sharp glance toward Souligne and gave a short, impatient shake of his head as if to emphasize the denial he thought but did not speak, lest he seem to take issue with the young Baron and chill his warmth. "If you can be persuaded to let us take along your furs?" he suggested easily.

Chalfonte smiled. "If it in no way binds me to hold my sales until your arrival, I can be. Provided, of course, that we agree on a price. Does that satisfy you, Lapiage?"

"Admirably," replied the trader. "In these uncertain times, one could hardly expect any sensible trader to wait for itinerant buyers, particularly when you're within easy distance of the Posts yourself."

"Good," said Chalfonte, nodding. "I'll have Fonda get the furs ready." He started away, but turned at the threshold. "Meanwhile, if you'd like refreshment of any kind, my wife will be glad to serve you. I know I can't ask you for supper, since you're already impatient to be off."

The traders shook their heads and looked dubiously after him.

His mother, turning, saw him come down the hall and said to Adrienne, "Here comes Chalfonte."

He passed her with a touch of his hand to her shoulder and said to his wife, "Adrienne, see if they will have anything."

"They're not staying?"

He shook his head. In a moment he was out of the house, crossing the yard, and Fonda's glance swung from the children to him.

"Bring our furs around to the front of the house, Edward," he said. "They've been sold."

Fonda's eyebrows went up. "All of them?"

"Move now. They're anxious to be off."

Turning, he paused briefly near the children, and the girl looked up at him, her broad mouth smiling happily. "I won, Pappa," she said. "I won." He nodded and smiled, though without being aware of what game the children played.

When he came back into the room, the men had finished a cup of hot oswego tea and a little cake or two. They looked up at him in faint surprise and half-smiled, as if in satisfaction now that they had agreed upon the sale, though its terms were yet to be decided upon.

"My man Fonda's bringing the furs around to the front of the house, "Chalfonte explained, again taking his stand before them with legs spread and fingers woven together behind his back.

Lapiage nodded absently, and the last of his cake disappeared into his mouth. Souligne sat with eyes half-closed, and in repose now, his face betrayed his tiredness.

Chalfonte looked at them and his brows drew slowly together. "If you came from the Portage, you might have some news of the Indians," he said tentatively. "I understand the Winnebagos are in touch with the Sacs, and keep Kinzie informed."

Lapiage looked at his companion, but the glance he gave him was without meaning. Chalfonte's eyes shifted.

"You, Souligne?"

Souligne pretended to an air of knowledge, the inevitable finger straying across his lean cheek to his nose. "There's going to be trouble. The Indians are irritable and restless—very restless."

"Who wouldn't be, with treaties broken and thrown back into their faces!" demanded Chalfonte angrily. "But they're always restless; that means nothing of itself." "No," agreed Souligne sagely, "but there's something in the air. Keokuk is always saying that the Indians must stay on the west bank of the Mississippi."

"He's been saying that for as long as I can remember," said Chalfonte. But he thought: They know nothing, nothing at all.

Lapiage nodded. "The trouble is, if there's unrest among the Indians, it's bound to affect trading."

"They're certainly the best trappers and hunters," agreed Chalfonte shortly. "And as neighbors—I could wish for none better, though I confess they're a little unorthodox at times." He coughed faintly, and the traders smiled, Lapiage wrinkling his nose with exaggerated meaning.

"Well," said Lapiage, "there ought not to be trouble, but I'm afraid it's coming."

"If the traders stood on common ground, something might be done," replied Chalfonte bitterly.

Lapiage shrugged. "The people are cattle; they listen to every story, no matter how stupid it might be."

Souligne said, "Might we look at the furs, Baron Pierneau?" his voice faintly apologetic, his eyes dog-like lest he offend his host.

Chalfonte eyed him and nodded.

They went out of the house by the wide front door into the slanting sunlight. Fonda came around from the outbuildings with the last furs thonged together in a great bundle and carried on his back. He put them down on the flagstones and stood aside while the men examined them. He glanced casually at Chalfonte, his eyes meeting his employer's briefly, then slipping away and losing themselves in the blue distance, his face tranquil, the first lines of age showing in the sunlight at his eyes and mouth.

Lapiage muttered under his breath.

"What do you say, Lapiage?" asked Chalfonte, a slight smile on his lips. He stood with his hands clasped behind him, easily confident in the excellence of his furs.

"These are very fine furs," said Lapiage, looking up with profound admiration. "They're the finest," said Chalfonte dryly.

Souligne ventured shrewdly, "You have a good source, Baron Pierneau?" his soft eyes narrowed and watchful.

"I have long received my best furs through the direction of Chief Black Sparrow Hawk of the Sac band."

"Small wonder you don't want to see trouble," put in Lapiage. "But it's that man who's stirring it up. Why don't you talk him into giving over these attempts of his?"

Chalfonte's fine eyes looked at him with scorn he took no trouble to conceal. "Black Hawk doesn't want war," he said.

Souligne looked incredulous. "You know damned well he threatened the settlers down along the Rock only this spring, and Governor Reynolds had to call out the troops."

"Reynolds is ten times a fool," answered Chalfonte bitterly. "He called for settlers to repel the invasion of the British band—twenty years too late!" He shook his head. "It's not Black Hawk, but the greedy white men he's had to deal with. If there's any Indian trouble-maker, it's the Prophet—White Cloud."

"You know, doubtless," said Lapiage lightly, and turned back to the furs.

They don't care, Chalfonte told himself. Hard upon the thought came the conviction that they would always be serving their own selfish ends, never uniting against a common enemy. They never see beyond their noses, they know no tomorrows—like all the others, he thought. Watching the two traders, he began to wonder whether his own interest was motivated as well by selfishness, knowing that trouble now or at any time would destroy the source of supply not only for many a buyer but for him also. For a moment he felt apart from the men, from the furs, and the trade, apart even from the house at his back; he raised his head and looked beyond the trees down the winding length of the river and the bottoms to the encircling hills, hazed in the sunlight. No, it isn't that, he told himself, and knew the sense of rankling injustice that stirred him. It's the way things change, the way they're brought about: by knavery and dishonesty, trickery and thievery: he thought, not the way of the upright man to whom justice and faith in his fellow men, whether red or white, are the sole measures of conduct. He stirred to realization that at the bottom it was not the fur trade at all, it was not anxiety about his existence primarily, it was concern for a way of life, a credo, a deep-grained belief in co-operation among men to effect change without violence and grief, without treachery and death. . . .

Spring deepened to summer; in the night the last pink blossoms of the sweet wild crab-apple were thinned by the wind; catalpa and locust flowered into June and dropped a carpet of blooms that lay briefly white and languorous on the prairie and at the edge of shallow woods along the river; wild roses came to bloom and made fragrant the air; the hill slopes were covered with columbines, whose faint delicate odor hung in clouds before the wind, with blue harebells, alum, and lupines, and in open places among the deep woods, the scarlet honeysuckles leaned into the sunny afternoons. The uncertain weather of April and May gave way to a quieter June, the sun shone more often, and rains came more seldom. The dark nights rang with the incessant cries of whippoorwills, the whooping of cranes and owls, and the deep swamps murmured with a multitude of voices the life and death of feathered and furred creatures, large and small. The solstice passed, the clear, cloudless days grew sultry and hot, and July came.

With the coming of summer, work on all the lines lessened, but there was always enough to keep them all busy. Kerry kept close to the house, for Kerith, approaching the day of her delivery, was irritable and discontented, and his power to soothe her was greater than that of any of the women. Clement and Fonda cared for the animals and the growing corn on the small piece of soil under cultivation; they took the scythes and went out to cut hay on the prairie, so that in the night the sweet smell of drying grass and flowers rose to the house and stayed in the air. The women were endlessly busy from dawn to night with countless tasks: making soap and candles, gathering and putting down the wild strawberries that grew profusely on the grassy slopes near the house, preserving mulberries and raspberries, washing and refilling the straw ticks under the feather-beds, making bonnets and homespun clothes for the children; they wove covers and canopies, and at night worked often on quilts and hooked rugs. In the heat of summer, they baked and cooked in the summer house, where the hearth fire was kept burning day and night; so the house itself remained cool even on the hottest days.

Throughout this time, Chalfonte could not keep hidden the wild restlessness that hounded him, and so revealed his knowledge of war to the south. Adrienne was briefly troubled, but in a few days appeared to quiet her fears, but the old lady held the trouble in her mind. Actually, Adrienne was no less disturbed, and continued to worry, but she concealed it better than either Chalfonte or his mother. Often at night she heard Chalfonte toss and was herself awakened; he slept poorly, though he did not appear to suffer from lack of sleep; and waking, she lay quiet, listening, wishing there were something she might do to alleviate his fears, but there was nothing, and she knew. If she thought about the war at all, she was convinced that sooner or later it would reach the prairie, reasoning simply that Chalfonte would not be so much upset if he himself did not fear this, too. But she was not afraid so much of what might happen then, as she feared for the effect of prolonged melancholy upon Chalfonte, and she strove from time to time, persistently, to take his mind from the war. But in this she failed.

The silence and isolation were chiefly unbearable for Chalfonte: never a word from outside, never a word to break the growing suspense, to lessen the feverish waiting for events to come to pass. Never had he noticed so insistently how alone they were on this hill, how empty the river was of traffic; never before had it come to him how sombre and still the wilderness could be, pregnant with a strange, mysterious waiting that presaged dire things to come. Sometimes he caught himself listening, and started awake in the night at the distant, growing murmur of wind in the trees; sometimes he lay wide-eyed in bed, and rose in the dark and went out of the house clad in trousers pulled over his nightgown and slippers, urged by his inner fear to see that all was right among the animals and the outbuildings; he went among the hens, bunched together on their roosts, he paused among the cows, whose velvet eyes were hung with sleep; he stood a while in the shadow of the haymow with his eye for the fork's dim shape in the early dawnlight, and sometimes he was held by the sight of the plow, remembering what Dousman had said of raising grain. He never saw Adrienne's anxious eyes watching for his return, because she was gone before he reached the house, the window empty of her.

Often he stood by day and looked over the prairie, as if expecting that any moment someone might appear in the distance and bear down upon the hill with news for them at the house. Such travellers as stopped were from the north, and came by river. At Fort Winnebago they knew little more than Chalfonte had heard from Dousman almost two months ago, or, if they hazarded anything in advance of Stillman's defeat, gave contradictory and garbled stories worse than nothing at all, since they but increased the uncertainty. Besides, all reports were made to Kinzie, and the agent was not likely to disseminate information which might frighten the women at the Fort, and so the traders knew nothing with authority.

Early in July, Chalfonte's watching the prairie was rewarded. He spied from the hilltop a solitary Indian making his way with some care to keep hidden along the prairie from the north. He was at first alarmed, but reflected presently that the Indian went too openly for danger, and, after a while, descried far behind him a tethered horse, unquestionably the Indian's, and beyond, in a grove of oak there, a man seated on a horse. So he divined that the Indian bore a message for him, having already seen that he was a Winnebago and not a Sac, and approached in this manner to attract his attention without alarming others at the house.

He mounted the bay mare and rode down the slope toward the Indian, unafraid to deal with him alone if his guess were wrong. But he was confident.

At his approach, the Winnebago stood waiting, one arm raised in a gesture of friendship, his face expressionless, his features typical of his tribe: nose large and much flattened, cheek bones high, lips thin and eyes hard; and his summer dress was the well-tanned skin of a wild animal worn loosely in a short apron as a loin cloth.

As Chalfonte came up, the Winnebago made a half-turn and extended his arm to the north, pointing toward the oak grove.

"Shaw-nee-aw-kee," he said slowly and distinctly.

Chalfonte knew this for the Indian name for Kinzie or any member of his family. He began to feel some alarm, lest something had happened at the fort; but in a moment this passed, for he reasoned that if Kinzie or anyone of his family were in flight he would have come directly to the house.

Not knowing the Winnebago language well enough, he asked in the Sac tongue, "Is he alone?"

"Shaw-nee-aw-kee alone," replied the Winnebago.

Chalfonte nodded and rode past him, urging the horse to a swifter pace. He did not feel the hot sun at his back in his eagerness to see Kinzie, for he knew that the agent would have news for him. He passed the Indian's horse and shortly came upon Kinzie.

The agent had dismounted and was striding back and forth in the shade of the oak trees there, watching Chalfonte come on, a half-smile of greeting touching his wide, firm mouth. He paused as Chalfonte rode up and dismounted, then came forward to shake his hand.

"Pierneau, I hope you weren't alarmed; I thought it best this way."

"I knew you must have some reason, knowing my hospitality is yours at all times. What is it? What do you hear of the war? Yes, I understood that this is what you have come to tell me, and this way so that the women might not know."

Kinzie's smile broke into a frank grin. "Of course, of course, Pierneau. I knew you understood. It's this. We know there are hostiles around here. I don't know who they are. If they're Sacs, of course, you have nothing to fear."

"I'm not too sanguine," said Chalfonte moodily.

Kinzie disregarded the interruption. "If they're not, heaven help us! Now I've sent Mrs. Kinzie, my family, to Fort Howard with a load of furs. They're fitted up comfortably enough, as comfortable as an open boat will allow, with a tentcloth on a hoop-pole framework, and enough provisions. Her brother and our blacksmith, Mata, accompanied them."

"When was this?" asked Chalfonte, his hand on Kinzie's arm. "Is danger so close?"

"On the fourth of this month, and I believe they had rain for most of their passage. But my wife has a stout heart and endless patience. As for danger— our Indian runners tell us frequently that the Sacs will fall upon the Portage and massacre us all, in the fort and without, except of course, my family and Pauquette's. But we've had no evidence of this and the Winnebagos have much imagination."

Chalfonte frowned and cast a glance over his shoulder to see whether the scout had returned; there was no sign of him. "And the Winnebagos— have they given any sign of joining Black Hawk if he reaches here?"

Kinzie shook his head. "No thought of it. . . . Come, let's walk a bit; I'm stiff from riding, and the horse had more spirit than I thought."

Chalfonte obediently fell in at the agent's side, and they walked among the oak trees there, talking the while and unmindful of gnats and mosquitoes that rose from the bushes they passed, slapping at them occasionally, but for the most part ignoring their attack.

"No, there's no danger in that quarter," continued Kinzie. "The Winnebago are on our side. You know, only a little over a month ago, Colonel Dodge and the agent, Gratiot, held a council with the Winnebagos at the Four Lakes, and received from the Indians their promise to remain neutral, or, in case of necessity, to join the whites against the Sacs. So you see we have nothing to fear from that source." He smiled wryly. "Unless they, too, have learned from us to break treaties, my friend."

"They've had enough examples, God knows," said Chalfonte bitterly.

Kinzie nodded thoughtfully, and stood looking out across the Wisconsin to the morain ridge on the other shore. "Of course, the settlements along the Barribault are much alarmed, but so far no harm has come to them. I doubt whether anything will happen."

"Yet you sent your wife away."

"I'm not taking chances. Myself, I shall stay. There was much alarm at the fort because after Hastings deserted his place on the creek, where he traded, some Indians burned his house. Don't ask me to tell you it was an act of war—no brave thing, certainly, to burn down an unoccupied house. It may as well have been a bad Winnebago. There are some."

"Of course. But everything now . . . What do you know of the war itself?"

Kinzie shrugged. "Probably no more than you. I believe the Sacs are here in the Territory, but I don't know where. Perhaps near the headwaters of the Rock; they would go there, I think."

He turned. "Let's go back. The Indian will be waiting, and I must return to the fort. You're all well, I hope?"

"Yes, as always."

"Good, I hope you keep so." He looked eagerly toward the horses and saw his companion. "Yes, he's there."

They came up to the horses and mounted, after which the Indian, too, got on his horse and rode a little before them, waiting in the shade of the oak grove, stolid and motionless, only the horse's tail flicking constantly at flies.

Kinzie's mount pranced. "Goodbye, Pierneau. I hope to see you soon again," he said, and was off, his high-spirited horse forging swiftly northward.

Chalfonte waved after him, watching him and the Indian ride rapidly into the north. Presently he turned the mare toward the hill in the south. Kinzie had not ridden down from the Portage simply to tell him these things; his words had been light enough, but the agent was himself alarmed, had come himself because he knew his passage would not be challenged by Indians, all of whom were attached to him. But the warning was there: the hostiles were in the Territory, and they were not all Sacs. . . .

Late in the afternoon of the twentieth, Kerry saw a canoe working up the river, and came around to where Chalfonte worked in the summer house, to tell him.

"Indians?" asked Chalfonte at once.

Kerry shook his head. "I don't think so. They don't look expert at paddling. For one thing, they keep in the current too much."

Chalfonte left his work and walked to where he could look down river, but by this time the canoe had passed out of sight, hidden by the thick growth of trees along the shore there, and Chalfonte swung impulsively away, striking rapidly down the winding, bushy path to the Wisconsin, Kerry after him, not without casting backward a worried glance to where Kerith stood framed in the south window of their room.

The canoe came into sight near the landing, and its occupants could be clearly seen; they were white men and, as they drew closer, Chalfonte saw that they were armed.

"They're from the Prairie," said Dave.

Chalfonte nodded, but said nothing until one of the men in the canoe hailed him.

"Pierneau?" The imperative question rang across the water.

Chalfonte held up his hand, partly to identify himself, partly in greeting.

"Good! shouted the young man again; for he was young, scarcely out of his teens, if Chalfonte were any judge.

A few minutes later, the canoe touched the shore, and the man in the prow jumped to land. Kerry laid hands on the craft and drew it up for the other to step out. The first of them had gone directly to Chalfonte.

"Mr. Pierneau, I'm John Legrande, with Tom Prillep," jerking his head backward. "We've been sent up by Mr. Dousman."

"With your mail," said Prillep, coming from the water's edge with a parcel and a pack of letters in his hands, his freckled face faintly red, as if sunburned, his grin uncertain and his brown eyes looking to Legrande for guidance.

Chalfonte glanced from one to the other of them, from the ingenuous Prillep to the dark and more certain Legrande. "Mr. Dousman would hardly have taken the trouble to send you here with my mail," he said dryly, observing that Legrande was slightly older than Prillep, as he took the things Prillep held out to him.

"Well, I guess that ain't all," admitted Prillep. "We're to stay here a few days, if you'll have us."

Chalfonte smiled. "Certainly. You're welcome to stay. But in what danger does Mr. Dousman think us?"

Legrande looked slightly puzzled. "It's the Indians," he replied finally, faintly apologetic, as if to say that Chalfonte might know as much. "They're heading for the Mississippi across country, at last reports."

"In flight?"

"I guess so."

"Where are they now?"

Prillep made a vague gesture embracing all the eastern horizon. "Somewhere off there."

Chalfonte turned abruptly. "Come along. You're just in time for supper."

He led the way, his thoughts beset with curiosity not untouched by amusement that Dousman should have done this thing; that, if he feared danger to the house and those in it, he should have the practical foresight to pause and send along what mail had accumulated at Prairie du Chien. He was perplexed because he had no clue to what might lie in Dousman's mind, but it was obvious to him that whatever it might be, these two young men were not fully aware of it. Nor was he certain of their status; whether they were of the fort, or whether part of Dousman's own private group of men; but this could be ascertained presently. If the Sacs were in retreat, with troops behind them, they had indeed little to fear from them, for, unless they were far in advance of the troops, it was not likely they would stop for plunder. Unless perhaps the Hawk's allies . . . ?

"Where are the Potawotomi?" he called back over his shoulder.

"Somewhere in Illinois," replied Legrande promptly. "They're out of it now."

Then it was not the Potawotomi. Chalfonte felt a faint vexation at Dousman's caution, even while feeling grateful for his consideration. Unless danger were very real, the presence of these men would serve only to alarm the women needlessly; and at present all of them were alert and watchful, and carefully concealed what fear they knew, by no sign betraying alarm that might become infectious.

That evening they sat in the front room: Adrienne and Chalfonte, his mother, and Kerith in the shadows, where only her face shown dimly in the flickering lamplight. The old lady was reading a letter from her cousin in Nantes, partly to herself, partly aloud, sometimes translating the French, sometimes reading it from the letter. Chalfonte only half listened, since his thoughts were possessed still by the significance of the soldiers' coming, for, despite their civilian clothes, they were from the fort at Prairie du Chien. One of them was now in the sheds with Fonda; the other was in the house with Clement. The animals had been getting restless of late, and one of the men regularly stayed near them. Usually it was Kerry, who early chafed under the restriction of abiding at the house, but tonight Kerry prowled somewhere about the grounds, and Fonda had taken his place.

In the room's occasional stillness, each of them pursued his own thoughts. Kerith listened eagerly for the old lady to read news from the world beyond the wilderness; Chalfonte thought from time to time of how Black Hawk fared; Adrienne held in her lap the package of books sent from France, and at her side, an argand lamp sent from Boston. None of them was entirely at ease, though the atmosphere of the room was soothing; the yellow glow of candles set in tin-backed sconces along the walls cast a pale illumination over the light blue wallpaper, revealing the faint outlines of the delicate French flower design. The camphene lamp, by the light of which the old lady read, shed a warm radiance that softened her face and outlined against the opposite wall a grotesquely exaggerated shadow of the barrel-backed chair in which she sat. . . .

The sound of her words had hardly died away before a faint whisper of padding feet came to ear, a subtle, intangible thrill of fear struck into Chalfonte, and he looked up, startled, to see Kerry standing on the threshold; he had come silently in the dark from outside, where his catlike walk had served him well, and now into the sudden hush that stood about them in the room, he dropped a single word, only half-spoken, as if for Chalfonte's ears alone.

"Indians!"

Chalfonte came to his feet, leaving the women speechless with sudden alarm; oddly, he was not himself fearful; he thought of the retreating Sacs, and he began to think only of giving them food and shelter; and with this in his mind he came undisturbed to where Kerry stood. But Kerry's first words shook him rudely from his security.

"I've barred the doors, and the shudders are tight on the windows—but for those on this room. They'd better be done at once." His words came out fast, sibilantly whispered, as if he spoke in urgent haste.

Chalfonte was astonished; his face underwent a change from quiet anticipation to quick alarm; his eyes narrowed, his lips came together, a frown came to his forehead.

Kerry, frowning fleetingly, said, "They're Sioux, Chalfonte!"

"Sioux!" He thought immediately of Dousman's sending the soldiers. "That was what he meant," he said aloud. "He knew it. That's what he meant!"

But Kerry had already passed him, gone to close the shutters, and the old lady was at his arm. Adrienne, too, had risen, and was now placing the books she had held at the side of her chair, next to the lamp, but Kerith still sat there, her eyes following her husband as he moved swiftly from window to window.

What is it, Chalfonte?" asked his mother.

He put his hand over hers on his arm and smiled confidently to reassure her. "It's Indians, maman. They're surrounding the house. Some Sioux—it can't be very many."

The fear that was in her betrayed itself so fleetingly that it might not have been at all: a swift widening of the eyes, a quick gasp and parted lips: then, after this moment of betrayal, the old woman seemed to grow in stature, she drew herself up, her head went up and back, and her mouth grew firm and faintly scornful.

"We can hold them off," she said proudly. "Your father and I did it twice."

Chalfonte only half heard, his mind busy with plans for withstanding attack. He understood now and was glad for Dousman's perspicacity in sending the soldiers. The military had joined forces with straggling Sioux, and these treacherous allies, as every trader and trapper well know, as Dousman had anticipated, would function best by attacking isolated whites, pillaging and murdering, and leaving behind the marks of the Sacs, so that the fear-stricken population might be still further inflamed against the Sacs, long the hereditary enemies of the Sioux, since they had long ago driven the Sioux from the valley of the Upper Mississippi into the west, even as they themselves were now being inexorably driven westward by the country's expansion. He anticipated no terrifying struggle, but did not minimize the danger that faced the. His thoughts were broken in upon by Kerry's steady voice.

The shutters closed, Kerry had paused before his wife, as if now for the first time having opportunity to be concerned about her, had bent toward her anxiously and asked, "Are you afraid, Kerith?"

She shook her head. "No, I've fought before—before I knew you; and it should be easier now. I'll stay with you and help reload."

The old lady thought with relief that Kerith was not afraid, that they would have one more hand in the battle, and considered where she should go.

"Perhaps you'd better take the turret, Dave," suggested Chalfonte.

The tense waiting was shattered abruptly by hideous yells and savage cries of Indians. A shot sounded, and was answered immediately from the rear of the house. Adrienne rose and with a swift movement, blew out the candles, lest their faint light betray them to the keen eyes of Indians, though from the east side of the house they had little to fear, since the approach there was too open, and the sharp descent lay immediately beyond, too close for any Indian to oppose himself successfully to the house. The old lady left his side for the kitchen, and Chalfonte turned to Kerry, who was coming toward him, eager now for battle.

"How many are there, Dave?"

"Not more than a score, or so, I think. It looks like a scouting party to me."

Shots sounded more closely now, and in a second they heard one of the men in the kitchen reply. Chalfonte went for his flintlock, Adrienne following him like a shadow, her skirts rustling and whispering in passage. Kerry and his wife vanished into the deeper darkness on the stairs, and from the kitchen rose the sound of repeated shots, to show that the old lady was already at work reloading for them there.

Clement's lusty shout came triumphantly. "Got one!"

Chalfonte went swiftly to the dining-room, from which he could command the front of the house to better advantage than from the room opposite. He dropped to one knee at the window's side, and, next to the jamb, pulled away an inset of stone, revealing a long slit, carefully disguised, through which his weapon might take a toll of the besiegers and his eye see where they were, though for sight, the window itself was better, for the walls were too thick to permit much scope through the narrow openings at the side.

Adrienne, the second gun ready in her hands, crept cautiously to the window and peered out into the dark as well as she could through a gap in the shutters there; but she saw nothing; only blackness and silence answered her, for the Sioux had momentarily withdrawn into the woods. Trees, however, were not thick enough near the house to encourage approach in the face of firing; but the woods were not advantageous enough for the Indians without exposure, owing to the conformation of the hill there, with uneven and sometimes treacherous descent to the river's shore on the southeast, to the prairie and bottoms on south and west; so presently there was movement again in the darkness around the house, vague shadows drifting with the blackness itself. An Indian hurtled suddenly forward out of the dark toward the house, but before Chalfonte could fire, Kerry's shot from above found its mark; the Indian half-turned and crumpled grotesquely into the bed of herbs before the verandah.

From the rear of the house came a desultory scattering of shots, and once more Clement's boisterous shout.

"That's three we know of," whispered Chalfonte. "And they may have picked one off from the summer house."

He did not hear Adrienne's reply, because he saw an Indian wriggling on his belly from the woods. He half waited for Dave's shot, smiling in anticipation, before he saw that the Sioux was trying to keep out of line of the turret window, keeping the bole of a tree between the south window of the turret and himself, in an effort to reach the porch unscathed. Then he drew a bead on the Indian, coolly, and pulled the trigger.

The explosion was louder than he had thought it would be, having accustomed himself to the more distant sounds around him; in this room the sound waited longer before dying out. But he did not wait; in an instant he had exchanged his weapon for Adrienne's, and she turned to reload. It was fortunate that he had acted quickly; the Sioux at whom he had aimed was unharmed and up; with the trunk of the tree still protecting him, he was sidling toward the verandah out of line with the window. But Chalfonte's second shot found him, and he dropped, rose once on all fours and attempted briefly to retreat, but collapsed and lay still before Chalfonte could fire again. He experienced a thrill of fierce, primitive joy rising within him, not alone because he had made a kill, but because he had slain an enemy, a relentless, cruel enemy of the Sacs, a treacherous ally of the Hawk's stupid pursuit.

There was silence now until Clement called from the kitchen, his voice distant and echoing in the house's vastness. "All right in there?"

"All right," Chalfonte shouted.

The silence grew. Outside, darkness shrouded movement, and it seemed that the Sioux, momentarily repulsed, were taking council in the woods down the slope, for the time being out of range of their fire. The house settled down to waiting. All was quiet in the room where Chalfonte and Adrienne were, the acrid smell of the black powder grew strong in their nostrils; from the kitchen and the turret came furtive small sounds, as if they hesitated to move there lest the besieging Sioux hear. Chalfonte sat back on his heels and smiled at his wife.

Her own warm smile answered him. She came to her knees at his side, her eyes kindling within him a deeply satisfying sense of contentment: danger for this instant remote and slight: he drew her unprotestingly close to him and kissed her, watching her eyes close softly as always, feeling her mouth tremble under his lips. Only a moment were they thus; then she drew away.

"They can't keep up much longer," she said, a faint line on her forehead. "If there were only twenty—let's hope Dave didn't miscount."

He laughed quietly. "Dave probably underestimated them, but there aren't many, even doubling their number. As for keeping up: well, they'll keep up until they're convinced it's hopeless. Sometimes it takes a long time for them to get that idea. But we're in no danger—unless they begin trying to fire the house."

Her hand tightened on his shoulder, but she gave no other sign of alarm, calm now, and knowing security at Chalfonte's side. She bent once more to the window and fixed her eyes into the darkness beyond, her sight ranging among the shadowed boles at the wood's edge. Chalfonte lowered his head to her side. The blackness gave way presently, but still there was no motion among the trees.

They crouched there for a long time, it seemed, before anything disturbed them; then it was the sharp, startling crack of Kerry's gun. In a moment, the Sioux were charging the house, yelling and shooting; the darkness was alive; and Chalfonte was firing as quickly as Adrienne could reload. A sudden, brief sortie, and the Indians were back among the trees again. Two more had fallen to Chalfonte's weapon, but one of them presently rolled back into the woods, rose, and limped away, out of range.

They renewed the attack almost immediately. Scarcely a breathing space afforded them. Chalfonte stiffened at the sight of flames among the trees; the Sioux were resorting to fire. He made a brief attempt to keep Adrienne from knowing, but this was futile; she betrayed her fear in no way, neither by sound nor action, for which he was grateful. But yes, she was afraid, she foresaw the direst consequences from the flaming arrows—the house fired, themselves forced out, exposed to the merciless savages; and she thought with a kind of dull, acquiescent emotion: So it must end this way!

The first two arrows fell short and lay smouldering harmlessly in the grass beyond the porch, but the third struck the floor of the porch, and Chalfonte knelt with eyes close to the window in sudden fright that he might see the growing fire-glow signifying that the wood of the porch burned. But there was nothing, and he reproached himself for needless fear, since the burning of the porch would not be nearly as likely to fire the house as arrows sent to the roof. Apparently the Sioux presently thought likewise, for the burning arrows began to soar higher. Chalfonte fired blindly at the row of trees behind which the Indians stood to draw their bows, and from above, Kerry kept up an unceasing assault. But throughout the ceaseless attack, only one Indian fell, on the point of firing, his flaming arrow beneath his gleaming body.

"They'll not get the house," said Chalfonte tensely. "But I'm afraid they may get the outbuildings—those of wood at least."

He flashed a brief, reassuring glance at Adrienne, as if to conceal from her the loss of the buildings would mean the loss of their stock as well: cows, horses, dogs, chickens, oxen, and perhaps also the death of the men in the summer house: but her troubled eyes belied her smile. From outside came a weirdly triumphant cry, and Chalfonte bent again to his weapon, now warm in his hands, his eyes grimly eager for sight of the Sioux; but suddenly he grew aware of an increased ferocity, a mounting rage in the yells and shouting that made bedlam in the woods.

"They've had reinforcements!" exclaimed Adrienne, her hands clenching. She drew instinctively closer to him.

He could not trust himself to reply, not even to nod; so he said nothing, only kept his eyes fixed upon the woods there. He waited for a renewed, more confident charge, but it did not come; in a moment he saw that the Sioux were venturing carelessly from behind the trees. Kerry dropped one of them, and the others, far from renewing a charge, began to run confusedly this way and that. He was mystified, because the shots and cries from without had increased so that there was no longer any doubt that there were now greater numbers of Indians.

He listened more intently, lest some aural hallucination had betrayed him; thus his ears began to pick out from among the noise in the woods individual voices and words; he heard that there was shooting there, and yet no bullets flattened against the walls of the house, nor thudded into the verandah. But it was the cries that told him finally, and despite the confidence he had felt, a great relief rose within him, and he turned smiling to Adrienne.

"It's the Sacs—they're attacking the Sioux from the rear!"

He got up and ran quickly into the kitchen, where Clement and the soldier waited with the old lady.

"Hold your fire," he directed. "Sacs are attacking the Sioux on the slopes."

"Hardly get rid of one before the others come," sighed Prillep. "Don't know which is worse."

Chalfonte was filled with quick, unreasonable anger. "We'll hold fire until we know whether or not these Sacs are hostile. If they're not, we're not firing on them."

He went out of the kitchen before his anger could further escape him, went to the turret and told Kerry, who had already guessed the situation, and was watching now from between slightly opened shutters.

"They're scattering. There were more Sioux than I thought," he said.

"They must have come in from the west, Dave. The firing came first from that direction."

Kerry nodded judiciously, he head half-cocked. His lengthening hair kept falling into his eyes as he stood, slightly bent, to watch, his wife pressing close to the shutters. "I judge so. More than likely it's a scouting party that passed from the east earlier in the day."

Chalfonte went downstairs again. Adrienne now stood in the hall, still holding a flintlock. He took it from her and went toward the great door. With his hands on the bar, he was halted by Adrienne who caught his arms and asked, "What are you going to do?"

"I'm going out," he said. "They're not hostile."

"No, no Chalfonte—you don't know!"

"Yes; the Sioux are in flight. I'll go out. I want to know where Black Hawk is . . ."

He opened the door as he spoke and stepped out into the darkness, now more quiet than it had been but a few moments before. Adrienne pressed after him.

"I'm coming, too," she said. "If you can expose yourself like this, I can."

He reply was on his lips when a Sioux, the last of the fleeing savages, seeing them, dropped quickly and fired. The ball struck Adrienne in the leg, but at first it was as if she did not feel it, a kind of stinging reaction at first being all; the sharp pain of the bullet's piercing her flesh was lost before a kind of numbness; she cried out briefly and looked once, reproachfully, at Chalfonte. He was stricken, and his dismay made him careless of danger.

"It's all right; I'm not hurt much," she said quickly. "It's just a flesh wound, I think."

But even as she spoke, she began to feel the pain of the wound anew; she took a step backward, and the pain became excruciating, so that she had to put out a hand and support herself against the wall of the house.

Chalfonte dropped the flintlock and caught her up, his face white and his eyes conscience-stricken.

"Adrienne!" he cried.

"It's nothing, it's nothing," she insisted. "Don't carry me in like this; maman will be frightened."

He did not heed her, but carried her quickly down the hall into the kitchen, meeting his mother's questioning eyes with a defensive, almost petulant glance, his eyes falling before the old lady's.

"Adrienne's wounded. A ball in the leg," he said shortly.

"It's nothing," repeated Adrienne, distressed, but by this time the pain was intense; her leg felt as if the flesh were seared to the hip, and she could hardly control her features to keep some sign of the pain she felt from showing there.

"It was my fault," said Chalfonte, answering his mother's unvoiced question.

"No," said Adrienne quietly, her voice tense. She winced, sitting down, and again when the old lady unceremoniously began to pull up her skirts.

"I'll see how they are out in back," said Clement apologetically, his big voice subdued. The soldier had already gone into the yard, and his voice rose in halloos to the summer house, from which muffled voices came in reassuring reply.

"There's hot water on," said the old lady crisply. "I thought someone might be hurt."

Adrienne's leg lay exposed, the blood-soaked stocking rolled down. The ball had entered the flesh midway between knee and ankle, had ploughed its way a short distance along the bone, and lay embedded not far beneath the skin.

"Someone's calling you, Chalfonte," said his mother, listening. "You'd better see who it is. I can manage Adrienne."

"I'll stay."

"I'd rather be alone," said the old lady firmly.

Adrienne looked up at him, the pain of her wound ebbing briefly. "It must be the Indians calling. I'll be all right, Chalfonte."

Thus urged, he frowned and raised his head to listen. The call came down the long hall through which he had just carried Adrienne: simply his name, sounded at regular intervals.

"All right," he said shortly. "I'll come right back."

He left the room without looking again at Adrienne, as if in shame at having so easily capitulated, and strode down the hall toward the front door, which he had left standing open. Just beyond the verandah he saw an Indian standing, arm upraised, the flat of his palm turned toward the house in gesture of friendship. Despite the war-paint, Chalfonte identified the Sac as a brave named Dark Thunder who had often accompanied Black Hawk on visits the chieftain had made to the house. He came out boldly, his own arm upraised, bent unconcernedly to pick up his flintlock and lean it against the wall, momentarily startling the Sac, and spoke to Dark Thunder in the Sac language.

"Where is the Black Sparrow Hawk?"

"He comes from the east," replied Dark Thunder, advancing uncertainly toward Chalfonte, with cautious glances and an attitude of alert listening for any sound behind him.

Chalfonte observed that the brave wore several scalps, among them undoubtedly that of the Sioux who had risked his life to send a last bullet vengefully toward Adrienne and him at their brief and impulsive appearance, for the Sioux lay dead in the place where he had paused to fire toward the house, shot but a moment after he himself had fired, Chalfonte recollecting now that he had heard a second shot within an instant of the shot that had wounded Adrienne. He warmed toward the Indian before him.

"Don't be afraid, " he said. "I am Black Hawk's friend. Black Hawk is my friend. I am friend to all the Sacs."

Dark Thunder drew slightly away, as if suspicious of this repeated protestation of friendship, and at the same time slightly offended, his dignity touched. "I am not afraid, but there are white scouts north of us, and some on the river," he said haughtily.

"When does the Hawk come?"

Dark Thunder shrugged. "He passes the Four Lakes perhaps tonight, perhaps at dawn. I go to meet him together with those who are with me."

"Where are the others?"

"They have gone after the Sioux who were here," replied the Indian, grimacing his hatred. "They are seeking scalps." Reflectively he added, with grisly complacence. "They will get them. There are more of us, and they are too well fed."

"How long since you left Black Hawk's side?" persisted Chalfonte.

The Indian appeared to ponder this, but his answer had been ready before he said, "Four days."

"He goes over the Father of Waters? Back to the western land? Things have not been well with him?"

Dark Thunder shook his head slowly, only the deliberateness of his act lending any pathos to it, for his painted face was more than ever immobile, incapable of any expression visible to Chalfonte. "We have come quickly from the sanctuary on the Rock because of the treachery of Winnebagos who guided the whites. Our women are tired and our children hungry. Our old men fall by the way and are shot by the whites. The way is hard: much swamp, deep waters under the grasses, much rain."

"There's food here. Tell Black Hawk it is his."

The Indian might not have heard. "We have been finding again the old fording places. There are many in the south, but here among the islands they are few."

Chalfonte took this to mean that the hungry Sacs would not approach near enough to the house for food, and nodded.

"I go now," said Dark Thunder abruptly. "Goodbye, Pierneau."

He turned and vanished into the darkness. Chalfonte stood looking at the place where he had faded into the woods, but there was neither sign nor sound of his going. There was within him a sense of unrest instead of the relief he thought he should feel, a sense almost of impending doom; he did not understand why it should be, unless it were the conviction of the Sacs' ultimate and final defeat and destruction. . . .

In the night clouds came upon the sky and darkened the stars. A wind rose and brought the smell of rain, and in the morning the birds were quiet, waiting, and the sky overcast; the cool smell of wet earth was stronger, and the lowering clouds gave promise of rain. The wind went down in mid-morning, and the heavy air grew still, but the rain held off. In the yard around the sheds, the chickens dusted themselves incessantly; toward noon the robins began to carol as at evening, and the roosters crowed. Over the river, the swifts and martins circled and soared, and the flies began to bite, as if to emphasize again the imminence of rain by a score of small, prophetic signatures.

Chalfonte did not once leave the house during the morning, save to cross the yard to the summer house and discuss the field work with Fonda. Kerry's restlessness made no impression on him, and he was not aware that Clement had gone off into the marshes. Chalfonte was occupied in the turret of the house with his spy-glass, watching the eastern horizon for any sign of the advancing Sacs.

Immediately opposite the house across the Wisconsin at that point rose a range of high hills curving irregularly to southward, and brokenly to northward along the northeast, none of them as high as the Pierneau hill, and most more rounded. Just north of him lay low rolling land in deep grass, and between the hills and the river, a deep meadow and a small thicket of trees crowded the Wisconsin's edge. The Four Lakes country lay directly east of the low rolling land adjoining the heights at that place, and it was here that Chalfonte thought the logical place for entry for the advancing Indians; it was this place that he watched, scanning the country from the blue line of the broad brook that came rushing down from among the low hills in the northeast to the heights themselves. The low grassland was bordered at its eastern extremity by a thick growth of trees; oak, ash, elm and birch: and the heights themselves were crowded from summit to base with old oak and poplar. Chalfonte kept a careful watch, for the grass there was so deep that a man might pass through it easily without detection if he took adequate caution that the waving blades might not betray his passage.

The haziness of the atmosphere made visibility poor, but his telescope was powerful enough to make out with ease over this scarce two-mile distance the occasional animals that crossed his field of vision: deer or bear, raccoon or opossum, mink or otter in the creek: and he had no doubt about his ability to see the Sacs if they indeed came this way. He chided himself repeatedly during that morning for his obstinate watching, knowing that the Indians might well cross to the north, or more likely still, to the south, for Dark Thunder had indicated that the river was easier to ford below, beyond the islands; yet he could not convince himself of the advisability of relinquishing his self-imposed task; he felt he must serve Black Hawk in this way and perhaps, having seen him, go out to him with an offer of food—unless the pursuit was too close. He ate his dinner hurriedly, solicitous about Adrienne, who was not permitted to move about, and who lay in bed with the old lady's promise that she might rise in another day or two to keep up her spirit.

As the afternoon lengthened, Chalfonte became convinced that Black Hawk had changed his plans; perhaps he had decided to stay where he was; perhaps Dark Thunder's information was in error. A thousand doubts assailed Chalfonte; perhaps Black Hawk had already been forced into battle, beaten, and taken; perhaps the Indians had passed in the night, after the Sioux had been buried and they had slept at last, save for Kerry, who stayed awake to serve as sentry. He rested now and then, impatient with himself and with the Sacs, as if by coming now they might benefit themselves, though there was no assistance he could offer them, save food.

At that time, too, a slight rain began to fall, further impairing his vision; though he was still able to see the heights and the rolling country to the north, he was unable to look as far eastward as he had hoped; he would no longer be able to see them enter the valley as soon as they came into the deep grass there. So he confined his vision to the immediate field below the heights, and to the hills themselves, with an occasional glance up along the brook that led so naturally into the valley, and which in all likelihood the Indians might desire to follow to the Wisconsin, since it emptied into the river's east channel at the long island above the hill where the house stood.

Toward late afternoon, Clement came up to into the turret to say that he had found the tracks of Indians to the south, along the river, and understood them to be the prints left by the Sac scouts on the previous day and night in search of a fording place there; the tracks lay at the mouth of the De Tour, and the concentration of footprints there led Clement to believe that it was at that place they planned to cross; though it was considerably below the boundaries of the valley at which Chalfonte had been looking most of that day, it was still possible for the Indians to make their way to the river here and pass down along its eastern shore to the ford where they might cross; it was, in fact, the most advantageous route to that place, since it was not necessary to climb hills and so lose time. Ordinarily the water at that point was too high, but the Wisconsin had fallen rapidly after the previous week's rainfall, and now stood near its lowest level, according to records kept by Chalfonte's father and continued by Chalfonte.

"There were no marks of numbers having crossed?" asked Chalfonte.

"None. Only the scouting party."

Thus reassured, he redoubled his vigilance, certain that he must see some sign of the Sacs before nightfall, if indeed

Dark Thunder had told the truth. As to that, there was no telling, since Dark Thunder may have thought it to the Sac's advantage to becloud their movements even to so old a friend as Pierneau. He swept the hills, the valley, and the line of the brook repeatedly until he began to feel the subtle discouragement he had known briefly during the day, but still he would not give up; as his discouragement grew, his stubbornness rose also; he became more and more convinced that he would yet see Black Hawk and his band, and he was determined to come to their assistance in whatever way he might be able to do so.

The drizzling rain was unsteady; it thickened and lessened, and at times the lowering sun shown through the clouds and the bright light lay flashing and gleaming on the wet blades of grass rolling and undulating in the occasional wind. The position of the sun now indicated that it was past four o'clock, but the clouds coming over it again made it seem later. It was at this moment that the moist air carried to Chalfonte's ears the muffled and distant sound of shooting, and at first, forgetting his telescope, he rose and peered excitedly toward the eastern horizon, but saw nothing, though he heard once more a brief exchange of shots before silence fell again.

He sat down to the spy-glass. He did not immediately see the Indians, but presently discovered them making their way cunningly through the long grass toward the heights; they were coming from the line of the brook, which they had evidently followed, children and squaws first, an occasional old man among them, and the braves last, travelling so as to shield them from the fire of their pursuers. Chalfonte was impatient at their slow progress, eager himself to see the chieftain; he looked at face after face, but found the Black Hawk among the last of the Sacs to enter the valley; the Sac chief was easily identified, not alone by his dress, but by the pride of his bearing, the white pony he rode, and by the fellow chieftain who rode at his side. Chalfonte guessed him to be Neapope.

They were halfway toward their objective when the soldiers appeared, horsemen rising against the eastern sky and growing in stature as they advanced, until they came to the edge of the grassland, in sight of the Indians, and there they halted and dismounted. The Sacs pressed steadily on, but among the pursuing soldiers there was bustle and excitement; shouts and cries; no effort at concealment being made. The soldiers were obviously preparing for a skirmish, for now certain among them dropped out of line and took up their places among the horses.

Chalfonte turned the glass back to the Indians. Without any disturbance in their ranks, the braves had separated; some stayed with the squaws and children, but the majority had dropped into the deep grass, and were even now retracing their way. Watching them, Chalfonte saw that they were about to attempt to flank the soldiers, and sat fascinated, moving his glass so as to keep them always within his sight. Suddenly the Indians rose, yelling madly and wildly, firing upon the whites, but in a moment the soldiers recovered from their surprise, a detachment drove in from the right, a second standing ground, and on the left, a third firing at the Sacs. For a few moments Chalfonte was unable to see what took place: the smoke and the drizzling rain which had begun again combining with the frenetic activity there to confuse his vision: he could not tell whether the Indians had been repulsed or whether the whites had given ground; he kept shifting his eyes from the glass to the window, vainly thinking he might be able to descry something on this larger if more distant canvas. But he saw nothing until the firing had ceased and the smoke had been dissipated; then he saw that the Indians had been beaten back, not without losses, though a group of ten or more soldiers were retreating toward the place where they left the horses, carrying among them at least five wounded men. A few, who lay motionless where they had fallen, Chalfonte assumed to be dead.

He looked toward the Sacs again. The Indians had dropped into the grass, and were now almost imperceptibly wriggling backward, changing position constantly, and yet lining up for further battle. Nor were the soldiers deceived. There ensued a brief lull before the firing began anew; at first it was desultory; a shot from the grass, another in answer, here now, now there. Presently there was a scattering of shots, and at last the engagement grew into a settled exchange, so that the sound of firing was steady, smoke began to form in vaporous wisps to spread a light pall over the field. Occasionally someone scored a hit, but not often; neither side seemed to be gaining any advantage, though the whites outnumbered the Indian braves by more than five to one. He swung his glass back to where the squaws had been, and failed to find them, though he spied the trail they had left and, following it, discovered them presently securely ensconced up upon the heights, well concealed among the trees and for the present safe from the shots of the soldiers in the rolling valley below.

Toward this same vantage point among the trees, the braves were now slowly retreating, one and one and one falling back in the grass, not so secretly now, since the whites pressed them hard and rashly. But at the same time, both sides were experiencing difficulty with their weapons: the moistness of the atmosphere, the drizzling rain, the wetness of the grass all making it increasingly difficult to keep the muskets dry. The firing became more desultory, and presently the whites drew back a little and ceased. For a moment Chalfonte was puzzled by this maneuver, because the Sacs were all too plainly retreating, even if slowly; but by keeping his attention upon the soldiers, he saw that they were affixing bayonets in preparation for a charge.

Turning from them to the Indians again, he saw with a small edge of bitter satisfaction that a majority of the Indians had already reached the heights, Neapope among them, that an additional fighting force had come down from the crest of the hill to join the retreating braves, thus forming a considerable adversary among the trees, not only protecting the women and children ensconced on the heights behind, but also guarding the retreat of the last line of braves yet in the deep grass.

Clement had come into the turret room behind him and stood peering out the window; he had been drawn by the sound of firing, which could be heard clearly, and was more than ever distinct because of the air's dampness. His vision at the pane was hampered, and he looked briefly through the glass which Chalfonte surrendered to him. But he relinquished it again to Chalfonte in a moment, having accurately gauged the field, and stood anticipating Chalfonte's comment.

"How will it go, Clement?"

"They won't dislodge the Indians. They might wear them out, but now, with night coming, they'll be making camp to take up with them again in the morning."

"Yes, so I thought," said Chalfonte, nodding and smiling. "Black Hawk has acquitted himself very well so far."

Chalfonte had thought that but a few minutes had passed, a quarter of an hour at best, but it was now already past five o'clock, an hour had gone since the engagement had begun. Since he had spoken to Clement without raising his eyes from the glass, he now saw Black Hawk, still mounted on his white pony, climb boldly to the top of a little knoll slightly to eastward of the slope where the Sac braves were now protected by tree-trunks and brush, and himself well hidden from the whites on the east and north by heavy foliage. Chalfonte focused his glass on the chieftain; he saw his lips move and knew that the Sac leader was shouting directions to his men, but he could not hear the words, nor more than an occasional sound, now that the firing had all but entirely ceased.

He looked again at the whites but was too late to witness the beginning of the bayonet charge. He swung his glass back to the Indians and so saw that what he and Clement had foreseen would happen; the braves broke and retreated, easily escaping the bayonets; they ran up out of the grass along a little slope, and before the advancing whites could take toll from them, they themselves had come within range of the second line of Indians there among the trees and received a volley that stopped them instantly, though the savages' aim was insufficient to drop more than three men, and apparently only one of these fatally.

The whites retreated in some confusion, and the Sacs rested.

Chalfonte leaned away from the instrument, sighing. "Yes, they're safe now—for the time being, the night at least," he said. "There are too few of the whites to encircle the hills there. All the same," he added as if in afterthought, "I think I'll stay here. Ask my mother to send up a little something to eat—not much; I have little appetite."

"All right," replied Clement.

He watched for a few moments more, looked again through the glass, and went out.

Eagerly, Chalfonte returned to the spy-glass, though his shoulders ached and he felt the strain of his position increasingly; but more than this, he was concerned for Black Hawk; he was heart and soul with him in the conflict he witnessed, even though he recognized that the ultimate defeat of the Sacs was not far distant; he foresaw the death or capture of Black Hawk, the end of Indian resistance east of the Mississippi. These things, however, remained distant in his mind; though he recognized their truth, his concern now was for the battle going on before his eyes, and he was filled with admiration for the way in which the Sac chieftain directed his badly outnumbered braves, so that even a final defeat might not come without honor.

The whites had now retreated to the middle of the valley, and from the rear, some of the horses were being moved up. Those in command had withdrawn a little way; they stood in a little group facing the slope upon which the Indians were now secure, and were discussing the situation: three men, one with a cape, another hatless, a third holding tightly to his musket, as if ready to charge the slope. Chalfonte recognized none of them; so far he had not seen Atkinson, and now began to doubt that these whites were under his command.

The Indians, meanwhile, waited; they were not sniping, and by this sign Chalfonte understood that they needed to watch their ammunition and not waste it; Black Hawk sat quietly now, ready for a charge; the braves were well distributed and clearly in the advantage even in the face of superior odds. Behind the first line of Indians, another had formed higher on the slope, some of them wounded; there were a few muskets among them, but this line was armed chiefly with bows and arrows. Above, on the crown of the hill, there was more activity: a few braves gathering wood for fires, with the evident intention of going into camp for the night.

The slopes held by the Sacs seemed secure to Chalfonte, not alone by virtue of the protecting trees, but because of the configuration of the land there; the ridge of hills began at this western extremity with a peaked rise that grew gradually from the rolling valley below until it reached the crest where the women and children were, turning in a great curve until it extended far to eastward, where it rose anew. The bowl of the curve was held by the Sacs; the slope there was not uniform, but rose in levels, with occasional knolls from behind which the Indians might inflict heavy losses upon the whites. One of these knolls was occupied by the Hawk; this to eastward, so that he might safely command the entire field of the battle without being himself endangered. To the south, the ridge sloped steeply away in a series of ravines and declivities hidden under foliage heavier than that growing on the north; at the same place, a secondary and equally high ridge appeared to grow out of this first and run southward into the marshes. Any attempt to encircle the slope held by the Indians was manifestly futile, because there were, as Chalfonte had seen, too few soldiers to adequately hold a line around the hill even if it could strategically be surrounded, and secondly, because the uneven configuration of the hill was such that any attempt in this direction would have resulted in an unnecessarily heavy loss to the whites.

This Black Hawk had shrewdly foreseen; hence his preparation to make camp, and his apparent calm in the face of a threatened charge. He was motionless now, and his braves might have been graven there behind the trees and rocks and ground rises. The soldiers, meanwhile, remained uncertain; some of them had fallen back to bring up the wounded to where the horses had been taken—beneath the shelter of an oak grove slightly to the northeast of the valley's rolling expanse, considerably south of the place where the brook meandered into the grassland, and yet sufficiently far from the besieged slope to be out of danger, though any charge from their vantage point on the part of the Sacs would clearly be fatal.

The three commanding officers parted suddenly; there was an abrupt bustle in the ranks of the whites; lines formed, muskets were got ready for firing, officers took their places in preparation for a charge. Black Hawk stirred briefly, peering through the foliage toward the soldiers, and turned to bawl a harsh order.

In a moment, the quiet scene sprang into action; the soldiers hurled themselves forward, discharging a volley toward the trees; the Indians answered their fire, and the whites fell back. Only Black Hawk sat unmoving, watching. On the sidelines, the white officers shouted orders; the lines, fallen back, began to re-form for another charge. Black Hawk rose slightly on his pony and shouted briefly to his braves.

Chalfonte, watching the field in his glass, began to feel, despite his sympathy for Black Hawk and his band, as someone remote, as some outsider viewing a drama in which he had no part, secure before a stage, and certain that none of the actors would cross the footlights. This made him momentarily uneasy, but even the conviction of his separation from the conflict before him was a thought far back in his mind, and his uneasiness fell away. But presently he began to be disturbed by the analogy drawn within the channels of his mind, he began to become conscious of a more significant conviction: that even as he knew himself now but a spectator before this battle, he might also be a spectator before the larger, greater scene—the backward stepping of the Indians, the dying away of the fur trade, the movement to westward; and from the sudden confusion of his thoughts rose up a feeling of panic, as if he had but dreamed his security and awakened to find that he had blindly enclosed himself away from his own life, a husk, a shell drawn and grown of his own impetuous desires. He drew away from the glass and pressed a hand to his tired eyes, but in his mind the image persisted, the conviction took on a malign existence; he could not shake himself free of it because he felt its validity.

So he sat until the sound of shooting drew his eyes again to the glass. The whites were charging once more; they had gone swiftly through the long grass and come to the edge of the slope before the Indians' volley broke their ranks, though only three or four of the volunteers dropped. Again the soldiers fell back, retreating hastily through the deep grass to the place from where they had come, and there they stood, uncertain whether to press forward again or go back still more, half expecting the victorious Indians to charge them. But the Sacs, knowing their security, made no move; in contrast to the numbers they had left behind them dead in the grass, here only one of them, wounded, was making his way painfully up the slope to the brow of the hill.

In the soldier's camp, the officers were drawing together again, converging toward the oak trees; there they stood to talk while the men drifted back toward the horses. The clouds broke briefly, and the sun shown redly there; it came to Chalfonte that the dusk hour was nearing, and he turned to see whether Clement had brought his lunch, and saw it on a chair behind him where Clement had obtrusively put it some time before. Because he had lost all sense of time, his camomile tea was no longer hot, as he found by rising and touching the pot; so he returned to his glass, and gave his attention once more to the battlefield.

The whites were now once more in a flurry of activity, but this time they were not preparing for a charge; instead, they were setting up tents; some of them gathered wood for fires, and a group had been detailed for sentry duty. On the hill the Indians had built huge bonfires, which were already flaming fiercely in the cloud-ridden dusk. Black Hawk had vanished from his knoll, and Chalfonte found him presently passing among the women and children as if to comfort them. The braves had moved; though a front line still held the first row of trees, it was thinned, and those behind had begun to slip farther up the slope; but here and there were certain Sacs who continued to snipe occasionally at the enemy, inevitably drawing the fire of the whites, with no casualties on either side that Chalfonte saw. The whites continued their preparations to make camp; the Indians held fast to the slopes and the hill.

So Chalfonte, in the face of growing darkness and the possibility that, apart from the infrequent and desultory shooting, the engagement was at an end until dawn, deserted the spy-glass and sat down to eat his lunch. He ate in contemplative silence; the tea was not too lukewarm to drink, and while he sat there, the dusk began to filter in to the room, the light darkened as if a loosely woven mesh of dark cloth had grown imperceptibly over the windows, which were casemented there, and high, with a ledge beyond, so that if Chalfonte cared, he might mount to the sill and step precariously outside. The rain had ceased, but the clouds loured down, and a wind began to grow from the southwest, not strong, but steady, drawing up the dampness of foliage and earth.

There was a sound of approaching footsteps, and in a moment Kerry came into the room, a brief interrogation in the upward movement of his eyebrows at the sight of Chalfonte still at the luncheon Clement had brought him an hour and more before. He stood indolently on the threshold, leaning against the jamb, with one arm braced against the opposite wall.

"Who won? The women are asking."

Chalfonte shrugged. "It's a draw so far. The Sacs took a beating at first, but they've held the heights without trouble. The soldiers were making camp when I last looked."

"There's still a little firing," observed Kerry.

"Yes, sniping on both sides."

He got up with the dishes and cups in hand. Jerking his head toward the telescope, he said, "Take a look if you want to, Dave—though it's getting pretty dark to see. I'm going down to see Adrienne."

He went down the narrow stairs to the second floor, and from there descended to the first, where he left the dishes in the kitchen, and made his way to Adrienne's room. She was sitting up in bed, candles not yet lit, since the room was not yet in total darkness, but only in that uncertain dusk so deceptive to the eye, when objects have not entirely lost their identity and yet take on occasionally strange shapes, changing outlines in baffling manner, and the eye is tricked. His mother sat at one side of the bed; he sat down on the other.

"How goes it?"

"It's healing," said Adrienne. "I wanted to get up but maman wouldn't let me."

"There are enough of us to take the work," said the old woman tranquilly. "Besides, it's a nastier wound than you may think."

Adrienne raised her eyebrows and pouted mockingly. "You see; I dare not move. How are your Indians faring?"

"They've held off the soldiers," he said briefly, but he thought: Why need she have said it so—*your Indians?*—and he felt that even she, with all her sympathy and understanding, was aloof and remote from his struggle, from his intensity of feeling about the cause of Black Hawk and his band, and the meaning they had in his existence, the thing for which their battle stood: the cause of all men against all aggressors, the oppressed driven to oppress and become outcast, hunted and shot, tricked and despised.

"I wondered," she replied quietly, her voice almost reproachful. "You haven't been here all day. I was afraid—afraid you might have gone over to them, to the Indians. We could hear the shooting."

The old lady's eyes punished him unflinchingly. "Chalfonte has a burden on his mind," she said, as if he were not there, her voice indulgently cold.

"I watched the battle all day," he said to Adrienne.

"Yes," said his mother brittlely.

He was suddenly suffused with shame and a feeling of guilt because he had not once looked in upon his wife since he had risen from bed that morning; he began to feel as if he had indulged himself at the expense of some one else, as he had often done as a child and sometimes as a young man; he began to feel again that uncertain, nagging awareness of remoteness from life, despite the intensity of his living within himself, the agony and constant flux of his emotions; so that he looked upon his wife as if she, too, were held within these invisible walls, she, too, a shell, a husk helpless and alone, powerless to break the enclosing bonds.

"I'm sorry," he said a little stiffly. "Of course, I should have come. I wanted to come. But the battle held me—I was afraid for Black Hawk's safety, but I guess he's safe enough for the time being."

"The wound is closing slowly," said the old lady quietly, looking away. "But the flesh is delicate."

"Or stubborn," said Adrienne, smiling. "You know the nature of the Defages."

The old lady's smile was fleeting; there was a certain gravity in her warm eyes not visible to Adrienne in the half-light, since she sat against the window, between the light and Adrienne, so that all Adrienne saw in the growing dark was the fine head sculptured in the fading light.

Adrienne turned to Chalfonte. "Tell us what's happened over there."

He told them succinctly, as impartially as he could, so that he might not seem to be unduly biased on the side of the Sacs, though his sympathies could not be entirely concealed.

"And what will happen to them now?" asked Adrienne.

He shrugged. "They may escape. They want to go back across the Mississippi, but they're closely pursued and I'm afraid they'll be taken somewhere on the way." He saw suddenly that his wife was tired, her lids heavy and her smile lax, and he got up, saying, "I must go back. Dave's there watching now."

He bent and kissed Adrienne and went rapidly from the room back along the way he had come, in his preoccupation only half hearing the sounds in the children's room, where Mrs. Fonda heard their prayers before bed; in the kitchen, where Kerith washed the dishes he had brought down from the turret.

It was dark now, though in the west a faint fringe of old rose pressed among the clouds lying there. Dave sat at the telescope still, having turned it to focus upon the great bonfires now making on the hilltops a distinct target for his sight. In contrast to these pillars of flame, the tiny campfires of the whites in the valley were minute indeed: pale yellow lights almost dimmed by the orange and red flares among the trees on the slopes and brow of the heights.

Kerry had heard him come in, and, without turning, he rose, indicated the glass, and said, "See what you can make out, Chalfonte."

Chalfonte fixed his eyes to the glass; for a moment he saw only a red blur and haze; the presently the trees took shape against the fires, and an occasional figure moved across the light. All firing had ceased now, and the camps had apparently settled down for the night. But why only this slight activity about the fires on the hill? Chalfonte wondered. Only a little while before, the squaws and children had been there, and the ponies with canoes and other baggage considered necessary to their retreat; but now only an occasional brave could be seen. While the telescope's efficiency was impaired to a great degree by darkness, still it was not so much impaired that it would not show him the squaws and children if they were there. But certainly they were not there. Then he struck upon it, he recognized Black Hawk's strategy, and he began to smile with satisfaction that grew into a feeling of personal pleasure the more he thought of the move the Indians had made. . . .

Dawn had risen into upper sky, the morning star had disappeared, and the early sunlight held Prairie du Chien in a haze of yellow when they turned into the Marais de St. Feriole. But for all the activity about the fort and in the river town, it might have been mid-day. East of the fort, several soldiers were moving rapidly across the prairie on their horses, and at the fort several more were mounted and ready to ride. Before the Lockwood house, women stood and talked together.

As the canoe turned toward the shore, a trio of traders rode over the bridge across the slough to the fort. Chalfonte recognized one of the horsemen as Dousman. At the same moment Dousman saw him, wheeled his horse about, and returned to the shore, cantering up to where their canoe struck against the bank even as Clement jumped out to moor it.

"I expected you," he said, dismounting. "Lapiage told me he had informed you of Black Hawk's surrender."

"Has he come?" asked Chalfonte, stepping from the canoe.

"Not yet." Dousman waved a hand toward the fort. "He's with Street, the Indian agent, at the Irish house; hence this early activity. Like vultures gathering for the kill."

At these words Chalfonte's heart sank, his dismay came into his eyes, and he exclaimed, "You don't mean they'll condemn him to death!"

Dousman smiled broadly, his deep-set eyes alight with gentle mockery. "Be at ease, my friend. Having slain most of his warriors, his women and his children, they can afford to be merciful. You shall see. At year in prison at best . . ."

"But he's no longer a young man."

"Well, perhaps less—but doubtless he'll be taken care of. Who can say? Afterward perhaps he may be put on exhibition as a living proof of how well the Indians are treated by the Great White Father."

"He would never permit that!"

"You think not?" Dousman looked at him quizzically. "But of course, you still have such faith; you have yet to learn how weak, how vacillating even the strongest among us is. Come now, let's join Taylor. I believe he's at the fort."

As he spoke, he led his horse back up to the road, stood there until he caught sight of one of his men, whom he hailed and called over to take his horse.

"After all, we'll not need to ride. They'll bring Black Hawk and the Prophet in to the fort, and he'll make his formal surrender to Taylor. The soldiers are merely a convoy.

It will make it look so much more impressive." He glanced around. "Does your man come also?"

Chalfonte shook his head. "He'll be kept occupied; he has some buying to do."

They crossed the bridge and mounted the slope to the fort, where the flag drooped in the windless morning; but the sunlight upon it lent its color brightness, and limned it more strikingly against the clear sky beyond. The fort in its newness untouched by the cold and snow of the past winter stood tan and yellow in the morning sun.

Inside the enclosure, a company had gathered. The soldiers were standing at ease near the buildings. Colonel Taylor sat in a chair facing the fort's entrance, while near him hovered Lieutenant Davis, somewhat ill at ease over the impending surrender of the chieftain. Dousman strode confidently forward until Taylor caught his eye and smiled.

"Hello, Dousman."

"Good morning," Dousman called out in a ringing voice. "Victors gathered to divide the last scalp, I see."

Lieutenant Davis shot a quick glance at Colonel Taylor, faintly alarmed lest Taylor's anger be aroused, but Taylor only smiled briefly and said placidly, "I thought he might be here by now." Then, seeing Chalfonte suddenly, he smiled anew. "Ah, Mr. Pierneau. What manner of man is this chieftain? I'm told you know him well."

Chalfonte made a small gesture of deprecation with his right hand. "As well as any man may known an Indian of his calibre, Colonel. As to what manner of man he is—he is honest and proud, impetuous, perhaps, but too easily misled, as he was in this war."

Taylor frowned as if in distaste, and his eyes left Chalfonte's momentarily, straying toward the gate and back again. "He's a man well along in years, I understand."

"In his middle sixties, yes," replied Chalfonte. "Which causes me to hope that he will not be too long imprisoned—if at all."

The colonel flashed a faintly reproachful glance at Dousman, who said nothing; then himself said shortly and a little stiffly, "I'm afraid we can't avoid that. After all, it's not entirely in our hands."

The ambiguity of his statement stirred Chalfonte to irritation, but he held his tongue, only inclined his head slightly and stepped aside.

"For the time being, of course, he'll be kept here," continued Taylor then, more to himself than to any other. "He might have been sent immediately to Fort Armstrong were it not for the cholera there; General Scott is desirous of seeing him; but as it is, he must presently go to Jefferson Barracks, whither Lieutenant Davis will take him."

He looked at the young lieutenant with a faintly ironic smile, as if by this decision he had somehow accomplished a clever stratagem.

Dousman pushed his lips outward, and his eyes laughed. To Chalfonte he whispered, "His daughter Knoxie is the apple of Davis's eye, but Davis, alas! is a cinder in the colonel's!"

At this moment there was a disturbance beyond the gate, and Chalfonte, turning, saw two soldiers ride into the enclosure to within a few feet of where they stood. They dismounted and saluted; one stepped forward.

"The soldiers have arrived, sir."

"Very well," said Taylor. "Let them come in at once."

A curious hush fell upon them as they waited. From beyond the gate came the sounds that gave evidence of the arrival not only of Black Hawk and White Cloud, but of their convoy: hoofbeats, shouts, bugle notes. Briefly now the August sun was hot, the air close, though a faint breeze had sprung up, and clouds had mounted the sky; the buzzing of gnats and the high stridulation of a cicada in a tree nearby seemed suddenly more portentous than the sounds beyond the enclosure; but in an instant the illusion had passed, for Chalfonte saw Black Hawk entering at the gate.

The chieftain walked slightly before White Cloud, General Street behind them. Black Hawk's head was held high and firm, his jaw tense, his eyes steady, fixed upon Colonel Taylor; he was dressed in a new deer-skin suit that shone whitely in the sun; on his head he wore a roach of hair dyed black, and feathers in red designating his rank. White Cloud approached in more submissive fashion, his head slightly bowed, though his eyes looked hatefully upward to observe what kind of men Black Hawk led him to.

Straight up to Colonel Taylor came Black Hawk, unfaltering, for he recognized the fort's commander. His step was firm, his eyes looked neither to right nor left; if he saw Chalfonte, he gave no sign, and no muscle moved in his dark face. Arriving before the colonel, he stood with arms at his sides and for a moment looked into Taylor's face. Then he spoke, as he had spoken before to the agent, Street.

"I am Black Hawk of the Sacs, surrendering. I am Black Hawk no longer fighting."

General Street moved forward and translated rapidly.

"You are our prisoner, Black Hawk. And you also, White Cloud," said Taylor.

The Prophet nodded, but Black Hawk made no sign; his eyes remained on Street until Colonel Taylor's voice commanded his attention.

"What have you to say to us of this war?"

Black Hawk looked at Taylor with a slowness that seemed infinite and calculated; his proud eyes met Taylor's unmoved, and he said as if from a great depth within him, "I loved my cornfields and the home of my people. I fought for them. Know that and remember it and do not speak untruths of the war after I am gone."

"As to the war . . ." interrupted Taylor shortly.

Black Hawk's eyes did not falter. He hesitated a moment; then he spoke again. "It is done. My warriors fell around me, and I saw my evil day at hand. The sun rose clear on us in the morning, and at night it sank in a dark cloud, and looked like a ball of fire. This was the last sun that shown on Black Hawk. He is now a prisoner to the white man. But he can stand the torture. He is not afraid of death; he is no coward. Black Hawk is a Sac; he has done nothing of which an Indian need be ashamed. He has fought the battles of his country against the white men, who came year after year, to cheat us and take away our lands. You know the cause of our making war—it is known to all white men—they ought to be ashamed of it. The white men despise the Indians and drive them from their homes. But the Indians are not deceitful. The white men speak bad of the Indian and look at him spitefully. But the Indian does not tell lies; the Indian does not steal. Black Hawk is satisfied. He will go to the world of spirits contented. He has done his duty—his Father will meet him and reward him. The white men do not scalp the head, but they do worse—they poison the heart; it is not pure with them. His countrymen will not be scalped, but they will in a few years become like the white men so that you cannot hurt them; and there must be, as in the white settlements, as many officers as men, to take care of them and keep them in order. Farewell to my nation. Farewell to Black Hawk. I loved my people and my cornfields; I fought for them."

His words seemed detached, but they struck deep into Chalfonte. They were heavy with a thousand things unsaid, they bore the burden of life and of a race. Behind them, as behind Black Hawk's immobile face, lay the tragedy that had overtaken his people, the destruction of all the aging chieftain had held close. His words were a barrier between his race and the white man's race; more, he could not say, because he had said all; his words were primal and final; as long as earth was, men would fight to preserve their homes and the homes of those they loved, and all battle so instituted would forever remain just. But Chalfonte looked in vain for any softness in the old man's eyes; there was none; the Sac chieftain had raised his eyes from Taylor and looked again to Street as if waiting; he was utterly immune to anything that might happen to him now, but he was proudly defiant even in defeat;

there was nothing of shame in the steadiness of his gaze, in the lines of his mouth.

For a few moments Taylor looked at him. Street glanced at Taylor, and back to the chieftain. "Come," he said shortly, and turned to lead the way.

Black Hawk turned to follow, but his way was intercepted by Chalfonte, who had walked quickly forward to stand before the Sac chief, hand outstretched. Black Hawk's eyes met his.

"Goodbye, Black Hawk."

For an instant it seemed as if the chieftain would brush past him but he did not. He did not take Chalfonte's hand, but his own descended upon Chalfonte's arm. "Farewell, Pierneau. You were my friend."

Then he passed on.

Chalfonte watched his retreating back briefly; then he turned abruptly and walked rapidly from the enclosure, unwilling to see Black Hawk locked into the guardhouse, and unaware of eyes upon him. Dousman followed more leisurely, bowing with a faint, intangible air of regret to Colonel Taylor and nodding to Davis.

Joining Chalfonte beyond the gate, he said, "You are impetuous, my friend."

Chalfonte shrugged. "It was difficult for me. The Hawk stood for something I could understand."

"As a symbol, I fear he has outlived his usefulness."

They walked silently to the slough, across the bridge, and were almost at Dousman's place before any further word passed between them. Chalfonte was occupied with what he had seen behind Black Hawk's eyes, what his sensitive ears had heard in his words, and he was angry, as always, at his own helplessness, at his inability to change even to the smallest degree the inexorable workings of time, even as he understood with faintly stirring alarm his continued inability to compromise with himself and with his existence. . . .

One evening toward the close of the second week in November, Chalfonte was called from the sheds, where he was at work among the pelts with Clement and Kerry. It was his mother's voice that called him, and he came out, wondering what the matter was.

"Chalfonte, see the sky," she said.

He looked and was amazed. From all points in the clear heavens came meteors; it was if all the stars were falling and, for a moment touched by fear, he sought the familiar ones he knew: Aldebaran, pale blue Vega, Altair, Capella, the Pleiades: but all were there, undisturbed, gleaming as always.

He could not determine a focal point for the shower, but he was astonished at its brilliance. He saw it as a rain of stars, and it was a full minute before he looked back to earth, seeing the women grouped in the yard just outside the kitchen.

"What is it, Chalfonte?" called Madeleine. "Are they all coming down?"

"No, no," he replied impatiently. "Just shooting-stars—meteors." He turned to the store-house and called Clement and Kerry. "Come out. See this."

They came and watched the heavens with him.

"We may be able to find one," said Chalfonte. "It's possible one may fall near here—with such a shower of them." To his mother he said, "Don't be alarmed, maman. It's nothing; it will pass."

There was no lessening of the shower. He moved away from the buildings so that he could see the sky more clearly, went out of range of the sheds there and to the path leading toward the cemetery. Clement leaned up against the fur-house, hands in his pockets, but Kerry went after Chalfonte.

"What's to look for?" he asked.

"Most of them will have burnt to cinder before hitting the earth," responded Chalfonte. "Or they may hit the river. Otherwise, we can look for fire. If one of them hits the earth without being burned out by the friction in passing through the atmosphere, there'll be fire."

Kerry halted and pointed. "What about that?"

Chalfonte saw a bright orange glow about a mile up the prairie not far from the river's edge. He was astonished and thrilled, because he had not hoped to see a meteor or evidence of one. Nor did he believe at once that it was evidence of a meteor's landing that glowed there on the prairie; he did not give way to the excitement he felt.

"Unless you came from there and left a fire burning," continued Kerry. "No one else has been up in that direction today—to my knowledge."

"It may be one," conceded Chalfonte. "I'll ride down."

He turned and walked quickly back to the stable, calling out to the women in passing to explain his going. He mounted the bay and guided the horse down the north slope. Kerry came after, catching up to him just as he struck out over the prairie toward the fire. The night air was chill, the moon waxed in the southwest, and there was no sound but that of their horses' hoofs in the darkness. The celestial phenomenon continued unabated; meteors coursed down the sky, some briefly aflame, some streaking down the sky from zenith to horizon, leaving long, quickly fading tails of light, an impressive, awe-inspiring sight. Chalfonte was puzzled about their source, but his knowledge was too limited to justify a guess in regard to it. He looked again to the fire toward which they travelled and, just before a grove of trees cut it from his sight, saw a figure move against the flames. He drew up until Kerry came alongside.

"It's a campfire, said Chalfonte.

"Take care, it may by Indians."

"I don't think so. We'll go close enough to see."

They rode through the grove, going as noiselessly as possible, and went forward cautiously until they had gone close enough to see that the three men around the campfire were not Indians. Chalfonte nodded reassuringly to Kerry and went forward less carefully.

The three men at the campfire jumped up, weapons in hand, and made for a crude shelter they had put up against the night.

"Friends!" shouted Chalfonte.

He rode up into the glow of the firelight and dismounted, looking rapidly around. Kerry remained in the background more cautious, alert for any sign of danger. There were instruments and papers in evidence; at least one of the men had been writing before their approach. All three were comparatively young, none was clean-shaven and all bore evidence of long and arduous travel. Some distance away their horse were tethered, standing quietly in the wan moonlight.

Chalfonte came forward confidently. "Good evening, gentlemen. I am Chalfonte Pierneau. Kerry behind me. I take it you gentlemen are surveyors."

They introduced themselves not without some manifest suspicion. Yes they were surveyors. They had reached the prairie at nightfall and had come to this lower plateau to spend the night after having worked along the hills in the north for most of the day.

"Your work must be almost done. I thought it would be finished by now," said Chalfonte.

"It is almost done. We'll have another month or so—barring bad weather and accidents."

One of them asked about the falling stars, with some nervous superstition. Chalfonte reassured him. Marking their rude shelter, he said, "You're welcome to stay with us on the hill until morning, if you wish. There are some bears around, though I don't think they'll bother you. Some lynx—but I suppose you've seen them before."

There was some indecision among them, but finally one of them spoke their minds. No, they would stay on the prairie. As long as the night was not cold, they were in no need of warmer lodgings. They could hold their own against animals. Perhaps in the morning one of them might ride to the house for provisions, if Pierneau would sell enough to hold them until they reached Fort Crawford.

Chalfonte mounted his horse again and turned away, bidding them good-night. He thought them cold and unfriendly, but reflected that perhaps they were overly tired. He waited until they were well out of hearing of the surveyors before he spoke his thoughts to Kerry.

Kerry agreed. "Poor shoats, the lot of them," he said. "But like as not, they're worn out. To look at their beards, they've been at it a long time."...

In the east the sky began almost imperceptibly to lighten; the flush of blue deepened toward the upper sky, changing from aquamarine to turquoise, and the stars began to fade, save for the red eye of Aldebaran and the great stars of Orion. Soon these, too, grew dim; the turquoise of heaven spread over the entire sky to where the last band of night lay along the western horizon; the moon had set, Mars and Jupiter alone gleamed. Now Jupiter was gone, the turquoise sky grew lighter, Mars faded, in the east bands of old rose and cerise lay from end to end across the sky, and the pale yellow of sunlight rayed up between; the sun's blaze of topaz pushed over the horizon, still invisible from the river, but all around them day began. The fingers of sunlight leapt from slope to peak to hill and bluff, crept down the side hills to the oak groves in low places, touched the long grass of the prairies, and lay gleaming there on the undulating green, where the wind blew from the southwest. From the rushes and overhanging bushes along the Wisconsin, the warblers sang, the thrashers mocked, the redwings swayed and cried *conqueree, conqueree;* from upland places the plovers cried wildly, the meadow larks sang, and deep in the woods the foxes slunk to cover, the lynx sought their lairs, the raccoon and opossum curled in sleep while squirrels began to race from tree to tree defying martens in the pine copses, and rabbits ventured out to dare the stoat's danger.

Sunlight slanted down to the river; it lay yellow on the earth. In the grass of prairie that sloped toward the river, the wild sweet william and pink mallow bloomed; on upland slopes the spicy beebalm had begun to flower, delicately lavender, and the first goldenrod stood out among the white and purple boneset near the river's edge. The Wisconsin gleamed in the sun, and its surface dwellers came to life with the light of day; ducks, whooping cranes, wild swans—all observed their passage placidly save the swans, who had known the anger of the long shiny weapons men carried into their haven; the swans trumpeted and scattered.

They swept down the Wisconsin, pausing only briefly for the lunch Madeleine had packed, passing a party of traders not far from the Mississippi, and reaching Prairie du Chien in early afternoon, swinging up to the river landing near Dousman's office.

"Come along and meet Dousman," said Chalfonte. "He's a market for your wheat—if you're going into raising it."

"I will," said Baxter.

Clement swung into shore, where he and Chalfonte shouldered the wheat. Baxter carried his baggage. They walked slowly up the street to Dousman's office, hailing acquaintances from time to time. Dousman was in; he had seen them coming and had shouted across the street for wine to be brought.

"Ah, the wheat," said Dousman. "But surely that's not all you're bringing me?"

"No, no, just a specimen," replied Chalfonte.

"And this," said Dousman, turning to look quizzically at the Virginian. "Not a new man, Pierneau?"

"No. Mr. Baxter is a Virginian who plans to become one of the first settlers on the prairie," said Chalfonte. To Baxter he said, "Mr. Dousman is a trader who plans to become the Northwest's first millionaire."

They shook hands. "Are you staying in Prairie du Chien, Mr. Baxter?" inquired Dousman.

"No longer than I can help. I'm on my way down river, going back to my home to wind up my affairs there."

"Then you've no time to waste," replied Dousman, glancing at his clock. "There's a keelboat leaving for St. Louis at three o'clock—it's almost that now. Unless, of course, you want to stay over until tomorrow. I believe M. Brisbois is sending a cargo down the Mississippi tomorrow."

"No, thank you; I'll go now."

"And I, too," said Chalfonte, to Dousman's astonishment. "I'm going up river to pay Black Hawk a visit. Can I make it before sundown?"

"Oh, yes, I think so," answered Dousman. "But why this haste? Why not stay here tonight and go on in the morning? You don't contemplate spending the night there, surely, Pierneau? Or do you?"

Chalfonte shrugged. "I know nothing about his accommodations, nor how tired we'll be."

Dousman wrinkled his nose faintly, his dark eyes probing Chalfonte's. He jerked his shoulders impatiently and said, "I'll wait up for you. I'll expect you around midnight or a little later."

The old woman who served him his meals came in scowling and muttering fiercely, a wine bottle and several glasses in her hands.

"There," she said. "I grabbed the first one."

She put it down before Dousman and handed him the glasses.

"You'll have a glass, gentlemen?"

They could not refuse, though the Virginian was nervous, his long, capable fingers fussing with his waistcoat. He drank his wine quickly and Dousman, seeing, did likewise. Clement put down his glass half emptied and turned away. They were ready to go, eager now. Dousman went out into the street with them.

"Look at the wheat, Dousman, and tell me what you think of it. And what you're prepared to pay for it. I'll expect your report on my return."

"You'll have it," promised Dousman.

He went down to the landing with them. There were just in time to catch the keelboat; indeed, the boat had already shoved off, and turned back only at Dousman's imperative shout. The Virginian clambered aboard, turned, and waved from behind the boat's railing, standing there among the horses. Dousman looked after him thoughtfully.

"That's the kind of man you'll want on that prairie of yours, Pierneau. Firm, certain of himself, not easily upset. He's a gentleman, all right; top to toe. Now, if they were all like that . . ."

"Wish for the moon," said Chalfonte, smiling. "How far to Black Hawk's place?"

"You'll make the best time along this side of the river for most of the distance; then across and go along the other side. Keep out of the central current—but, of course, I don't need to tell you that. The Iowa's just across the Mississippi from the Bad Axe. He lives not far up on the river; you can find the place easily enough if you get there before sundown, I think you will. But why go?"

"I want to see him," answered Chalfonte shortly.

Dousman nodded. "I see. I understand. This dies hard in you, Pierneau. But go." He grinned, the obvious sincerity of him stemming Chalfonte's quick resentment. "I'll wait for you."

They got into their canoe and were about to shove off when they thought of the other craft, in which Clement had brought down the wheat.

"Keep an eye on that canoe, will you, Dousman" asked Chalfonte.

"I'll do better. I'll keep the canoe."

He bent down and, with easy strength, pulled the canoe from the water, took the paddle out, and shook it so that drops of water showered from it. They saw him last, going up the street with the canoe on his back.

They made time going up the Mississippi along the comparatively quiet water close to its banks, and came to the mouth of the Iowa before sundown, though the sun was low, and the evensong of birds already rose from the rushes along the river and from upland slopes where the sun shown.

Black Hawk's home was not far from the Mississippi: a log cabin, stoutly built and set well before the others that made up the village where he lived.

Here and there were wigwams, but the majority of the shelters there were cabins, though all were not of logs. The chieftain's cabin stood on a slight eminence facing the setting sun, and Black Hawk himself sat before it, his old face turned westward.

Chalfonte approached him with mingled feelings; he was curious, half afraid of what manner of man the past two years had made of Black Hawk; he was eager, and his mind was full of memories of those early years, the years when he and his father had traded with the Sac chieftain; and he thought of how he had seen him last, but two years ago—how long before it seemed! His first impression, when he came within sight of Black Hawk's features, was how the lines of his face had deepened, how age had taken hold of the old man.

The chieftain was not dressed in the habiliments so familiar to Chalfonte, but in civilian clothes: a dignified black coat and trousers of similar sombreness; he had a red handkerchief around his neck, and a white shirt beneath. His hair had greyed and had receded from the high, dome-like brow, where now the last sunlight lay with a faint saffron glow, lending the old man a singular austerity of spirit.

There had come over his aging features an aura of peace, but his dark eyes had not changed. He looked at Chalfonte and recognized him. He did not rise, but drew himself up, investing himself with even greater dignity not untinged with warm friendliness. To Chalfonte he indicated a seat at his side; Clement he waved to the ground before him.

"My friend Pierneau," he said.

Chalfonte felt a faint misgiving. The air with which Black Hawk had waved him to a seat was regal. "I came a long way to see you, Black Hawk," he said. "I came to know how you are, how you fare." As he spoke, he looked around him and saw that just within sight at the corner of the house, a woman, who might have been the chieftain's wife, was cutting up bear meat, a circle of dogs watching her with greedy anticipation.

"Come, sit beside me," said Black Hawk. "You see I am well. I am an old man, my friend. But I am still a Sac, a leader among the Sacs. I am honored alike by your people and mine, and this honor is dear to my heart."

Chalfonte sat down. "The trader, Dousman, told me you had gone on a long trip in the east."

The old man's eyes sparkled, and a faint suggestion of a smile touched his lips. "Yes, he speaks the truth," he said eagerly. "We went on a long trip, and I saw many things. I saw the greatness of the whites in their cities. I learned that in those places where we went, the whites have a different belief than do these settlers I have known. There their belief is to do unto others as you wish them to do unto you; that is not true of the whites I knew in those days now past. We went many days up the Ohio, and we came at last to a road more wonderful even that the smooth road through the mountains. They call it a railroad, and I examined it carefully. But you, Pierneau—you know all about this; so I need not speak of it. I prefer riding horseback to any other way, but I suppose those people prefer riding in their new-fashioned carriages, which run by steam, as do the boats on the rivers. After many days we came to Washington and went before the Great White Father."

"What did you think of him, Black Hawk?"

The chieftain nodded thoughtfully. "He has seen as many winters as I have; he is a great brave. I had little talk with him, though he asked me why I went to war against his white children. I thought he ought to have known this and said little to him about it. I went to Fort Monroe at his wish, and stayed there a few weeks, after which I was sent home by a route leading through the big towns of the whites. In all of these I was well received, I was greatly admired and entertained. The President was there, too, and he said to me that I would see the strength of his white children. And I saw that his young men were as numerous as leaves in the wood, and that we could do nothing against them, not all the Sacs, the Foxes, nor even all the Sioux, of whom there are many in the West. Then he told me to go back, to bury the tomahawk; to which I replied that the tomahawk had been buried so deep that it would never again be resurrected.

"Then we went by steamboat to a city where they make medals and money, and in this place saw a militia training. I watched this for some time, and it was good; but I think our system of parade is better than that of the whites, though now I am done with war. We went to New York and I saw a man go up into the air in a balloon. In this place, too, I was given many gifts, and wise counsel, and the squaws were very kind to us. Many of them were very pretty, for palefaces. I saw there, too, my old friend Crooks of the American Fur Company. In this fashion many days passed, and we visited many cities, but soon we came to Detroit, and then were in Prairie du Chien, where the Agent, General Street, received me kindly and returned to me my great medicine bag, the medicine bag of my nation given me by Old Thunder, which he had kept for me after I had forgotten it when I was last taken from that place a prisoner.

"Now my travels are over. Now I am an old man, content to live in peace with the whites. I have my medicine bag, and the years are heavy on my shoulders. A few more moons and I must follow my fathers to the shades. I hope that the Great Spirit may keep our people and the whites always at peace."

Chalfonte listened to Black Hawk's narrative with mingled emotions; he had not believed that Black Hawk would speak in this manner, but he reproached himself for expecting otherwise. Dousman had told him before this. He wondered why he had come, why he had sought to find in seeing Black Hawk once more an outlet for the intangible nostalgia that harried him ceaselessly, a means of escape from the fugitive memories and old ghosts that plagued his night hours. He had come filled with things to say to the old Sac chieftain, but now he could think of nothing; no words came; he saw the old man as a stranger might see him: proud, contented, vastly pleased by flattery and attention. He was not unbowed, but he was resigned, he was content and satisfied with his lot; he sat waiting here for the years to overtake him. So Chalfonte listened to words that fell hollowly upon his ears, while deep in the channels of his memories echoed those proud one-time words of the spectral Black Hawk he had known: *Is Black Hawk a woman? No, Black Hawk is no woman. I cannot endure this. No! I am a Sac; my forefather was a Sac; and all the nations call me a Sac. I am the Black Sparrow Hawk, leader of my people, chieftain of the Sacs!* Chalfonte felt a violent resentment, a sick fending against himself; it was against no tangible thing, rather against time itself, against the harrying years, the inevitable years that changed all things. Time lost, time past, time gone—and with all time the ghosts of men who were, who lived no more, whose once proud deeds, whose once unbroken words echoed dimly in the vast abysses of the past.

He was conscious that Black Hawk had ceased to speak and was regarding him now with an attitude that was almost benevolent, sitting as if waiting, expecting some word of praise, some commendation.

"You are happy here?" asked Chalfonte.

"I am content," replied Black Hawk gravely. "I live in peace with the whites, and I am looked upon as a chieftain of my people. I have my family around me, my lands, my hunting grounds, and the shackles are no longer on my feet. I am content."

Chalfonte was baffled. There was nothing for him to say. There was no reason why Black Hawk should not be content; and yet, yet—somewhere something was not as it should be. He began to think: better he had died fighting, better that. But it was irrational.

Now the sun was gone, the soft twilight dwelled upon the land and trees, the small river, wigwams and cabins blurred in their outlines; the smell of wood smoke rose from the open fires of the Indians, the pleasant water sound rose up from the Iowa's stream, a gentle wind blew coolly upon the lingering heat of the day. A few dogs came and snuffled at Clement, who sat unmoving; and on the river bank were three squaws carrying naked children, whom they threw casually into the water, pulled them out, and wiped them vigorously, while the children squalled and bawled, a disturbing sound into which the sweet cry of a whippoorwill at no great distance fell gently.

Black Hawk regarded him soberly. "Are you going back home tonight, friend Pierneau?"

Chalfonte shook his head. "I think not. Only to Prairie du Chien, where Dousman is expecting me. He is examining my wheat."

The chieftain expressed a polite interest, and Chalfonte explained.

"And the trapping?" asked Black Hawk.

"There's no longer much to be done," replied Chalfonte. . . . "Prices are not what they were, and the markets are crowded."

Black Hawk nodded slowly, his expression indicating that he had known. "The animals move west with the red men, friend Pierneau, and the white man's bird, the honey bee, sings in the woods where they were."

Clement stirred and got up. Chalfonte took a deep breath and got up, too. "I go now Black Hawk," he said. "See, the night comes. I must meet the trader at Prairie du Chien."

The chieftain rose, clasped Chalfonte's arms briefly, strongly, as of old. "Goodbye, friend Pierneau, I will remember you. You were my friend and the friend of my people. You are always welcome at my wigwam."

"And my doors are open to you, Black Hawk."

They parted, Black Hawk standing with an arm raised in the familiar gesture of farewell until they were out of sight. But Chalfonte saw him not as he was, but as he had been; he saw not the dark cloth coat, but the white buckskin of the wartime chieftain. Black Hawk was lost in the twilight, a dim figure shrouded in the darkness that followed dusk there. At the last, only the dim outlines of houses remained, the red glow of fires, the barking of dogs. The village was gone, the river lay before, the great Mississippi flowed deeply quiet ahead. In a little while they swung out into that larger stream and were carried swiftly down.

They reached Prairie du Chien just before midnight, having travelled with greater speed than they had calculated upon for being on strange waters, since moonlight made the river's surface almost as bright as day. Chalfonte turned to Clement.

"Can you stand going on?"

"If you can," answered Clement gravely.

"Good. Wait for me."

He went up the deserted street to Dousman's office, where a light still burned in the windows, a pale yellow in the shadow where no moonlight fell. He went in.

Dousman was bent over a ledger, his head concealed behind a stack of account books and papers on the table before him. "Is that you, Pierneau?" he asked, without looking up for more than enough to glance at the hour-glass before him.

"Yes." Chalfonte sat down wearily, sighing.

"Tired?"

"Tired and weary."

"You were disappointed, *hein*?"

For a few moments only the scratching of Dousman's pen was heard. Failing Chalfonte's reply, Dousman said, "You won't mind my finishing this, Pierneau. It must be done. I thought of doing it in the morning, but now I'll probably sleep in the morning. Tell me about Black Hawk."

"There's nothing to tell. An old man who lives in the present and dreams of his greatness and the greatness of the whites and their power."

There was an edge of bitterness in his voice. It did not escape Dousman. "Ah," he said dryly. "But what did you expect? To see him on a charger ready for battle? He's no fool. But of course, what you expected, Pierneau, was to see him unchanged, as always; you were prepared to be enheartened by his firmness, to carry his image home with you and feed upon it for years to come. Better you had not seen him at all, in that case. As it is, seeing him has done you good, though, perhaps, you won't see it."

"Nor am I a fool, Dousman, " said Chalfonte with unwonted spirit.

Dousman cocked an eye at him, one raised eyebrow giving his face a satanic expression. He sat for a moment touching the feather of his pen to his pursed lips. Then he shrugged and bent again to his work. "Perhaps not. We shall see. Tell me what you expected of him, Chalfonte."

Chalfonte hesitated. "I don't know," he confessed after a bit. "I can't tell you, can't put it in to words. I was disappointed, that's all."

"What dreams a man has!" murmured Dousman. "Was he happy?"

"He said so; he looked so."

"And you resented it?"

"It was the way he spoke of his trip—as if it were the greatest thing that ever happened to him," said Chalfonte bitterly.

"Perhaps it was," said Dousman gravely.

"Perhaps it was, indeed!" exclaimed Chalfonte angrily. "If he experienced anything greater, more noble than his defiance of the men who tricked him and his people, I don't know of it. Certainly not this—this prostitution of all he stood for, this lending himself to his victorious foes . . ."

"But he didn't know that," interjected Dousman gently.

". . . as an example of the conquered. And he enjoyed it, he enjoyed every moment of it. The women, he says, were kind to him; the white chiefs were generous. And he thinks of it, speaks of it as a great experience, a great thing to happen to him; he sits there dwelling upon it, receiving homage, and he rots!"

Dousman laid down his pen and raised his clasped hands for his chin to rest upon. He looked at Chalfonte with a slightly bemused smile. "My good friend, my earnest friend," he said softly, cogently, "Joshua stopped the sun; that was a great thing, an immortal thing. No other man has ever succeeded in doing it. Black Hawk has come to that wisdom in his age. What must happen to you before you know it? Was it a great thing of him to seek to stop time in its inexorable march across the pages of history? I say nothing of nobility, which perhaps lies differently in our minds; nor did he; at least, you said nothing of it if he did. Black Hawk has learned that compromise is the only alternative to death. And life, being all we have, should not be so easily given. God knows, a man has enough to fight against without battling the world for ideals which, however noble, depend for their existence upon things outside, beyond his control. Look, Chalfonte," he said, striking his breast, "keep them here."

Chalfonte gazed at him. "At least we understand each other. I haven't come away from him defeated. But I have learned something, nevertheless. Now I'm tired, yet I'm going on. I want to get home. There's much to be done there."

"Why not rest? Don't drive yourself so!"

"No, I'm set on it. We can rest on the way, if need be. Besides, it's already past midnight. Did you look at the wheat? How was it?"

"Good," answered Dousman, nodding. "I'll send a flatboat up after it when it's ready, and I'll make you a good price on it, never fear. When do you estimate the threshing will be finished?"

"In two weeks or so. Come then, in any event."

"Very well." He closed his ledger and rose. "Now, in regard to this man Baxter who will take up land on the prairie . . ."

"Nothing's happened to him?" Chalfonte betrayed alarm.

"No, no—only this: I met another like him today. A young man named—let me see—Leland; yes, that was his name. Looking for country to settle in. Wilderness, he said. So I sent him up the Wisconsin in your canoe, the extra one, and told him to look for your place. No doubt he's resting somewhere along the river. You may encounter him, or, perhaps, meet him tomorrow. He left here close to six, eager and afire to move. He's another of Baxter's calibre, and I hope he may be pleased by the look of the land there. You'll be interested in him for another reason—he's a graduate of Harvard, in law."

Chalfonte's interest was aroused despite his tiredness. "I'll look for him—though to see him in the dark calls for better sight than mine."

"He may not have rested." Dousman came around his desk. "Now, the wheat; if you find it impossible to complete the threshing in the time specified, let me know. As to Black Hawk—don't think too harshly of him; resignation to defeat is better than futile struggling. Only a fool refuses to recognize futility, only a fool sacrifices himself to a cause manifestly lost."

Chalfonte put his hand affectionately on Dousman's arm. "But a cause is never lost so long as it exists in the heart of one living man," he said.

"And never harms a man so long as it is kept there," replied Dousman smiling. He pointed to a small bag near the door. "There's your mail. I had Lockwood send it over."

Chalfonte thanked him, took the bag, and went out.

Dousman stood on the threshold looking after him thoughtfully, his lips pursed, pushing out and in, his eyebrows raised. Darkness engulfed Chalfonte, and Dousman turned and went into his office again. He took up his hour-glass and put it beside the clock, turning it presently, and he stood there watching the sand trickle down as the moments passed. "What dreams rule a man's life!" he muttered. "Even as it ebbs away! Yes, yes, and you, too, Hercules!"

Chalfonte, meanwhile, had come upon Clement pacing the shore. He told him that the other canoe was gone, volunteering no explanation because of his preoccupation. They got into their canoe, shoved off, and paddled swiftly downstream toward the mouth of the Wisconsin.

Chalfonte's thoughts were troubled, agitated partly by his sight of the aging Black Hawk, partly by his brief conversation with Dousman. He was filled, moreover, with a sudden sharp longing to be home, to be back to his land, to his beautiful prairie and the wood country there; he experienced an urgent desire to see the wind blowing there in the long grass, to see the oak leaves turn their silver undersides in the sun, to hear the voices his animals, of the women in the house, of the men on the threshing-floor, and the intimate murmuring of the river around the hill. He was not homesick, no; it was something deeper; it was the conscious flight to a haven, the sick animal's seeking his burrow so that he might lick his wounds and wait in familiar security for recovery.

This had been growing in him for a long time, ever since Black Hawk's defeat, ever since Adrienne's death. It was inevitable that his restlessness, his moodiness, his ceaseless dwelling in past years, in that halcyon time, that his lack of direction come so suddenly after his own bitterness at the defeat of his friend and the death of his wife, should come now at last full circle, should come to this climax. Seeing Black Hawk so had done this to him; this had brought him out of himself more than anything before had done, and as he paddled, not feeling the tiredness of arms and shoulders, he looked at himself, at his past years, at the time just gone: the two years since Adrienne's death: and he found them not good. He thought of what Dousman said, of what his mother had said: A man adjusts himself—yes, spiritually as well as physically. Years, age, the combination of kindness and well-being had brought Black Hawk down, even as some day the innumerable events and occasions of years, the small ironies of time would ultimately defeat him, too, would bring him, too, to this end.

Now he was overwhelmed with a tremendous conviction of time lost, a desire to be up and doing; it seemed to him that he had only now awakened from a long semi-sleep, and he was filled with a nervous eagerness to go about the business of living, to change his lot from trapper and trader to farmer's. This, too, lay behind the urgence which impelled him homeward despite the tiredness of his body; this was his reaction in the face of necessitating some compromise between the ideals he held true and the physical truths of existence. But he held too, to a belief that somehow the turmoil of his thoughts would work out without aid, that some solution to the morass of doubt and self-pity in which he lived would come about.

They went up the winding Wisconsin without stopping. Chalfonte was not aware of the passage of time; he did not see the stars wheel over, the moon set, the day break until the first light fell upon the hills. He searched the recesses of his mind and memory for a way of escape from his lack of direction these past two years, and still felt the gnawing agony of Black Hawk's defeat and decay, of Adrienne's death—distant now, but still conspiring to keep him enslaved. But his land was vital, alive, final; nothing in his time could change it very much; the face of it was eternal, whether grass waved there in the wind, or grain; whether a village grew there or not. He found himself contemplating the establishment of others on the prairie with equanimity, with acceptance, but he had no time to ponder this, for his imagination carried him ahead by leaps and bounds to a time when, indeed, a village might lie there, north of the house on the hill, and the land might yield wheat and corn and rye, and men might be born and grow old on the land, and die there. And he felt at one with Dousman in seeking to bring to the prairie men like Baxter. If settlers must come—and come they would, without doubt; he understood that—then let them be like Baxter: not rough and raw, but men who had known land before, and knew how to care for it. He could smile now, catching himself thinking as a farmer might think: no longer the trapper, the trader, but a landsman—a man whose life must come now from the land rather than from other creatures that lived, like himself, on the land.

His thoughts returned to Black Hawk, and he called up from his immediate memory the image of the old chieftain sitting before his cabin, heard again his words, and in the deep channels of his memory heard still the faint echo of the embattled chieftain's speech. How long ago now? Two years, three years? No more. But a century in spirit!

He could hear Dousman: God knows, a man has enough to fight against without batting the world for ideals which, however noble, depend for their existence upon things outside. And his mother: A man adjusts himself, he makes the best of things, he meets things as they are and doesn't stand idly by and hope that things might have been otherwise. Both right, yes. And still he was not wrong. Could he be satisfied to hold his truths in the secret places of his heart, in the recesses of his mind, keep these ideals still? Life itself asked nothing more. Life asked nothing more than that a man live securely in his ideals, but not that he give his life itself trying to impose their pattern upon his fellowmen in the world around him.

*In the nights now the animals come from their lairs: the opossum, the raccoons, the foxes, and the weasels—*les fouines, *the trappers called them: the animals come forth and prowl as always: the timid rabbit fearful of the predatory owl, the otter in the streams, the marten and the muskrat; and by day the chattering squirrel, the fearless skunk. Hawks wheel as always high above the hills and prairie, the herons feed along the river, the eagles mount the buttes of air. The bears, the wolves, the whistling swans, the passenger pigeons, the curlews and the paroquets are gone; all are gone, their voices heard no more where once they echoed in the wilderness. Gone as the Indians went, as leaves before the wind, driven before time and years into the past, into the lost places of time. And the ghost of Soft-Walker, the quiet one, the ghosts of his family, of his band and nation: these range the woods where once they hunted, loved, fought and died. The fragrance of wilderness is no more; in its place rises the sweet richness of turned soil. And the prairie grass is gone, the oak groves gone. Nothing is left to remember now, nothing to say how the Indians went, how trappers went, how river men, voyageurs, traders, miners, pioneers passed down the stream of time and disappeared; none but the landsman on the prairie, and the village grown . . .*

Wisconsin Saga

from Leave To Ponder

STAMBAUGH WENT DOWN to the boat with Hercules. It was too early to open the store, he maintained, and the October morning was so pleasant that it was good to be out in it before the day's confinement. Besides, Hercules was a customer of many years's standing. Stambaugh was a tall, saturnine man, with a sharp look about him, gaunt-faced, with a kind of tic below one eye, which caused his skin to twitch from time to time. His hair was graying, and he walked with hands clasped behind him, in the manner of a man given to age.

"I said to myself the other day," he said in his reedy voice, "it's been more than twenty years that Hercules Dousman has been buying from me. I remember that you took over Joe Rolette's account." He chuckled. "Then his wife, eh? Oh, all right and proper—don't mistake me, I don't mean any disrespect."

"Don't apologize," said Hercules shortly. "Just don't forget to send those new dresses for Madame before we freeze in for the winter."

"If they get here in time, Mr. Dousman, certainly," said Stambaugh. "How have you found St. Louis, sir?"

"Growing—as is all the Middle West."

"Middle West," repeated Stambaugh, tasting the words. "Now, that's good. St. Louis has always been the gateway to the West—I suppose, when you think it over, we're not the West at all."

"Far from it."

They reached the docks. Here, for all the bustle of activity, the hour might have been midday. The river outward from the landing was a sea of stacks, most of them belching black smoke into the morning sun. Some barges were to be seen, but not a keelboat, not a flatboat, not a bateau was in sight. The Mississippi, which had once been the province of canoes and bateaux, then of pirogues and keelboats and flatboats, was now the domain of steamboats. Even as the keelboats had once increased travel and commerce on the river,

---

The House on the Mound, 1958

so now the steamboats were bringing vastly greater traffic to all the rivers of the Middle West. The sea of smokestacks was testimony of the steamboat's popularity.

Observing Hercules' calculating glance, Stambaugh hastened to say, "Most of these are for the upper Mississippi trade, Mr. Dousman. Fully seven hundred boats docked here last year—all from the upper Mississippi—and that was just about a quarter of the total we had from the lower Mississippi, the Ohio, the Illinois, and the Missouri, together with the upper Mississippi. And this,"—he gestured—"this has been a common scene throughout the entire season."

Stambaugh referred to the patient crowd of immigrants. Men, women, and children, standing or sitting among all their worldly possessions, were to be seen the length of the docks, waiting to board the steamboats, anxious lest they be left before the season closed.

"Some are going West, but most of them are heading for points north," said Stambaugh. "Minnesota Territory, particularly. A great many Germans, but a lot of Irish, too. The Irish are replacing the roustabouts up North—you've probably noticed . . . . "

"Where's the *Galena Belle*?" asked Hercules.

"Over this way. I see her, Mr. Dousman."

The boat on which Hercules had taken passage stood on the ready. Smoke poured from her twin stacks. She was a stern-wheeler, destined to travel no farther north than Prairie du Chien, under the command of Captain Albert Dreiburgh. Roustabouts were loading her, and the ship's clerk was measuring wood to be taken aboard. Immigrants already crowded her lower deck.

"I hope Phillips hasn't forgotten to get my piano on board," said Hercules.

"Ah, you bought Madame a piano, Mr. Dousman?"

"A Lemuel Gilbert—one of the best, I'm told, although, being no hand at playing myself, I wouldn't know."

"Trust Phillips, Colonel."

"I have to. I paid three hundred fifty for it. That's a good price and I expect a good instrument."

"What is the wood?"

"Rosewood."

"Oh, fine, fine! Couldn't do better. Phillips has done himself proud. You'll never regret it, sir! That piano will hold its tune. It will serve you a hundred years, mark my words."

"Not me, it won't," said Hercules with a grin.

"That boy of yours, then."

"Well, I'd better get on board, Stambaugh. I'll look to you for your customary service, sir."

"I've never disappointed you yet, Mr. Dousman. I won't start now. Some of your goods have been loaded, and the rest will follow just as soon as I can find the space."

Hercules moved down among the roustabouts, past passengers bidding final good-bys to friends and relatives, though a medley of shouting and bawling of orders from boats to shore and back. It was the landing at Prairie du Chien, multiplied many times over. Watching the bustle, listening to the excitement of arrivals and departures never failed to please Hercules; in this lay ample proof of the westward expansion, of the growth of the valley of the upper Mississippi, of the triumph of man over the wilderness, which had once seemed so awesomely forbidding. Yet Hercules never recognized this without a concomitant feeling of regret at the inexorable passing of that wilderness. He remembered how his friend, Baron Pierneau, had railed against the westward expansion, and mourned the loss of his Indian friends, Chief Black Hawk and his Sauk band. He understood now how Pierneau had felt at that time, fifteen years ago. How much had happened to the frontier in those years!

He went on board the *Galena Belle.* He pushed through the immigrants on the lower deck, past bales of goods, and mounted to the upper deck. He found a place at the railing where he was out of the way and stood to look back at the city, glowing in the morning sunlight. St. Louis was now a city of 75,000. The innumerable stacks of the boats tied up along the river were matched by the steeples and spires gleaming in the morning sun. Hercules counted more than a dozen church steeples before he stopped. The skyline was dominated by the white dome of the new courthouse and beyond it by an almost Byzantine structure rising up among rows of red-brick houses. The city, below its towers looked, like an army of chimneys flowing back from the river's edge. Adding to its color, the city's trees were resplendent in yellow and claret, at the height of brilliance before the season turned. How well Pierre Liguest had chosen, when he picked the site of St. Louis almost a century ago!

Hercules left the rail and sought out the captain. He found him down off the texas, watching the last load being put on board, tense and impatient. Captain Dreiburgh was a short, pudgy German, with a florid face and a fierce mustache which jutted forth on both sides of his mouth. His sharp eyes saw Hercules coming.

"Yes, Mr. Dousman," he said before Hercules could speak, "your piano's on board—and precious room it took, too!"

"Thank you, Captain. That was what I wanted to know."

"It's the first piano I've taken North, Mr. Dousman."

"It won't be the last."

Hercules looked across to the neighboring steamboat, which had come in to unload. It was the *Dr. Franklin II*, under the command of Captain Daniel Smith Harris, one of the most daring and skillful captains on the upper Mississippi. The boat had come in from Galena, for the roustabouts were carrying lead down her plants. Beyond her another side-wheeler was pulling out. As far as he could see in either direction steamboats were loading or unloading; Hercules estimated that at least forty boats were in dock; others stood offshore waiting to come in. The complexion of the dock had not changed since his arrival; some of the immigrants had got on board; others had moved in to take their places, waiting; draymen, boatmen, roustabouts swarmed over the docks, voices raised in song or curses. Barrels of flour, bags of corn, piles of lead, hogsheads of tobacco, barrels of whiskey and cider, lumber, farming implements, brick, crackers—all were stacked waiting to be loaded for the journey upriver or the Ohio River run, and activity from one end of the docks to another, between boats and landing, was indescribable.

A shout from below interrupted his reverie. The last load had been brought aboard; the roustabouts were signaling to the captain. Captain Dreiburgh immediately cupped his mouth in his hands and shouted, "All aboard! Up Planks! Loose the ropes!" The roustabouts fell back; some ran to the ropes to loosen them; the two planks at the head of the *Galena Belle* were raised to stand out at an angle. The departing bell began to ring. Captain Dreiburgh turned toward the pilothouse. "Are you ready, Mr. Brown?" The pilot waved his hand.

The *Galena Belle* backed out into the current, widening the water between her head and the dock. A roustabout stood at the bow with a measuring line in his hand, although there was no need for him in these familiar waters; yet he stood ready to call back the water's depth to another black beneath the pilothouse. The paddle-wheel churned water, brown with silt, into yellow and white foam. The boat moved out among others standing off, carefully edging past another boat bound upriver with a barge filled with cattle lashed to its side, and swung out into the current, pointing upriver.

Hercules looked back. Already St. Louis was diminished in perspective. Across the river, on the east shore, Illinoistown looked like the merest hamlet by comparison; beyond it the low, rolling country of Illinois stretched limitlessly away toward the horizon, lost in the blaze of the morning sun. Blue herons and white sandhill cranes flew along the river's shore, sunlight gleaming on their wings.

The boat leaped forward, filled with life; the throbbing of the engines made a steady pulse; the smokestacks began to sigh; the movement of the water seemed to communicate itself to the boat.

Captain Dreiburgh leaned past the upright to which he clung, swinging out over the water. "Tell me, Mr. Dousman, is it true you're thinking of starting a line?"

Hercules smiled. "I take it you've been hearing talk, Captain. I've had a hand in the game for a long time. Captain Throckmorton and I bought the *Chippewa* nine years ago; she weighed in at a hundred seven tons. Four years later I owned half the *Lynx*. But it's true, I am thinking about expanding my steamboating interests."

"The way the river towns are growing—I don't know of another investment that pays off so well.

"Is that so?"

"Take it from me, Mr. Dousman—the average steamboat plying the upper Mississippi—that is, if she's kept up and keeps her engagements—clears about eight thousand a season."

"That's an impressive figure, Captain," said Hercules, who had reason to know that the average earnings of boats were closer to twelve thousand.

"I say we're just beginning on the upper Mississippi, Mr. Dousman."

"You may be right, but remember, the keelboats had hardly begun when the steamboats came along. And now the railroad's pushing toward the river."

"That won't matter." He swung around again. "Stop in at my cabin any time, Mr. Dousman."

"Thank you, Captain."

Hercules made his way to the main cabin, and into his stateroom, which opened off it. The day glowed with sunlight; the trip North promised to be swift and easy.

At the breakfast table Hercules said matter-of-factly, "Mr. Sark has left us."

Jane stared at him. "When did he go?"

"He left in the night. I lent him two of my horses. As a matter of guesswork, I believe he eloped with Annette Gaucher, or he wouldn't have needed a second horse."

Jane turned this over in her mind. "Why did he go all of a sudden this way?"

"I believe these things usually happen suddenly, Jane," said Hercules, laughing.

"But what will Mistaire Dousman do now?" she cried.

"All my life I've been accustomed to doing for myself. Someone to help me is a convenience—but only as important as someone to talk to, and not much more so. Just the same, I've been thinking about the time Jonas would go; I knew he'd leave us someday."

Hercules turned and looked at Louis LeBrun, who sat quietly at the table eating bacon and eggs. Louis had grown from a diffident boy to almost a young man. His skin had darkened, his hair seemed even blacker than it had seemed that first night he had come into the house in the shadow of Alexander Fisher. As he had learned to speak English, he had become more confident and poised.

Jane followed his gaze. "Not Louis!" she cried.

"Why not?" To Louis he said, "Louis, when you've finished, come to the office."

"I'm done now, sir," said Louis eagerly, his bright eyes alert.

"Then come."

Hercules got up, went around the table, kissed Jane and Dede at her side, bade Miss McCleod good morning, and went out of the house. Louis excused himself and followed.

At the office he bade Louis sit at Sark's desk until the mail could be examined. Louis sat down expectantly, his eyes following Hercules' every movement. He was aware that Hercules had plans for him that went beyond his status as houseboy, and he waited patiently while Hercules went over the letters on his desk.

Hercules did not intend to do more than ascertain where the mail had come from, but among the little stack of letters was one without one of the new stamps which had been in use for a few years now, nor did it have the scrawled fee written by a postmaster in such part of the western territories as stamps might not yet have reached. It was a free letter from Washington.

Hercules slit it open. It came from the Commissioner of Indian Affairs. He looked past the superscription and the initial paragraph, which he knew by experience would be a compound of formal introduction and not so subtle flattery.

> We believe, in view of your many past services to us, that you are the best man fitted to represent us in two matters. The one is as yet in the future—perhaps next year—and that is the matter of the Sioux lands west of the Mississippi in Minnesota Territory. There is some reluctance on their part to sell. [No wonder, thought Hercules, at the exchange offered!] . . . The other, however, is more imminent, and I propose to outline it herewith. We are trying to persuade the Menominees under Chief Oshkosh to move into the Crow Wing country of Minnesota Territory. This is the same general region to which the Winnebago we put at Long Prairie have now gone. Oshkosh has proved extremely unwilling to leave his ancestral lands about Lake Winnebago, but

he has at last consented to go with a party of his Menominees to look at the Crow Wing country. He will come down to Prairie du Chien with his party by wagon early in June, and expects to go up river from Prairie du Chien on the seventh. We do not know the day of his arrival in Prairie du Chien, but we will try to find out and let you know. Once they reach Minnesota, Fletcher will take them in charge.

Will you use your good offices to talk with Oshkosh anddo what you can to put him in the proper frame of mind sothat he will be amenable to our suggestion that he removehis tribe to the Crow Wing country? He is a stubborn man . . .

And who would not be? thought Hercules wearily, against such a history of unfairness and duplicity practiced upon the Indians. He put down the letter and turned to Louis LeBrun.

"Now, Louis," he said, "we begin."

Louis was an apt pupil. In three weeks he had learned all Sark's office work, and Hercules did not doubt that he would be as quick to learn what he had to know about furs and the trade. Hercules rapidly grew accustomed to him, and as the days passed Sark became inexorably part of past time—only one brief message came from him, sent from Fort Laramie, then no more; and it began to seem as if Louis LeBrun had been part of the office for a long time.

One day late in May LeBrun came for Hercules just as Hercules had got out Major and was preparing to mount.

"Mr. Dousman," he said deferentially. "I know you said not to bother you, but there's a man at the office who says he must see you. I thought, sir, since he's the sheriff . . ."

"That's right, Louis. Go back and tell Mr. Fonda I'm at his disposal."

The boy ran fleetly back. Hercules followed more leisurely, on his horse. He dismounted at the office just as Sheriff Fonda came out of the building.

"Sorry to disturb you, Dousman," said the sheriff. "But as you know most of the *voyageurs*, I wonder if you might be able to identify a body Alex McGregor turned up over at his ferry landing on the other side of the river. Man has been dead some time—been in the water at least six weeks, Dr. Foote said."

"Oh, Foote's had a look at him, has he?"

"I called him."

"What's his verdict?"

"Drowned. Misadventure, he called it." He grinned under his discolored moustache. "You've got a suspicious mind, Dousman. This fellow just drowned, that's all. Probably got pickled and fell in—you know what a rough and fast life those men lead."

"I'll take a look at him."

He thought he might recognize the body; he might be known to him, as Doutard was; but he had forgotten that the river was not kind to flesh—the face had been partly eaten away, and the limbs as well. Hercules did not know him, or, had he once known him, he could not identify him. The body was that of a *voyageur*, judged by such of his clothing as still remained with it, a man over fifty, Dr. Foote had said.

"I'm sorry," he said, after looking at the body. "I don't know him."

But he had no doubt that this was Doutard's companion, Thunder Walker's victim. So this was an end to that matter. The body would be taken out and buried with no name on the stone above it—if a stone was put there: a fate which had once come uncommonly often to the independents who fought the Astor Company, and which now came, thought Hercules, with fitting irony to one of the men who had not hesitated to murder the innocent individualists who had stood fast by their idealism in opposing Astor.

On the tenth day of June the Menominee party reached Prairie du Chien to rest but a night before embarking by steamboat for St. Paul. Hercules went over to where they were encamped. There were eighteen men in the party—eleven Menominee chiefs, headed by Oshkosh and Carron Glaude, two braves, and five white men, including the interpreter, and the Indian Agent, William Bruce, a young man who seemed earnestly convinced that the Crow wing country of Minnesota Territory was the ideal place for the Menominees to go. After five minutes' conversation with him, Hercules was not convinced that Bruce knew much about either the Crow Wing country or the character of the Menominee, although he was sincere enough.

The Indians themselves seemed passive and resigned. But Hercules, accustomed to dealing with Indians for decades, saw at once that they were glum and hostile. They had come all the way from the Lake Winnebago country in wagons—a distance of more than a hundred miles. Wagons! thought Hercules, when canoes, to which they were accustomed, would have carried them up the Fox and down the Wisconsin to the familiar meeting place at the juncture of the rivers. It was a particular kind of madness to which officials of government were prone, to subject the Menominees to this ordeal by wagon, particularly at a time when the government was attempting to cajole them to accept an exchange of property which was not at all to the Indians' advantage.

"I met Oshkosh some years ago when he was at a council here," said Hercules. "But I'm not sure I could pick him out."

Bruce pointed. "He's an ugly one. And if he gets any liquor in him, he's as likely to kill you as look at you."

Hercules paid no attention to this. He decided that Bruce was an easterner. He looked at Chief Oshkosh. True, the old fellow did look somewhat dissipated. Moreover, he was shorter than most Indians, chunky of figure, with a badly wrinkled face. Yet his face was not without character, and his almost absurdly pathetic look might have been the result of the ride he had been forced to take and to which his flesh was unaccustomed. He was dressed partly in tribal regalia and partly in white men's clothing, but he wore his headband and three feathers in it. His black, oily hair glistened in the late-afternoon sunlight.

"I'll talk to him," said Hercules.

"I'll call Powell or Pickett."

"Don't trouble yourself, Mr. Bruce. I don't need interpreters. I can get along in their language. I understand them and they understand me."

He walked over to face Oshkosh, raised him arm, palm outward, and sat down before the chieftain, pronouncing his name for him.

Oshkosh held out his hand. They shook hands.

"I meet Dousman many years ago at this place."

"Are we not old friends?" demanded Hercules. "Have we not looked upon each other before that?"

Oshkosh been forward and peered into Hercules' face with narrowed eyes, as if seeking some clue to where they might have met before the time of the council to which he referred.

Hercules went on. "Was not the great chief, Oshkosh, then but a young brave, among the Indians who fought with the Redcoats to seize the Island of the Turtle when the Americans and the Redcoats were locked in battle?"

"It is true," said Oshkosh wonderingly.

"I was then a boy on Mackinac—that is to say, the Turtle. Oshkosh was in one of the boats. He was a brave young Indian, good to look upon. He was with Tomah. He stood out among his fellow braves. He did not stain his tomahawk with innocent blood."

The Menominee smiled, pointed to Hercules, and looked proudly around to the other chiefs who accompanied him. "See!" he cried. "This man is our friend. He has known us in other times." He turned again to Hercules. "You know why we are here?"

Hercules nodded.

"Say to us what we must do, friend of the great White Father."

"I say to you go to this country of the Crow Wing, look upon it, and do as your heart tells you to do."

Hercules' words aroused a murmur of approval.

Chief Oshkosh sprang to his feet, nodding his head in fierce agreement. "We come here," he said. "We shake hands with you. We do so with a good heart. I have seen many years. I was but a young brave when the Americans came to my place at Green Bay. This was in 1816. This was after they had taken back the Island of the Turtle, where we fought with the Redcoats. The Americans shook hands with us. They told us they had come to live among us and make us happy. They promised us if we followed their counsel we would have no trouble.

"At the council we held in 1827 . . ." He stopped suddenly, and peered intently at Hercules. "It was there that we first saw each other, Dousman."

"It was there."

"At this council," continued Oshkosh, "General Cass said the same thing to us—that Americans were our friends, we should always follow their advice. Again, in 1836, at Cedar Point, we met Governor Dodge, who came to treat with us. He told us that what he promised our Great Father, the President, would perform. We submitted to our Father's wish and ceded part of our lands. Governor Dodge promised that our Great White Father would always protect us as his own children and would always hold our hands in his.

"We always thought much of governor Dodge as an honest man. We believed all he told us. But he said the government would not ask more of our lands from us. How is this, then, that now these white men have come to us and say they have a place in the Crow Wing country for the Menominee, and ask us to surrender our land in Wisconsin for this land we have never seen? How is this?" He turned to his fellow chiefs. "Do I not speak for us all?" he demanded. "You, Souligny? Na-Molte? Carron? Oshkeehenawniew? Ahkenotoway? Casgascegay?"

Each of the chiefs nodded solemnly as his name was called.

Oshkosh turned to Hercules and waited for an answer.

Hercules got to his feet. He began to talk slowly, choosing his words with great care. He explained that many moons had passed since the first Great White Father had spoken to the Menominee. In this time many changes had come about. Many of those who had spoken for the White Father had been gathered to their ancestors. Others were no longer in the government. Even the Great White Father had changed, for now he was that man who had commanded Fort Crawford in the old days, who had taken Black Hawk prisoner, and who had fought with Mexico. Now even he lay ill in Washington. All things must change, said Hercules, for such was the law and order of life.

"The Menominees do not change," cried Oshkosh to the accompaniment of an approving mutter.

Nevertheless, Hercules went on, it was not the fault of Governor Dodge that this request was now made. It was not the fault of General Cass, who had tried to become the Great White Father two years ago but had failed because General Taylor had been the choice of the white men. He explained patiently that many many white men were coming into America from far countries across the sea, that the Great White Father was trying to find more land for them.

"He may send them to Crow Wing country," said Oshkosh with admirable simplicity.

Hercules restrained a smile.

"We wish to stay in our lands," Oshkosh continued. "We have great love for our lands. We have remained there many generations. We do not wish to exchange for other lands. We are content to die there."

How many times had he heard Indian chiefs express similar sentiments! thought Hercules. Red Bird of the Winnebagos! Wabashaw! He recalled with every intonation of the words the moving speech of the Black Sparrow Hawk when he had surrendered to Taylor eighteen years ago. "We loved our land!" Was it not a constant refrain, a continuing lament? It had been spoken by Indians of the eastern seaboard, and was perhaps even now being said in many places west of the Mississippi as the ravenous land seekers pushed toward the West Coast. "We loved our land. We fought for it!"

"Is it our fault that the land around Lake Poygan is coveted by the white men?" cried Oshkosh. "It is our land. Is the land of the Crow Wing rich in wild rice? The blackrobe among us says it is not. We are gatherers of rice. We are not tillers of the soil. We are not farmers. We are hunters." Abruptly Oshkosh shook his head. "Now I have spoken. I will say no more." Then he sat down.

Hercules knew that the government expected him to persuade the Menominee to accept the Crow Wing country. Had they not agreed to go to this country in the treaty of 1848? he asked Oshkosh.

"But only if the country is fit for us—and we shall judge that," answered Oshkosh.

Hercules agreed that this was fair. He could not say to them to obey the wish of the White Father if the agents of the government had accepted the Menominee proposal of approval of the country west of the Mississippi.

"Then go to the Crow Wing country and look upon it. The Crow Wing River is fair. Its valley is good to look upon. I do not know it as a country of wild rice. You must decide as your hearts tell you. I can say no more."

Then he bade Oshkosh and his companions a ceremonious farewell and walked back to where the Indian Agent waited for him.

"What's this about the blackrobe who tells the Menominee the Crow Wing country isn't good?" he asked.

"He's a Jesuit priest—a troublemaker. Father Bonduel. Half these Menominees are Christian, half are not. The Jesuit has a great influence among them."

Hercules shook his head. "They use him, not he them. Mr. Bruce, you're making this journey in vain. These Menominee will never accept the Crow Wing country."

In a way, he hoped they would not. He had seen so many Indians betrayed and misled by the government that he could not help wishing the tables might be turned. In the midst of Bruce's voluble attack on Father Bonduel, Hercules excused himself and walked away, lest it become too clear where his sympathies lay.

from Tranquility, Farewell

THE AFTERNOON OF the October day was approaching the hour of sundown and twilight, and already the distances were lost in a pale, lavender haze. Along the ridge a stage moved steadily in a generally northeasterly direction, at a pace which suggested that its goal was not far distant, though no dwelling was in sight in all that wild country of hills and valleys. Still visible along the horizon to the southwest rose the Platte and Belmont Mounds, passed more than an hour ago—twin, rounded hills standing forth like dark, grave sentinels in a land of silence and strangeness, dominating the face of the earth at that place. An illusion of level land lay between the blue peaks and the ridge road, a tranquil country of high plateau and deep valleys, but at this hour the valleys were lost in the last sunlight lying in a soft pink and copper haze along their slopes, complimenting the colors of ivy, sumach, birch trees, and hazel brush which grew at the edge of every copse and thicket. In the ravines nearby, sunlight lay pooled and warm; a kind of shimmering, colorful and mystic, filled the air,

The Hills Stand Watch, 1960

but beyond, in the deep, wooded valleys between the ridges, the first dusk already flowered where sunlight and day were withdrawn.

The two passengers who rode through the Territory of Wisconsin on this autumn day of 1844 were beset by conflicting emotions. David Pengellen was quietly happy to be so close to home once more, and proud in his young wife, Candace, whom he was bringing to her new home from Providence. He had observed her excitement, but did not know whether it rose from the unfamiliar wildness of her surroundings, from uncertainty, or from perturbation. She was pretty—dark with hazel eyes, a small, thin-lipped mouth, a pert, slightly foreshortened nose. Her long-fingered hands lay laxly in her lap, ready instantly to seize hold of him or some part of the coach each time the stage tipped and leaned or jolted and swayed on the rough roads over which they traveled.

Pride in her shown in his honest, clean-shaven face; he had the look of a scrubbed schoolboy just passed in his examinations, though he was twenty-five to her twenty. He had short, dark hair, almost black, cut close to his head, but betraying a tendency to curl; his eyes were a strong blue, his mouth was wide, his lips were dominant and sensitive. He was powerfully built, broad-shouldered, and his hands were wide and strong, with spatulate fingers. In profile, his chin had a prognathous appearance because of the fullness of his mouth. His skin was dark, in contrast to her fairness, and he stood a half head taller than she, though, because of the amplitude of her clothing, in concession both to fashion and the chill of the weather, she seemed in some respects as large of frame.

The stage was now moving toward a broad thicket. She turned from the window and looked anxiously at him. "David, you said we'd be home today. It's almost dark. I hope we won't have to spend another night at an inn."

"We're almost there," he said tranquilly. "Mineral Point lies down under that ridge up ahead. Our house is the nearest one to the stage route half way up the slope—but we don't stop there." He leaned forward, with one arm about her shoulders, turning her to the window of the stage once more. "See there—it's down past these trees. If you watch, you'll see a little of the house when we turn down High Street."

She peered intently into the glow of sunlight. Out of the corners of her eyes, she was uncomfortably aware of the sunlit mounds they had left behind, reared up like sentinels out of the plateau, like watchers on the threshold of her new world. The stage, which had traveled into the northeast ever since leaving Galena, was now describing a curve into the west, turning slowly along the ridge through a stand of thin timber toward the slope to which David had pointed. As attentively as she could, for the uncertain jolting progress of the stage, and the surrounding trees, she examined the landscape.

A wild place, certainly. A place of high hills, woods, deep valleys. Indians, too. She remembered one spot on the road not far along into the territory northeast of Galena where a colorful party of Indians had stood on horseback off to one side of the road, watching the stage roll past. Impassive, dark-skinned men, wearing little clothing. She had been briefly terrified at sight of them, recalling instantly all the horrors of massacre of which she had read. But they had made no hostile move; one of them had even offered a gesture which might have been a reply to a hail from the driver.

The country which the stage passed was spread over with the haze of sunset glow, so that it appeared to exist on two planes—the unreality presented to the eye, the reality below. Its wildness was apparent on both; here was untamed country, a far cry from that pleasant farming land around Providence, out of which she had come as a child. She looked upon it with a troubled foreboding. It had seemed romantic from the perspective of the east; the thought of being alone in the west with her husband, in the lead mining country of the Wisconsin Territory, seemed attractive; but the realities of the frontier had grown steadily less romantic with every mile west of Vincennes. The roughness of Galena had repelled her, though it was a considerable settlement by any standard, it had attractive houses and churches, it teemed with life; but the brawling frontiersmen at the inn and in the streets of the village had filled her with apprehension. Nor had the country north of Galena offered anything to assuage her disappointment. All the inns and stopping-places along the way seemed hastily put up to accommodate the travelers in the Territory at the least expense to the innkeepers; all of them, from the Four Mile House just out of Galena to the Olmstead Inn near Belmont, were rough, barren places. So were the settlements—Hazel Green, Platteville, Belmont—crude hamlets, with none of the graciousness of similar villages in the east. The frontier was not as she had imagined it, but her confusion was such that she no longer remembered how it was she had conceived it.

In topography, the Territory here was not unlike the land around Providence, except that on occasion it was higher. But the marks of civilization were absent—there were no stone or rail fences, no old houses, no good roads, none of the signs of human habitation save only this rough, jolting road over which they had traveled since early in the day. There had been a moment of sharp familiarity at the sight of Galena, for that settlement, like Providence, lay along a stream, and was built up on the slopes on both sides; but this moment had passed, for the Galena River was not the

Seekonk, and the frontier houses bore little relation to the gracious homes of Providence.

The Wisconsin country was dominated primarily by three tall domes of earth, blue against the sky now—the Platte and Belmont mounds rising out of the high plateau to the southwest, the even higher Blue Mound rising out of the northeast, on the way to the territorial capital of Madison; secondarily by the ridge along which they rode. Almost from its beginning at Galena, forty miles south, the road had followed the ridge as steadily as possible, clearly because it would have prolonged the journey and increased the difficulties to go more directly up and down hill. It was no level route; in some places the ridge was broad, in some narrow: once it was a succession of sloping knolls, again stretches of long, flat terrain, prairie-like, but not true prairie, for it was a high succession of level areas broken by low, rolling regions, grass-covered except for little thickets, which flowed from around the Platte and Belmont Mounds and constituted a true plateau, which was lost, after some miles, in the customary declivities and deep valleys. Along the ridge at this hour the sun still shown with a soft, ever-reddening glow.

Sloping away from the ridge was a succession of shallow valleys, where centuries ago erosion had taken place and been healed over; beyond these, the slopes descended less gradually but farther still to the deeper valleys. These were often very long, though never wide; they lay among the hills, with their slopes rising and flung away toward higher slopes and the ridge on all sides, for that along which the stage made its way was not the only such ridge in this portion of Wisconsin Territory. It was into one of these deeper valleys that the stage was now beginning its descent through a growth of trees.

She thought she caught a glimpse of a house among the trees, but it was a phantom; she could not recapture it, and the stage was now proceeding along an undulating road, from slope to slope, past rows of ancient oaks and flaming maples, leaving the ridge behind. The sky which only a moment ago held the setting sun, shown now only with the afterglow; the sun had vanished behind the hills rising higher and darker as they went down.

The stage lurched out of the grove, and there before her lay Mineral Point, spectral in twilight—a long, winding street of small, compact houses, stone buildings of two and sometimes three storeys, crowding almost upon the street toward which the stage moved. There were a surprising number of buildings, some of frame construction; they stood immediately before them and grouped along both sides of the street toward the north. Some of the houses had the appearance of having grown out of the slopes, though along that part of the street which led south the houses stood only on one side, along the east; across the road was a swale, with massed willows here and there, a brook, and rising land, with earthworks and crude buildings adjacent. These, then, must be the lead mines, she reasoned, and the street they were now almost upon must be Shake-Rag Street, where most of the miners lived in little homes, to which they were summoned at mealtime by wives who waved white rags to signify the hour.

The stage traveled more slowly now. From the window, Candace saw enough of the near houses to be unimpressed with them; she did not like their smallness, the few windows, the cold stone exteriors, the way in which they were grouped, some of them almost eave to eave, all set into the slope behind, like outcroppings from the dark hill. A few pale yellow lights burned in scattered windows, and just ahead, a lantern hung out on a hook before a building, casting a wan light into the dusk. It was this building which was the object of the stage's journey to Mineral Point, a three-storey, clapboard building, painted or whitewashed, with porches running across the full face of every storey. The stage reached the bottom of the slope and came to a stop. A simply lettered board above the porch announced it to be the Mansion House.

"We're home, Candace," said David.

She made no answer.

The driver was dropping to the ground amidst a flurry of sudden activity. A short, hunched-over man came running toward the horses with fodder and water. A fat man wearing a white apron and carrying another lantern came out of the building. He was followed by three others, two of them dressed for travel, the third the innkeeper himself; he stood in the doorway bidding the travelers godspeed. One addressed him briefly as "Mr. Nichols," after which Nichols retired into the building once more, and the travelers, coming forward, stood aloof while the aproned man exchanged words with the driver, who had by this time come around to the door of the stage and flung it open.

"Watch en step, Ma'am," cautioned the driver.

David leaped out and stood waiting for her. She felt a pang of hesitation, as if stepping forth now she would commit herself irrevocably. Then she gave him her hand and stepped from the stage. Behind her, the driver climbed to the top after their baggage, while the aproned man moved around him with the lantern held ineffectually low, complaining, "Why doan't 'ee come on time, Lanyon? T' Governor's bin waitin'."

At the same moment a lusty, resonant vice rang out. "Well, Pengellen—I've not seen you in almost a year. Been away?"

"Only two months, sir." David caught hold of her hand and drew her forward. "I have the honor to present my wife, Candace—General Henry Dodge, late Governor of the Territory, now Delegate to Congress."

"Madam, I'm charmed and delighted to find one so fair come to our Territory."

She smiled and gave him her hand. Even in the half-light of dusk and the reflected glow of the lanterns, she was aware of his wide-set, keen eyes, which dwelt upon her without faltering, of his firm, prominent nose, of his high brow and moulded mouth, about which a faint smile seemed to linger with an air of singular permanence. A man of character and strength, she thought. A man of determination, of purpose and power. He was rugged in appearance, and yet well dressed; his paradox was briefly inexplicable to her, until she divined that he was a frontiersman risen to leadership in his domain, and the marks of his early years were still apparent.

But he was turning. "Allow me. My companion, Lieutenant Nathaniel Parr. Mr. and Mrs. David Pengellen."

The other traveler stepped casually forward and bowed. He shook the hand David offered him; Candace did not extend her hand, but she could not help taking notice of Parr, who was a much younger man than the Governor—near David's own age, tall, dark, thin, with brooding eyes and a sullen mouth. His cheeks were a little hollow, and his eyebrows dark and arched, so that he had a faintly sardonic expression.

"I'm in haste for Dodgeville," said Dodge. "And then I must get back to Washington."

"I tell General Dodge we'd much rather have him back in Madison as Governor," said Lieutenant Parr.

"Iss, we'd all as lev see 'im back," muttered the aproned man, passing.

The Delegate chuckled. "Tallmadge has half the legislature against him now, has he not? An honest man, but stubborn. Who can tell? I may be back. Washington often seems to me cold and alien."

"But not half so cold as here, certainly," ventured Candace.

Dodge eyed her speculatively, and at his side, Parr looked at her with some frank interest which he made no effort to conceal, his dark eyes fixed on her, hovering about her, cradling her.

"I marvel at your husband's courage at bringing you here, Madam," observed Dodge. "The cold months are coming soon, too." He turned to David. "Where did you find her, Pengellen?"

"In Providence, General."

The driver came around his six horses, touching his hat to General Dodge. "Wessen 'ee git in, Governor?"

"Are you ready to be off, Lanyon?"

"Iss, tidden far to go. I mean t' git there 'fore dark."

General Dodge bowed again to Candace. "By your leave, Madam." He walked past her and got into the stage, followed by Lieutenant Parr. The lieutenant leaned from the stage, smiling, and said politely, "I look to see you again."

The stage rolled off in a swirl of dust and fallen leaves, revealing the aproned man still standing there, his lantern held laxly.

"Arr'y hastis for hoam, Pengellen, or can 'ee step ento t' Mansion House for a spur?"

"Thank you no, not tonight, Kit. We're tired and for home."

"Do as thee wool," answered Kit, moving toward the porch. "Aunt Marget's leve a braave fire. She knaw'd ye war comin'."

There was a brief surge of voices from the Mansion House as the door closed on Kit; then David and Candace were left alone in the wan glow of the hanging lantern, against which the deepening dusk on all sides seemed suddenly profoundly dark. The impression was fleeting, for the village began to give voice almost at once in the sounds of dogs barking, the neighing of horses, distant talk and laughter, and the lights in windows shown through the twilight up and down the long street, where it turned further and seemed to dip even deeper into the valley past the Mansion House. Here and there a few lights shown on the slope which rose on the east side of the street.

"We've got a way to walk, Candy," said David. "I'll carry the portmanteau and one of the bags, if you can manage the two small ones."

"Oh, yes," she said, eager now, anxious to see the home to which her husband had brought her. "Which way is it?"

He gestured. "Over there—on a hilltop past the edge of town. We won't be alone there for long," he added, as if to reassure her. "In a few years there'll be houses all around us. Why, there are over a thousand people and more than two hundred buildings in the Point now!"

Shouldering the portmanteau and picking up the bag, he started away. She followed. The bags she carried were light; they held mostly her own things, and she wondered whether she would ever have opportunity to wear them in so rough a setting. She smiled at the thought of the stage depot's being called the Mansion House; but in a moment she sobered—if so unpretentious a building had so pretentious a name, what could she expect of her own home in this settlement? And the man, Kit, with his strange language . . .

"David?"

"Yes?"

"David, why did that man call her 'Aunt Marget'? I thought she was your aunt."

He laughed. "I should have explained. She's neither. It's just one of those Cornish customs you'll have to get used to, Candy. Older folks are often referred to as 'Aunt' or 'Uncle'. Marget Hoskins is just the widow of an old fellow who mined here ten years ago. She works around for a living."

She turned this over in her mind. "Does she have a key to our house, then? He said she'd left us a fire."

"Why, yes. You'll meet her in the morning. She's to come and help you till you get settled. And I want her to teach you something about making the Cornish dishes I like. Do you mind?"

"Oh, no," she cried quickly. "I don't want to be alone every day—at least not at first."

They left the street and began to mount the hill. He cautioned her to watch her step, for the way was rough—only a wagon trail. She went so carefully that twice David paused to wait for her. And once he turned her around, so that she might look down into the valley from which they had come and see among the trees the pale eyes of the houses, yellow with candle-light and lamps. From this perspective, under the boundless stars overhead and the pale glow of the orange sickle of new moon low in the west, the valley had a kind of wild, warm beauty.

"There aren't any street-lights," she said.

"They'll come," he answered confidently.

"Oh, David," she cried suddenly. "I feel so far away from home."

"But you aren't—you're only a few steps from the house. Come on."

"It was at her lips to say that she meant Providence, but she did not speak; David was right; Providence was no longer home; this was home, Mineral Point in Wisconsin Territory—a strange place in an alien country where she might never again see Benefit Street or College Hill or Prospect, or her mother or ailing father . . .

The house loomed up before her, dark against heaven. It stood among trees, neither numerous nor dense enough to obscure it; a square building. The windowpanes shown in the moonlight; there were enough of them, and from one pair came the flickering glow which could only mean a hearth fire. The house was of two storeys, a boxlike building; from one of its chimneys came a steady column of smoke, spectral on the starlit sky.

The front door opened into a small vestibule, into which he carried her, gravely. The vestibule in turn gave into a long hall which divided the lower storey and gave access to a broad stairway to the second floor. The fire was in the living-room, which was to the right of the hall in the northwest corner of the ground floor. Beyond, on the southwest, was a bedroom. Across the hall was a spacious dining-room, and behind this a kitchen and pantry. Another door led out of the house from the kitchen. As soon as David had lit a lamp, she took it and went through the house, examining each room in turn, with David following, saying nothing, watching her intently, to detect if possible any mark of displeasure, any sign of dissatisfaction. The uncertain light of the lamp told him nothing.

She could not complain for lack of space. The rooms were amply large, even to the two bedrooms and upstairs storeroom; but, by the very absence of all the furniture it might have held, the house seemed empty. The barrenness of these rooms affected her disagreeably; she felt cold, lost, ill-at-ease; she was relieved to be back in the living-room once more, where the fire dancing on the hearth created an air of coziness.

"Do you like it, Candy?" he asked finally.

"Yes, David—it's very nice—much nicer than I thought it would be, truthfully." She smiled as he took her into his arms and kissed her. "I was afraid we might have a log cabin with two rooms instead of one. Of course,"—he kissed her again—"it needs things."

"Sure it does. But what it needed most it has now you're here."

She hugged him with a brief, shuddering fierceness.

"Tired? Aunt Marget has turned the bed down . . ."

"Can't we just sit here by the fire a while? It seems such a long time since I saw a fire."

"Last night, in Galena . . ."

"Oh, last night's so far away," she cried, sinking to the floor on the rag rug before the fireplace. "And the night before that—and the one before that—and before that—does that take us no farther than Ohio, David? How far are we, then, from Providence?"

He came down beside her and held her close, putting his cheek against her hair. "Homesick—already?" he murmured. "And but come here! A thousand miles, perhaps. But it doesn't matter, for the railroads will soon be here, and once they've come, why, a thousand miles will be as nothing."

She did not answer. She looked into the flames, seeing there all she had left behind—the familiar streets of Providence, old decades before this town of Mineral Point had come into being, before even the first white man had walked here; the old buildings, the steeples and towers of that city of her birth; the long-known faces. The log on the hearth fell apart, sending a shower of sparks up the chimney; a few of them leaped past the stones to the wooden floor and faded there.

"It's comfortable just this way, David." she whispered. "I wish we didn't have to stir—ever. I'm so tired now."

"Then come—we'll go to bed. Mr. Trelawny will expect me as early as possible tomorrow, and Aunt Marget'll be here soon after sun-up."

She lay for a long while in bed, looking toward the windows, where the outline of the panes was set forth by the contrasting lightness of the sky, and broken by the windy branches of a tree. She thought of all that had taken place since she had bidden her parents farewell, spirited and excited as she was that day, anticipating the wildness of the west, the challenge of living there at her husband's side. Somehow it seemed no different to be in this house than it did to be at an inn along the way; she felt that in the morning they would once again have to be roused in haste and hurry through breakfast in order to be on time for the stage; it seemed that they were destined to hasten on and on, blindly, pushing ever farther away from the haven of Providence, of childhood and youth, toward some destination which was unknown in an alien place beyond maps, where they would be forever lost to the world to which she had grown accustomed.

She felt indeed like one lost in a wilderness; all the events of the journey to Wisconsin Territory pushed up in her thoughts, and in this darkness all the hardships were magnified, all the difficulties promised on the horizon of tomorrow seemed insurmountable; she dreaded the adjustment which would be necessary; she dreaded the thought of meeting people; she viewed with uncertainty her own ability to meet the challenge of living in a frontier town like Mineral Point, the roughness of which David had not tried to hide.

But I will try, she told herself earnestly, with a kind of desperation that spurred her sincerity. Though everything in this dark hour was covered over and colored by her homesickness, by the nostalgic longing to wash away the memory of the past days, to be back again in the home of her childhood and youth, she told herself sensibly that the past was done, there was no returning to it, she must fit herself and conform to this new way of life she had chosen when she had told David she would become his wife. She was confident that she could overcome her doubt.

She sank at last into a troubled sleep to the keening of the October wind at the eaves and the melancholy song of a screech owl not far away.

It was dawn when she awoke.

It took her a few moments to realize where she was. She looked to David, but he still slept, turned on his side, his dark head deep in his pillow. She slipped quietly out of bed, but the room was cold. She unfolded a blanket which lay at the foot of the bed and wrapped it around her; thus clad, she walked to the window and looked into the southwest.

Beyond the house rose the grove through which the stage had made its way the previous night; great old oak trees, together with maples fired with red autumn, covered the ascending slope. The sky was visible here and there, and on the top of the slope the stage road ran; beyond loomed the Platte and Belmont Mounds—thrusting out of the morning sun as they had reared up against the stars during the night. But from here, no fence-post, no sign of an axe—nothing was there to say that any other human being lived in all this wilderness.

She walked into the living-room and crossed to the windows in the northeast. Down the slope lay the village. She studied the roofs crowded along the long winding road that was Shake-Rag Street. A few small houses stood on the rise flung up from the street—of stone, of logs, of clapboards, and brick. Across, on the eastern slope, were the lead diggings, some of them but pits, wide at the mouth, narrowing toward the bottom, others shaft mines with windlasses and little sheds at their openings.

Under the morning sun, the village seemed twice as large as she had thought it on their arrival. Despite its roughness, there was a tidiness about it, a compactness which belied the appearance of being strung out along one long street. Two hundred buildings, David had said. Surely, among all these people, she ought not to be lonely.

Beyond the village rose the high ridge, along which lay the road to the outside. She recalled the names of the neighboring towns—on the southwest, Belmont, which had been the territorial capital until a short time ago—a small, scattered settlement, through which they had passed yesterday; to the northeast, Dodgeville, and past that on the one side Helena and the Wisconsin River, on the other, Madison, the new capital. The ridge towered over the settlement, flung up proudly upon the sky—and the Blue Mound above, like a great sentient beast reclining there in an attitude of watchful waiting, as beneficent under the sun as it could be malign under cloud and storm. For an instant she saw the house and the town as a kind of prison, and the three great dome-like hills as guards—with an effort she thrust this thought from her.

David came up silently behind her, saying, "You'll take cold, Candy." He put his arms around her, kissed her, held her close, blanket and all. "What are you doing? Looking over the Point?"

She nodded. "I'm glad I don't have to live in any of those little houses."

"They're not all houses. There are eight dry-goods stores, four groceries, two churches, a brewery, four public houses—the Mansion House in the biggest. There are tailor shops—there's even a cabinet-maker. And, of course, there are more smelting furnaces than just Trelawny's."

"And are all these people employed in the mines?"

He laughed heartily. "Lord, no, Candy! Those are just a few of the mines. There are lead mines all over around the village. Two miles northeast of here are the copper mines—though they're not doing so well since Mr. Ansley's plan to sell stock in London fell through. I'd say there are between four and five hundred miners. And many of them also have farms of some sort, with livestock."

"You didn't say . . . is there a school?"

"Trust an ex-school teacher to think of that! Certainly—a fine brick building. It was enlarged only this year."

She turned to say something further when the sound of a key fitting into the lock of the back door arrested her.

"Here comes Aunt Marget," said David. "Go and get dressed."

Aunt Marget Hoskins was plump and apple-cheeked, with soft, warm eyes and a pleasant smile. Though she lived in reduced circumstances, she never failed to dress neatly; this morning she had come over from her home on the slope above Shake-Rag Street, behind High, dressed in a tight bodice and so many skirts beneath her apron as to create the illusion that she still had a waist line. Her brown hair, parted in the middle and worn straight to a pug behind, was covered with an ample brown shawl, which more than half swathed her.

"Mister Pengellen!" she cried at the sight of him. "'Tis good to see 'ee. I knaw'd ye'd be hoam last night. And' t' bride?"

"She's dressing, Aunt. She'll be out in a few moments."

"I'll get a crum o' fire goin'."

As she worked, she made a detailed recital of everything that happened to her since David had gone east, and ended with the hint of a pressing problem with which she hoped he could help her. Would he?

"Of course," said David, curious to know what it might be.

She told him. Her youngest sister—"that were Bess Bishop, her that was livin' in Tintagel"—had died, leaving her child an orphan. Hard upon the letter announcing her sister's death, her orphaned niece herself came, having obtained passage to America through the kindness of a distant relative in London, who had occasion to be traveling to St. Louis, and had come as far as Galena with her. Now the girl was to live with her, but it was certain that she would have to find some kind of work to keep herself. She was too fine a girl to go into ordinary service for long, but her speech was so Cornish that she would find adjustment difficult. She should be taught to speak as Americans spoke, so that she might improve her prospects. "Oh, 'tes suant she talks, but the cheel caa'nt go on to speak in the ould way!" she cried.

"She could go to school here, Aunt."

"Aye, but she wedn't. P'raps she's toytish, but I do thenk she's too old."

"How old is she, then?"

"Seventeen."

"Yes, she'd be uncomfortable in school. How can I help, then?"

She explained volubly. She hoped that David, who had had an education in America, might help her niece to free herself from the Cornish pattern of speech. "She's cruel smart some ways," she finished, looking at him hopefully.

"I'll see, Aunt. I'll be quite busy at the store for the next few days. Meantime, she can study in Mr. McGuffey's newly revised speller. I'll set it out. You can take it to her when you go home. You've not told me her name."

"Tamson—Tamson Bishop, Mister Pengellen."

"A pretty name."

"Iss, 'tes that."

Candace came across the hall into the kitchen, dressed plainly in brown broadcloth, which became her. She walked already with an air of possession, thought David; this pleased him. He introduced her to Aunt Marget.

"I'm fixin' a dish 'o tay, Missus," said Aunt Marget respectfully.

"You'll have to be patient with Mrs. Pengellen, Aunt," said David. "I'm afraid she'll take a while to understand you. But you'll do what you can to help her?"

"I'facks, I wool."

"I'm sure we'll get along, David," said Candace.

"Once 'ee're settled, we'll make a paasty," promised Aunt Marget enthusiastically. "I fetched some 'taties, steak, and onion to fill et ento the paasty. Ye'll soon be setten' en afore him, es good es any paasty en t' Point."

The two women took each other's measure unobtrusively. Candace offered to help prepare breakfast, but Aunt Marget would not permit it—"not this first day," as if somehow her first day in her new home ought to be set apart. As Aunt Marget chatted of news in Mineral Point, she flashed hurried glances at Candace, trying to take her measure, while Candace attempted earnestly to understand the older woman's burring dialect, the rolled 'r,' the over-emphasized vowels which confused her. Candace's eyes baffled Aunt Marget; they told her less than she thought they should, no matter how much she tried to see behind them. Aunt Marget saw nothing but their blandness, like a wall shutting away her sight. Of what Candace thought, she knew nothing. She felt in Candace a burning desire to please, to like and be liked, but decided that Candace was withholding judgement on her, on the house, on Mineral Point . . .

from New Country

A SQUALL KEPT Alex below deck for most of the way from Chicago, but just before noon the rain stopped falling, the wind died down, and the sun came out. Alex came up from below and stood on the deck of the laker steamer looking toward the land which loomed closer as the steamer moved in. Indeed, they were about to reach Milwaukee; Alex could already see the river mouth, and the line of high land tapering down toward the mouth of the Milwaukee was clearly recognizable in his memory of the map he had seen.

The clouds scudded rapidly eastward, diminishing into the lake. A west wind blew across the water, bearing the musk of the land. The air was rain-washed and fresh, and now and then Alex thought he detected the fragrance of some kind of blossoms. Could it be apple? he wondered. It smelled like apple blossoms, and the month lacked three days of being June. The trees of the low hills along the shore were still green with the yellow-green of spring; behind them, the rolling country looked darker in color.

He sought and found the light-house at the foot of Wisconsin Street. Then, as the boat drew in closer, he saw other buildings. As they approached the mouth of the Milwaukee, the buildings along the shore stood out more clearly. They were all of logs, save one, which seemed to be of wide planking and stood just south of the mouth of the river on a sandy point of land. They were widely separated. Until the boat entered the mouth of the Milwaukee, nothing but these few houses of the settlement could be seen.

Then, past the Kinnikinnic, across the swamp to the west, other houses came into sight, at first but two or three, then groups of a dozen or so. According to the map he had seen, Alex concluded that these were the houses on Walker's Point. There were enough of them to be impressive. But at the same time, he was dismayed at the magnitude of the marshland between the river and Walker's Point. Indeed, it lay on both sides of the river, and seemed to be ever widening, except for the narrowing point of land which came down to the river itself and divided the swamp before the boat reached the mouth of the Menominee River. And along this stream coming in from the west, the swamp was equally wide. Here and there small

The Wind Leans West, 1969

islands broke its expanse, but there were no buildings of any kind in the bogland. Yet it was not uninhabited; wild fowl were abundant.

Here and there, Alex caught glimpses of places where ground had been filled in; but they were so small, in comparison to the whole, that he hesitated to contemplate how long it would take to fill in all the swamps—if indeed it could be done. For the first time since he had left Aberdeen, he began to doubt the wisdom of his course. How different was the Will Fortrie farm from this desolate place! Yet alone he had made the decision. He had listened to such advice as had been offered him; he had weighed it all carefully, and he had made his choice between remaining where he was, with the certainty of advancement in the bank at Peterhead, or of casting of his lot with George Smith in America.

Not far past the mouth of the Menominee, the marsh gave way to higher ground, first upon the right, and then later on the left. But whereas on the left there were many trees, on the right there was a large area of cleared land. There stood the heart of the settlement, for it was plainly the cluster of buildings there that was the ship's goal. Alex could even make out the place where they were to drop anchor, for a crowd of people had assembled there, and more were running down toward the end of the street toward which the ship was patently making its way. The ship's whistle set off a clamor of voices from the waiting crowd—a bedlam of shouts, from among which rose the voice of one man imitating a rooster.

As the ship came to a stop at the end of the street, Alex picked up the carpetbag which he had not left out of his sight since he had first taken hold of it. His portmanteau he swung under one arm. The deck was crowded now. New settlers, like himself, were eager to see all they could of the place that might be their home, if they decided against going to the interior of Wisconsin Territory. Alex took his time, letting those who were in haste precede him. When at last he reached the street, he found it a morass of mud; however, a wooden walk had been laid not far away, and to this he made his way.

He paused on the walk and looked around him. Already the ship he had just left seemed like a haven. The buildings, many of which had been put up with no semblance of order, had a look of impermanence, as if at any moment the carpenters were to come and take them down. Except for a scattered few, which were of weather-worn logs, and usually surrounded by lesser out-buildings, most of the structures he faced were new. Behind him, the crowd still milled about the boat, where supplies of various kinds were being unloaded. Perched high on a post not far from the river's edge, a man crouched crowing like a rooster!

No one paid attention to Alex until he was part of the way along the wooden walk. Then two rough-looking men stopped and guffawed at the sight of his plaid pantaloons.

"Lookit the little ladies' man," said one, pointing to Alex's trousers. "Boy, have ye got ye're didies on?"

Alex turned and walked casually up to him. "What was that?" he asked, as if he had not heard.

The man repeated what he had said and added an obscene epithet.

Alex dropped his portmanteau, clenched his fist, and swung at his chin. The fellow went down and off the boards into the mud.

His companion stood with his mouth agape. Alex's sudden attack had taken him as much by surprise as it had the other.

"The name is Mitchell—Alexander Mitchell," he said. "And see to it you don't forget it."

The man he had knocked down got up, rubbing his jaw. He looked qizzically at Alex. For a moment the cloud lingered on his stubbled face; then a smile broke through. He stuck out his hand.

"Rab Harker, Mitchell," he said. "Never'd a thunk a man with such fancy pants could hit so hard."

Alex took his hand.

"I'm new here, gentlemen," he said. "I'm looking for the home of Daniel Wells. Can you direct me?"

"Sure," said Harker. "Everybody knows Dan Wells here. Let me give you a hand. I'll walk you over." He turned to his companion. "So long, Aaron." Then he picked up the portmanteau Alex had dropped and started striding along the board walk.

"You gonna settle here, Mitchell?"

"I'm thinking about it."

"Well, there's something doing all the time. If you want a lively time, there's the Cottage Inn . . ."

Alex chuckled. "I'm not settled yet, Harker."

Harker changed his tack. "That's Judge Fowler's house over there. He's been here about as long as anybody since Juneau. This one's George Dousman's place . . ."

Alex let him talk, expressing a polite interest now and then. Harker did not seem to be a bad sort. Lively, full of the old Harry, with too much vitality for his own good. He was like a young animal. He could not be over twenty-five Alex thought. He had dancing blue eyes and curly hair. His smile was as engaging as his jeer was insulting. If he were shaved and presentably dressed, he might even pass for a gentleman.

Around them the village unfolded. In every direction there were buildings in the process of erection. An air of haste and bustle lay over the settlement like a cloud. Here change was the order of the day—expansion and growth, quite as if, thought Alex, the swamp did not loom immediately nearby on the west, and the lake not far away on the east. Wherever he looked were men who worked with such a will it did not seem likely that either swamp or lake would stop them if they had a mind to move in either direction.

"Well, here we are, Mitchell," said Harker suddenly, stopping before a modest frame house. "This is Wells' house." He put down the portmanteau, stuck out his hand once more, and said, "Just the same, if I was you, I'd get rid of them pants you wear."

Alex thanked him. His offer to pay him was indignantly refused.

"Maybe you can do something for me sometime—but I doubt it," said Harker.

Then he turned back toward the river's edge.

Alex had just raised his hand to knock, when the door was opened. The young man who stood there was tall. His eyes were as piercing as a bird of prey's, his brows were shaggy, and his hair was worn long, in a pompadour back on his head. The most extraordinary feature of his face was his nose, which was large, though well-shaped, and surmounted a mouth that spoke voicelessly of reticence and caution. He stood waiting for Alex to speak.

"I'm looking for Daniel Wells—junior," said Alex.

"I'm Wells, "he said. "Come in."

He stepped aside, as Alex walked in, introducing himself.

"I guessed as much," said Wells. "You're the picture of Scotland, Mitchell. Though how you took up with a fellow like Rab Harker beats me."

Alex explained. "He didn't strike me as a bad lot," he added.

"He's not. Just lazy and inclined to mischief. But let me take your bag. You're to stay with me—as you'll know if you've seen Smith."

"This bag stays with me, Mr. Wells," said Alex. "Where I go, it goes. Here, let me show you."

He put the bag down on the table in the sparely furnished room where they stood, opened it, lifted out two garments and stood aside so that Wells could look into it.

An exclamation escaped Wells. "You carried that all the way from Chicago!"

"From Aberdeen," replied Alex.

"Great God! It's not yours?"

"No, sir. it's Mr. Smith's. The money's been sent from his backers in Aberdeen; I was entrusted with it."

"It looks like a good deal."

"In American currency, it's the equivalent of fifty thousand dollars. We can't start a business such as we propose to start without capital. And if we succeed . . ."

"We must succeed, Mitchell. The people need something which can serve them as a bank, no matter what we call it." He smiled. "Of course, we'll succeed," he went on. "Though I'm bound to tell you that the successful man on the frontier can count ten enemies for every friend. You'll find that out."

"People are pretty much the same everywhere, Mr. Wells."

Wells gave Mitchell a curious glance from his deepset eyes. "But you saw Smith in Chicago," he said. "Why didn't you leave the money with him?"

"He wants it here, Mr. Wells."

"Then he has good reason for it. If you've talked with him, you'll know we've sold stock—over four thousand shares at two dollars a share. When is he coming, by the way?"

"He expects to call a meeting of the stockholders early in June," said Alex. "Since today is the twenty-eighth, he'll be here within the week."

Wells shrugged. "He's been and gone so much, a man has a hard time keeping track of him, especially since I have to go to Madison from time to time for meetings of the Territorial Council. But I'm doing you an injustice—keeping you from something to eat—I know they didn't feed you on the steamer. Let's put that carpetbag in my safe."

In the afternoon Wells took Alex down to show him the building in which the Wisconsin Marine and Fire Insurance Company would conduct its business. Wells owned it. It stood on Broadway, within easy walking distance of Wells' home. It was a sturdy, if small frame building, built flush up to the wooden walk which ran before it. An oak door opened squarely in the center of the front wall; it was flanked by a window on each side, and two more windows were set in the second storey. The side walls were windowless; the rear had but one window and a door which led out into a back yard, partly fenced in.

The building inside was all but barren. Wells had made some primary alterations in preparation for its new role; he had built a simple enclosure, to fence off the working quarters of the single large room which made up the first floor from the space before the door.

"The equipment and furnishings will be left up to you, Mitchell," Wells explained. "Smith suggested that as you're to be in charge, these matters should best be left to you."

Though the building was still new, Alex could not help comparing it with the Peterhead bank which he had left only a few weeks ago—not yet two months. Yet it seemed years since he had bid them at Peterhead goodbye; he had had so many varied experiences since then, he had seen so many different places, that already Peterhead and even Scotland's faces seemed almost impossibly remote. But the barrenness of the building, the rawness of the settlement did not discourage him; on the contrary, now that he was face to face with Milwaukee and began to see the immensity of the task which lay before him, the challenge emboldened him. There was no denying that the security of the Peterhead bank was more than balanced by the opportunity offered by his new position; advancement at Peterhead was severely restricted; here it was virtually limitless.

"There's plenty of room," said Alex thoughtfully.

"We'll need more before long," said Wells with confidence. "Once you get it furnished, you'll find it more cramped than it looks. You'll need a safe, for the first thing, and a stove—it gets devilish cold here, Mitchell, once the winter sets in." He pointed to the opening in the floor almost in the exact center of the second storey. "There's your vent for the chimney."

"I suppose I might as well get at the outfitting without delay. Mr. Smith will expect it to be done before the meeting," said Alex.

"Oh, let that wait a day or so. It's the middle of the afternoon now—you could barely get started."

"A man never gets back a minute lost, Mr. Wells," said Alex.

Wells nodded. "True, true." He shrugged. "Well, here's your key. You do as you like. If you take my advice, you'll look about a little and get acquainted with Milwaukee."

"Thank you, sir. I may do that."

"I'll go along, if you like. But to tell the truth, I've one or two things to do."

"I'll be all right, Mr. Wells."

"We'll look for you at supper time."

Wells strode off, in haste now, suggesting that whatever he had to do he was late about doing it. Alex locked the building behind him and walked in the opposite direction. Wherever he looked, he saw new structures taking shape. Most of them were rough and crude, but here and there were beginning to appear more decorative facades. Rounding a corner he came full upon the most magnificent building he had yet seen, for all that it, too, was frame. It was utterly unlike anything else in Milwaukee, for it was an imitation of Tuscan architecture. It was a long building, over fifty feet in length, and almost as wide, of two stories, with a Belvidere of one section and a pediment front which extended nine feet from the wall of the building and was supported by four Tuscan columns. If he had any doubt about the nature of the building, Alex was soon convinced, because of an obvious jail which stood not far beyond it, that it was a court house. So at least law and order had made an impressive appearance upon this frontier scene!

Beyond these two buildings, there were comparatively few others. Alex turned west. He walked the rough streets to the river's edge, where, finding a boat for hire, he rowed across to Kilbourntown. He was started to discover that the streets in Kilbourntown were not aligned with those of Milwaukee's east side, and resolved to ask Wells about this curious way of laying out a town. Kilbourntown was less settled than Juneautown. Less land had been cleared here; the streets were rougher and muddier; there were no wooden walks; buildings were fewer and farther apart. Here, too, all was a-bustle. Here Alex saw his first Indians, a trio of whom were coming in from the west, walking toward the river.

In one place before what Alex guessed was a tavern, a group of shouting, laughing men were gathered about one who was mounted on a keg, declaiming something. Could it be a political speech? Alex grew closer and joined the group, listening. But, no, the fellow was reading what was apparently a poem from the pages of the Milwaukee *Sentinel*.

" 'The Indian on the high bluff stood,'" he read. "'Alone, and nobody 'round him, Save tenants of the ancient wood, That always did surround him. He folded his arms and lit his pipe,'—get that. Try it sometime—or ask Egbert Smith how it's done. I got all I can do to light my pipe without folding my arms first!" His laughter joined the crowd's. He went on. "'He took a good look of the village and town—With its thousands of houses and people; And cast his bold eye up and down, O're many a mansion and steeple,'—You fellows see any mansions or steeples hearabouts?—'Then, throwing one more look adown, He gathered his blanket tight, And taking one long, unwavering step, Flung himself off the height.'"

"What is it?" asked Alex of the man who stood next to him.

"Oh, some school teacher from Oak Grove writ a poem," he answered. "He let the *Sentinel* print it. Old Limpy they call him. He's a greenhorn, all right—limps a little, wears green spectacles. If you'd ever see him, you'd likely not forget him."

A poet in this wilderness! thought Alex, drifting away. Of course, what he had heard was not much of a poem—but, still, it was an attempt to reflect the new milieu in which the writer found himself. Alex could appreciate how he must feel, for he himself was bounded by strangeness.

A horseman stopped suddenly before him. The tall rider hailed Alex. "A newcomer to our fair city?" he asked. "Permit me—my name is Kilbourn—Bryon Kilbourn." He waved one hand in a half-circle around him. "Are you thinking of settling, sir?"

Alex measured him. He face was sharp, his eyes were observant, but there was a certain softness about his features, nevertheless. A man who was a leader, though Alex, but one in whom leadership was not consistent with excellence of judgement. Yet Alex liked the way his gaze did not waver.

"My name is Mitchell," he said.

"A Scot, I'm bound!" exclaimed Kilbourn.

He slid down off his horse. "Would you like to look around a little, sir? I have business over yonder." He pointed to the tavern before which Alex had listened to Old Limpy's poem being read. "I'll be there a good hour. Why not take my horse and ride him around?"

"Thank you. I will."

"Bring him back to the tavern when you've finished, and perhaps we can talk over some lots."

Alex smiled. He preferred not to tell Kilbourn that he had come over from Juneau's side of the river. He mounted the horse and rode west, his quick eyes taking in every detail of the landscape. He was now well away from the bottoms, with their tamarack thickets; he had also passed beyond a band of cedar. He rode among low hills, some of them shorn by time to bluffs, but all covered alike with a growth of oak trees which were not yet in full leaf and stood as if cloaked in the ghosts of leaves, hung with blossoms and unfolding small ears of leaves that were so pale a green as to seem spectral.

These small hills dominated the country away from the river. They were broken by occasional ravines and by low swales which were even more thickly wooded than the slopes. Alex followed a well-defined road, which, like almost all the other streets and lanes in the settlement, was muddy in many places. He was beyond the region of houses now, however, though he was not past human companionship, for he was not alone on the road. At a narrow place he passed a traveler struggling to get his wagon through the mud; at the mouth of a ravine well away from the settlement, he went by two men who appeared to be in early middle age sitting beside the road; they eyed him boldly and did not respond to his greeting; still farther along he met an old Indian walking on foot toward Milwaukee. He was burdened with things of Indian manufacture which Alex could not recognize, since Indians were something of America of whom he had no knowledge; perhaps he hoped to trade them for this wants in the settlement. The Indian appeared to be quite elderly; he was clad in a white man's hat, and, though his legs were naked, he wore a heavy blanket over his shoulders.

Presently the woods came to an end. Before Alex stretched westward a marvelous expanse of green, where the grass waved in the late afternoon sun. As far as the eye could see there was rolling prairie country, broken here and there by groves of trees. Flowers Alex could not name shone in the grass; they were pink, yellow, white; some of them resembled roses, not unlike those in the highlands; some were grass-flowers of a delicate blue and a vibrant chrome color. As he sat astride Kilbourn's horse, Alex could understand Smith's enthusiasm; the possibilities of the land before him seemed to be boundless indeed. He wondered where the road led; certainly to no near farm, for none was in sight. Perhaps to an inland settlement.

He measured the distance of the sun from the western rim, and concluded that he had better turn around. He had taken this look into the country to assuage his curiosity. He was well pleased with himself for having done so, for he was now satisfied that the land was all George Smith had suggested it was. It lacked only settlers to turn it to use.

He rode back toward Milwaukee as swiftly as he could, lest darkness overtake him and Wells begin to worry what had happened to him.

As he came toward that ravine where he had passed the two men who had not spoken to him, he was aware of the sound of cries and blows. Despite his natural caution, he pressed forward, rode off the road and to the mouth of the ravine. The two men were still there; they had set upon the old Indian and were beating him. It was clear to Alex that they meant to rob and perhaps kill the Indian.

He dug his heels into the horse's belly and rode straight at the men. Without hesitation, he leaped from the horse and began to rain blows upon the nearer of the men, who had been so busy with their quarry that they had not heard him come. At his sudden appearance, the Indian, seeing help, began to fight with renewed strength.

One of the would-be robbers broke free, and began to run up the ravine. The other turned to follow, but, unhappily for him, Alex struck him such a blow as to knock him out.

The struggle had taken but a few moments. Alex had an impulse to run after the other robber and bring him down, but a glance served to tell him, in the crooked way he ran, that he had been drinking. The two men were clearly trash, the kind he had understood followed the frontier in this country, and he realized now that their scrutiny of him, when he rode by, was solely to determine whether or not he were worth robbing. The Indian must have been poor prey, and perhaps if they had not been drinking, they would have permitted him to pass peacefully.

Feeling a little absurd now, Alex turned to the Indian.

The old fellow was on his feet again. He limped badly now; they had evidently hurt his leg.

"Are you hurt?" he asked.

The Indian looked up at the sound of his voice, but he only shook his head. Plainly, he was hurt, thought Alex. Why should he deny it? Then he realized that what the Indian met to say was that he could not understand English. Even as he thought this, the Indian spoke a few words in his own language.

This time it was Alex's turn to shake his head.

There was nothing for it but to resort to sign language. With infinite patience, Alex tried to tell the Indian by means of gestures that it would be better for him if he mounted the horse and rode into the settlement, while Alex walked beside him.

The Indian seemed a little distrustful.

At this moment, however, the man Alex had knocked out came to. With cat-like quickness, the Indian seized a small rock and hit him with it. Of the other robber, there was now nothing to be seen; he had made good his escape. Startled as Alex was by the Indian's angry attack on the prone robber, he could not act quickly enough to prevent the man from being hit; and on second thought, he told himself, it was probably a good thing; the blow had served only to knock him out a second time. He would give them no trouble.

The Indian, at least, now understood Alex. Having gathered up his things, and put his blanket once more about his shoulders, the Indian waited for Alex to help him on Kilbourn's horse.

This done, they set off.

It was almost sunset when they reached the tavern where Byron Kilbourn waited for his horse. Kilbourn stood outside, talking with two men, as Alex came walking up. Seeing them, Kilbourn stopped talking and stared.

"I've brought you a new settler, Mr. Kilbourn," said Alex dryly.

Kilbourn did not know what to say; his companions began to laugh.

Alex explained what had happened and motioned the Indian off the horse.

"That looks like old Bright Cloud," said Kilbourn.

"Well, he's not very bright, now," said one of his companions, laughing heartily at his own quip.

They helped the Indian off the horse.

"I'll see him to the river," said Alex, "and across. After that he's on his own."

"He'll be your friend for life," said Kilbourn. "That could prove embarrassing." He shrugged. "However—it's your embarrassment. Tell me, Mr. Mitchell, did you see any lots that interested you?"

"Almost everything I saw interested me," answered Alex. "I think it very likely I may want to invest in some. For the time being, though, I'm staying with Daniel Wells."

"A Juneau towner!" exclaimed Kilbourn in disgust. "Man, that place has no future but here and west of us."

"They can't very well expand into the lake, can they?"

Kilbourn grinned. "It takes a stranger or a Kilbourntown man to see that. Look me up, Mitchell, when you're in the mood to buy."

"I'll do that."

Alex thanked him for the use of his horse. Then he gave his arm to the Indian.

They made their way to the river, where Alex helped the Indian into a boat, and rowed across. Once on the other side, the Indian made signs to express his gratitude; then he bade Alex farewell and went limping off in the direction of the dock where the boats came in.

Alex hastened back to Wells' house.

They were waiting supper for him. Mrs. Wells had now returned to the house from which she had been absent before. She was a small woman, compared to her husband, with fine, grey eyes and sandy-colored hair. She said very little, however, beyond greeting Alex and explaining that the children had already had their supper, and she maintained a reticent silence while her husband and Alex talked.

Alex talked with enthusiasm of the country he had seen to the west. He mentioned meeting Kilbourn.

Wells' eyebrows rose. "What did you think of him?" he asked.

Alex told him.

"I reckon that's about right, Alex," said Wells. "He's a fine man in many ways—even brilliant. But he does petty and short-sighted things. Like those streets . . ."

"I meant to ask why they weren't in line with those on the east side."

"He never expected the streets to be joined by bridges," explained Wells. "Yet at the same time he recognized that our only expansion lies westward. He deliberately laid out his streets so they'd be out of line. And nothing will move him, even though its as plain as the nose on his face that we're going to have to build bridges." He shook his head. "He thinks his boats are enough. He runs the *Badger* and *Menominee*, and he has them put in only on the west shore of the Milwaukee."

Alex praised Milwaukee and its setting with all the enthusiasm of George Smith himself. This pleased his host.

"You'll never regret coming here, Alex," said Wells fervently. "We expect great things of Milwaukee. And it'll take great men to bring them about."

"And great women," observed Mrs. Wells tranquilly. "But you'll hear less about them, Mr. Mitchell."

Wells smiled tolerantly. "The people must come into the Territory somewhere," he continued. "And this is the only natural harbor for miles around. In fact, I'm inclined to think it's a lot better than Chicago's if we have to make a comparison. It's the natural setting for a city, and our rate of growth in the last two years shows that we're well on the way."

How long would it take to bring the dreams of the city's founders to reality? wondered Alex, as Wells spent his enthusiasm. And those of George Smith—with his hopes for his insurance company that was really to be a bank?

That night, as he lay in his narrow bed in that interval before sleeping, Alex pondered his changed circumstances. He had not slept well since leaving Scotland. But then, with the dubiety of all who came to America, he had not really expected to. He had eaten such food as he would have shunned at the best table in Aberdeen. And found he liked it, too, for that matter. He had met so many men filled with the spirit of the adventurous frontier that he had become imbued with the same spirit—but he knew that it was only a veneer. Beneath it lay still untouched the same Alex Mitchell who had grown up on Will Fortrie farm, the same youngster who had studied so hard to make his people proud of him, who had gone to Adams & Anderson and then on to the Peterhead Bank—and now to America, that wild country which had torn itself by force of arms from its mother country and flourished now as it might never have done had it not gone its own way. Here he was now—twenty-one—young as the country itself was young.

He had not conquered a nostalgia for his native country, but he was prepared to crush it ruthlessly. If he permitted himself now to yearn for what he had put behind him, he would only complicate the way ahead. He must accustom himself to this Milwaukee, raw and brutal as it was; he must learn to think of Milwaukee as home. If, in the end, he could not come to grips with this land, he could turn back. But he did not think he would turn back, and he fell asleep with serenity and confidence . . . .

Poetry

Deer in Snow

Silent walking in the silent deeps of wood,
going as slowly as slow I ever could
and snow, snow falling thick, snow falling fast,
no sound, no creature passed:
walking among the strange world's white
emptiness, the pale half-light
of the snowstorm's heart,
walking alone, alone and silent, silent and apart:
I came upon the one live thing
in that snow-hung and silent place, watched him spring
to being there, in the moment's fading dread
saw how the proud and antlered head
held to the bush and the clear
eyes velvet without fear
looked briefly, briefly, briefly so—
and he went, was gone in silence into the world of silent snow.

1938

American Portrait: 1877

I am Crazy Horse. Do not touch me!
All of lost America in his eyes, all the wild land in his burning eyes, the
deep forests and the wind-swept plains,
all the remembering: buffalos thundering along the prairies, antelope in
the wooded hills, and the fair earth flowering after rains
in April, here in his eyes all of lost wild America taking a last breath
but not afraid of passing. Back of his proud and fearless eyes,
grief and the face of death.

(This is the way they went: one and one and one
by hundreds down the way of the setting sun:
after Narragansetts, Seminoles, Ojibwas, the Minneconjous, Aparahoes,
Commanches, all the Sioux,
all the last of the Lakotas pushed down the night's retreating blue,
like purple clouds spread fanwise from the afterglow
into the darkening sky and lost.)

His the slow
backward stepping, the unashamed defeat and the heart's cone
of bitterness; his the proud, fearless turning upon the centuries;
his the turning alone. . . .

I am Crazy Horse. Do not touch me!

1938

Man Track Here

Less than this my lone path is:
a deermouse track in winter's snow—
less than any mark of hare of crow.
Than the least falling leaf from the most crabbed, most aged tree
in the least wind, than the least pebble dropped into the stillest pool,
than the most secret ways of the foolish, obscure bee,
no path of mine is now as much, nothing of mine is
more. Through wood, way over meadow and plain,
footprint on hill and river sand, by moonlight and by rain,
where laboringly my clear path went, there
lordly strides now windy snow, and where
my challenge sounded to the wind, now looms the blank, unheeding air.

1939

Little Elegy: Herons At Dusk

Down toward the distant dusk-held ridge
from which the river bends away,
I looked in twilight stillness from the bridge,
and listened to their talk above the sound
of pewees mourning nearer ground.

Across the evening's fading blue,
ponderously the herons flew,
where nighthawks swooped to feed
and the cricket trembled on his reed
with night drawn down to tree and slough,
while I stood watching how the last of day
went down the west
as air went past the heron's breast.

They went into the east's retreat to meet the night;
for me there is no ambuscade to hide me from its sight.

1940

Elegy: On a Flake of Snow

for Zona Gale

Dusk-bound with snow, with snow and winter cold,
the ever new year comes, and newly passes now the old

in voiceless whispering of flakes upon the pane;
all breath as vapor passes in the air,
and hushed the hours, hushed eternal moment where
comes over wire, telephone, out of snow-held space
the hallowed word,
the word of shadows:
death.

Dusk-bound with snow, with snow and winter cold,
new year as always comes, as always newly goes the old

in year's last stirring air, snow's lulling sound,
in sibilant lost whispering of flakes among the ground,
among barren hills, last lingering, forgotten, last one leaf,
now flowers heart's deep wordless grief:

dusk-bound with snow, with snow and winter cold,
new year as always comes, as always newly goes the old.

Over the river soar the gulls, over river
and the snow-clad hills
like distances now tangible upon the brittle sky:
where summer-long fly hawks, spills
swallows' song from slopes of June, the sky's blue
space—

gone now without a trace
to mark their going, and far, and farther still—Zona!

1940

gone beyond the dusk, the moonlight, summer sun and winter dawn:
she who loved them all, a dove
who passing left an eagle's trail above
the year's corrosion, gone now where,
spectral as snow in winter air,
in deeper shadows wait the children of her mind:

Miss Lulu Bett, Papa La Fleur, and Mr. Pitt; the young, the old, the kind
—still bound around
by glance of eyes, her smile, her voice's sound.

Dusk-bound with snow, with snow and winter cold,
new year as always comes, and always newly goes the old,
while over hills, the prairie, rivers and the sea,
in space of snow-filled air, lonelily
the word, the shadowed word:
death.

Dusk-bound, snow, winter cold:
new year as always comes, and goes the old
in hushed lost whispering of flakes upon the pane,
stirring memories again, again,
in intimate communication intricately snow:
the calm, appraising eyes; her slow,
her quiet smile; and here within this brief,
    this fleeting moment unconfirmed,
the people of her mind:

while over hills, the rivers, prairie and the sea,
over the wire, telephone, in falling hush of snow, the threnody
resounds, snow-held in whispering air,
the words fallen dustily upon the year, all years
now gone, down to the shadows where now stand,
now wait, the lasting children of her mind's familiar land:

borne by each whispering flake,
the word now tangible in air,
over the prairie, river, lake,
land once she loved, over country, towns apart
to linger in the forest-places of the heart—

the hallowed word,
the word:
death

death—
and death's eternity,
her life's death the life of shadows:

her dying's death,
her immortality.

Brush Fire

Red blossom in the winter wood,
red burning in the winter dusk:
windless now the trees
stand silent, snow-held, on the turn
and bank of hill where brush,
the limb and twig of axe-slain, fallen tree
burst into final, one last bloom:
orange flower of fire,
blossom of burning bole, of birch
and elm
aflower now this brief last hour
in winter's dusk, in twilight wood,
where hill meets stubbled field
and pasture-land retreats.

Red burning in the winter dusk,
red blooming in the snow-held wood:
pillar of flame to greet the dark,
the fire's body, bright as bloom,

1941

burning glory in the winter wood,
last flowering of limb, of branch and tree,
burns soundlessly, where no wind is,
and dusk-cloaked trees are gaunt around.
Above, the starless sky
bears snow
to quench the fire's ruddy glow.

Red blossom in the winter wood,
red burning in the snow-hazed dusk:
squirrel and bird who watch in awe,
and rabbits' great-eyed wonder
at this flaming with no shotgun's thunder
after . . . No wind blows.

Brush fire burning winter dusk,
brush fire blooming in the dead and dying wood,
breathing here its little warmth,
spreading here its little death.

For one last hour, one swift, swift hour still
these ancient limbs are great upon the hill.
Red blossom in the winter's snow-blue wood,
red burning in the woodland's early dusk.

The Solitary

The secret of stars is distance, their splendid isolation,
as anyone's secret is the unrevealed motive, the hidden relation
of self to another and another and the world.
As a cocoon lost within a curled
leaf, the self hides within you; and the self that is mine

1945

seeks the same refuge, unhoused of peace, lost to the heady wine
of self assurance.

The secret of stars yields to an equation;
not so the intricate, the complex and incomprehensible relation
between act and memory, motive and impulse, word and deed,
each the casual planting of an unknown seed.
What it yields is unknown,
perhaps joy, perhaps sorrow, perhaps the misshapen stone
of resignation carried in the heart—the plain
endurance of the plain man of complex pain.

The secret of stars is neither premeditated nor forever forbidden to man;
but, like the hidden self, is part of a pattern, the same plan
perhaps, one in its relation to the other
antipodal, not of necessity bound to another;
the stars' geometry has its parallel in the geometry of love,
the eyes, the lips, the word of the unknown quantity, of
which the solution is never quite evident, never quite seen,
but lies for any two forever intangible between.

The Hawk as Time

The anonymous, inscrutable hawk moves from behind your hair
where your head is sharp in October smoke-sweet air,
with sun in it as aureole.
The hawk's orbit is no precise line between earth and heaven; he flies
on motionless wings, and he is in your eyes;
yes, he is there as time, flies there as on the clock's face the minute hand
makes its round interminably: his shadow dark upon the autumn land,

---

1945

dark within your eye and brain,
dark where you and I have lain
on the sweet grass, but yesterday alive and green.

Oh, the hour suddenly is lean
with hunger, and the mortal ear listens, listens
for what the hawk cries
where he goes in and out your hair, where he
flickers in your eyes,
aloof, inscrutable with the golden aureole,
waiting too for the whine of death to make him whole.

Elegy: Autumn

Everywhere the smell of drying leaves,
the smell of bonfire smoke in quiet air,
the dry sound underfoot of autumn . . .

Footsteps sound hollowly where
you walked before unleafing time. (Darks
outside and darks within.) No voice but scuttering leaves
licking flames, smoke smell.

(What walks beside that has no need
to speak?)
Streetlights make their pools of light
as always, every night—
as windows lit in childhood's long lost house,
as stars in adolescent dream. Mouse-
footed time leaves no footprint there.

1946

Everywhere the smell of drying leaves,
the smell of bonfire smoke in windless air,
the dry sound underfoot of autumn . . .
and the years gone by
under that same, that unchanged evening sky . . .

(What walks beside that has no need
to speak?)
Everywhere the disembodied voice that speaks
of love, that quickens pulse and heart and makes
the signature of grief
plain as the gathered sheaf

(Oh, hush! whose footstep there?
Who cries love, love answered
in the batflit evening air?)

Rendezvous in a Landscape

Walden: 1845-1847

i. Private Business

> *My purpose in going to Walden Pond*
> *was . . . to transact some private business.*

Having been for many years each day
about his business long before
his neighbors stirred, Thoreau made his way
to quarters shared more privately
with thrush and whippoorwill and veery.

1952

A good post and a good foundation:
advantages it may not be good policy
to divulge . . .

He counted years at but a score
and eight, his occupation many-
faceted, to wit: inspector
(self-appointed) of snow-storms, rains,
of lightning and the thunder;
accountant of man's humble wonder
under heaven;

You must build everywhere
on piles of your own driving.

surveyor
of forest paths, ravines, of woodland lanes,
of bridges, watchman of the wild stock
of the town, of unfrequented nooks
and corners on the farm, of jutting rock
and fern-grown dell, of murmurous brooks;

Strict business habits
are indispensable to every man . . .

caretaker of red huckleberry, nettle tree
wild crab, of red pine, black ash, and bumblebee,
of cross-lots routes, of leaf
and blade, of insect's private grief;
cliff-top sentinel to mark
the comings and goings of hawk
and tern, merganser and of meadow lark,
to keep a record of the forest talk
within the province, to telegraph the word
of any new arrival, and to wait
each evening for the sky to fall,
for the first bright star to call
down night, to see the late
huntsman home and the last bird
in;

Most luxuries, and many
comforts of life are not only
indispensable, but hindrances
to the elevation of mankind.

listener, to hear
what was the wind, and in the wind, to hear
and carry it express; herald of the sun
each morning, present at its rising and again
its setting, a matter to be done
unfailingly, of last importance for the plain,
indigenous American.

Talk of a divinity in man!
What a man thinks of himself,
that it is which determines
his fate.

He went to build himself a house
which might surpass the best on Concord's Main Street,
yet one that he could share with mouse
and ant, a house where me might meet
the sun each day without disturbance
to his neighbors, at a place where
he could root himself most firmly into earth
to rise at last into the upper air
of heaven in the same proportion, a rebirth
quietly desired, so that with less chance
of interruption he might pursue
his various enterprises and earn the due
reward of merit . . .

Not to live cheaply nor dearly there,
but to transact some private business
with the fewest obstacles . . .

ii. Solitude

The time at Walden was his own;
he could look out or inward. Alone,
he had no social contacts to fulfill, he found

all his occasions in himself, got down to bottom ground
to discover all around him ample space,
his horizons never at his elbows any place
he chose to be. His visitors all marvelled at his lack
of loneliness, and urged him back
to Concord.

Why should I feel lonely?
Is not our planet
in the Milky Way?

He was no lonelier than sorrel on a hill,
a single mullein, a bean leaf, a nocturnal whippoorwill;
he shared the isolation of the North Star,
a weathercock, the south wind moving far
up country, no more away of loneliness than mouse,
or bee, the Mill Brook, the first spider in a house.

This whole Earth
is but a point in space.
How far apart dwell
the two most distant habitants
of yonder star?

And as he spent his days and months alone,
he found life sweetest near the bone.
Being human—the sentient scene
of thoughts, affections, and conceits—the lean
ascetic hours gave him choice of being
what he chose to be: driftwood in the stream, or seeing
Indra far above. He learned his kind of doubleness, a duality
by which he stood remote from self as well as others, an actuality
independent of his station,
impervious to misinterpretation.

Life is a kind of fiction,
a work of the imagination.

His solitude was relative; of companions a few
were constant—bird, vole, mouse, and shrew;
he had a kind of understanding with owl and hawk

that transcended common talk,
though it was a primal communication
which existed long before man's conversation.
He found this way of keeping whole
in solitude an illumining of the soul,
implicit in the instinct toward a spiritual plane,
manifested now and again,
dividing him between the higher good
and the savagery of dwellers in his wood.

I love the wild
not less than the good.

Peace lay in being where
few other human voices echoed in the fragrant air,
and something he had known before—
he found the thick wood and pond not just at his door—
was emphasized anew; there was a kind of space
that kept him from his fellowmen and bade him
seek a solitary place

No exertion of the legs
can bring two minds
much nearer to each other.
I never found the companion
so companionable as solitude

iii. Track-Repairer of the Planetary Orbit

His retreat was linked alone, he said,
to all society by the railroad along whose bed
he walked to Concord and returned; and often on his way
was hailed by men passing on trains; who, seeing him from day to day
doubtless thought him an employee of the road.
So in a sense he was; he had a share in every load
of cotton that went up to town
and every one of woven cloth that came back down,
of silk and wool, of wood and chair,
and of the wit that made a book, had more than one man's share.

I too would fain be
a track-repairer somewhere
in the orbit of the earth.

His purpose was related,—as recorder
of a cosmic plan and order—
to keep intact the planetary courses and all such other right-of-ways
as pertinent—the migrant's path from north to south and back,
the seasons' days,
the rising and the setting of the sun, the stars, the moon,
the comings and the goings of the peregrine,
wild roses' blossoming in June,
the redwings' gatherings and the locusts' cycle, the green
and yellowing of leaves, the insects's hours,
the paths of sparrow and hawk
as well as all their devious ways of private talk.

I meet the engine with its train of cars
moving off with planetary motion,
with its steam-cloud like a banner
unfolding in the light . . .

He had his private speech with the whistle of the train
that passed along the line a hundred rods away, snow, rain,
or sunny day, morning, afternoon, or night; a kind of muted conversation,
one-sided, to be sure, but still communication
A breaker and enforcer of his solitude,
each passing train only the more imbued
his chosen refuge with taste enough of what lay yonder
to satisfy the daily measure of his curiosity and wonder,
and left him quite content to be
the confident alone of bird and tree

This traveling demigod,
this cloud-compeller,
would ere long take sunset sky
for the livery of his train . . .

A mutual respect informed his purpose, where he stood
offside to watch it pass, where he moved from woodland depths
when he could

to see the locomotive and the cars go by
and the smoke like clouds rise into sky,
his purpose was but clearer for the train,
nothing daunted by weather of storm or snow or rain.

> *I watch the passage of the morning cars*
> *with the same feeling I do*
> *the rising of the sun . . .*
> *When I hear the iron horse*
> *make the hills echo*
> *with his snort like thunder,*
> *shaking earth with his feet,*
> *breathing fire and smoke from his nostrils,*
> *it seems as if earth had got*
> *a race now worthy to inhabit it.*

Something in the locomotive's voice to him was kin to hawk's scream
over pasture, field, waking owl and fox as well as farmer
  from his dream—
a track-repairer in the orbit of the earth, he said,
going on his way where he by self alone was led . . .

> *Every path but our own*
> *is the path of fate.*
> *Keep on your own track . . .*

iv. Essential Facts

> *I went to the woods because*
> *I wished to live deliberately.*

He lived not by hours marked on an employer's clock,
but rather by cloud-shadows on the face of rock;
not by wall-bound commerce, by merchandise,
but by sunlight on the water, and by simpler things that give rise
to no complexities of dollars and cents,
nor greed and avarice, envy and concupiscence.
He knew one could not take the measure of a man by height, his look,
his clothes, or the resources of his pocketbook,
but by the potentials of his mind;
no man's bank account informs one—is he kind?

is he considerate? does he love his fellowmen?
is he patient, tolerant, humble, joyful? does he work and when?

To front only the essential facts
of life, and see if I could not learn
what it had to teach,
and not, when I came to die,
discover that I had not lived.

He knew home men live meanly, like ants upon the crowded plains;
how men like pygmies spend themselves in fights with cranes,
pile error upon error, clout on clout,
and beg the unfit among them to wield the knout,
frittering lives away by complex detail, self-doubt, and infelicity,
instead of honest and exacting simplicity.

I did not wish to live what was not life
living is so dear;
nor did I wish to practice resignation, . . .

He would not be thrown off the track
by every nutshell or mosquito's wing, by looking always back,
nor, sleeping, wake to ask, "What's the news?"
as if mankind had stood his sentinels, nor refuse
to understand that all the news concerning him was carried
in his pulse, his respiration, his senses, or buried
deep within his brain. News indeed! The cable stretched to Spain
could not carry news of such importance as that
  between his heart and brain.

I wanted to live deep
and suck out all the marrow of life,
to put to rout all that was not life,
to cut a broad swath and shave close,
to drive life into a corner,
and reduce it to its lowest terms . . .
to be able to give a true account of it.

The child lives far more worthily; to him alone
reality is fabulous, whereas to man, who would own
shams and delusions as the truth, what has a right to be—

the beautiful, music, poetry—reality
is lost behind the so-called wisdom of experience,
which is to say
behind his failure to live worthily, even for a single day.

> *What a man thinks of himself,*
> *that it is which determines*
> *his fate.*

v. Every Man Is an Inlet

> *Every man is an inlet*
> *yet unexplored by him . . .*

At Walden he had leisure
to explore himself, be it with pain or pleasure;
he had no need of ships and men to be
the navigator of his private sea,
for this Atlantic, his Pacific were reduced to one
small pond, and yet, a paradox, were all in one,
were Concord, Boston, London, Rome, the planetary spaces,
were Emerson, Alcott, Shakespeare, mother, brother, the countless faces
of millions yet to come and here before.
He found a "Symmes' Hole" by which to get inside, a door
in introspection which led him to his private sea
upon which England, France, Portugal, Norway, Italy
all fronted. This alone was the uncharted ocean, the way
no coward could escape by enlisting for the wars. None could say
what might be found along its coasts, tangent to the sphere
sun down, moon down, and at last earth down, too; the way was clear,
the path uncertain, but he undaunted
at possible discoveries by which another might be haunted.

> *I learned . . . that if one advances*
> *confidently in the direction*
> *of his dreams,*
> *and endeavors to live the life*
> *he has imagined,*
> *he will meet with a success unexpected*
> *in common hours.*

He learned to greet the day and night with joy,
to know that he had been far wiser as a boy,
to drink deep, to fish the stream of time and heaven, too,
to enter into secrets of all things and mine all veins.
old, as well as new

Rather than love, than money,
than fame, give me truth.

What truths he found were there for every man to see: to wit—
the pungence of the bergamotte, the gentian's heavenly blue, the sky lit
by the rising and setting sun, the hyla choir, the chipmunk's curiosity,
the scent of herbs, the vesper sparrow's threnody,
killdeers' nostalgia, the phases of the moon, the perfume of the grass,
the bat-flit evenings, the drone of summer's bee, the richness of each
  hour to pass,
the immortality of truth and beauty in themselves, the cricket's churr,
the lark's dawn song, toad's trill, the pewee's invitation to share
  his small domain, the cat's warm purr—
all the homeliness of common things: the trees,
the clouds, the birds, the stars—these
were the ultimate realities.

He will put some things behind,
pass an invisible boundary;
new, universal, and more liberal laws
will establish themselves
around and within him;
he will live with the license
of a higher order of beings.

He never took these truths for granted, and he had cause
to bless himself. Blind men doubted their existence
  and knew no higher laws;
the greatest gains and values were out of reach,
none knowing what the commonest flower had to teach.

The true harvest of daily life
is as intangible and indescribable
as the tints of morning or evening . . .

These were the fruits of all his days
at Walden: these that he could not communicate—the ways
of wasp and bird, of flower and fish
and all the dwellers of earth and air;
these were the things he could not persuade
another to share,
for these were part of what each man could find on the shore
of his own private sea, were he but to sail and explore
that inner ocean.

In proportion as he simplifies his life,
the laws of universe
will appear less complex,
and solitude will not be solitude,
nor poverty poverty,
nor weakness weakness.

He learned the immortality of simple things—of flower, bird;
the grain of sand, the drop of water, the wind's least whispered word.
From his good post he knew
the universe was wider than any one man's view
of it, and if the mass of men led lives of quiet desperation
too often they alone were authors of their private desolation.

He could go from Walden and not come back, yet never be far
away from it, for he had Walden in his private ocean,
had it to its farthest star
and he knew its formal plan
as surely as the limitations of the inner man.

If you have built castles in the air,
your work need not be lost;
that is where they should be
Now put the foundations under them.

Sirius: Midnight

I woke in dark and thought by the illumined pane
the waning moon had risen once again,
and rose to see all bright and glowing there
Sirius in the wintry air,
the Great Dog looking in to see how well I kept
while earthly dogs and keepers slept.

Cold blue, far and crystal clear—
yet it was uncanny now it seemed so near
there in the midnight dark where it was framed
by trees outside and walls within, and flamed
the brighter for the black of cedar and wall,
standing there was wide as the horizon and as tall
as heaven, and making all the pane to glow
as if a miniature moon had come to show
how neighborlike it was.

I knew it was a star,
and yet it seemed more near than far,
come close to the window to look in
and find what might be next to being kin.

How many worlds were we apart?—
as close as two beats from a single heart,
or as distant as a million light-years across space
a fan would blanch to face ?
No star might ever come as near again
as Sirius in that one moment just beyond the pane
to make man know through star and dark and windy tree
such kinship with eternity.

1956

On a Locomotive Heard in the Forest

This voice, though alien to these woods,
is close as any sound of vole or deer,
and echoes here as one long known,
where it goes crying past from far to near
and on to far again, to leave but ghost of sound,
like a beloved footstep that has gone to ground.

What man who hears it so but stands to listen,
to mark it where it goes; a great beast
sped in but a trice the confines of the wood,
flung westward out of the green east,
and briefly, intimate as one leaf curled,
combines this solitary wood with all the world.

Wild creatures fall to stillness as it goes
and listen, filled with wonder, while its cry
mourns down the wood, rising, falling,
where it passes fleetly by—
and yet, of all the motes that tremble in the wood,
only man, in all his vaunted power, should.

1956

Windy Trees and Evening Star

The peepers hold the meadow side, between me and the
eastern rim, but on the west are
wind and trees, lithe young blooming limbs and evening star,
the peepers singing spring, the wind here in these vaulting
trees and the star
just past the farthest twig, among the windy, lashing branches
and their swollen buds—not far—
past woodcock rising to his mating dance, and wind drawn
across the lute
of flowering maples, these too shout April to the burgeoning
night; nothing is mute
on such an evening, the very earth pulses and throbs with
hyla cries,
the sky explodes with life anew where the woodcock flies,
but here on this heaven still pale with dying day, Venus
among the windy branches
unfolds first leaves, announces spring's avalanches,
and not all the birds and frogs now giving tongue
can make the year, the earth, the heart so young.

1960

Old Turtle

This eye of basilisk looks up at me
from cycles of time past
and tells me knowingly of two of us
he will be last.

He may be well as wise
as he is old,
but there's no warmth in him;
his eye is cold.

He watches me as if he took
my enmity for granted;
he makes no move and sits
as were he planted
ages long gone by. Nothing here
is more sure than this—
each looks at each across
a bottomless abyss.

1960

Eine Kleine Nachtmusik

Here on this abandoned, night-held road deep
in the wood, snow imprisons all the cusped moon's light
and makes of this remote and shimmering space
an intimate, enchanting place,
makes iridescent this corner of the night.

All earth is still, the wood's asleep,
but I stand here beside the trees
and look far in. Something is here that calls
me to come in, yet something other keeps me where
I am, standing in the chill, hushed air,
as if between the wood and me were walls
only sight could breach. Something inside sees
deep, each to each, and what is here
between the sickle moon so wan above,
shining like foxfire on this forgotten lane,
speaks with fierce joy akin to pain,
circumscribing birth and death with love,
speaks with a voice no ear can hear.

I will stand here a little while and look,
I will stand here now and see,
until what gazes out from deep inside
and recognizes what verities do here abide
speaks from lonely place to lonely deep, of windy tree
and man and mute, white snow, of leaf and brook.

I have not far to go
to children, home, to bed and book;
I will not step inside the virgin snow
or violate my own deep lonely place. I will only stand a while and look.

1960

In the End Was His Beginning

Henry David Thoreau
July 12, 1817-May 6, 1862

The neighbor's children passed the house.
Why don't they come to see me?" he said
to birdsong and the stirring of a mouse.
"I love them as if they were my own." He read
the morning star, the sunrise, the crying
of a meadow lark on the brightening edge of day.
Sam Staples said, "Never saw a man dying
with so much pleasure and peace." Time ticked on its way,
at Walden, at Fair Haven, and in the town
where his steps had scarcely ceased to stir the dust.
To that one who stood beside him looking down
and asked, "Have you made your peace with God?" he must
make such an answer as he did: "I did not know
that we had quarreled." And had he thought
about the other world? Light made show
in his reply: "One world at a time!" They ought
to have known him better after forty years—
surveyor of forest paths, bridges, dells and ravines,
inspector of snowstorms, student of wild careers
and hidden ways, knowing where the sassafras leans
upon the air, and the wild duck reared her young,
caretaker of beanrows and the bumblebee . . .
"I regret nothing," his words true on the tongue,
as the wind in the loneliest Concord tree.
The sun came. He spoke of moose
and Indians. At nine that May morning quietly, he died.
None knew his end was not yet to be. Children were loose
upon the town. Outside, a robin cried.

1965

Morel Morning

Neighbor to orchid and Solomon's Seal,
they came over night, each six inches high
and bearing a little of the night still
in the feel of cool flesh when I pick them.
Nearby a whippoorwill starts up from its nest
soundlessly and a pewee cry inquires
what I am about where I stand
laved by the soft wind out of the west
in the dew-wet plum-blossom morning
holding morels in my fingers,
smelling the musk of semen spilling out,
as always, old leaves and soil, the sweet land—
and remembering last year you were along
on such a morning, picking morels, too—
and the hour is suddenly charged with love
as were I speaking to you of all
that binds us each to each through
the morels thickly phallic in my hand.

1966

A Little Elegy for My Father

William J. Derleth: 1883-1965

The echo of his whistling at work
stalks the rooms of this house he built,
like a ghost never to be laid.
How he loved the feel of wood
in his hands! He built to last.
Strange in this house he wrought
with such capable hands
to think of him as past.

He who was yesterday is gone today:
what he left stands.
He loved work; he must be doing,
shaping, building, repairing,
with the same hands that now and then held
a small boy's fishpole, patient with his son
impatient for Wisconsin sunfish,
bluegills,—strong wandering the hills
for butternuts, hickorynuts, wild cherries.

I hear his whistle echo still, bell-clear.
Oak and pine give it back,
with a tantalizing hint
of the smoke from his cigar.
In all he did, love was understood,
as tangible as wind's rune in the aspen tree,
the saw's song cutting through the wood
against his knee.

"We listen to the dead.
We are sure they will not deceive us . . .
with words unbiased by greed, love, anger."

1967

I listen, Father.
I listen, listen, and I hear
the echo of that whistling joy
in work, sweetening life
for man and boy. I listen, Father. Speak,
who said enough in happiness at work
to make the lesson clear.

Apologia

Early, early in my young and tender years
led astray by wind and air, by lonesome water
talking to the core inside, charmed away
by sunlight dappling pond and forest floor—

oh, early, early drawn from phantom fame
and siren wealth by grace of tree and hill,
wind's rune in the aspens, pale flame of dawn,
the April promise of new moon and evening star,
the robin's matins and far, the solitary whippoorwill,
song sparrow's threnody, the pewee's pensive cry,
nighthawk's sky-coasting and the lyrics
of the hermit thrush—

early bewitched by the unplumbed well of night
and the spill of owl call, the bell-voiced hylas
and the trill of toadsong—early, oh early
fallen to the spell of hawks aloft, riding wind
and the invisible currents of air,
and no less to nature's aloof disposal of the plans
of men as well as those of mice—

1969

early, early lost to the affairs of men in worlds
away from all green and sunlit days,
enticed away by wild plum and cherry, and the ways
of ant and bee, by cowslips and wild roses,
violets and columbines, strange mushrooms;
drowned in lilac fragrance and sweet fern,
caught up in arrogance of crows, by wild geese over,
the towering majesty of thunderheads and storm,
by fireflies in clover, by boneset purpling meadows—

early enchanted by sunset and afterglow,
the witchery of northern lights, by rain and snow
and the solitudes of men; early, early
in my young and tender years; trading avarice
and the show of ownership, the mean pursuits of envy
and of greed for quiet valor and for love,
for hawk's eminence on the high, blue stair
of heaven, for the least blade of grass,
the last pedal of flower, for earth and running water,
for wind and all green and gold leaf-hushing air.

Juveniles

from The Moon Tenders

THAT EVENING WE reached Bogus Bluff. We saw it first when we came around a curve in the Wisconsin and passed between two large sand bars still gleaming in the light of the westering sun. There it was, straight ahead of us, on the west bank of the Wisconsin where the river turned south once more. It was a tree-girt hill, with some rock showing near the crown. The mouth of the cave was plain to see among the trees from this distance, but as we drew closer, it fell behind the treetops and was hidden.

Filled with visions of that Fort Winnebago gold lying somewhere there just waiting for us to find it, we did everything we could to hurry the raft along. Even so, it was the edge of dusk when we tied up along the shore just below the bluff. It loomed over us, almost straight up, separated from us by a road that went past, and the wooded stretch between the road and the water's edge.

Sim leaned his head back and looked straight up the bluff. "Maybe we better wait till morning to go up to the cave," he said. "We're in strange country. Looks like rattlesnake country, too."

"Why wait?" I wanted to know. "We got flashlights. And there seems to be a path of some kind."

We took a couple of sandwiches—the last of those Great-aunt Lou had made for us to take along—and set out. The sun had just gone down and there was still plenty of light. Besides, as long as the sky was clear, the moon would soon be giving its light, and it wouldn't be as if we had to proceed in pitch blackness.

There were three trails up the bluff. At first, what we thought was the trail that led straight up turned out to be a cow path that angled over to the side. We found a better trail coming up on the northeast side, and it was that one we followed. It looked as if people came in from the yard of an abandoned pasture shed and went up the bluff. Sim looked at it close once or twice as we went along, beginning the steep climb. Then he stopped.

Bogus Bluff, 1958

"I though your grandpa Adams said people didn't come here much any more," he said.

"He did. Used to be a place to go when people didn't have anything but horses and buggies."

"Well, look at this. Leaves turned. Twigs broken." He pointed them out. "Somebody's been using this path lately. Looks to be quite a lot, too."

I examined the evidence. Someone had been passing up and down the old trail. Yet there was every sign to show that the trail had been unused for a long time—little runnels of erosion right in the middle of it, for instance—until recently.

I dropped to my knees and turned on my flashlight. I crawled forward a little way. I studied the footprints, wherever I could find them. Here and there I found fairly clear prints in the sandy loam. There were also cow tracks.

"Well, it's not kids," I said. "The footprints are too big. I'd say two men—one heavy, one light."

Sim peered over my shoulder. "That's elementary," he said.

"Anyway, the last footprints lead down—so we don't have to worry about them."

"You don't suppose the heavy one was carrying the Winnebago gold, do you?" asked Sim, grinning.

"You'll laugh out of the other side of your mouth if we do find it," I said. "Come on."

We pushed on up the steep hill that seemed almost as broad as it was high.

Bushes and treetops pretty well screened the mouth of the cave when you looked up toward it. It opened right out of the rock, and the last ten feet or so were the hardest part of the climb. From the mouth, I looked back and saw the broad Wisconsin, with the two sandbars still showing sunlight and the bottomland trees a green sea on both sides of the river.

It was dusk at the cave. I turned on my flashlight. You could walk into the cave, the mouth was that wide. A lot of earlier visitors had cut marks into the rock on both sides. "Sue and Elmer," I read, "July, 1871." And "Jo, Mattie, and Chris, May 11, 1901."—"I met Molly here Aug. 7, 1899. Came back on honeymoon, June 10, 1900. Elgin Platt." And hundreds of other names and dates carved into the soft stone.

"Lookin' for somebody you know?" asked Sim. "Or can we go in?"

"Grandpa Adams always says it takes a special kind of fool to carve his name in a place like this."

"Or somebody showing off for his girl," said Sim. "Go on in. You can take all day tomorrow to read what's on the walls. I don't know, Steve, but you got too much curiosity."

"I like to know about everything," I admitted.

We walked into the cave. About thirty feet back it began to narrow. We dropped to our knees and began to crawl. It was damp and cool-smelling, as if springs or some other running water wasn't very far away.

After a little way on our knees the cave got higher again. At the same time, we came up against three openings.

"Now what?" asked Sim.

"You take the right one, I'll take the left," I said. "Crawl as far as you can go, then come back here and we'll both take the middle. If you find anything, holler."

Sim turned off into the one passage, and I took the other way from the main cave.

I crawled until I came to another opening out of the hill. I could look down the river from it, and figured I was on the south side. I turned around and went back.

Sim was just coming out of his passage when I came back into the main cave.

"Just a lateral" he said. "I came out on the north side."

"I came out, too," I said. "It's only a narrow passageway."

"Same here."

We turned into the main cave once more and went on, still on our knees. We came to another room, not quite high enough to stand up in, and crouched through it, to the opening at the far end. Then we had to crawl again. We crawled until we came to a place where the passage began to widen once more. Just when we thought we would be able to stand up again, we came up against a wall of rock.

I examined the side walls carefully. The more I looked, the more disappointed I felt.

"I don't know where the soldiers'd find a place to hide the gold here," I said.

"Was it soldiers?" insisted Sim.

"Well, it was soldier's pay—must have been a detachment bringing it up from Fort Crawford at Prairie du Chien. What difference does it make, anyway? This wall's solid. Whenever I find a chink in it, it's hardly big enough for my hand."

"How much gold you figure it was?"

I shrugged. "Oh, I don't know."

"How many soldiers were at Fort Winnebago at that time?"

"Two or three companies," I said. "Everything I read about the Black Hawk War tells about two companies coming from Winnebago. They'd hardly have left less than one company to hold the fort, would they? Then there'd be officers and the regular help at the fort and the Indian Agency?"

Sim did some silent computing. "Well, that might come to quite a lot of money," he admitted.

"That's what I said," I answered.

Sim began to flash his light around. "But there wasn't anything in that book that said they hid the gold here, was there?" he demanded.

"Not exactly, no. It just said it was around here that the boat was sunk. So they went ashore with the gold and hid it. The book says, 'on or in the vicinity of Bogus Bluff.' That's the story."

"But was it true?"

Sometimes Sim could be the most trying person on earth. He always had to know every last detail. He called it "the scientific method," and he thought as much of his science books as of the Bible.

"It didn't have any footnotes on it, if that's what you mean," I said. "If all the soldiers got killed and the gold was never found, who do you suppose could prove it?"

"Oh, that's simple. They'd have some record of it at Fort Crawford, and that would be passed down. All you'd have to do would be check back."

"You mean, write the War Department down in Washington and have them look it up? Fort Crawford's been abandoned sixty, seventy years—it'd take years for the government even to find out there was such a fort in Wisconsin Territory."

Sim didn't answer. His light wasn't moving, either. I looked over at him. The light was directed down at a sizable cedar branch lying over against the wall at the end of the cave, and he was peering at it with frowning attention. His lean, hawklike face was all scrounged up to show that he was thinking.

"What's up?" I asked.

"Now that's a funny thing," he said. When Sim said "funny" he meant "strange," unlike the rest of us to whom "funny" meant something to laugh at most of the time. "What's that cedar limb doing here?"

"Somebody dropped it," I said. "You know how people are always breaking off branches. They carry them around till they get tired of 'em, then they just drop them wherever they are."

Sim shook his head. "No, this limb's too big for that. Besides, you know how hard it is to break cedar. This one's been cut. It's all dirty on the branches, too. It's been used for something."

"Maybe somebody brushed the cobwebs off the wall," I said.

Sim just shrugged.

I shot my light down, too. "Look at the marks on the floor," I said. "Somebody's been brushing the floor with that cedar limb, that's what."

"What for?"

"Why, to hide something," I said, excited now. "Maybe that's where the gold's buried!"

Sim laughed.

"Laugh!" I said. "I'll be the one who laughs last."

"You and your imagination!" said Sim.

"You and being practical!" I retorted.

Just the same, when I simmered down and looked at it, of course the cedar branch would never hide anything except maybe marks of some kind in the sandy floor—the sandstone worn away from the rock in all these years to lie as a thin covering on the floor of the cave. Something like an outline marking the place where something had been buried—that cheered me a little. But most likely it was just to erase what somebody had scrawled into the sand. Or maybe just footprints.

"Footprints," I said. "See."

I took the branch, turned around, and swished it over the sand, obliterating my footprints.

"But why?" asked Sim.

I put the branch back. Sim turned his light on the back wall and began to scrutinize it.

"If you can wait, Sherlock," I said, "I'll fun back to the raft and try to find our magnifying glass."

He paid no attention. He turned around, picked up a fair-sized stone, and began to pound on the back wall. The wall was a kind of limestone—not so soft as that used at the lime kiln at Mill Bluff—maybe part sandstone.

"It sounds hollow," said Sim finally. "Could be there's another room in back—another cave."

"Then that's where the gold must be," I said.

"Sim had been crawling along the wall. Now he stopped at one corner where the rocky side wall was especially craggy. "Hey!" he cried out. "These stones are fitted. Hold your light up here."

I turned my light on the wall, while he put his light out and slipped it into his pants pocket. While I held the light, he worked away at the back wall. He had hold of a good-sized slab of rock. It was plain, after only a few moments, that he was moving it.

I looked around for something to prop my light on. There was a little projecting ledge up the wall just about level with the place where Sim worked, so I put the flashlight on that. It threw a steady glow on the back wall. Then I gave Sim a hand.

The slab of rock came out.

We put it down on the floor at the side of the cave. Sim took out his flashlight once more and shot it through the hole we had made. He let out a whistle of astonishment. I crowed close and peered over his shoulder.

The light fell upon a lot of things no one would ever expect to find in a cave—a table, rickety chairs, pots, what looked like machinery of some kind—just the kind of stuff you'd think kids would get together and put into a hut in the woods somewhere. I'd found it a half-a-dozen times on Third Island or on Bergen's or in the bottoms woods near the brook coming down from behind Roxbury—lugged in by kids and abandoned.

"Kid stuff," I said disgustedly.

Sim put out his flashlight and put it back into his pocket. "Let's move a few more of these stones," he said. He couldn't help jeering. "You and your men, one heavy, one light! A fat boy and a thin one, most likely.

I didn't say anything. By the glow from the flashlight on the ledge we cleared a door-sized opening right down to the cave floor. Then I picked up the flashlight and we went into the real rear of the Bogus Bluff cave.

Sim's light flickered over everything. It fell on an old cane rocking chair. He promptly sat down in it.

"Here's solid comfort," he said. "Or would be, if I had more bottom to fit the chair. This is the fat boy's chair," he decided.

I kept on looking around. My light fell on a pile of blankets all laid out on the floor. Pillows, too. "Look at that," I said. "Sometimes they even sleep here."

But of course boys slept in the log huts they made in the woods around Sac Prairie, too. That was part of the fun of it—no mother, no father, nobody around to say "Do this," "Do that," or "Don't, don't, don't!" Almost every kid I knew who had any ambition or any self-reliance went into the woods at some time or other to came out at least, if he didn't build himself a hut with the help of a few other kids.

Sim got out of the chair and gazed at the blanks. "It's pretty damp to be sleeping in here," he said.

"Not for just once in a while," I said. "You have to get used to things like that when you're not home.

"I can see your ma or mine letting us do that," said Sim.

"I, too."

"There's a funny smell in here," Sim went on.

"The whole place smells," I said. "It's not just one smell—it's a whole lot of 'em. Something real sharp—metallic like."

"And something that smells like an old battery," added Sim.

"You know how kids lug those things around. Smells like they've been smoking, too. Cigars, at that." I had to laugh. "Every little kid think's he's a man as soon as he can put a cigarette in his mouth—the poor dumb shoat!"

"They've got more junk here than I ever saw in a hut," said Sim. "But no sign of your treasure. Maybe they found it."

"If they did, they wouldn't be here."

"They aren't."

"Don't be so encouraging," I said. "Nobody knows how long this place has been empty."

"Would it still smell like this if it had been empty a long time?" wondered Sim.

"How would the smell get out, with the wall shut off like that? Leave those stones down for a while, and all you'll get in here is that wet ground smell you always find in caves."

"There's a draft," said Sim. "That means openings somewhere."

"There wouldn't be a draft with the wall up."

Sim had turned his flashlight from the blankets. The light now lay on the table. There were two kitchen chairs drawn up to it. Like the table, they looked like junk-heap discards.

"Where do you suppose they got all this stuff?" asked Sim. "Looks like chunks of metal."

It did, too. What was on the table was the strangest mixture of stuff I ever saw. I couldn't imagine what kids might be doing with it. Chunks of metal. An iron pan that looked as if it had had fire in it many times. Other iron pans, smaller in size, which had been used to boil something in; they were all discolored inside. But what had been boiled hadn't been something to eat, because there were pieces of kitchenware stacked to one side. There were tools there, too. Some were like needles with handles on. Some were more blunt. Some seemed to be carving tools. Two or three had the look of being used to stamp designs.

"Dies," said Sim.

"Kids'll pick up anything," I said. "It takes a while to grow before they become selective—like your and me."

"I think these kids are up to something," said Sim.

"Most kids are up to something. We weren't any different when we were younger—except that you were always going on about being caught and never got to do much."

"Ha! Have your little joke," said Sim.

He examined the tools with puzzled interest.

I flashed my light all around. The rear part of the cave was the best part of the Bogus Bluff cavern. I wondered how it could have been sealed off like this without somebody noticing, but then I reasoned that if few people came up here anymore, there wouldn't be anyone to know the difference. Besides, most of the visitors probably wouldn't go much beyond the laterals.

My light fell upon a folded newspaper stuck behind a box against the wall. I went over and pulled it out.

"Here's a copy of the Chicago *American*," I said.

"What's the date on it?"

"Wait till I read *Krazy Kat*," I said. I read the comic strip and had a good laugh. Then I looked at the date. "May seventeenth, this year."

Sim thought about this for a while. "Well, I suppose Gotham or Muscoda boys get to see a Chicago paper just the way we do in Sac Prairie," He said. "Anything else back there?"

I looked. There were a few more newspapers pushed back there. There was also a copy of *The Atlantic Monthly*. And a badly worn book, *Essays of Emerson*, which I knew practically by heart. Next to *Walden*, it was one of my favorite books.

Sim stared, jaw agape. *"The Atlantic Monthly!"* he exclaimed. "That don't add up."

"What's the matter with it?" I asked. "I look at Grandpa's copies once in a while."

"I can't figure out what kind of kid would come up here to live in a cave and read such a magazine," he said.

That made sense.

"And Emerson to boot! Say, there's something mighty fishy about all this."

"Who's got the imagination now?" I wanted to know. "The kids might have picked up the magazine and the book the same way they got everything else they lugged up here."

"Funny papers, maybe—but not *The Atlantic Monthly*."

"Maybe they couldn't find any funny papers," I said. "They aren't all as lucky as we were. Shumow's had their junk yard only a block from our house, and I could go down there any time with Sollie and they'd give me funny papers. My aunt Bertha keeps sending them down from Minnesota to this day—about every two weeks I get a pack. So maybe they couldn't find funny papers."

"What issue of the magazine is it?"

"June," I said. "This month."

"They never found that on a junk pile."

"Well, could be somebody gets it."

"There'd be a label on it—you know, an address label."

I examined the magazine carefully by flashlight. There was no mailing label on it.

Sim came over and looked through the newspapers.

"No label here, either. They didn't get these at home, then," he said. "They weren't discarded by a drugstore or anybody else that sells papers, either," he went on, "because they always have to cut off the top of the front page and send it in for credit. These are whole."

"Couldn't they buy 'em?"

"Kids buy papers?" he said scornfully. "Not when they can buy ice-cream cones."

"Their folks might have bought 'em," I said.

"Speaking of ice cream cones," Sim said, "I'm getting hungry." He took his sandwich out of his pocket, unwrapped it, and began to eat.

I followed his example.

"We'd better get back to the raft and make camp," I said between mouthfuls. "We can camp right on shore. Then tomorrow, we can really begin to hunt the whole bluff top to bottom."

Sim might just as well have been in another world. "I can't figure this out," he said. "It wouldn't be like kids. Maybe you were right, Steve, about those footprints."

"Sure I was right," I answered confidently. "But anybody could've made them any part of the day."

He finished his sandwich and was just about to throw the wrapper away when he thought better of it. He began to fold it up. "Better not leave anything here," he said. "You never can tell."

I bent and retrieved the wrapping I had dropped.

"Do we put back the stones?" I asked. "I suppose we'd better."

"Sure," said Sim.

"It's a lot of work," I said. "We could come back in the morning and do it."

Just then my flashlight went out.

"There goes your battery," said Sim. "Lucky we got more on the raft."

"Your own's getting a little weak, too," I said. "We'd better get out while we still have a little light left."

"Well, well," said a rich, oily voice out of the darkness behind us, "it seems we have visitors, Mr. Tom."

Sim turned and shot his light at the opening we had made in the wall.

It was filled. Two men stood there, looking in.

Beast Signs

FOR A LONG moment neither of us said anything.

Then Banny shrugged nonchalantly and said, "Ja, I guess we are."

"You're Dora Carey," I said. "I've seen you in school."

"Dody," she said scornfully. "Nobody calls me 'Dora.'" She jumped from the limb on which she had been sitting. She was a little shorter than I, but about as tall as Banny. "What're you doing out in the woods?"

"Hiking," I said quickly, before Banny could give us away.

Banny was blushing. I could hardly believe it. He was acting like a kid. Blushing!

"Hiking!" she said. Then she laughed.

It antagonized me. I held my tongue, though, and it was a good thing Banny was sort of hypnotized.

"I could think of half a dozen better places than this to hike without even waking up," she said.

I could see she was the kind of girl who didn't care what she said.

Banny found his tongue. "Well, we were sort of trying to get to Lily Lake overland."

"Oh, is that it. Well, then, just follow me."

She started off at an angle from where we stood, Banny after her. I had no choice but to follow. We were backtracking. We had gone past the lakes, just as I had figured, but out of sight of them.

I could tell she knew these woods. She never made a false start. She seemed to know where every swale was and went around without having to try the way first. It wasn't until we had the lake in sight that she began to falter.

"What's the matter?" I asked. "You lost?"

"No," she said. "I just wanted to make sure."

"How come you knew the woods we came through so well, and you don't know this part?"

"My grandma lives back there," she said.

"In the woods?"

"Sure," she said. "She likes the woods better than town."

She stopped now, so suddenly, that Banny ran into her.

The Beast in Holger's Woods, 1968

"There," she said, pointing to where we could see the blue water. "That's the lake."

"Thanks," I said and walked around her, poking Banny, who was still standing still.

"Anytime you're lost," she called after us, "just holler."

"Thanks," I said again.

"Keep your ears open," said Banny.

He meant it, too. You'd think he was expecting to get lost again, as if we hadn't fumbled enough already.

"Come on, come on," I said. "We're losing time."

I risked looking back. She was standing there watching us. She was certainly pretty enough, but her eyes seemed to be laughing at us and there was a sort of half-smile on her lips.

"She's sure easy to look at," said Banny.

"Skin deep," I said.

We lost sight of her. Banny looked back once or twice, but since he couldn't see her any longer, he got back to work looking for tracks or anything he could find. The lake was only a little way ahead; already we were in soft ground. There, if anywhere, we should have seen prints if any large animal had been in the area. There was nothing, not even a human footprint until we left ours.

We began to go north around the lake, back from the shore. The trees and bushes were thicker there. It was hard going, but it was a likely place for an animal to hide out.

Banny stopped short. "Hey! Look at that!"

I look where he pointed. Through an opening in the brush he had caught sight of an arrow-shaped sign pointing toward the lake. It had been there a long time, for it was weather-beaten, and the stake that held it leaned crazily.

The sign read *Cook Lake.*

"That Dody's not so smart, after all," said Banny.

"Lily Lake can't be any wilder than this," I said.

Just then I caught sight of something stuck to a pine tree, right to the rough bark. It was a tuft of fur, black fur, on the trunk as high up as my shoulder.

I went over to it. Only a big animal of some kind could have left it. Like a bear. Now and then somebody reported a black bear in the woods around Rhinelander. Once they had been common—when the pine forests were still all over northern Wisconsin; now they were rare. It could have been a black bear.

Banny came over. "That's it!" he said excitedly when he saw the tuft of fur. "Only something as big or bigger than a man could have left that there."

"I don't know," I said.

"Oh, you're always looking for anything but the obvious answer," said Banny impatiently.

I broke away a little of the bark and carefully took out the tuft of hair. It looked as if a piece of skin was still attached to the root of it. But it wasn't fresh. Yet, since it had been fairly loosely lodged in the bark, it couldn't be very old.

"I'll just take this along," I said.

"This is the place to look for tracks," said Banny.

He dropped to his hands and knees and began to crawl all over the ground around the tree. But it was all brush and pine needles, and dry. There wasn't a chance that there would be a print of any kind.

I pointed this out to him.

"I'm looking for bear sign," he retorted. "If we can be sure it was a bear, then we know it's not the animal we want. Cliff said it wasn't a bear—or anything he ever saw before."

I looked at the trees. The one I had taken the tuft from hadn't been used as a rubbing tree. Neither had any other tree I could see nearby. It was possible the bear had come up against the tree so hard as to lose some of its fur, but it hardly seemed likely without some of the bark being torn off. And the only bark torn off I had taken off myself.

Banny was scrambling about on all sides. He wasn't finding a thing. He could hardly have expected to, the ground being so dry. But his imagination wouldn't let him think so.

The tuft of hair bothered me. It was coarse and it felt like bear hair. It wasn't fresh enough to have been left there recently, and it was too loose to have been there long.

I tried to halt Banny long enough to let him know what I was thinking.

"I don't know what's the matter with you, for a fact," he said, without getting up from his knees. "We came out here looking for proof that Cliff saw some kind of animal, and we got it."

"No such thing," I said.

"You think a bird left that there?"

"No," I said, "but it doesn't prove that Cliff saw a big animal."

"It came from an animal, didn't it?"

I had to admit that.

"Well, that's enough for me."

"Not for me," I said.

"That's the trouble with being so practical. You can reason yourself right out of the evidence."

There was no use saying anything. Banny had made up his mind that we had evidence. It *was* evidence, but not of what Banny thought.

"At least," I said, "you might stop that silly horsing around here in the dry woods and get to some softer place where a print would be likely to take. You won't find anything here."

Banny stopped long enough to think that over. He had by this time covered a good-sized circle around the tree. After a while he scrambled reluctantly to his feet.

"Sometimes you make sense," he said.

He walked back to the place where I had taken the tuft of fur off the pine, and stood looking at it and trying to take a line from it.

"If that thing, whatever it was, bear or else, left fur here, he was going either this way or that way," he said.

I could hardly argue about that.

"That means," Banny went on, "if he was anywhere near the lake, it would be over there."

He pointed ahead a little way, following the animal's imaginary line—the line Banny imagined. It intersected the lakeshore not far away. I didn't say anything, but it didn't seem likely that a bear or any other animal would be traveling in a straight line, short of following a trail, and there was no evidence of a trail anywhere. That animal could have been wandering around in all sorts of patterns and directions.

Having decided, however, Banny set out along the line as he saw it, keeping his eyes open for any other evidence.

I took a parallel course, so as to cover as much territory as possible, and followed him.

It wasn't until Banny got close to the lake that he saw anything. He had reached a little open place where patchy reeds were growing. I saw right away that somebody or something had been through it not long ago—the reeds were broken down and there were places where the grass had been pressed down and away.

"Look at that!" cried Banny triumphantly, pointing down ahead of him.

He stood on the edge of a bare place of muck and sand.

There was a print there, a paw print. It was bigger than a bear's. And it went in deeper, I thought, unless the ground there had been wetter when it was made. And you could see great long claw prints in front and at both sides of it, longer than I had ever seen before.

"That's it," said Banny, just dancing with excitement. "That's it, all right."

I wasn't so sure.

"What's the matter?" asked Banny. "Did you ever see a print like that before?"

I had to admit I hadn't.

But the more I looked at it the more puzzled I got. It was a crazy kind of print, because the paw was pressed in good and pretty sharp, but the claw prints were hardly more than scratches.

Banny said. "You don't believe it."

"I see it," I said. "But I can't figure it out."

"It's that hodag come to life," cried Banny.

"That hodag was a humbug."

"Well, this is here. You see it. You can touch it."

"It's what I see I can't figure out," I said. "Take a good look at that print."

But Banny had wandered a little further along the swale, and now he sang out again. "Here's another one!"

I went over and looked at it. It was just like the first.

"What I mean," I went on, "is that if an animal with claws like that were walking along in this soft ground, the claws would've cut in more."

Banny gave me a baffled look. "You're always talking about my imagination. What about yours?"

"It's not imagination," I said. "It's scientific fact."

Banny just looked painfully tolerant.

"Look at your own footprint," I said. "Right there. What comes out the strongest? It's the ball of your foot, not your heel."

Banny shook his head. "I don't dig you, Rick. Here we go looking for evidence and we find it and you start doubting it."

"There's all kinds of evidence," I said. Dad being a lawyer, I knew it.

"Let's start with Cliff Potter's story. He said he saw a beast of some kind he never saw before somewhere hereabouts. Now we've got a footprint we never saw before. That adds up."

"It adds up to something, all right," I agreed. "I just don't know what. It won't figure up for me."

I got down on my knees beside the paw print and took a good look at it. Judging by the size of it, there never was a bigger animal in the woods around Rhinelander. The print, counting the claws, was a good foot across. It was fuzzy at the edges, strong only in the middle, and deeper at the forward end rather than at the back. It was the strangest paw print I ever saw.

"Let's try to track it," said Banny.

He was off at once, along the way the beast might have gone. He found three more prints, and I looked at each one in turn. They were all alike—deep in the center and forward, toward the ball of the foot. By that time we were out of the soft ground and there wasn't anything more to be seen.

"I don't like it," I said.

"Scared?" jeered Benny.

"No. It's just that I never saw an animal track like it. I mean, it's not the way animals walk. Not at all. An animal print spreads out, with the walking weight on the toes, and it leaves strong claw prints. Come over here—I saw coon prints—and see what I mean."

Banny followed me. The coon prints were little prints—like the prints of long, miniature hands, delicate and clear. The claws showed plain all the way to the end.

We might have gone on arguing for a while longer if I hadn't heard the rustling of leaves off to one side of us.

Banny heard it, too. He froze.

"It's back there," he whispered.

Whatever it was, it was moving.

"Let's get up a tree," said Banny. "I'm not hankering to come up against Cliff's beast."

I shook my head. "It's not that big."

We stood listening.

Whatever it was, it was moving with some caution.

"Come on," I said, starting out toward the place I last heard the sound of movement.

"Wait," said Banny. "Take it easy."

"I'm just going back to take another look at one of those prints," I said. "I just thought of something else."

I headed for the place where the prints showed.

When I got there, I looked at the pattern of the prints. Just as I had at first only fleetingly noticed, they were pretty much in a straight line—more like the prints of a two-legged animal, not four. The beast didn't walk like a bear.

I pointed that out to Banny.

"Now, look," said Banny. "You don't believe it in the first place and now you're trying to say how it walks." He pointed to the nearest footprint with a big flourish; Banny liked to be dramatic. "You believe what you see, don't you?"

"I believe that," I said. "Trouble is, I think you and I believe different things. For instance, if that thing's as big as that footprint suggests, we ought to see some other evidence of its passage, shouldn't we?"

"Like what?" demanded Banny.

"Oh, like scraped bark and broken twigs and limbs."

Banny's glance darted all around, sort of jabbing into the woods here and there. Right off he found a broken twig. He bounded over and took hold of it in triumph.

"There!" he said, as if it were all the proof anybody in his right mind would need.

"Anything as big as that ought to leave a trail about six feet wide at least. We can't even see much sign of where it went—just some footprints to show where it put a foot down here and there."

"Well, that's so," agreed Banny reluctantly.

"This is pretty overgrown," I said. "Bushes and stuff all over."

"Anything could hide in it," Banny said.

"Anything could hide forever," I agreed. "But something that'd leave a footprint like that could hardly get through without leaving a trail."

"Unless," said Banny, "it was like Cliff Potter said. But more like a bear—and a bear on all fours isn't so high."

"I though we just demonstrated that whatever it was wasn't walking on all fours," I said.

Banny looked thoughtful. "Well," he said presently, "what do you figure it is?"

"I'm not ready to say."

"Big deal!" said Banny. "You know something I don't know."

I shook my head. "Maybe I don't know as much," I said. "But there's something wrong with this, Banny."

"Show me."

"Don't you feel it?"

Banny shook his head. "I want the evidence."

"It's all around us. I just got through showing you. It doesn't add up to what it's supposed to."

"Let's start from the beginning," said Banny. "Do you believe Cliff Potter saw an animal like he described?"

"It's possible."

"Well, that's something," said Banny. "Do you believe this might be its footprint?"

"It might be."

"Then what's it apt to be?"

"I don't know yet, and suspicions don't count."

Banny looked exasperated. He was getting ready to explode when he heard what I had been hearing and stood with eyes widening and alert.

"There's been something back of us for quite a while," I said, dropping my voice. "I'll give you two guesses."

"Whatever it is, it's not big," said Banny.

He pushed past me and plunged into the underbrush.

I went after him.

I wasn't surprised at what we saw. It was Dody Carey again. She was squatting beside one of those footprints making a drawing of it on a sheet of paper she must have been carrying in a pocket of her jeans. The folds in the paper could be seen even from where we stood.

She never looked up. "So this is what you were hunting for," she said. "I didn't think you were just hiking."

It was a good drawing, butter than I could have done.

"Keen!" said Banny, with admiration written all over his face.

Keen! I could have kicked him.

A Warning from Mrs. Moon

"WHAT'RE YOU DOING that for?" I asked her.

"I'm going to show it to my grandma. She might know what made it." Then she gave me a long level look and said, "But maybe you know?"

"I don't," I said. "Thanks." She had known very well I didn't know any more than she or Banny; she must certainly have heard the two of us talking about the footprints.

"There," she said, "it's finished."

She got up, brushing off her knees. She folded the drawing and slipped it back into her jeans.

"Let us know what she says," said Banny.

"Come along and find out," she said.

Banny was ready to go. He didn't have a speck of pride. He could see I was hanging back, too.

"Come on, come on, Rick." he said impatiently. And then he added, "It's a good thing somebody had sense enough to make a drawing of one of those footprints."

He didn't see the look I gave him. He was already trotting after Dody.

I swallowed my pride and went, too.

The Beast in Holger's Woods, 1968

She went through the woods like a homing bee. Only a little while ago she had got us to Cook Lake instead of Lily Lake; she hadn't known where she was. But now she was going along as if she were on a familiar trail. There were no footprints, but I noticed that her head kept turning this way and that, and saw that she was looking for something. So I did the same thing.

She was backtracking herself. She was doing it by keeping a lookout for turned leaves and brush, a twisted twig here and there where she had marked the way she went. I had to admire the way she did it.

In no time at all we were back where she had originally left us.

"Boy, that was fast!" cried Banny. "I don't see how you did it. Why, you led us to Cook Lake before, not Lily."

Banny would say it. I flashed her a quick look, but there wasn't any resentment in her blue eyes.

"Dumb, wasn't it?" she said cheerfully. "We've still got over a mile to go." She pushed on.

This time she knew her terrain without looking for signs. We crossed a brook on a fallen tree that been used for crossing many times before. We jumped a creek at a narrow bend that had the marks of being narrowed for just that purpose.

We followed a winding trail, but never once crossed a road other than a long-abandoned logging road. Then suddenly we burst into a little clearing in the middle of which stood a tight little cabin faced with pine slabs. It was an old building, weather-beaten, with a few flowers growing in front, and a garden out in back.

There was a cane rocking chair as old as the cabin out on a little porch that ran across the front of it. An old woman sat in it, rocking and smoking a corncob pipe! I saw right away that she was an old Indian woman, a Chippewa, for, though she had on a white woman's dress, she still wore some beading and her hair was long and very black.

Dody went right up to her and said, "Grandma, I'm back."

The old lady took the pipe out of her mouth and said, "Hm! Found company, hm?"

Dody introduced us. Her grandmother's name was Mrs. Moon. I figured she was on her mother's side.

Then Dody took the drawing she had made out of her jeans, unfolded it, and put it down in front of her grandmother.

"What kind of animal made that, Grandma?"

The old woman studied it with a baffled look on her face. Then she shook her head. "No such animal," she said.

"Give me your pencil, Dody," I said.

When she handed it to me I walked over and shaded in the indentation at the center and foreground of the imprint. She had forgotten that.

"That's right, Rick," said Dody, watching me.

Mrs. Moon studied it again. Once more she shook her head, firming her lips. "No such animal," she said again. "I never saw such an animal. I never saw such a print."

She looked searchingly at her granddaughter. "Where did you find this?"

Dody gestured in the direction of Cook Lake. "They were in the soft ground near the lake."

Mrs. Moon continued to look at the drawing. She traced it with one dark finger, noting especially the claws. Then she got up unhurriedly, still carrying the paper, and went around the house toward the garden. Reaching there, she got down on her knees, beckoning us to stand near.

She leaned forward on one hand, spread out her other hand, and pressed it into the soft garden ground. Then she flexed it forward, leaning with it, fingers outspread.

"This is the way an animal walks," she said, leaning back again. She tapped the paper. "Not like this. There is no such animal."

What she was telling us was crystal clear. Any animal with claws, even retracted claws, would leave clear prints of the claws digging and cutting into the ground. This print showed no such marks. It was if the claws were only appended and not in the toes proper at all. Mrs. Moon was saying she had never known any animal that would leave such a print.

"That's what I thought," I said, and Dody nodded.

Mrs. Moon, still sitting back on her haunches beside the garden, looked again, very puzzled, at the drawing Dody had made. When she looked at us once more, she was plainly troubled.

"This is bad," she said, tapping the paper again. "You keep away, Dody. And you boys better keep away, too."

"But there was nothing there," said Banny.

She shook her head. "No animal, no." she said. "But something was there to make this print."

She got up and made her way back to the rocker.

Banny was excited. He was on fire to get back into the woods and dare whatever danger was there.

Mrs. Moon wanted to know just where we had seen these "marks." That was what she called them, not "tracks."

Dody did her best to explain.

While she was talking, I thought of the tuft of hair. I took it out of my pocket and put it down on Mrs. Moon's knee, telling her where I had found it. The old lady picked it up and carried it to her eyes, narrowing them to look at it, which made all the wrinkles deepen around her eyes.

"Bear," she said, without hesitation.

Then she examined the piece of hide to which it was attached.

I was pretty sure I know what she would say. I watched her. Impassive as her face was, her eyes were bright and alert. But now once again they grew clouded, as they had when she saw the drawing Dody had made.

"You found this on a tree?" she asked.

"Caught in the bark, yes Ma'am," I said. "Just as if it got torn off when the bear brushed it."

She shook her head. "No bear. This is bear fur, but no bear brushed it off on a tree. It's from a treated bearskin."

With a satisfied nod, she handed the tuft of fur back to me.

"We've got to go back there," Banny said.

"Somebody is making fun," said Mrs. Moon. "Bad fun. You boys had better stay away. The woods are deep. Old Rain Feather had a cabin there long ago. Now there is much underbrush there."

She took up her pipe again.

"We've got to get home," I said. "The sun says it's the middle of the afternoon."

"My stomach told me that a while ago," said Banny. "Just the same, I think we ought to go back there and look around a little more."

"We're going home," I said.

"I'll show you," said Dody.

She took us around the house to a little lane that led in from the west.

"Just follow that road and you'll come to a county trunk. That'll take you up between Cook and Lily lakes and back to the highway."

"Thanks," I said. "See you around."

"Thanks for finding us, Dody," said Banny. He had a genius for saying the wrong thing.

We walked along the lane. It was little more than a wagon track—just enough to bring Mrs. Moon out from town for the summer, with her groceries and whatever else she needed. It was bowered by trees and deeply shaded in many places, which was a good thing because the day had grown very warm.

Banny didn't say anything until we were well away from Mrs. Moon's cabin. Then it was only, "I'm hungry."

"You're always hungry," I said. "But we can eat."

"We sat down on an old log and ate the food Mother had sent along. I gave Banny more than his share of donuts because he liked them so.

Once his hunger was satisfied, however, Banny was all for going back into the woods again.

"Nothing doing," I said. "Not now, anyway. It's beginning to look as if we're on to something a little deeper than we think."

"We can get up to the highway just as easy though the woods."

"You only think so," I said. "You figure Dody'll be back there to find us again if we get lost."

"She knows her way around there better'n we do."

"There," I said. "She ought to—staying there with her grandmother."

"I never knew Dody was part Indian," he went on. "That's probably why she knows the woods so well."

He went on about Dody for half a mile. I lent him one ear. I kept thinking over what we had found in the woods—what Mrs. Moon had said—that there wasn't any animal that made such a footprint as we had found, but that something was there. I figured I knew what she meant, all right. Cliff Potter had seen something, just as we had seen something. He had seen the beast and we had seen its tracks. Cliff had been sure of what he saw, but Mrs. Moon seemed to be equally sure there was no such animal. There was an outside chance that something had come down from Canada, but I wasn't ready to believe that. Some of the Indians used to talk about something they called the "wendigo" up in the Canadian wilderness. It might be something like that. Nobody had ever seen it near Rhinelander, Indian or white man. Maybe a thing like that, if it had paws, walked like a man.

It was late afternoon when we got back to Rhinelander.

I left Banny at his place and headed for the public library.

Mrs. Evans was there. She was a tall, angular woman, and wore spectacles on a gold chain. She frowned every time I took out a detective story and beamed when I settled on a historical novel.

I went straight up to her. "Mrs. Evans, where can I find out something about the wendigo?"

"Whatever is that?"

I tried to explain.

"Oh, superstition!" she said. "I think your best chance of finding something in that field would be in the *Standard Dictionary of Folklore.*

I thanked her.

"Over there, Rick. The second shelf," she directed me.

I found the book and carried it over to one of the tables. I found the entry all right, even if they did spell it "windigo." I read it carefully.

The wendigo, according to the entry, was a man-eating monster of the forest. It was part of the mythology of the Algonquin tribes. According to some beliefs the wendigo was a lost hunter who became cannibalistic, but the Ojibwa believed that it was a genuine ogre. Sometimes it was a giant. But it seemed to be always in the general shape of a man. And there was nothing in the entry about paws or claws or even fur.

I replaced the book, and went back to the desk.

"Did you find it?" asked Mrs. Evans.

"Yes, I did. But it's not what I want, Mrs. Evans. Now I want to learn a little more about the hodag."

Mrs. Evans chuckled. "You really are out after monsters today, Rick," she said. "Look on page thirty-four of *The Rhinelander Story*."

She showed me where that was.

The Rhinelander Story was mostly the history of the town and the area, but you could hardly tells the story of Rhinelander and leave out Gene Shepard and his hodag. There was a picture of it there, all right, and it looked just like the wooden models Banny's dad made. It had long claws on its paws. It looked like a lizard, right enough. The text said it weighed three hundred pounds, was seven feet long and almost three feet tall. It was black and hairy with horns along its spinal ridge. It even had claws for eyebrows, to say nothing of an almost foot-long spike at the end of its tail.

But it walked on four legs. What was in the woods and left that track we had seen walked on only two.

Anyway, Gene Shepard had made it all up. He had gone to the trouble of having a wood-carver make the frame—its spikes were bull horns—the eyebrows were bear claws, the skin was oxhide. He even had rigged it to move and make sounds, and put it on exhibit at county fairs.

Oh, he was a joker, all right! And he made such a hit with it and gave Rhinelander so much publicity, we even called our high school annual *The Hodag*, and our teams "Hodags." But what was in the woods in the vicinity of Cook Lake had nothing to do with Gene Shepard. Maybe Mrs. Moon was right in suggesting that it might be dangerous.

It was almost suppertime when I got home. . . .

Tales of the Weird

The Dweller in Darkness

> Searchers after horror haunt strange, far places. For them are the catacombs of Ptolemais, and the craven mausolea of the nightmare countries. They climb to the moonlit towers of ruined Rhine castles, and falter down black cobwebbed steps beneath the scattered stones of forgotten cities in Asia. The haunted wood and the desolate mountain are their shrines and they linger around the sinister monoliths of uninhabited islands. But the true epicure in the terrible, to whom a new thrill of unutterable ghastliness is the chief end and justification of existence, esteems most of all the ancient, lonely farmhouses of backwoods regions; for there the dark elements of strength, solitude, grotesqueness and ignorance combine to form the perfection of the hideous.
>
> —H. P. Lovecraft

UNTIL RECENTLY, IF a traveler in north central Wisconsin took the left fork at the junction of the Brule River highway and the Chequamegon pike on the way to Pashepaho, he would find himself in country so primitive that it would seen remote from all human contact. If he drove on along the little used road, he might in time pass a few tumble-down shakes where presumably people had once lived and which have long ago been taken back by the encroaching forest; it is not desolate country, but an area thick with growth, and over all its expanse there persists an intangible aura of the sinister, a kind of ominous oppression of the spirit quickly manifest to even the most casual traveler, for the road he has taken becomes ever more and more difficult to travel, and is eventually lost just short of a deserted lodge built on the edge of a clear blue lake around which century-old trees brood eternally, a country where the only sounds are the cries of the owls, the whippoorwills, and the eerie loons at night, and the wind's voice in the trees, and—but is it always the wind's voice in the trees? And who can say whether the snapped twig is the sign of an animal passing—or of something more, some other creature beyond man's ken?

Something Near, 1944

For the forest surrounding the abandoned lodge at Rick's Lake had a curious reputation long before I myself knew it, a reputation which transcended similar stories about similar primeval places. There were odd rumors about something that dwelt in the depths of the forest's darkness—by no means the conventional wild whisperings of ghosts—of something half-animal, half-man, fearsomely spoken of by such natives as inhabited the edges of that region, and referred to only by stubborn head-shakings among the Indians who occasionally came out of that country and made their way south. The forest had an evil reputation; it was nothing short of that; and already, before the turn of the century, it had a history that gave pause even to the most intrepid adventurer.

The first record of it was left in the writings of a missionary on his way through that country to come to the aid of a tribe of Indians reported to the post at Chequamegon Bay in the north to be starving. Fr. Piregard vanished, but the Indians later brought in his effects: a sandal, his rosary, and a prayer-book in which he had written curious words which had been carefully preserved: "I have the conviction that some creature is following me. I thought at first it was a bear, but I am now compelled to believe that it is something incredibly more monstrous than anything of this earth. Darkness is falling, and I believe I have developed a slight delirium, for I persist in hearing strange music and other curious sounds which can surely not derive from any natural source. There is also a disturbing illusion as of great footsteps which actually shake the earth, and I have several times encountered a very large footprint which varies in shape. . . ."

The second record is far more sinister. When Big Bob Hiller, one of the most rapacious lumber barons of the entire midwest, began to encroach upon the Rick's Lake country in the middle of the last century, he could not fail to be impressed by the stand of pine in the area near the lake, and, though he did not own it, he followed the usual custom of the lumber barons and sent his men in from an adjoining piece he did own, under the intended explanation that he did not know where his line ran. Thirteen men failed to return from that first day's work on the edge of the forest area surrounding Rick's Lake; two of their bodies were never recovered; four were found—inconceivable—in the lake, several miles from where they had been cutting timber; the others were discovered at various places in the forest. Hiller thought he had a lumber war on his hands, laid his men off to mislead his unknown opponent, and then suddenly ordered them back to work in the forbidden region. After he had lost five more men, Hiller pulled out, and no hand since his time touched the forest, save for one or two individuals who took up land there and moved into the area.

One and all, these individuals moved out within a short time, saying little, but hinting much. Yet, the nature of their whispered hints was such that they were soon forced to abandon any explanation; so incredible were the tales they told, with overtones of something too horrible for description, of age-old evil which had preceded anything dreamed of by even the most learned archeologist. Only one of them vanished, and no trace of him was ever found. The others came back out of the forest and in the course of time were lost somewhere among other people in the United States—all save a half-breed known as Old Peter, who was obsessed with the idea that there were mineral deposits in the vicinity of the wood, and occasionally went to camp on its edge, being careful not to venture in.

It was inevitable that the Rick's Lake legends would ultimately reach the attention of Professor Upton Gardner of the State university; he had completed collections of Paul Bunyan, Whiskey Jack and Hodag tales, and was engaged upon a compilation of place legends when he first encountered the curious half-forgotten tales that emanated from the region of Rick's Lake. I discovered later that his first reaction to them was one of casual interest; legends abound in out-of-the-way places, and there was nothing to indicate that these were of any more import than others. True, there was no similarity in the strictest sense of the word to the more familiar tales; for, while the usual legends concerned themselves with ghostly appearances of men and animals, lost treasure, tribal beliefs, and the like, those of Rick's Lake were curiously unusual in their insistence upon utterly outre creatures—or a "creature"—since no one had ever reported seeing more than one even vaguely in the forest's darkness, half-man, half-beast, with always the hint that this description was inadequate in that it did injustice to the narrator's concept of what it was that lurked there in the vicinity of the lake. Nevertheless, Professor Gardner would in all probability have done little more than add the legends as he heard them to his collection, if it had not been for the reports—seemingly unconnected—of two curious facts, and the accidental discovery of a third.

The two facts were both newspaper accounts carried by Wisconsin papers within a week of each other. The first was a terse, half-comic report headed: *Sea Serpent in Wisconsin Lake?*, and read: "Pilot Joseph X. Castleton, on test flight over northern Wisconsin yesterday, reported seeing a large animal of some kind bathing by night in a forest lake in the vicinity of Chequamegon. Castleton was caught in a thundershower and was flying low at the time, when, in an effort to ascertain his whereabouts, he looked down when lightning flashed, and saw what appeared to be a very large animal rising from the waters of the lake below him, and vanish into the forest. The pilot added no details to his story, but asserts that the creature he saw was not the Loch Ness monster." The second story was the utterly fantastic tale of the discovery of the body of Fr. Piregard, well-preserved, in the hollow trunk of a tree along the Brule River. At first called a lost member of the Marquette-Joliet Expedition, Fr. Piregard was quickly identified. To this report was appended a frigid statement by the President of the State Historical Society dismissing the discovery as a hoax.

The discovery Professor Gardner made was simply that an old friend was actually the owner of the abandoned lodge and most of the shore of Rick's Lake.

The sequence of events was thus clearly inevitable. Professor Gardner instantly associated both newspaper accounts with the Rick's Lake legends; this might not have been enough to stir him to drop his researches into the general mass of legends abounding in Wisconsin for specific research of quite another kind, but the occurrence of something even more astonishing sent him posthaste to the owner of the abandoned lodge for permission to take the place over in the interests of science. What spurred him to take this action was nothing less than a request from the curator of the state museum to visit his office late one night and view a new exhibit which had arrived. He went there in the company of Laird Dorgan, and it was Laird who came to me.

But that was after Professor Gardner vanished.

For he did vanish; after sporadic reports from Rick's Lake over a period of three months, all word from the lodge ceased entirely, and nothing further was heard of Professor Upton Gardner.

Laird came to my room at the University Club late one night in October; his frank blue eyes were clouded, his lips tense, his brow furrowed, and there was everything to show that he was in a state of moderate excitation which did not derive from liquor. I assumed that he was working too hard; the first period tests in his University of Wisconsin classes were just over; and Laird habitually took tests seriously—even as a student he had done so, and now as an instructor, he was doubly conscientious.

But it was not that. Professor Gardner had been missing almost a month now, and it was this which preyed on his mind. He said as much in so many words, adding, "Jack, I've got to go up there and see what I can do."

"Man, if the sheriff and the posse haven't discovered anything, what can you do?" I asked.

"For one thing, I know more than they do."

"If so, why didn't you tell them?"

"Because it's not the sort of thing they'd pay any attention to."

"Legends?"

"No."

He was looking at me speculatively, as if wondering whether he could trust me. I was suddenly conscious of the conviction that he did know something which he, at least, regarded with the gravest concern; and at the same time I had the most curious sensation of premonition and warning that I have ever experienced. In that instant the entire room seemed tense, the air electrified.

"If I go up there—do you think you could go along?"

"I guess I could manage."

"Good." He took a turn or two about the room, his eyes brooding, looking at me from time to time, still betraying uncertainty and an inability to make up his mind.

"Look, Laird—sit down and take it easy. That caged lion stuff isn't good for your nerves."

He took my advice; he sat down, covered his face with his hands, and shuddered. For a moment I was alarmed; but he snapped out of it in a few seconds, leaned back, and lit a cigarette.

"You know those legends about Rick's Lake, Jack?"

I assured him that I knew them and the history of the place from the beginning—as much as had been recorded.

"And those stories in the papers I mentioned to you. . . ?"

The stories, too. I remembered since Laird had discussed with me their effect on his employer.

"That second one, about Fr. Piregard," he began, hesitated, stopped. But then, taking a deep breath, he began again. "You know, Gardner and I went over to the curator's office one night last spring."

"Yes. I was east at the time."

"Of course. Well, we went over there. The curator had something to show us. What do you think it was?"

"No idea. What was it?"

"That body in the tree!"

"No!"

"Gave us quite a jolt. There it was, hollow trunk and all, just the way it had been found. It had been shipped down to the museum for exhibition. But it was never exhibited, of course—for a very good reason. When Gardner saw it, he thought it was a waxwork. But it wasn't."

"You don't mean that it was the real thing."

Laird nodded. "I know it's incredible."

"It's just not possible."

"Well, yes, I suppose it's impossible. But it was so. That's why it wasn't exhibited—just taken out and buried."

"I don't quite follow that."

He leaned forward and said very earnestly, "Because when it came in it had all the appearance of being completely preserved, as if by some natural embalming process. It wasn't. It was frozen. It began to thaw out that night. And there were certain things about it that indicated that Fr. Piregard hadn't been dead the three centuries history said he had. The body began to go to pieces in a dozen ways—but no crumbling into dust, nothing like that. Gardner estimated that he hadn't been dead over five years. Where had he been in the meantime?"

He was quite sincere. I would not at first have believed it. But there was a certain disquieting earnestness about Laird that forbade any levity on my part. If I had treated his story as a joke, as I had the impulse to do, he would have shut up like a clam, and walked out of my room to brood about this thing in secret, with Lord knows what harm to himself. For a little while I said absolutely nothing.

"You don't believe it."

"I haven't said so."

"I can feel it."

"No. It's hard to take. Let's say I believe in your sincerity."

"That's fair enough," he said grimly. "Do you believe in me sufficiently to go along up to the lodge and find out what may have happened there?"

"Yes, I do."

"But I think you'd better read these excerpts from Gardner's letters first." He put them down on my desk like a challenge. He had copied them off onto a single sheet of paper, and as I took this up he went on, talking rapidly, explaining that the letters had been those written by Gardner from the lodge. When he finished, I turned to the excerpts and read.

> I cannot deny that there is about the lodge, the lake, even the forest an aura of evil, of impending danger—it is more than that, Laird, if I could explain it, but archeology is my forte, and not fiction. For it would take fiction, I think, to do justice to this thing I feel. . . . Yes, there are times when I have the distinct feeling that *someone* or *something* is watching me out of the forest or from the lake—there does not seem to be a distinction as I would like to understand it, and while it does not make me uneasy, nevertheless it is enough to give me pause. I managed the other day to make contact with Old Peter, the half-breed. He was at the moment a little the worse for firewater, but when I mentioned the lodge and the forest to him, he drew into himself like a clam. But he did put words to it: he called it the Wendigo—you are familiar with this legend, which properly belongs to the French-Canadian country.

That was the first letter, written about a week after Gardner had reached the abandoned lodge on Rick's Lake. The second was extremely terse and had been sent by special delivery.

> Will you wire Miskatonic University at Arkham, Massachusetts to ascertain if there is available for study a photostatic copy of a book know as the *Necronomicon,* by an Arabian writer who signs himself Abdul Alhazred? Make inquiry also for the *Pnakotic Manuscripts* and the *Book of Eibon,* and determine whether it is possible to purchase through one of the local bookstores a copy of The *Outsider and Others,* by H. P. Lovecraft, published by Arkham House last year. I believe that these books individually and collectively may be helpful in determining just what it is that haunts this place. For there is something; make no mistake about that; I am convinced of it, and when I tell you that I believe it has lived here not for years, but for centuries—perhaps even before the time of man—you will understand that I may be on the threshold of great discoveries.

Startling as this letter was, the third and last was even more so. For an interval of a fortnight went by between the second and third letters, and it was apparent that something had happened to threaten Professor Gardner's composure, for his third letter was even in this selected excerpt marked by extreme perturbation.

> Everything evil here . . . I don't know whether it is the Black Goat With a Thousand Young or the Faceless One and/or something more that rides the wind. For God's sake . . . those accursed fragments! . . . Something in the lake, too, and at night the sounds! How still, and then suddenly those horrible flutes, those watery ululations! Not a bird, not an animal then—only those ghastly sounds. And the voices! . . . Or is it but dream? Is it my own voice I hear in the darkness? . . .

I found myself increasingly shaken as I read those excerpts. Certain implications and hints lodged between the lines of what Professor Gardner had written were suggestive of terrible, ageless evil, and I felt there was opening up before Laird Dorgan and myself an adventure so incredible, so bizarre, and so unbelievably dangerous that we might well not return to tell it. Yet even then there was a lurking doubt in my mind that we would say anything about what we found at Rick's Lake.

"What do you say?" asked Laird impatiently.

"I'm going."

"Good! Everything's ready. I've even got a dictaphone and batteries enough to run it. I've arranged for the sheriff of the county at Pashepaho to replace Gardner's notes, and leave everything just the way it was."

"A dictaphone," I broke in. "What for?"

"Those sounds he wrote about—we can settle that once and for all. If they're there to be heard, the dictaphone will record them; it they're just imagination, it won't." He paused, his eyes very grave. "You know, Jack, we may not come out of this thing?"

"I know."

I did not say so, because I knew that Laird, too, felt the same way I did: that we were going like two dwarfed Davids to face an adversary greater than any Goliath, an adversary invisible and unknown, who bore no name and was shrouded in legend and fear, a dweller not only in the darkness of the wood but in that greater darkness which the mind of man has sought to explore since his dawn.

II

Sheriff Cowan was at the lodge when we arrived. Old Peter was with him. The sheriff was a tall, saturnine individual clearly of Yankee stock; though representing the fourth generation of his family in the area, he spoke with a twang which doubtless had persisted from generation to generation. The half-breed was a dark-skinned, ill-kept fellow; he had a way of saying little, and from time to time grinned or snickered as at some secret joke.

"I brung up express that come some time past for the professor," said the sheriff. "From some place in Massachusetts was one of 'em, and the other from down near Madison. Didn't seem t' me 'twas worth sendin' back. So I took and brung 'em with the keys. Don't know that you fellers 'll git anyw'eres. My posse and me went through the hull woods, didn't see a thing."

"You ain't tellin' 'em everything," put in the half-breed, grinning.

"Ain't no more to tell."

"What about the carvin'?"

He sheriff shrugged irritable. "Damn it, Peter, that ain't got nothin' to do with the professor's disappearance."

"He made a drawin' of it, didn't he?"

So pressed, the sheriff confided that two members of his posse had stumbled upon a great slab of rock in the center of the wood; it was mossy and overgrown, but there was upon it an odd drawing, plainly as old as the forest—probably the work of one of the primitive Indian tribes once known to inhabit northern Wisconsin before the Dacotah Sioux and the Winnebago—

Old Peter grunted with contempt. "No Indian drawing."

The sheriff shook this off and went on. The drawing represented some kind of creature, but no one could tell what it was; it was certainly not a man, but on the other hand, it did not seem to be hairy, like a beast. Moreover, the unknown artist had forgotten to put in a face.

"'N beside it there wuz two things," said the half-breed.

"Don't pay no attention to him," said the sheriff then.

"What two things?" demanded Laird.

"Jest things," replied the half-breed, snickering. "Heh, heh! Ain't no other way to tell it—warn't human, warn't animal, jest things."

Cowan was irritated. He became suddenly brusque; he ordered the half-breed to keep still, and went on to say that if we needed him, he would be at his office in Pashepaho. He did not explain how we were to make contact with him, since there was no telephone at the lodge, but plainly he had no high regard for the legends abounding about the area into which we had ventured with such determination. The half-breed regarded us with an almost stolid indifference, broken only by his sly grin from time to time, and his dark eyes examined our luggage with keen speculation and interest. Laird met his gaze occasionally, and each time Old Peter indolently shifted his eyes. The sheriff went on talking; the notes and drawings the missing man had made were on the desk he had used in the big room which made up almost the entire ground floor of the lodge, just where he had found them; they were the property of the State of Wisconsin and were to be returned to the sheriff's office when we had finished with them. At the threshold he turned for a parting shot to say he hoped we would not be staying too long, because "While I ain't givin' in to any of them crazy ideas—it jest ain't been so healthy for some of the people who came here."

"The half-breed knows or suspects something," said Laird at once. "We'll have to get in touch with him sometime when the sheriff's not around."

"Didn't Gardner write that he was pretty close-mouthed when it came to concrete data?"

"Yes, but he indicated the way out. Firewater."

We went to work and settled ourselves, storing our food supplies, setting up the dictaphone, getting things into readiness for a stay of at least a fortnight; our supplies were sufficient for this length of time, and if we had to remain longer, we could always go into Pashepaho for food. Moreover, Laird had brought fully two dozen dictaphone cylinders, so that we had plenty of them for an indefinite time, particularly since we did not intend to use them except when we slept—and this would not be often, for we had agreed that one of us would watch while the other took his rest, an arrangement we were not sanguine enough to believe would hold good without fail, hence the machine. It was not until after we had settled our belongings that we turned to the things the sheriff had brought and, meanwhile, we had ample opportunity to become aware of the very definite aura of the place.

For it was not imagination that there was a strange aura about the lodge and the grounds. It was not along the brooding, almost sinister stillness, not alone the tall pines encroaching upon the lodge, not alone the blue-black waters of the lake, but something more than that: a hushed, almost menacing air of waiting, a kind of aloof assurance that was ominous—as one might imagine a hawk might feel leisurely cruising above prey it knows will not escape its talons. Nor was this a fleeting impression, for it was obvious almost at once, and it grew with sure steadiness throughout the hour or so that we worked there; moreover, it was so plainly to be felt, that Laird commented upon it as if he had long ago accepted it, and knew that I too had done so! Yet there was nothing primary to which this could be attributed. There are thousands of lakes like Rick's in northern Wisconsin and Minnesota, and while many of them are not in forest areas, those which are do not differ greatly in their physical aspects from Rick's; so there was nothing in the appearance of the place which at all contributed to the brooding sense of horror which seemed to invade us from the outside. Indeed, the setting was rather the opposite; under the afternoon sunlight, the old lodge, the lake, the high forest all around had a pleasant air of seclusion—an air which made the contrast with the intangible aura of evil all the more pointed and fearsome. The fragrance of the pines, together with the freshness of the water served, too, to emphasize the intangible mood of menace.

We turned at last to the material left on Professor Gardner's desk. The express packages contained, as expected, a copy of *The Outsider and Others*, by H. P. Lovecraft, shipped by the publishers, and photostatic copies of manuscript and printed pages taken from the *R'lyeh Text* and Ludwig Prinn's *De Vermis Mysteriis*—apparently sent to supplement the earlier data dispatched to the professor by the librarian of Miskatonic University, for we found among the material brought back by the sheriff certain pages from the *Necronomicon*, in the transcription by Olaus Wormius, and likewise from the *Pnakotic Manuscripts*. But it was not these pages, which for the most part were unintelligible to us, which held our attention. It was the fragmentary notes left by Professor Gardner.

It was quite evident that he had not had time to do more than put down such questions and thoughts as had occurred to him, and, while there was little assimilation manifest, yet there was about what he had written a certain terrible suggestiveness which grew to colossal proportions as everything he had not put down became obvious.

"Is the slab a) only an ancient ruin, b) a marker similar to a tomb, c) or a focal point for Him? If the latter, from outside? Or from beneath? (NB: Nothing to show that the thing has been disturbed.)

"Cthulhu or Kthulhut. In Rick's Lake? Subterrene passage to Superior and the sea via the St. Lawrence? (NB: Except for the aviator's story, nothing to show that the Thing has anything to do with the water. Probably not one of the water beings.)

"Hastur. But the manifestation do not seem to have been of air beings either.

"Yog-Sothoth. Of earth certainly—but he is not the 'Dweller in Darkness.' (NB: The Thing, whatever it is, must be of the earth deities, even though it travels in time and space. It could possibly be more than one, of which only the earth being is occasionally visible. Ithaqua, perhaps?)

"'Dweller in Darkness.' Could He be the same as the Blind, Faceless One? He could be truly said to be dwelling in darkness. Nyarlathotep? Or Shub-Niggurath?

"What of fire? There must be a deity here, too. But no mention. (NB: Presumably, if the Earth and Water Beings oppose those of Air, then they must oppose those of Fire as well. Yet there is evidence here and there to show that there is more constant struggle between Air and Water Beings than between those of Earth and Air. Abdul Alhazred is damnably obscure in places. There is no clue as to the identity of Cthugha in that terrible footnote.

"Partier says I am on the wrong track. I'm not convinced. Whoever it is that plays the music in the night is a master of hellish cadence and rhythm. And, yes, of cacophony. (Cf. Bierce and Chambers.)"

That was all.

"What incredible gibberish!" I exclaimed.

And yet—and yet I knew instinctively it was not gibberish. Strange things had happened here, things which demanded an explanation which was not terrestrial; and here, in Gardner's handwriting, was evidence to show that he had not only arrived at the same conclusion, but passed it. However it might sound, Gardner had written it in all seriousness, and clearly for his own use alone, since only the vaguest and most suggestive outline seemed apparent. Moreover, the notes had had a startling effect on Laird; he had gone quite pale, and now stood looking down as if he could not believe what he had seen.

"What is it?" I asked.

"Jack—he was in contact with Partier."

"It doesn't register," I answered, but even as I spoke I remembered the hush-hush that had attended the severing of old Professor Partier's connection with the University of Wisconsin. It had been given out to the press that the old man had been somewhat too liberal in his lectures in anthropology—that is, that he had "Communistic leanings!"—which everyone who knew Partier realized was far from the facts. But he had said strange things in his lectures, he had talked of horrible, forbidden matters, and it had been thought best to let him out quietly. Unfortunately, Partier went out trumpeting in his contemptuous manner, and it had been difficult to hush the matter up satisfactorily.

"He's living down in Wausau now," said Laird.

"Do you suppose he could translate all this?" I asked and knew that I had echoed the thought in Laird's mind.

"He's almost a day away by car. We'll copy these notes, and if nothing happens—if we can't discover anything, we'll go to see him."

If nothing happened—!

If the lodge by day had seemed brooding in an air of ominousness, by night it seemed surcharged with menace. Moreover, events began to take place with disarming and insidious suddenness, beginning in mid-evening, when Laird and I were sitting over those curious photostats sent out by Miskatonic University in lieu of the books and manuscripts themselves, which were far too valuable to permit out of their haven. The first manifestation was so simple that for some time neither of us noticed its strangeness. It was simply the sound in the trees as of rising wind, the growing song among the pines. The night was warm, and all the windows of the lodge stood open. Laird commented on the wind, and went on giving voice to his perplexity regarding the fragments before us. Not until half an hour had gone by and the sound of the wind had risen to the proportions of a gale did it occur to Laird that something was wrong, and he looked up, his eyes going from one open window to another in growing apprehension. Then I, too, became aware.

Despite the tumult of the wind, no draft of air had circulated in the room, not one of the light curtains at the window was so much as trembling!

With one simultaneous movement, both of us stepped out upon the broad verandah of the lodge.

There was no wind, no breath of air stirring to touch our hands and faces. There was only the sound in the forest. And both of us looked up to where the pines were silhouetted against the starswept heavens, expecting their tops would be bending before a high gale; but there was no movement whatever; the pines stood still, motionless; and the sound as of wind continued from all around us. We stood on the verandah for half an hour, vainly attempting to determine the source of the sound—and then, as unobtrusively as it had began, it stopped!

The hour was now approaching midnight, and Laird prepared for bed; he had slept little the previous night, and we had agreed that I was to take the first watch until four in the morning. Neither of us said much about the sound in the pines, but what was said indicated a desire to believe that there was a natural explanation for the phenomenon, if we could establish a point of contact for understanding. It was inevitable, I suppose, that even in the face of all the curious facts which had come to our attention, there should still be an earnest wish to find a natural explanation. Certainly the oldest fear and the greatest fear to which man is prey is fear of the unknown; anything capable of rationalization and explanation cannot be feared; but it was growing hourly more patent that we were facing something which defied all known rationales and credos, but hinged upon a system of belief that antedated even primitive man, and indeed, as scattered hints within the photostat pages from Miskatonic University suggested, antedated even earth itself. And there was always that brooding terror, the ominous suggestion of menace from something far beyond the grasp of such a puny intelligence as man's.

Thus it was with some trepidation that I prepared for my vigil. After Laird had gone to his room, which was at the head of the stairs, with a door opening upon a railed-in balcony looking down into the lodge room where I sat with the book by Lovecraft, reading here and there in its pages, I settled down to a kind of apprehensive waiting. It was not that I was afraid of what might take place, but rather that I was afraid that what took place might be beyond my understanding. However, as the minutes ticked past, I became engrossed in *The Outsider and Others*, with its hellish suggestions of aeon-old evil, of entities co-existent with all time and conterminous with all space, and began to understand, however vaguely, a relation between the writings of this fantasiste and the curious notes Professor Gardner had made. The most disturbing factor in this cognizance was the knowledge that Professor Gardner had made his notes independent of the book I now read, since it had arrived after his disappearance. Moreover, though there were certain keys to what Gardner has written in the first material he had received from Miskatonic University, there was growing now a mass of evidence to indicate that the professor had had access to some other source of information.

What was that source? Could he have learned something from Old Peter? Hardly likely. Could he have gone to Partier? It was not impossible that he had done so, through he had not imparted this information to Laird. Yet it was not to be ruled out that he had made contact with still another source of which there was no hint among his notes.

It was while I was engaged in this engrossing speculation that I became conscious of the music. It may actually have been sounding for some time before I heard it, but I do not think so. It was a curious melody that was being played, beginning as something lulling and harmonious, and then subtly becoming cacophonous and demoniac, rising in tempo, though all the time coming as from a great distance. I listened to it with growing astonishment; I was not at first aware of that sense of evil which fell upon me the moment I stepped outside and became cognizant that the music emulated from the depths of the dark forest. There, too, I was sharply conscious of its weirdness; the melody was unearthly, utterly bizarre and foreign, and the instruments which were being used seemed to be flutes, or certainly some variation of flutes.

Up to that moment there was no really alarming manifestation. That is, there was nothing by the suggestiveness of the two events which had taken place to inspire fear. There was, in short, always a good possibility that there might be a natural explanation about the sound as of wind and that of music.

But now, suddenly, there occurred something so utterly horrible, something so fraught with terror, that I was at once made prey to the most terrible fear known to man, a surging primitive horror of the unknown, of something from outside—for if I had doubts about the things suggested by Gardner's notes and the material accompanying them, I knew instinctively that they were unfounded, for the sound that succeeded the strains of that unearthly music was of such a nature that it defied description, and defies it even now. It was simply a ghastly ululation, made by no beast known to man, and certainly by no man. It rose to an awful crescendo and fell away into a silence that was more terrible for this soul-searing cry. It began with a two-note call, twice repeated, a frightful sound: *"Ygnaiih! Ygnaiih!"* and then became a triumphant wailing cry that ululated out of the forest and into the dark night like the hideous voice of the pit itself: *"Eh-ya-ya-ya-yahaaahaaahaaahaaa-ah-ah-ah-ngh' aaaa-ngh 'aaa-ya-ya-yaa . . ."*

I stood for a moment, absolutely frozen to the verandah. I could not have uttered a sound if it had been necessary to save my life. The voice had ceased, but the trees still seemed to echo its frightful syllables. I heard Laird tumble from his bed, I heard him running down the stairs calling my name, but I could not answer. He came out on the verandah and caught hold of my arm.

"Good God! What was that?"

"Did you hear it?"

"I heard enough."

We stood waiting for it to sound again, but there was no repetition of it. Nor was there a repetition of the music. We returned to the sitting room and waited there, neither of us able to sleep.

But there was not another manifestation of any kind throughout the remainder of that night!

III

The occurrences of that first night more than anything else decided our direction on the following day. For, realizing that we were too ill-informed to cope with any understanding with what was taking place, Laird set the dictaphone for that second night, and we started out for Wausau and Professor Partier, planning to return on the following day. With forethought, Laird carried with him our copy of the notes Gardner had left, skeletal as they were.

Professor Partier, at first reluctant to see us, admitted us finally to his study in the heart of the Wisconsin city, and cleared books and papers from two chairs, so that we could sit down. Though he had the appearance of an old man, wore a long white beard, and a fringe of white hair straggled from under his black skull cap, he was as agile as a young man; he was thin, his fingers were bony, his face gaunt, with deep, black eyes, and his features were set in an expression that was one of profound cynicism, disdainful, almost contemptuous, and he made no effort to make us comfortable, beyond providing places for us to sit. He recognized Laird as Professor Gardner's secretary, said brusquely that he was a busy man preparing what would doubtless be his last book for his publishers, and he would be obliged to us if we would state the object of our visit as concisely s possible.

"What do you know of Cthulhu?" asked Laird bluntly.

The professor's reaction was astonishing. From an old man whose entire attitude had been one of superiority and aloof disdain, he became instantly wary and alert; with exaggerated care he put down the pencil he had been holding, his eyes never once left Laird's face, and he leaned forward a little over his desk.

"So," he said, "you come to me." He laughed then, a laugh which was like the cackling of some centenarian. "You come to me to ask about Cthulhu. Why?"

Laird explained curtly that we were bent upon discovering what had happened to Professor Gardner. He told as much as he thought necessary, while the old man closed his eyes, picked up his pencil once more and, tapping gently with it, listened with marked care, prompting Laird from time to time. When he had finished, Professor Partier opened his eyes slowly and looked from one to the other of us with an expression that was not unlike one of pity mixed with pain.

"So he mentioned me, did he?" But I had no contact with him other than one telephone call." He pursed his lips. "He had more reference to an earlier controversy than to his discoveries at Rick's Lake. I would like now to give you a little advice."

"That's what we came for."

"Go away from that place and forget all about it."

Laird shook his head in determination.

Partier estimated him, his dark eyes challenging his decision; but Laird did not falter. He had embarked upon this venture, and he meant to see it through.

"These are not forces with which common men have been accustomed to deal," said the old man then. "We are frankly not equipped to do so." He began then, without other preamble, to talk of matters so far removed from the mundane as to be almost beyond conception. Indeed, it was some time before I began to comprehend what he was hinting at, for his concept was so broad and breath-taking that it was difficult for anyone accustomed to so prosaic an existence as mine to grasp. Perhaps this was because Partier began obliquely by suggesting that it was not Cthulhu or his minions who haunted Rick's Lake, but clearly another; the existence of the slab and what was carved upon it clearly indicated the nature of the being who dwelled there from time to time. Professor Gardner had in final analysis got on to the right path, despite thinking that Partier did not believe it. Who was the Blind, Faceless One but Nyarlathotep? Certainly not Shub-Niggurath, the Black Goat of a Thousand Young.

Here Laird interrupted him to press for something more understandable, and then at last, realizing that we knew nothing, the professor went on, still in that vaguely irritable oblique manner, to expound mythology—a mythology of pre-human life not only on the earth, but on the stars of all the universe. "We know nothing," he repeated from time to time. "We know nothing at all. But there are certain signs, certain shunned places. Rick's Lake is one of them." He spoke of beings whose very names were awesome—of the Elder Gods who live on Betelguese, remote in time and space, who had cast out into space the Great Old Ones, led by Azathoth and Yog-Sothoth, and numbering among them the primal spawn of the amphibious Cthulhu, the bat-like followers of Hastur the Unspeakable, of Lloigor, Zhar, and Ithaqua, who walked the winds and interstellar space, the earth beings, Nyarlathotep and Shub-Niggurath—the evil beings who sought always to triumph once more over the Elder Gods, who had shut them out or imprisoned them—as Cthulhu long ago slept in the ocean realm of R'lyeh, as Hastur was imprisoned upon a black star near Aldebaran in the Hyades. Long before human beings walked the earth, the conflict between the Elder Gods and the Great Old Ones had taken place; and from time to time the Old Ones had made a resurgence toward power, sometimes to be stopped by direct interference by the Elder Gods, but more often by the agency of human or non-human beings serving to bring about a conflict among the beings of the elements, for, as Gardner's notes indicated, the evil Old Ones were elemental forces. And every time there had been a resurgence, the mark of it had been left deep upon man's memory—though every attempt was made to eliminate the evidence and quiet survivors.

"What happened at Innsmouth, Massachusetts, for instance?" he asked tensely. "What took place at Dunwich? In the wilds of Vermont? At the old Tuttle house on the Aylesbury Pike? What of the mysterious cult of Cthulhu, and of the utterly strange voyage of exploration to the Mountains of Madness? What beings dwelt on the hidden and shunned Plateau of Leng? And what of Kadath in the Cold Waste? Lovecraft knew! Gardner and many another have sought to discover those secrets, to link the incredible happenings which have taken place here and there on the face of the planet—but it is not desired by the Old Ones that mere men shall know too much. Be warned!"

He took up Gardner's notes without giving either of us a chance to say anything, and studied them, putting on a pair of gold-rimmed spectacles which made him look more ancient than ever, and going on talking, more to himself than to us, saying that it was held that the Old Ones had achieved a higher degree of development in some aspects of science than was hitherto believed possible, but that, of course, nothing was known. The way in which he consistently emphasized this indicated very clearly that only a fool or an idiot would disbelieve, proof or no proof. But in the next sentence, he admitted that there was certain proof—the revolting and bestial plaque bearing a representation of a hellish monstrosity walking on the winds above the earth found in the hand of Josiah Alwyn when his body was discovered on a small Pacific island months after his incredible disappearance from his home in Wisconsin; the drawings made by Professor Gardner—and, even more than anything else, that curious slab of craven stones in the forest at Rick's Lake.

"Cthugha," he murmured then, wonderingly. "I've not read the footnote to which he makes reference. And there's nothing in Lovecraft." He shook his head. "No, I don't know." He looked up. "Can you frighten something out of the half-breed?"

"We've thought of that," admitted Laird.

"Well, now, I advise a try. It seems evident that he knows something—it may be nothing but an exaggeration to which his more or less primitive mind has lent itself; but on the other hand—who can say?"

More than this Professor Partier could not or would not tell us. Moreover, Laird was reluctant to ask, for there was obviously a damnably disturbing connection between what he had revealed, however incredible it might be, and what Professor Gardner had written.

Our visit, however, despite its inconclusiveness—or perhaps because of it—had a curious effect on us. The very indefiniteness of the professor's summary and comments, coupled with such fragmentary and disjointed evidence which had come to us independently of Partier, sobered us and increased Laird's determination to get to the bottom of the mystery surrounding Gardner's disappearance, a mystery which had now become enlarged to encompass the greater mystery of Rick's Lake and the forest around it.

On the following day we returned to Pashepaho, and, as luck would have it, we passed Old Peter on the road leading into town. Laird slowed down, backed up, and leaned out to meet the old fellow's speculative gaze.

"Lift?"

"Reckon so."

Old Peter got in and sat on the edge of the seat until Laird unceremoniously produced a flask and offered it to him; then his eyes lit up; he took it eagerly and drank deeply, while Laird made small talk about life in the north woods and encouraged the half-breed to talk about the mineral deposits he thought he could find in the vicinity of Rick's Lake. In this way some distance was covered, and during this time, the half-breed retained the flask, handing it back at last when it was almost empty. He was not intoxicated in the strictest sense of the word, but he was uninhibited, and he made no protest when we took the lake road without stopping to let him out, though when he saw the lodge and knew where he was, he said thickly that he was off his route, and had to be getting back before dark.

He would have started back immediately, but Laird persuaded him to come in with the promise that he would mix him a drink.

He did. He mixed him as stiff a drink as he could, and Peter downed it.

Not until he had begun to feel its effects did Laird turn to the subject of what Peter knew about the mystery of the Rick's Lake country, and instantly then the half-breed became close-mouthed, mumbling that he would say nothing, he had seen nothing, it was all a mistake, he eyes shifting from one to the other of us. But Laird persisted. He had seen the slab of craven stone, hadn't he? Yes—reluctantly. Would he take us to it? Peter shook his head violently. Not now. It was nearly dark, it might be dark before they could return.

But Laird was adamant, and finally the half-breed, convinced by Laird's insistence that they could return to the lodge and even to Pashepaho, if Peter liked, before darkness fell, consented to lead us to the slab. Then, despite his unsteadiness, he set off swiftly into the woods along a lane that could hardly be called a trail, so faint it was, and loped along steadily for almost a mile before he drew up short and, standing behind a tree, as if he were afraid of being seen, pointed shakily to a little open spot surrounded by high trees at enough of a distance that ample sky was visible overhead.

"There—that's it."

The slab was only partly visible, for moss had grown over much of it. Laird, however, was at the moment only secondarily interested in it; it was manifest that the half-breed stood in mortal terror of the spot and wished only to escape.

"How would you like to spend the night here, Peter?" asked Laird.

The half-breed shot a frightened glance at him. "Me? Gawd, no!"

Suddenly Laird's voice steeled. "Unless you tell us what it was you saw here, that's what you're going to do."

The half-breed was not so much the worse for liquor that he could not foresee events—the possibility that Laird and I might overcome him and tie him to a tree at the edge of this open space. Plainly, he considered a bolt for it, but he knew that in his condition, he could not outrun us.

"Don't make me tell," he said. "It ain't supposed to be told. I ain't never told no one—not even the professor."

"We want to know, Peter," said Laird with no less menace.

The half-breed began to shake; he turned and looked at the slab as if he thought that at any moment an inimical being might rise from it and advance upon him with lethal intent. "I can't, I can't," he muttered, and then, forcing his bloodshot eyes to meet Laird's once more, he said in a low voice, "I don't know what it was. Gawd! it was awful. It was a Thing—didn't have no face, hollered there till I thought my eardrums 'd bust, and them things that was with it—Gawd!" He shuddered and backed away from the tree, toward us. "Honest t' Gawd, I seen it there one night. It jist come, seems like, out of the air and there it was a-singin' and a-wailin' and them things playin' that damn music. I guess I was crazy for a while afore I got away." His voice broke, his vivid memory recreated what he had seen; he turned, shouting harshly, "Let's git outa here!" and ran back the way we had come, weaving among the trees.

Laird and I ran after him, catching up easily, Laird reassuring him that we would take him out of the woods in the car, and he would be well away from the forest's edge before darkness overtook him. He was convinced as I that there was nothing imagined about the half-breed's account, that he had indeed told us all he knew; and he was silent all the way back from the highway to which we took Old Peter, pressing five dollars upon him so that he could forget what he had seen in liquor if he were so inclined.

"What do you think?" asked Laird when we reached the lodge once more.

I shook my head.

"That wailing night before last," said Laird. "The sounds Professor Gardner heard—and now this. It ties up—damnably, horribly." He turned on me with intense and fixed urgence. "Jack, are you game to visit that slab tonight?"

"Certainly."

"We'll do it."

It was not until we were inside the lodge that we thought of the dictaphone, and then Laird prepared at once to play whatever had been recorded back to us. Here at least, he reflected, was nothing dependent in any way upon anyone's imagination; here was the product of the machine, pure and simple, and everyone of intelligence knew full well that machines were far more dependable than men, having neither nerves nor imagination, knowing neither fear nor hope. I think that at most we counted upon hearing a repetition of the sounds of the previous night; not in our wildest dreams did we look forward to what we actually did hear, for the record mounted from the prosaic to the incredible, from the incredible to the horrible, and at last to a cataclysmic revelation that left us completely cut away from every credo of normal existence.

It began by the occasional singing of loons and owls, followed by a period of silence. Then there was once more that familiar rushing sound, as of wind in the trees, and this was followed by a curious cacophonous piping of flutes. Then there was a recorded series of sounds, which I put down here exactly as we heard them in that unforgettable evening hour:

> *Ygnaiih! Ygnaiih! EEE-ya-ya-ya-yahaahaaahaaa-ah-ah-ah-ngh'aaa-ngh-aaa-ya-ya-yaaa!* (In a voice that was neither human nor bestial, but yet of both.)
>
> (An increased tempo in the music, becoming more wild and demoniac.)
>
> Mighty Messenger—Nyarlathotep . . . from the world of Seven Suns to his earth place, the Wood of N'gai, wither may come Him Who Is Not To Be Named . . . There shall be abundance of those from the Black Goat of the Woods, the Goat With the Thousand Young . . . (In a voice that was curiously human.)
>
> (A succession of odd sounds, as if audience-response: a buzzing and humming, as of telegraph wires.)
>
> *Ia! Ia! Shub-Niggurath! Ygnaiih! Ygnaiih! EEE-yaa-yaa-haa-haaa-haaaa!* (In the original voice neither human nor beast, yet both.)
>
> Ithaqua shall serve thee, Father of the million favored ones, and Zhar shall be summoned from Acturus, by the command of 'Umr At-Tawil, Guardian of the Gate . . . Ye shall unite in praise of Azathoth, of Great Cthulhu, of Tsathoggua . . . (The human voice again.)
>
> Go forth in his form or in whatever form chosen in the guide of man, and destroy that which may lead them to us . . . (the half-bestial, half-human voice once more.)

(An interlude of furious piping, accompanied once again by a sound as of the flapping of great wings.)

Ygnaiih! Y'bthnk . . . h'ehye-n'grkdl'lh . . . Ia! Ia! Ia! (Like a chorus.)

These sounds had been spaced in such a way that it seemed as if the beings giving rise to them were moving about within or around the lodge, and the last choral chanting faded away, as if the creatures were departing. Indeed, there followed such an interval of silence that Laird had actually moved to shut off the machine when once again a voice came from it. But the voice that now emanated from the dictaphone was one which, simple because of its nature, brought to a climax all the horror so cumulative in what had gone before it; for whatever had been inferred by the half-bestial bellowings and chants, the horribly suggestive conversation in accented English, that which came now from the dictaphone was unutterably terrible.

Dorgan! Laird Dorgan! Can you hear me?

A hoarse, urgent whisper calling out to my companion, who sat white-faced now, staring at the machine above which is had was still poised. Out eyes met. It was not the appeal, it was not everything that had gone before, it was the identity of that voice—*for it was the voice of Professor Upton Gardner!* But we had no time to ponder this, for the dictaphone went mechanically on.

"Listen to me! Leave this place. Forget. But before you go, summon Cthugha. For centuries this has been the place where evil beings from outermost cosmos have touched upon Earth. I know. I am theirs. They have taken me as they took Piregard and many others—all who came unwarily within their wood and whom they did not at once destroy. It is His wood—the Wood of N'gai, the terrestrial abode of the Blind, Faceless One, the Howler in the Night, the Dweller in Darkness, Nyarlathotep, who fears only Cthugha. I have been with him in the star spaces. I have been on the shunned Plateau of Leng—to Kadath in the Cold Waste, beyond the Gates of the Silver Key, even to Kythamil near Acturus and Mnar, to N'kai and the Lake of Hali, to K'n-yan and fabled Carcosa, to Yaddith and Y'ha-nthlei near Innsmouth, to Yoth and Yuggoth, and from far off I have looked upon Zothique, from the eye of Algol. When Fomalhaut has topped the trees, call forth to Cthugha in these words, thrice repeated: *Ph'nglui mglw'nafh Cthugha Fomalhaut n'gha-ghaa naf'l thagn. Ia! Cthugha!* When he has come, go swiftly, lest you too be destroyed. For it is fitting that this accursed spot be blasted so that Nyarlathotep comes no more out of interstellar space. Do you hear me, Dorgan? Do you hear me? Dorgan! Laird Dorgan!"

There was a sudden sound of sharp protest, followed by a scuffling and tearing noise, as if Gardner had been forcibly removed, an then silence, utter and complete!

For a few moments longer Laird let the record run, but there was nothing more, and finally he started it over, saying tensely, "I think we'd better copy that as best we can. You take every other speech, and let's both copy that formula from Gardner."

"Was it . . . ?"

"I'd know his voice anywhere," he said shortly.

"He's alive then?"

He looked at me, his eyes narrowed. "We don't know that."

"But his voice!"

He shook his head, for the sounds were coming forth once more, and both of us had to bend to the task of copying, which was easier than it promised to be for the spaces between speeches were great enough to enable us to copy without undue haste. The language of the chants and the words to Cthugha enunciated by Gardner's voice offered extreme difficulty, but by means of repeated playings, we managed to put down the approximate equivalent of the sounds. When finally we had finished, Laird shut the dictaphone off and looked at me with quizzical and troubled eyes grave, with concern and uncertainty. I said nothing; what we had just heard, added to everything that had gone before left us no alternative. There was room for doubt about legends, beliefs, and the like—but the infallible record of the dictaphone was conclusive even if it did no more than verify half-heard credos—for it was true, there was still nothing definite; it was all as if the whole were so completely beyond the comprehension of man that only in the oblique suggestion of its individual parts could something like understanding be achieved, as if the entirety were too unspeakable soul-searing for the mind of man to understand.

"Fomalhaut rises almost at sunset—a little before, I think," mused Laird—clearly, like myself, he had accepted what we had heard without challenge other than the mystery surrounding its meaning. "It should be above the trees—presumably twenty to thirty degrees above the horizon, because it doesn't pass near enough to the zenith in this latitude to appear above these pines—at approximately an hour after darkness falls. Say nine-thirty or so."

"You aren't thinking of trying it tonight?" I asked. "After all—what does it mean? Who or what is Cthugha?"

"I don't know any more than you. And I'm not trying it tonight. You've forgotten the slab. Are you still game to go out there—after this?"

I nodded. I did not trust myself to speak, but I was not consumed by any eagerness whatever to dare the darkness that lingered like a living entity within the forest surrounding Rick's Lake.

Laird looked at his watch, and then at me, his eyes burning now with a kind of feverish determination, as if he were forcing himself to take this final step to face the unknown being whose manifestations had made the wood its own. If he expected me to hesitate, he was disappointed; however beset by fear I might be, I would not show it. I got up and went out of the lodge at his side.

IV

There are aspects of hidden life, exterior as well as of the depths of the mind, that are better kept secret and away from the awareness of common man; for there lurk in dark places of the earth terrible desiderata, horrible revenants belonging to a stratum of the subconscious which is mercifully beyond the apprehension of common man—indeed, there are aspects of creation so grotesquely shuddersome that the very sight of them would blast the sanity of the beholder. Fortunately, it is not possible even to bring back in anything but suggestion what we saw on the slab in the forest at Rick's Lake that night in October, for the thing was so unbelievable, transcending all known laws of science, that adequate words for its description have no existence in the language.

We arrived at the belt of trees around the slab while afterglow yet lingered in the western heavens, and by the illumination of a flashlight Laird carried, we examined the face of the slab itself, and the carving on it: of a vast, amorphous creature, drawn by an artist who evidently lacked sufficient imagination to etch the creature's face, for it had none, bearing only a curious, cone-like head which even in stone seemed to have a fluidity which was unnerving; moreover, the creature was depicted as having both tentacle-like appendages and hands—or growths similar to hands, not only two, but several; so that it seemed both human and non-human in its structure. Beside it had been carved two squat squid-like figures from a part of which—presumable the heads, though no outline was definitive—projected what must certainly have been instruments of some kind, for the strange, repugnant attendants appeared to be playing them.

Our examination was necessarily hurried, for we did not want to risk being seen by whatever might come, and it may be that in the circumstance, imagination got the better of us. But I do not think so. It is difficult to maintain that consistently sitting here at my desk, removed in space and time from what happened there; but I maintain it. Despite the quickened awareness and irrational fear of the unknown which obsessed both of us, we kept a determined open-mindedess about every aspect of the problem we had chosen to solve. If anything, I have erred in this account on the side of science over that of imagination. In the plain light of reason, the carvings on that stone slab were not only obscene, but bestial and frightening beyond measure, particularly in the light of what Partier had hinted, and what Gardner's notes and the material from Miskatonic University had vaguely outlined, and even if time had permitted, it is doubtful if we could have looked long upon them.

We retreated to a spot comparatively near the way we must take to return to the lodge, and yet not too far from the open place were the slab lay, so that we might see clearly and still remain hidden in a place easy of access to the return path. There we took out stand and waited in that chilling hush of an October evening, while stygian darkness encompassed us, and only one or two stars twinkled high overhead, miraculously visible among the towering treetops.

According to Laird's watch, we waited exactly an hour and ten minutes before the sound as of wind began, and at once there was a manifestation of which had about it all the trappings of the supernatural; for no sooner had the rushing sound begun, than the slab we had so quickly quitted began to glow—at first so indistinguishably that it seemed an illusion, and then with a phosphorescence of increasing brilliance, until it gave off such a glow that it was if a pillar of light extended upward into the heavens. This was the second curious circumstance—the light followed the outlines of the slab, and flowed upward; it was not diffused and dispersed about the glade and into the woods, but shown heavenward with the insistence of a directed beam. Simultaneously, the very air seemed charged with evil; all around us lay thickly such an aura of fearsomeness that it rapidly became impossible to remain free of it. It was apparent that by some means unknown to us the rushing sound as of wind which now filled the air was not only associated with the broad beam of light flowing upward, *but was caused by it;* moreover, as we watched, the intensity and color of the light varied constantly, changing from a blinding white to a lambent green, from green to a kind of lavender; occasionally it was so intensely brilliant that it was necessary to avert our eyes, but for the most part it could be looked at without hurt to our eyes.

As suddenly as it had begun, the rushing sound stopped, the light because diffuse and dim; and almost immediately the weird piping as of flutes smote upon our ears. It came not from around us, but from *above,* and with one accord, both of us turned to look as far into heaven as the now fading light would permit.

Just what took place before our eyes I cannot explain. Was it actually something that came hurtling down, streaming down, rather?—for the masses were shapeless—or was it the product of an imagination that proved singularly uniform when later Laird and I found opportunity to compare notes? The illusion of great black things streaking down in the path of that light was so great that we glanced back at the slab.

What we saw there sent us screaming voicelessly from that hellish spot.

For, where but a moment before there had been nothing, there was now a gigantic protoplasmic mass, a colossal being who towered upward toward the stars, and whose actual physical being was in constant flux; and flanking it on either side were two lesser beings, equally amorphous, holding pipes or flutes in appendages and making that demoniac music which echoed and reechoed in the enclosing forest. But the thing on the slab, the Dweller in Darkness, was the ultimate in horror; for from its mass of amorphous flesh there grew at will before our eyes, tentacles, claws, hands, and withdrew again; the mass itself diminished and swelled effortlessly, and where its head was and its features should have been there was only a blank facelessness all the more horrible because even as we looked there rose from its blind mass a low ululation in that half-bestial, half-human voice so familiar to us from the record made in the night!

We fled, I say, so shaken that it was only by a supreme effort of will that we were able to take flight in the right direction. And behind us the voice rose, the blasphemous voice of Nyarlathotep, the Blind, Faceless One, the Mighty Messenger, even while there rang in the channels of memory the frightened words of the half-breed, Old Peter—*It was a Thing—didn't have no face, hollered there till I thought my eardrums 'd bust, and them things that was with it—Gawd!*—echoed there while the voice of that Being from outermost space shrieked and gibbered to the hellish music of the hideous attending flute-players, rising to ululate through the forest and leave its mark forever in memory!

Ygnaiih! Ygnaiih! EEE-yayayayayayaaa-haaahaaahaaahaaa-ngh'aaa-ngh'aaa-ya-ya-yaaa!

Then all was still.

And yet, incredible as it may seem, the ultimate horror awaited us.

For we had gone but half way to the lodge when we were simultaneously aware of something following; behind us rose a hideous, horribly suggestive sloshing sound, as if the amorphous entity had left the slab which in some remote time must have been erected by its worshippers, and were pursuing us. Obsessed by abysmal fright, we ran as neither of us has ever run before, and we were almost upon the lodge before we were aware that the sloshing sound, the trembling and shuddering of the earth—as if some gigantic being walked upon it—had ceased, and in their stead came only the calm, unhurried tread of footsteps.

But the footsteps were not our own! And in the aura of unreality, the fearsome outsideness in which we walked and breathed, the terrible suggestiveness of those footsteps was almost maddening!

We reached the lodge, lit a lamp and sank into chairs to await whatever it was that was coming so steadily, unhurriedly on, mounting the verandah steps, putting its hand on the knob of the door, swinging the door open . . .

It was Professor Gardner who stood there!

For one cataclysmic moment, we sat open-mouthed and gazed at him as a man returned from the dead.

Then Laird sprang up, crying, "Professor Gardner!"

The professor smiled reservedly and put one hand up to shade his eyes. "If you don't mind, I'd like the light dimmed. I've been in the dark for so long . . ."

Laird turned to do his bidding without question, and he came forward into the room, walking with the ease and poise of a man who is as sure of himself as if he had never vanished from the face of the earth more than three months before, as if he had not made a frantic appeal to us during the night just past, as if . . .

I glanced at Laird; his hand was still at the lamp, but his fingers were no longer turning down the wick, simply holding to it, while he gazed down unseeing. I looked over at Professor Gardner; he sat with his head turned from the lights, his eyes closed, a little smile playing about his lips; at that moment he looked precisely as I had often seen him look at the University Club in Madison, and it was as if everything that had taken place here at the lodge were but an evil dream.

But it was not a dream!

"You were gone last night?" asked the professor.

"Yes. But, of course, we had the dictaphone."

"Ah. You heard something then?"

"Would you like to hear the record, sir?"

"Yes, I would."

Laird went over and put it on the machine to play it again, and we sat in silence, listening to everything upon it, no one saying anything until it had been completed. Then the professor slowly turned his head.

"What do you make of it?"

"I don't know what to make of it, sir," answered Laird. "The speeches are too disjointed—except for yours. There seems to be some coherence there."

Suddenly, without warning, the room was surcharged with menace; it was but a momentary impression, but Laird felt it as keenly as I did, for he started noticeably. He was taking the record from the machine when the professor spoke again.

"It doesn't occur to you that you may be the victim of a hoax?"

"No."

"And if I told you that I had found it possible to make every sound that was registered on that record?"

Laird looked at him for a full minute before replying in a low voice that of course, Professor Gardner had been investigating the phenomena of Rick's Lake woods for a far longer time than we had, and if he said so . . .

A harsh laugh escaped the professor. "Entirely natural phenomena, my boy! There's a mineral deposit under that grotesque slab in the woods; it gives off light and also a miasma that is productive of hallucinations. It's as simple as that. As for the various disappearances—sheer folly, human failing, nothing more, but with the air of coincidence. I came here with high hopes of verifying some of the nonsense to which old Partier lent himself long ago—but—" He smiled disdainfully, shook his head, and extended his hand. "Let me have the record, Laird."

Without question, Laird gave Professor Gardner the record.

The older man took it and was bringing it up before his eyes when he jogged his elbow and, with a sharp cry of pain, dropped it. It broke into dozens of pieces on the floor of the lodge.

"Oh!" cried the professor. "I'm sorry." He turned his eyes on Laird. "But then—since I can duplicate it any time for you from what I've learned about the lore of this place, by way of Partier's mouthings—" He shrugged.

"It doesn't matter," said Laird quietly.

"Do you mean to say that everything on that record was just your imagination, Professor?" I broke in. "Even that chant for the summoning of Cthugha?"

The older man's eyes turned on he; his smile was sardonic. "Cthugha? What do you suppose he or that is but the figment of someone's imagination? And for the inference—my dear boy, use your head. You have before you the clear inference that Cthugha has his abode on Fomalhaut which is twenty-seven light years away, and that, if this chant is thrice repeated when Fomalhaut has risen Cthugha will appear to somehow render this place no longer habitable by man or outside entity. How do you suppose that could be accomplished?"

"Why, by something akin to thought-transference," replied Laird doggedly. "It's not unreasonable to suppose that if we were to direct thoughts toward Fomalhaut that something there might receive them—granting that there might be life there. Thought is instant. And that they in turn may be so highly developed that dematerialization and rematerialization might be as swift as thought."

"My boy—are you serious?" The older man's voice revealed his contempt.

"You asked."

"Well, then, as the hypothetic answer to a theoretical problem, I can overlook that."

"Frankly," I said again, disregarding a curious negative shaking of Laird's head, "I don't think what we saw in the forest tonight was just hallucination—caused by a miasma rising out of the earth or otherwise."

The effect of this statement was extraordinary. Visibly, the professor made every effort to control himself; his reactions were precisely those of a savant challenged by a cretin in one of his classes. After a few moments he controlled himself and said only, "You've been there then. I suppose it's too late to make you believe otherwise . . ."

"I've always been open to conviction, sir, and I lean to the scientific method," said Laird.

Professor Gardner put his hand over his eyes and said, "I'm tired. I noticed last night when I was here that you're in my old room, Laird—so I'll take the room next to you, opposite Jack's."

He went up the stairs as if nothing had happened between the last time he had occupied the lodge and this.

V

The rest of the story—and the culmination of that apocalyptic night—are soon told.

I could not have been asleep for more than an hour—the time was one in the morning—when I was awakened by Laird. He stood beside my bed fully dressed and in a tense voice ordered me to get up and dress, to pack whatever essentials I had brought, and be ready for anything. Nor would he permit me to put on a light to do so, though he carried a small pocket-flash, and used it sparingly. To all my questions, he cautioned me to wait.

When I had finished, he led the way out of the room with a whispered, "Come."

He went directly to the room into which Professor Gardner had disappeared. By the light of his flash, it was evident that the bed had not been touched; moreover, in the faint film of dust that lay on the floor, it was clear that Professor Gardner had walked into the room, over to a chair beside the window, and out again.

"Never touched the bed, you see," whispered Laird.

"But why?"

Lard gripped my arm, hard. "Do you remember what Partier hinted—what we saw in the woods—the protoplasmic, amorphousness of the thing? And what the record said?"

"But Gardner told us—" I protested.

Without a further word, he turned. I followed him downstairs, where he paused at the table where we had worked and flashed the light upon it. I was surprised into making a startled exclamation which Laird hushed instantly. For the table was bare of everything but the copy of *The Outsider and Others* and three copies of *Weird Tales*, a magazine containing stories supplementing those in the book by the eccentric Providence genius, Lovecraft. All of Gardner's notes, all our own notations, the photostats from Miskatonic University—everything was gone!

"He took them," said Laird. "No one else could have done so."

"Where did he go?"

"Back to the place from which he came." He turned on me, his eyes gleaming in the reflected glow of the flashlight. "Do you understand what that means, Jack?"

I shook my head.

"They know we've been there, they know we've seen and learned too much . . ."

"But how?"

"You told them."

"I? Good God, man, are you mad? How could I have told them?"

"Here, in this lodge, tonight—you yourself gave the show away, and I hate to think of what might happen now. We've got to get away."

For one moment all the events of the past few days seemed to fuse into an unintelligible mass; Laird's urgence was unmistakable, and yet the thing he suggested was so utterly unbelievable that its contemplation even for so fleeting a moment threw my thoughts into the extremest confusion.

Laird was talking now, quickly. "Don't you think it odd—how he came back? How he came out of the woods *after* that hellish thing we saw there—not before? And the questions he asked—the drift of those questions. And how he managed to break the record—our one scientific proof of something? And now, the disappearance of all the notes—of everything that might point to substantiation of what he called 'Partier's nonsense'?"

"But if we are to believe what he told us . . ."

He broke in before I could finish. "One of them was right. Either the voice on the record calling to me—or the man who was here tonight."

"The man . . ."

But whatever I wanted to say was stilled by Laird's harsh, *"Listen!"*

From outside, from the depths of that horror-haunted dark, the earth-haven of the dweller in darkness, came once more, for the second time that night, the weirdly beautiful, yet cacophonous strains of flute-like music, rising and falling, accompanied by a kind of chanted ululation, and by the sound as of great wings flapping.

"Yes, I hear," I whispered.

"Listen closely!"

Even as he spoke, I understood. There was something more—the sounds from the forest were not only rising and falling—*they were approaching!*

"Now do you believe me?" demanded Laird. *"They're coming for us!"* He turned on me. "The chant!"

"What chant?" I fumbled stupidly.

"The Cthugha chant—do you remember it?"

"I took it down. I've got it here."

For an instant I was afraid that this, too, might have been taken from us, but it was not; it was in my pocket where I had left it. With shaking hands, Laird tore the paper from my grasp.

Ph'nglui mglw'nafh Cthugha Fomalhaut n'gha-ghaa naf'l thagn! Ia! Cthugha! he said, running to the verandah, myself at his heels.

Out of the woods came the bestial voice of the dweller in the dark. *"Ee-ya-ya-haa-haahaaa! Ygnaiih! Ygnaiih!"*

Ph'nglui mglw'nafh Cthugha Fomalhaut n'gha-ghaa naf'l thagn! Ia! Cthugha! repeated Laird for the second time.

Still the ghastly melee of sounds from the woods came on, in no way diminished, rising now to supreme heights of terror-fraught fury, with the bestial voice of the thing from the slab added to the wild, mad music of the pipes, and the sound as of wings.

And then, once more, Laird repeated the primal words of the chant.

On the instant that the final guttural sound had left his lips, there began a sequence of events no human eye was ever destined to witness. For suddenly the darkness was gone, giving way to a fearsome amber glow; simultaneously the flute-like music ceased, and in its place rose cries of rage and terror. Then, there appeared thousands of tiny points of light—not only on and among the trees, but on the earth itself, on the lodge and the car standing before it. For still a further moment we were rooted to the spot, and then it was borne in upon us that the myriad points of light were *living entities of flame!* For wherever they touched, fire sprang up, seeing which, Laird rushed into the lodge for such of our things as he could carry forth before the holocaust made it impossible for us to escape Rick's Lake.

He came running out—our bags had been downstairs—gasping that it was too late to take the dictaphone or anything else, and together we dashed toward the car, shielding our eyes a little from the blinding light all around. But even though we had shielded our eyes, it was impossible not to see the great amorphous shapes streaming skyward from this accursed place, nor the equally great being hovering like a cloud of living fire above the trees. So much we saw, before the frightful struggle to escape the burning woods forced us to forget mercifully the other details of that terrible, maddened flight.

Horrible as were the things that took place in the darkness of the forest at Rick's Lake, there was something more cataclysmic still, something so blasphemously conclusive that even now I shudder and tremble uncontrollably to think of it. For in that brief dash to the car, I saw something that explained Laird's doubt, I saw what had made him take heed of the voice on the record and not of the thing that came to us as Professor Gardner. They keys were there before, but I did not understand; even Laird had not fully believed. Yet it was given to us—we did not know. "It is not desired by the Old Ones that mere man shall know too much," Partier had said. And the terrible voice on the record had hinted even more clearly: *Go forth in his form or in whatever form chosen in the guise of man, and destroy that which may lead them to us. . . .* Destroy that which may lead them to us! Our record, the notes, the photostats from Miskatonic University, yes, and even Laird and myself! And the thing had gone forth, for it was Nyarlathotep, the Mighty Messenger, the Dweller in Darkness who had gone forth and who had returned to the forest to send his minions back to us. It was he who had come from interstellar space even as Cthugha, the fire-being, had come from Fomalhaut upon the utterance of the command that woke him from his eon-long sleep upon that amber star, the command that Gardner, the living-dead captive of the terrible Nyarlathotep had discovered in those fantastic travelings in space and time; and it was he who returned whence he had come, with his earth-haven now forever rendered useless for him with its destruction by the minions of Cthugha!

I know, and Laird knows. We never speak of it.

If we had had any doubt, despite everything that had gone before, we could not forget that final, soul-searing discovery, the thing we saw when we shielded our eyes from the flames all around and looked away from those beings in the heavens, *the line of footprints that led away from the lodge in the direction of that hellish slab deep in the black forest, the footprints that began in the soft soil beyond the verandah in the shape of a man's footprints, and changed with each step into a hideously suggestive imprint made by a creature of incredible shape and weight, with variations of outline and size so grotesque as to have been incomprehensible to anyone who had not seen the thing on the slab—and beside them, torn and rent as if by an expanding force, the clothing that once belonged to Professor Gardner, left piece by piece along the trail back into the woods, the trail taken by the hellish monstrosity that had come out of the night, the Dweller in Darkness who had visited us in the shape and guise of Professor Gardner!*

Fool Proof

DR. JASPER CONSIDINE'S car came around the corner and stopped before the house. The doctor pushed the felt hat back from his rubicund face and leaned out. "Want to come along out into the country? George Tomson's been found dead."

"Lorin? Want to come too?" Judge Ephraim Peabody Peck looked at me over his spectacles, his opaque eyes casual.

"Okay by me," I said.

We went out to the curb after the judge had told his niece where he was going. He climbed into the front seat next to his old crony, and I got into the back.

"What happened?" asked the Judge as we started off.

Dr. Considine shrugged his heavy shoulders. "They found him in bed half an hour ago. It could have been anything—though it's his brother John who's got heart trouble and has to take it easy. A lucky thing, because John never liked work and George always did. Emma found him."

"Who are these people?" I asked.

"Tomsons?" said the Judge, without turning. "Oh, a couple of old bachelors and their spinster sister. Fairly well-to-do, but disagreeable. Crotchety, rather. Can't seem to get along too well with one another, though John lives with his sister, Emma, and George lived alone."

"I never know what you mean by 'well-to-do' when you talk about Sac Prairie people," I said. "A lot of money?"

Dwellers in Darkness, 1949

He laughed. "No, just comfortable. Each one is or was worth probably as much as twenty-five thousand, exclusive of real estate. John might have a little less than the others, because he spends it more freely. Emma's the youngest, George was the closest—almost to parsimony, I'd say—and John the most careless with money. I drew up George's will not long ago; he leaves everything to Emma."

"That so?" said Dr. Considine with interest. "I don't know why some of these old bachelors don't leave their money to some community interest, like the school or the library, for instance."

"Probably nobody asks them," observed the Judge. "How old was George?"

"I think about sixty."

The surviving Tomsons waited on the porch of George Tomson's house, set well back from the highway, and backed by a cluster of long-unused farm buildings. Emma was a small, prim woman, with thin lips and a pinched face out of which her dark eyes looked like strangers. John was more portly, but tall. He had graying hair, and the veins of his face stood out.

He was breathing fast, a laboring of excitement.

"He's inside, in bed," said Emma. She had come to her feet but John remained sitting in the rocker.

"Forgive me for not coming along," said John. "The shock's been bad enough. My heart, you know."

"Yes, take it easy, John," said Dr. Considine sharply, in passing. "No exercise whatever. You shouldn't have come over here at all."

The doctor knew his way around. He went through the kitchen and the dining room to the bedroom. We followed him. The light was on in the bedroom. George Tomson's body lay across the bed. The bedclothes were torn up quite a bit. It looked as if he had got up, put on the light, and tried to get out. Perhaps to call the doctor.

"It looks like convulsions," I said.

Dr. Considine nodded judiciously. He had already bent to his examination.

"I saw him two mornings ago when he was out hunting mushrooms," said Emma from the hall. "Then this morning when I walked over—" Her house, she explained needlessly, was a mile down the road.

"He appears to have died last night," said Dr. Considine.

"Yes," said Emma faintly.

"Mushrooms," murmured the Judge. "Did he often gather them, Miss Emma?"

"Oh, yes, Judge. He's been getting them for twenty years. Just morels, though. He wouldn't trust himself with any other kind."

Judge Peck smiled, but his eyes flickered.

"I don't know what this is," said Dr. Considine, puzzled. "There'll have to be an autopsy." He straightened up. "Better call Dr. Enderby down from Baraboo, Emma. I'll just have a look at the kitchen."

He went back into the kitchen. Some dishes still stood on the table, but those Tomson had used had all been washed and stacked on one side of the sink. The dishes on the table were covered. Dr. Considine uncovered them one after the other. Cold steak. Cheese. Celery. Finally an unsavory-looking dark-colored mess.

"Ugh! What do these people eat? I wanted to know.

"Morels," said Judge Peck. "But unusually dark, aren't they?"

"Yes," answered the doctor dubiously, his normally cheerful face wrinkled in puzzlement.

"Let's have a look at that," said the Judge.

He went over and got a plate, hunted up a long-handled spoon, and came back to the dish. Emma, coming from the telephone, stood on the threshold watching with marked disapproval on her severe features. John, too, had got up and come into the house; he stood just behind her, looking apprehensive, one hand held to his chest; his breathing was still labored. The Judge dipped a few mushrooms out of the dish and spread them on the plate. They were cut up.

"He fixed them in butter sauce," said Emma. "That's the way he always did. Maybe he parboiled them in a little salt water; then he poured water and all into the spider and fried them in butter."

Judge Peck took out another spoonful and emptied it on the plate. A third and fourth followed. He got another plate and went on. He hesitated over his seventh spoonful, until finally he got a fork and fished a piece of mushroom out of the mess. It was a good-sized, limp mass, a kind of chestnut-brown in color. He held it up without comment before Dr. Considine's eyes.

"Ah. *Gyromitra esculenta*," said the doctor.

"I thought so. Deadly, isn't it?"

Dr. Considine nodded. "Some people seem to have eaten it without ill effect. But the species is listed as poisonous. The poisonous principle is helvellic acid, soluble in hot water. But then, he used hot water."

"Cause of death?"

"I think so."

"Oh, no!" exclaimed Emma.

"Everybody around here's been expecting that for years," said John. "I wouldn't touch them. Emma wouldn't either."

Judge Peck looked at them speculatively for a moment. His opaque eyes seemed to pass them, looking beyond the walls into the distance. He stood quite still for almost a minute, his long frock-coat with its brass buttons bright in the May sunlight which streamed in through the windows, his green-tinted black umbrella tight in his hand like a weapon. I knew he was thinking of something Dr. Considine had not caught.

"Poor devil! He had a hard time of it," said the doctor. He turned to Emma. "Is Dr. Enderby coming?"

"Yes, Doctor. Right away. It'll take fifteen minutes or so yet, I expect."

"Miss Emma, you knew George had left everything to you, didn't you?" asked the Judge.

"Why, yes. He told me when he made his will."

"He said he was going to."

"He and John always argued about things. But John and I get along—at least as well as we should. And I guess George figured John would have the benefit of it anyway, as long as he lived with me. I don't really need it. I've got money." She said this a little proudly.

The Judge nodded. He had that faraway look again, and his long, almost equine face, with its strong jaw and the pursed lips, was setting in an expression of firmness.

"I sometimes think there's no such thing as a fool-proof mushroom, Ephraim," said Dr. Considine, moving out of the kitchen once more. "They call the morel that. But the *Gyromitra esculenta* is also called 'the false morel,' which is probably another way of saying that nature sets a trap for over-confident fools."

"You're philosophically inclined today, Jasper," said the Judge.

We followed him to the porch and off it, where he stood in the shade of a spreading elm tree. Miss Emma came out and sat down once more, this time in the rocker John had been using. John, too, came out, walking slowly, almost painfully; he came down the steps and leaned up against a nearby maple tree.

"Do you suppose any stranger lurking around here that morning or noon, or any visitor to George, would have been seen?" asked the Judge.

Dr. Considine looked at him queerly. "Perhaps."

"I should say absolutely," said the Judge pensively. "There is that all-seeing eye, Jasper."

But Dr. Considine was no longer listening. He had taken out his watch and was looking at it, muttering that it was high time Enderby had got here; so he could go on about his business.

"So that anyone visiting here would have been seen. Because someone did come here while George was getting his last dinner ready."

"Eh? How do you know that?" asked Dr. Considine sharply.

Because, in my mind's eye, I saw him," answered the Judge imperturbably, the hint of a grim smile lurking at his lips.

He walked away from us toward the place where John stood.

Dr. Considine looked at me, somewhat bewildered, as if to say, "You live with him, but I've known him longer and I still don't always know what he's up to."

What he was up to this time was clear. He bent to John Tomson's ear and whispered something. I saw Tomson's hand drop from his side; it hung there for a moment, shaking. I looked at his face. He was staring at the judge. He was afraid. For only a second, though—then he set out awkwardly running across the fields, away from the house.

Emma got up, her hand at her throat. "John! You shouldn't run!"

But he ran faster.

"What on earth did you say to him?" demanded Dr. Considine.

"Not much, Jasper. I only asked him why he put that poisonous mushroom into his brother's dish—all cut up, too, so that George would hardly notice it in the frying pan."

"For God's sake, Ephraim! What are you saying?"

"That John killed his brother. And he may very well kill his sister next."

"Ephraim!"

"Why, Jasper, John told us himself he had done it. He said, 'Everybody around here's been expecting that for years.' But that wasn't quite true, because John hadn't been expecting it, or he wouldn't have brought it about. And Emma put it clearly when she said that he never picked but one kind of mushroom. Morels. You know what a morel looks like, Jasper. Its appearance resembles a smooth sponge. A *Gyromitra,* on the other hand, has brain-like convolutions. Only a fool could mistake them. Certainly no man who had been gathering only morels for twenty years could make such a mistake. George wasn't a fool. But John is."

"Why didn't you hold him?"

"Because I can't prove a word of it. I just know it's so. It has to be. And see him run! 'The guilty flee when no man pursueth!' I think we'll find out he hadn't any more money, and probably Miss Emma hasn't as much as she thinks she has, either. John could have managed that. Neither you nor I can do a thing to him, Jasper. But perhaps Providence can. There's Emma to think of—if he comes back."

They found John Tomson's body next day only two miles from George's house. His heart had given out. Nobody had to tell me that was the way the judge had planned it . . .

The Extra Child

"NOW THIS THE picture I'm telling you about," explained Hannibal Corscott, "My uncle was a little queer about that. I remember seeing it a long time ago, when I was a kid. It's a picture of six kids three boys and three girls—playing in a circle around a big old tree that looks to be deep in some woods. It's autumn; the leaves are all colored,—rich yellow, brown, sienna, not much red, only a little. The kids have the color in their clothes. They're small kids—oh, about nine, ten, eleven years old. He was crazy about that picture."

He laughed silkily.

"I wonder, if he went off, that he didn't take it with him. The reason he liked the picture is that it was so good; it was a good job, though; no, it went back further than that. When Uncle Jason was a boy, well—say twelve or so—something like that, he was in love with a girl. You know how young people talk, and they were planning on getting married, and he used to say he wanted three kids and she said, no, six. Well one day they were going along Madison Avenue, passing the show windows of some art association, when they saw that picture. 'Look,' she cried, 'there they are—our six kids.' Well, later he bought the picture. Something had happened. I don't know, but I think she died or went off, and he never looked at another woman. Some men are like that, you know.

"Now this picture, Inspector, had a good deal of meaning for him. It belonged to something important in his life—I guess you can see how that would be so. He made a lot of it. You'll see it in a few minutes."

"The picture, however, seems to have had nothing to do with your uncle's disappearance," said Inspector Gryce.

"Now that's a matter I'm not prepared to make a statement about, and that's a fact," said Corscott. "Those six kids in that picture—my uncle got it in his head that they were what his kids might have been, or some such notion. He lived too much alone; he got lonely. My uncle was a little queer; I've said that. If you could understand how he lived—but then, even I don't know just exactly how he lived; I didn't see him so very often. He was a fairly handsome fellow, even at his age, but sedentary, sedentary: a solitary . . ."

Lonesome Places, 1950

It was on a morning in May when Jason Corscott first noticed the alteration in the picture. An hallucination, he thought. The illusion was of someone looking out just momentarily from behind the great old tree—as if a seventh child were concealed there, waiting his turn to come forth and join in the circle around the tree. Or was it a girl? For one brief moment he considered this question before he dismissed the hallucination from his mind.

At seventy, he was austere, almost forbidding in the face he presented to the world. He had made a modest success of his career, but he had long felt that his retirement had been ill-advised. He was lonely. He missed the steady flow of people in the office, though he had no question of his nephew's competence. People could speak of him as a person of some consequence in the financial world, no Morgan, to be sure, but nevertheless one of the soundest figures on the Exchange.

The austerity vanished in the privacy of his apartment. Here he was, in reality, as so many men and women are, when alone, entirely himself. Here he sloughed off all the masks he wore to protect himself from the world, and became someone markedly different. To tell the truth, he favored an aspect of himself few people suspected, the arrested youth in his early teens who had loved Evelyn Howe, and who never got over her defection, her going away finally, her marrying another man. To the idyl of their love he returned again and again; to its symbol, the picture of the frolicking children on the wall, he turned his eyes repeatedly during his waking hours. And with each year of age, he looked back ever more fondly to that halcyon time when Evelyn and he and all the world were young.

But now, in a subtle way, something had altered. Up to yesterday, Evelyn had still lived somewhere in the world. Ceylon. Far away, but still, she was alive somewhere, and the tenuous bond that had been removed from time to time in little chance notes at Christmas and birthdays, was forever severed. "Mrs. Thomas Bainbridge, the former Evelyn Howe, died today at her plantation in Ceylon—" He had not read beyond that; nothing could add to or diminish the fact that she was dead, gone out of his world, so that the sight of the picture on the wall, the picture of their six children who had never been born and were destined to remain forever the creatures of an artist's imagination, should stir him to hallucination.

For that, certainly it was. There were six of them—the three boys, the three girls—the one in the purple shirt, the one in the blue dress, the one in yellow; oh, yes, all were there, unchanged, in a world where nothing ever changed, and their shouts and their joyous laughter might ring out forever.

But at this moment, at the instant of his dismissal of his hallucination, he saw once more what appeared to be the head of another child looking out from behind the trunk of the tree. He went directly to the mantel, over which the picture hung, and peered at it. How extraordinary that he should not have noticed it before! Still, the child's head—a girl's—was so placed as to blend with a branch swinging low and also seem to be an outgrowth of the tree-trunk. Yet he had always had the conviction that the trunk was symmetrical.

He pulled over a hassock and stood on it in order to scrutinize the picture more carefully. What else might he not have missed? The extra child was there, beyond question, just turning her head to look out from behind the tree; beyond her, beyond the six frolicking children, the woods seemed to stretch limitlessly toward a place where the sun shown even more brightly, a glade similar to this one in which the children played, but somehow larger, more significant. Instead of being enclosed within a frame—whether the obvious wooden border or the frame of the woods—the picture seemed to have gained in depth and meaning; it was as if the discovery of this extra child had added a kind of revelation to the picture.

But there was also another factor, Corscott thought as he went down the elevator afterward; the children were no longer six, the children Evelyn had marked as their own in those magic years of their youth. By all standards, the picture should have lost some of its meaning to him; yet it did not. If anything, this discovery so many years after the picture had been bought to hang over the mantel enhanced it in his eyes. Secretly he fancied that this one, this extra child, was the unplanned one, the unpredicted, unforseen child, come to remake their dream.

It was difficult, in his preoccupation with the picture, to remember that Evelyn had died, shattering the bond which had been so strong between them for so many years.

Perhaps because he glanced at the picture each time he passed it, he was not aware of increasing change for some days. May passed into June; the summer grew hot, and his associates, few in number, were getting ready to go up the coast to the seashore. One of his oldest friends stopped in one evening to bid Corscott goodbye.

"Tell me, Joel," said Corscott in the course of their conversation." How do you explain hallucinations? You're a doctor; you encounter these things."

Doctor Matthews shrugged. "There are all kinds of hallucinations, Jason."

"Well, I don't mean the kind that come with liquor or daydreams—nothing of that sort. I mean something you see which ought not to be there."

"Have you been having them, Jason?" the doctor asked with a hint of anxiety in his voice.

"I'm beginning to think so. Come here."

He took him over to the picture.

"Oh, yes, this picture. I've seen this before, Jason."

"Well, look at it. Don't you see anything different about it?"

"Not a thing, no."

"How many children do you see?"

"Good heavens, Jason! How intense you sound!"

"I mean it. Count them, will you?"

"Why there are seven—six playing, and another coming out from around the tree."

Corscott swallowed. "But, you know, I was convinced there were only six children there. So was Evelyn. We saw them quite clearly. Now this extra child . . ."

Dr. Matthews looked at him professionally. "Look here, Jason. Why don't you run up to Maine with me? Do you good. You need to get out of the city once in a while. You lock yourself up here too much."

"No, that isn't it, Joel. Just stand here a moment," he asked, putting a hand on one arm of the doctor, who had begun to move away. "I've had that picture for fifty years, you know. I never saw that extra child until a few days ago. And the dimensions seem to have altered—a subtle thing; I am hard put to explain it—as if to invite me to look into another world beyond that frame. I mean, you seem to see a country beyond the children, and yet part of their lives, an integral part, a place of sunshine and light and laughter . . ."

"Without a stock market," added the doctor dryly.

"Yes," agreed Corscott with a small laugh. "Without that and a great many other things. But what I wanted to say is that I noticed this extra child just a few days ago, a week or ten days; I couldn't tell you any longer which day it was. She was just turning her head to look out from behind the tree."

"She would appear to be making ready to run out," said the doctor. "See, she's getting ready to toss her hair back out of her face so that she can join the others. I'd hardly describe her as just turning to look out from behind the tree."

Corscott coughed. "That's what I mean," he said. "Exactly. But the other day, you know, I am quite certain—believe me, I really am certain—that there was nothing more than a part of her head showing. Do you see what I mean?"

Matthews looked at him with more care than before. "Yes, I see. Really an extraordinary hallucination, when you think of it. But then, you've always thought a lot of this picture, Jason; you've had it on your mind a great deal, perhaps because of that youthful romance of yours."

"She's dead, you know."

"Yes, I saw it in the papers." He considered for a moment, turning away from the picture. "I could give you some advice, but I don't know whether you'd take it or not."

"What is it?"

"Why don't you sell this picture or put it away for a while?"

"No," said Corscott quietly. "I think it means a little too much in my life."

"That's just it. That's the entire basis for your hallucinations, Jason. A kind of wishful identification with the world of this picture which has come in your mind to represent the world of your adolescence. This is, in fact, a kind of arrested development; you never looked at a woman after Evelyn Howe, did you? No. When she went away . . ."

"Oh, come, Joel. That's over and done with. A long time ago."

"In a sense, nothing a man does is ever over and done with. It leaves a mark on him and his world. And this picture is the world you somehow never knew—the world of Evelyn and the six children—love, romance, ideals—a world of childhood and youth divorced from the business world in which you spent your life." He took his old friend by the shoulders. "Come along with me. We'll rot in the sunlight and swim out to sea. Believe me, Jason, you need that kind of relaxation. You're growing farther and farther away from life."

"No. I have my own life."

"Inside, yes. A dream, an hallucination."

"We were talking of hallucinations, Joel," said Corscott, smiling. "After all, your world might as well be an hallucination as mine."

"You're philosophical today."

"And there are quite possibly planes of time and space with which mankind is not yet familiar."

"Take care. You'll become a spiritualist and take to seances."

"No, never."

"Promise me something at least," urged Matthews.

"If I can."

"Don't look at the picture for a week or so. Cover it up. Do something about it. But don't look at it."

"Very well. I won't."

"I'll look in when I get back. If you change your mind, you have my address. Just follow me up. There's plenty of room for you, and we'll vegetate."

"Thanks. But I'll probably stay here. My roots are down too deep."

During the week he kept the picture covered, he was disturbingly aware of a kind of life beneath the cloth. This was, he felt certain, another hallucination, this feeling of standing on the portal of another world, of looking into a world that might have been his own. If I were a child again, he caught himself thinking repeatedly, I would like to be there. To be the age he was when Evelyn and he had discovered the picture—so young, in love, their first love, his only love!

The sense of throbbing life persisted from beneath the covering cloth with an extraordinary vitality. But he refused to yield to his impulse to remove the cloth before the promised week was up. He had, in fact, been in receipt of a brief letter from his old friend cautioning him jokingly against dwelling upon the picture and warning him, with equal facetiousness, of the serious consequences of hallucinations. "After all," Matthews had written, "every dreamer reaches a point at which he no longer knows where reality begins and where it ends. And he asks himself quite seriously whether the welcome dream he has is the real world or whether the world in which he lives is just a bad dream."

The conviction of life beneath the cloth haunted him day after day. He could not take his mind from the picture, but he confided to no one else anything of what troubled him. Yet he was not so much aware of being troubled as he was of a kind of anxiety, as if—however absurd it was—the extra child might run out from behind the three, beyond the circle of frolicking children, out of his sight beyond the boundaries of that world caught within that frame, before he could lift the cloth. It was important that she should not; it was important that he see her face to face.

He restrained his eagerness until the Monday a week after he had last seen Joel Matthews. Then he waited until evening to lift the cloth, so that the sunlight of the picture might meet the soft evening glow of his apartment. His eyes sought at once for the seventh child, the extra girl.

There she was, free of the tree, her arms extended as if to join the circle of the six frolicking children. And yet, she did not seem to be looking at the children at all; she seemed to be looking directly ahead, out of the picture, at him. A fresh, beautiful girl, thirteen or fourteen, he thought, perhaps a little older than the others, with something so familiar about her that he felt a pang of nostalgic pain.

Like Evelyn, he thought, even to the dress.

He turned up the lights, pulled up the hassock, and mounted it, leaning over the mantel. He stared. His mouth went dry. The extra girl was in the likeness of that Evelyn Howe he had known and loved more than fifty years ago, and, seeing her so, standing in that sunlit glade waiting to resume a time of joy and laughter, he was overwhelmed in the pent-up rush of emotion which had been too long locked away. All the love withheld, all the affection he had longed to lavish on someone came pushing up like a tidal wave, engulfing him.

He could almost hear the shouts and cries of the children. He could almost feel Evelyn's impatience where she stood with her arms extended to him, waiting. The scene invited him.

He put his hands on the frame of the picture. His fingers reached beyond, into the picture, into space. The frame dissolved, vanished. The room around him blackened, swam in a mist of darkness.

He climbed up the mantel, over the frame.

"Now there it is," said Hannibal Corscott. "Just as he always had it, over the mantel. He used to sit by his fireplace and look up at it and dream. Of his six children that he never had, no doubt."

"I would hardly think of your uncle as a dreamer, Mr. Corscott."

"Ah, who would? He was a financial wizard. In his way, of course. No Hetty Green, no Morgan. And perhaps just as well. He was reasonably content. Or was he? I wonder. Now just take a look at that picture."

"I thought you said there were six children—three boys and three girls. There are eight—four boys and four girls."

"Yes, there are, aren't there? I saw the picture first when I was quite young. There were six children. And what do you make of that spot over to the left?"

"It looks like an old man sleeping in the shade."

"Sleeping or dead, yes. He wasn't there, either. But of course you can say that children don't see these things. Perhaps they don't. Perhaps children see just what they want to see. But I know I didn't see it this way. There were six children and nobody else in the picture. What do you think of it?"

Inspector Gryce laughed brittlely. "I should say that someone certainly had an hallucination."

"Yes. But whose hallucination? His or ours? I leave that for you. I find it impossible to answer."

The Night Road

THERE IS SOMETHING about out of the way country places which suggests the adventurous unknown, the strange, the mysterious, as were these things inherent in the human lives so remotely lived out in such places. People born and dying far away from the centers of civilization, people who may never use a telephone or listen to a radio, locked away in the hollows of the hills, with little-used roads connecting them to the highways, which for many of those country people must mark the known boundaries of their world.

The little-used roads. Rutted and grass-grown sometimes. Or, like the one Evelyn called the "road that just seems to come out at night," with what was meant to be a note of gay enchantment and turned out to be something more. I could set down here that I had passed it a score of times, but would it be true? I don't know. It led off the ridge road between Green Spring and Logtown in southern Wisconsin, a smooth gravelled road that didn't stay gravelled or smooth.

Evelyn noticed it first. We were coming back from a movie at Green Spring late one night before we were married, and Evelyn said, "There's a road off here to the side somewhere. It's a strange road. Nobody ever turns off on it. It's a road that just seems to come out at night."

"Do you want to take it?" I asked.

"I hate to park on the highway. There's so much traffic."

I drove slower, until she caught sight of the turn.

"There it is. Drive in."

I drove in from the ridge. The road that was so inviting soon became rutted and difficult, and it went almost straight down off the ridge, a dark road with trees crowding close upon it. I had to slow down, shift, pull forward, maneuver the ruts, the washed out portions of the road, the muck and mud.

"Where does it lead to?" I asked at last.

"I don't know," Evelyn confessed. "You always talk about the charm of country roads."

"By day," I said.

Dwellers in Darkness, 1952

"Well, it goes somewhere," she said, laughing. "Every road has to go somewhere."

"It doesn't even look modern," I said. "Like nothing put here this year or ten years ago."

Nor, in fact, did it. Country roads are narrow, dusty, sometimes overgrown. But this one was rocky, rutted, muddy, with a look of such age that it might have been a road used long ago and long since abandoned.

There was not a mark on it of a tire, but here and there a wagon wheel, or a buggy's narrower track. And the trees that pressed so closely upon it and were so young at the place where we had entered it were older and older the farther we went. Where at first there had been fence-lines, here now and there was nothing.

Two miles, three—we were at the bottom of the hollow, and Evelyn sat silent at my side.

I slowed up and came to a stop.

"Where are we?" she asked in a small voice.

"I don't know."

"There should be a turn somewhere, or a crossroads."

"We'll see."

But at this point, our venturesome drive turned into an unnecessary chance. The car would not start.

"Well, here we are in the middle of nowhere," she said. "Better put out the lights or you'll wear the battery down."

I did so.

We sat for a moment in absolute stillness. Not a bird's voice, not the rustle of a mouse in the grass, not an animal's cry. I reached for her through the darkness, drew her close and kissed her long.

"We always wanted to be shut away from the world, didn't we?" I said. "Now here we are, maybe three miles from the highway, but a thousand from anywhere."

"Will we have to walk back?"

"No, the car'll start after it rests a little—I hope!"

I kissed her again.

"Is that a light over there, Will?"

I turned. Back from the road shone a pale yellow glow.

"Must be."

"We'd better find out where we are, just in case the car doesn't start."

The moment I stepped outside the car, I felt it. Something wrong, some note of error, something not as it should be. In the car there had been no sound from the outside, but now, outside, the air was filled with sound—the thousand small rustlings in the grass of mice and voles and shrews, the indistinguishable hum of life in the woods, the almost deafening chorus of the whippoorwills, for the month was June of a late spring, and the whippoorwills were mating. But of all this, in the car, nothing.

I went around and opened the door for Evelyn. How small and frail she looked against that vaguely menacing darkness pressing in from all sides! The light in the farmhouse window was a welcome haven.

"I can't see," she said. "And listen to those whippoorwills!"

"I'm listening," I said. "Wait a minute. I've got a keyring flashlight—it'll help a little."

I turned it on. There was a kind of path, or a place where not much grew. We walked along it, Evelyn closed behind me. The house grew out of the darkness, dark, like the night and the woods, a stone house which was old, so old that vines covered all one wall of it, creeping even upon the window.

"There's the door," said Evelyn.

I went up to it and knocked. It opened under my knock, and the light shown out of the room. There was a young woman standing up against one wall there, dark-skinned, lustrous-eyed, a beauty. And two men were sitting across a table paying no attention to anything but each other. The woman was watching them; her eyes were scornful, aloof, remote, and yet she was intensely interested in what was gone on. A game? I wondered.

"Can you tell us where we are?" I asked.

None of them looked toward us. No one answered.

There was a broad-shouldered man. He said, "It's your cut, Neil."

And a slender man. He said, "How many times?"

"Three. This is your last cut."

They were dressed like country people, but in old-fashioned clothes. The young woman had on a dress which came up to just under her ears. Of some black material. Evelyn said later it was taffeta; I wouldn't know.

"Paul, you can't do it," she said.

"I can do anything," He answered.

"Even to this," she said bitterly. "I never wanted to come to Lost Hope Valley. There is a curse on it, there's a curse on us all."

The broad-shouldered man looked at her and said, "If there is, it's a woman's curse—the curse of a woman who couldn't be satisfied with one man."

"You could die of loneliness here," she said.

I coughed, loudly. "Could you tell us—" I began. But no one was listening. I felt Evelyn take hold of my arm, pull it. I looked at her. She inclined her head a little; her motion and her eyes said urgently, "Out!"

I went back to the porch, leaving the door stand open.

"Something's going to happen," she said.

"Something's always going to happen, sure."

"No, no," she said, and bit her lip. "Something terrible. Please, I feel it!"

I chuckled. "Let that be a lesson to you. Don't go leading men down strange roads at night." I made a half-hearted attempt to leer at her. But her eyes were closed tightly now.

At any rate, I thought, I knew where we were—in a sort of way. Long ago I had found an old copy of the *Green Spring News*, a weekly paper with country correspondents who filled its inside pages. There was news from Logtown and Black Hawk and Cross Corners, Little Bear Valley and Bear Junction. Yes, and Lost Hope Valley. All the others were still in the *News* today, but not Lost Hope Valley. That had retreated into silence. Small wonder!

I looked back into the room, examining the two men. They looked alike. Brothers, perhaps. The woman had a wedding ring on. Perhaps she was married to one of them. There was a little smile on her lips now, and for one moment the scene held; nobody moved, waiting for the slender man, Neil, to cut his card. Then he cut and turned the cards over. I could see the card in the yellow light of the kerosene lamp on the table.

The seven of spades.

The woman gave a sharp cry. "You cut the seven of spades! Oh, Neil—spades! It's a death card."

He paid no attention to her. "Beat that," he said to his brother.

The broad-shouldered man cut the five of hearts.

"You won, Neil," said the woman.

"All fair and square," said Neil, laughing.

"Yes, now," said Paul. "Now, by the cards. But how was it before, when my back was turned, when I was out in the fields, off in the woods—how was it then?"

"You said you'd abide by the cards."

"I did. I said it, and I will. But I didn't say how."

With that, he pushed his chair away from the table and stood up. There was a pistol in his hand. He pulled the trigger, and the slender man fell forward on the table. The woman screamed and came at him like a tiger; she had a knife. He shot her, too, but she fell on him, stabbing him, a cry of rage and despair tearing from her lips. They fell together. Blood ran off the table to the floor, blood pooled from the man and woman lying together beside the table.

It all happened so fast that there had been no time for a cry of protest. But now I ran into the room, to give what help I could. The men were both dead; the woman was dying. If she saw me, she gave no sign. She bled from the wound in her breast, she bled from her mouth. She murmured, "Neil, Neil!" and died.

Behind me, Evelyn came to the threshold. I had forgotten her. She looked in and saw what I saw. I heard her scream, and got to her in time to catch her when she fainted. I carried her back to the car, some intuition guiding my steps. The whippoorwills cried from all sides, flying up silently, brushing past. Crying for somebody's soul, my grandmother used to say.

I got her to the car and put her in. I got in on the other side, hoping the car would start now. I knew what had to be done. There had been no telephone in the house, not even electricity. Logtown was closest, once I got back to the highway. I would have to report what I had seen.

The car started. I pulled forward a little, knowing there must be a driveway of some sort to the farm.

There was. It was used even less than the road, but I could turn there. The road was too narrow of its self, the shoulders too soft or too steep. I turned around and headed back. The light was still burning in the house.

Evelyn stirred.

"Take it easy," I said.

"God! she cried.

"Listen," I said. "We're all right."

"Were they all dead?"

"Uh-huh. All we can do is report it."

"How awful!"

"Sure," I said. "But things like that happen. It's our unlucky night.

She was silent for a little while. Then, "The whippoorwills!"

I noticed it the moment she spoke. Not a sound. Dead silence. Outside I knew the whippoorwills were calling, filling the night with their wild, nostalgic crying; but here in the car there was no sound.

"It's some quirk of space and sound," I said. "A pocket in space."

"What happened back there?"

I tried to explain things the way I had seen them, but somehow the whole thing now had an air of unreality, of dream; and the farther I got along that road, escaping the dark, wooded hollow, the less real it seemed. But what I had seen, I had seen; nothing could alter that. Evelyn said nothing.

We got back to the highway after what seemed an interminable ride. The car balked on the steep slope, just where the road was so steep that even the emergency and the regular brake could hardly hold it there; Evelyn had to push the accelerator in while I shifted and got started again. The highway never looked so good. Cars going back and forth between Green Spring and Logtown. I had the wild impulse to flag them down and tell them what had happened down in Lost Hope Valley.

I didn't. I drove into Logtown. I reported what I had seen to the village constable, who got on the telephone and talked to the sheriff. I took Evelyn home and came back to help guide the deputy-sheriff who turned up at the sheriff's order, back to the scene of the crime.

I led the way back. There were three or four cars. It was about four miles from Logtown that the road had turned off into that precipitous descent into Lost Hope Valley. I knew the place, I thought, so well that I could lead someone there blindfolded.

But try as I would, I could not find the turn. I could not find the road.

When I stopped at the place where I thought it had been, there was a grassy shoulder. I got out and examined the ground by the glow of the headlights. It had the look of once having been a road, long ago. Certainly no one could travel it now. And yet there were exactly what looked like tire tracks over that grass, moving in the direction of the downgrade.

A road "that comes out only at night," indeed!

I felt like a dozen kinds of fool, and I was growing momentarily more frantic, let we would not get there in time to do anything for any one of them just in case I should have been mistaken in thinking them all dead.

But the road was not to be found. I drove to Green Spring and back to Logtown, looking at every side-road. I found nothing. The men thought I had been drinking. I could understand how they would.

The deputy-sheriff was bound to make a report to the sheriff's office, just the same. I could imagine what would be in it. He took down everything I deposed in the most minute detail.

We never spoke of it. We never took strange roads at night after that.

One day I had a note from the sheriff asking me to pick up Evelyn and run up to the county seat and call on him. It was convenient to do so; the day he named was the day Evelyn and I planned to go up for our license.

After we had it, we went over to the sheriff's office. He was a fat, good-natured man. I introduced Evelyn and myself.

"You're the folks had that funny thing happen to you that night last June," he said, identifying us. "I remember now I wrote you a letter. Got something here to show you."

He pulled open a drawer, talking as he did so. "Got to thinking. Says to myself there's something familiar about that story. And sure enough—but look at these."

There were three old photographs. Two men and a woman.

Evelyn's fingers tightened on my arm. She put her other hand over her lips, pressing down.

I nodded. "It's them."

Evelyn nodded, too.

"You'd have no call to think up a thing like that," the sheriff went on. "You can see for yourself how old the pictures are. Don't figure you'd know a thing about it. Now here's another photograph we took the other day."

The ruins of a house, a stone house. I recognized it, for all that not a wall was left intact.

"That's what you'll find in Lost Hope Valley today. How you got down that road, the Lord only knows. That's the Manadal farm. She got to fooling around with her husband's brother, and he shot 'em both. She got him with a knife before she died, though."

"That's it," I said. "I saw it."

"Yeah, that's it. Only it happened in 1891—sixty years ago. Maybe that's why nobody lives down in Lost Hope Valley now."

Something strange about remote country places, and the roads that lead into the pockets in the hills. We could understand, Evelyn and I, why that Lost Hope Valley road had been like a road "that just seems to come out at night."

The Place in the Woods

THOSE OF YOU who live in cities have little conception of isolated country places, where one is alone with sky and trees, with the soil and the waters of the earth, with the invisible dwellers of the woods. There must be many hidden places on the face of the earth like the place in the woods on my grandfather's farm, places with trees and a pool in a brook, where the earth has never been turned and nothing has ever disturbed the haunts which were occupied by unknown dwellers ages before any human being walked there.

Grandfather never forbade us to go to the place in the woods. Indeed, we went everywhere—my sister, my cousin, and I—but there was no other spot on the farm we liked so well as the place where the brook made a pool

---

Lonesome Places, 1954

under the great old trees, the beech and the oak, the scarlet maple and the birch, all unaware that it was a place set apart.

It was an idyllic woodland setting. The great trees were three and four feet in diameter; their limbs hung low, pressing groundward; and they were thick there, making a kind of haven of the place, a haven in which the voice of the brook was constant, and, in summer, the hushing of the birch and beech leaves, whether wind blew or not; though otherwise it was still, with few bird voices raised there, drifting in from outside, as if this little place were reserved for us.

It lay perhaps a mile from the farm buildings, for my grandfather's was a large farm of almost three hundred acres, and the woods alone was close to one hundred acres in low rolling land and small hills, from the crowns of which you could look far in every direction to the distant hills which lay blue against every horizon. Whenever we tired of playing in the haymow—on which grandfather frowned—or tormenting the animals, or fishing in the lower brook where chubs and a species of trout abounded, or running the dogs, we went off to play in the place in the woods which we had come to think of as our own.

Despite old Tom. Tom was the hired man, an old fellow who had lived in the neighborhood for many years and had at last come to work for my grandfather.

"There's things in the woods," he used to say. "Stay out."

"What things?" my sister would demand challengingly.

"Things," he would answer darkly.

Never anything more—only his ambiguous words, his dark hints, and his brooding fear of something he could or would not define. We paid no attention to him, except to tease him from time to time, in the way of children; he was so old that he went about muttering to himself, talking about the small events of his life. Later on, we understood that grandfather had taken him on because he felt sorry for the lonely old man, though he was only a little older than grandfather, if more worn.

The place in the woods lay southeast of the farm buildings. I think it was sister Evelyn who first discovered that the trees were arbored over a kind of bank or rise in the earth, which faced westward and on which, just at sunset, the sunlight fell redly, lending to the place a kind of strange, almost unearthly light. The sunlight at this hour penetrated no other part of the place of the pool—only this one, slanting across the landscape, though the woods, to fall from among the boles of the trees to this one spot, and from this spot seeming to reflect in a roseate glow over all the hidden place. And it was my sister, too, who conceived the idea of making of that spot an altar, at which the three of us could celebrate the end of the day and the coming of night.

Of such fantasies is childhood made.

We did not always go to the glade together. Sometimes grandfather put us boys to work at the corn-sheller or in the hay-mow; sometimes Evelyn refused to go fishing with us, having a horror of worms; sometimes she herself was busy in the kitchen with grandmother. She had just turned eight, and was already indulging her imagination by seeing herself a matron who excelled in all the culinary virtues.

One night, after the house was asleep, Evelyn came to the room I shared with cousin Richard.

"Nick, I was at the place in the woods this evening," she whispered, for Dick was asleep.

"Uh-huh," I answered.

"Nick, there was something there."

"Oh, you and old Tom," I said, grinning.

"No, really, cross-my-heart-and-hope-to-die," she said earnestly.

"What, then?"

"An animal, I think."

"Oh, rabbits," I said in disgust.

"No, a big animal. And someone looked at me from out of the trees."

"You mean a man?" I asked, incredulous.

"I think so."

I wanted to make fun of her, but she was trembling and scared. She stood there biting her lip, wanting me to believe her. I pushed away the book I had been reading and slipped out of bed.

"What did he look like?"

"I'm not sure. An old man. I ran."

"Could it have been Tom?"

"Oh, no—I know Tom."

But I knew it couldn't have been Tom, for he had been with us. At this moment Dick woke up, irritated.

"What's going on?" he demanded, rubbing his eyes sleepily. I told him.

"Girls are always seeing things," he said.

"I swear," Evelyn said.

"Well, you just go back to bed. We'll investigate," said Dick importantly.

"I want to go along."

"Not now. Tomorrow night."

She went back to her own room then, leaving Dick and me to talk about what she might have seen. He preferred to believe it was all Evelyn's imagination. I was not convinced of that. Besides, I did not want to be convinced of it, because the prospect of someone or something actually being in the place of the pool was too exciting to brush away so casually. We tried to guess who or what it might be, but of course, we could not. If it were an animal, then of course there must have been a man there, too, to account for the face Evelyn had sworn she had seen. The investigation promised excitement.

None of us thought of saying anything to our grandparents, and our parents were seldom there; they spent most of the week in the city, during our holiday time, and showed up only on the weekends. This was our secret alone, and the place in the woods took on new significance, held new promise.

That next evening we went out to it, though Evelyn was hesitant now that she must again face the mystery which had so seized upon her imagination. It was a beautiful summer evening, with a light west wind blowing. The day had been hot, but was cooling now, and all around us the countryside rang with the songs of larks and thrushes, of robins and killdeers. It was just at sundown that we pushed into the place of the pool.

The reddening light of the setting sun lay against the little knoll. There was something on it.

What's that?" demanded Dick, looking accusingly at Evelyn.

Evelyn made futile gestures with her hands. She explained, haltingly. On her way to the place yesterday she had found a dead sparrow. She had intended to bury it there. But once she had put it down, she had become convinced that the dead bird ought to be given a funeral by fire.

"I know it's funny, but I thought it ought to be cut open and bled only of course it was dead and wouldn't bleed and so the next best thing was to build a fire under it; so I gathered all the twigs and some of those dry leaves and put them on the altar . . ."

"What altar?" I asked.

"Why, that altar," she said, pointing to a rise in the bank.

Dick looked at me and sniffed. "Girls are like that," he said heavily.

"Only I didn't have a match," finished Evenly.

"Well, I have," said Dick, grinning.

And off he went to set fire to the leaves and twigs under the dead sparrow. It started to blaze at once with an orange flame. For a moment the glade shown with sunlight and fire; then the sunlight faded as the sun slipped under the horizon, and only the little fire burned there.

It was then that the first change came to the place in the woods. Suddenly out of the hush came a feeling of ineffable wildness; it was if trees, leaves, grass, even the water were springing to life against our intrusion. And at the same time we were conscious of this, we heard what was undeniably the sound of somebody blowing on a flute or something of that sort, making a kind of weird, piping music, followed the sound of something jumping up and down on the ground—an animal. And the limbs of the trees began to move as if a wind was in them.

I glanced at Dick. He, too, had heard.

I looked toward Evelyn. But she was standing transfixed, staring at the little grove of cedars just beyond the altar; her eyes were wide, and her lips were parted. On the instant she gave a wild cry of terror and ran back, right into Dick, knocking him in turn into me, and she went out of the place in the woods, screaming in fright.

Had she seen something? Had we? I thought there had been something in the cedars. I did not stop to look. Neither did Dick. Both of us ran pell-mell after Evelyn, and we did not stop until we were half way back to the farm, and all alone in a wide expanse of pasture which still seemed to glow a little from the declining day shining yet in an afterglow to the west, where the evening star and the new moon hung pale yellow.

"Well, what did you see?" I demanded.

"Didn't you see it?"

"Don't think so," I answered. "Did you, Dick?"

"How could I? With her carrying on like that."

"I saw him again. That man."

"I think there was something there," said Dick thoughtfully. "But if I can depend on my nose, it was an animal. It smelled like an animal—you know the kind of smell animals have. Strong."

Now that he had mentioned it, I too knew that I had smelled something. A musk. It might have been an animal. On the other hand, that sparrow's feathers were beginning to burn and it might have been that. I pointed this out.

"I saw a man," my sister said stubbornly. "He had a little beard."

"An old man?"

"I'm not sure."

"You said he had a beard."

"I know. But I don't think he was old.

"Dick looked at me and shrugged as much to say, "That's girls for you."

We talked for a while longer. We couldn't get anywhere. We decided at last that each of us had felt or seen something strange. We decided, too, that the burning sparrow had had something to do with it. And we agreed to go back there, just as soon as we could find something to sacrifice, something alive that we could kill without doing anybody any harm.

It was three days before our chance came.

That morning Tom came in while we were eating breakfast and said to grandmother that three chickens appeared to be sick, and ought to be killed. He had been watching them for two days now, and they weren't improving. Better to kill them than to let them infect the whole flock. Grandmother agreed and said simply, "Kill them, then."

The moment he left the kitchen, I was after him.

"Tom, we want one of those sick chickens," I said.

"Taint no good, Nick. It's gonna die."

"We want to kill it," I said.

"Bloodthirsty, ain't you? Why don't you take 'em all three?"

"We just need one."

He looked at me with a sideways glance. "What're you up to?"

I assured him we weren't up to anything, and keep on badgering he until he agreed that we might have one of the chickens. Without delay, I went with him—I suppose because I didn't entirely trust him—and got the chicken immediately, tying a string to one of its legs to make sure it wouldn't get away. I took the chicken away from the barnyard and tied it to an ash tree on the way to the pasture. Old Tom watched me with grave curiosity and frowning disapproval.

That evening, just as soon as supper was done, the three of us collected the chicken, which was all but dead, and set out across the pasture for the place of the pool. We were all wildly excited. The quick fear we had known before was already lost in the past, and we were anxious to try again. This time, we vowed, we would not break ranks and run, but would stand our ground to see what might be there. Somehow, we were convinced the chicken and the sacrifice were important.

It was a wonderful night, just like the other, except that there were a few dark, louring clouds in the west. From among them, now and then, the sunlight streaked through, over the fields and pastures, against the hills, showing rose and lavender. Already the pale moon showed in the sky, though the sun was still above the horizon.

The place in the woods was lighted by the setting sun; a haze of old rose bathed the tree-trunks and the place that Evelyn had called an altar. We had not been back there since the night we had burned the sparrow; now only ashes lay there, black where the grass had been burned away.

I carried the chicken and took it over to the altar.

The sunlight shown redly on its white feathers.

"Do we have to have a fire?" asked Evelyn.

We had not thought of that.

Dick said, "Not yet. We can kill it first. Then we can burn it."

That was agreed upon. Then it was a matter of how it should be killed.

My sister thought it ought to be stabbed to death. Girls always seem to be more bloodthirsty than boys. Dick was for more refinement than that, and so was I. The poor chicken was hardly able to sit erect; its head drooped, and you could see that it would probably not last till morning. It was a mercy to kill it.

"We'll slit its throat," said Dick.

He had brought his jack-knife, and now he took it out and opened it.

"I won't look," said Evelyn, staring right at the chicken to make sure she wouldn't miss a drop of blood.

I raised an objection. If we were making a sacrifice of the chicken, we ought to know to what we were sacrificing it. We couldn't sacrifice it to God, because chickens were not the kind of sacrifice to make to Him. We couldn't sacrifice it to an animal or a face, either, Dick pointed out.

"I know," said Evelyn. "We'll make the sacrifice to the place—the place of the woods and the pool."

To this we all agreed.

Dick took his place beside the chicken.

"Somebody ought to pray," he said.

"We will," said Evelyn.

She knelt down. Somewhat reluctantly, I followed her example.

My sister knew just what to say. "To you, woods' spirit, we offer up this chicken. We make this sacrifice to the oaks and the birches, to the beeches and the cedars, to the water of the brook and the pool, to the fish and sky and the birds and the animal we can hear, but cannot see, and the player of the music . . ."

So she had heard that music, too! I thought.

The last sunlight slipped away from the mound where the chicken lay just as Dick made a dramatic gesture and pulled up the chicken's head. With one sweep, he bent and slit its throat. The blood ran redly down the white feathers.

Suddenly, just as before, everything was changed.

The place in the woods which had always seemed a haven for us seemed suddenly charged with danger. It grew darker than the pasture beyond the woods, the hushing of the leaves sounded more loudly, and the limbs and branches began to thresh together as if a storm were brewing among them. The cedars began to tremble and I could hear that music again, a think, far-away piping, growing steadily more loud, coming closer. And I could hear the tapping of feet.

"He's coming," said Evelyn huskily. She reached for my hand and clung to me.

"Remember," said Dick in a trembling voice. "We don't move."

"We're waiting," I said with a stoutness I did not feel.

Then I knew it was bad to stay, I knew there was terrible danger. The wind was pulling at us, and Evelyn's face was white, and that music was wild, wilder than the wind, and a horrible face, a face that was both old and young, peered out of the cedars. With one accord, we broke away from the altar and ran.

But the very trees had turned against us. Now their branches swept down to make a kind of prison, barring our way. We flung ourselves upon them, screaming for help now, spurred by a terrible fear. Behind us came the sound of oncoming feet, like a deer's, almost overcoming us with dread. None of us dared turn to look.

At that moment old Tom burst into the place in the woods. He came fiercely in among the trees, swinging his arms, breaking the branches which barred us from the pasture and the farm buildings still held in the half-daylight, half-moonlight so near and yet so far. Gratefully we flowed around him, past him, and streaked across the pasture for the safety of the house, never pausing a moment, but running wildly for the house where our parents had just come for it was Friday night, and midsummer eve, the eve of their holiday, too.

"Indians!" said my father laconically.

"Oh, be quiet, children," said my Aunt Leonie. "I've such a headache.

But grandfather sensed at once that something was wrong.

"What's up?" he demanded. "What have you children been up to?"

Breathlessly, we told him, each of us, in snatches of words. And at last, we turned back the way we had come in and in one voice cried," Ask Tom!"

But Tom was not there.

Tom had not come with us.

Tom was nowhere in the house or the barn or the barnyard.

They set out at once for the place in the woods and would not let us come along. And when they came back and told us Tom wasn't coming back again, Tom was dead, he had had a heart attack, we could hardly believe it, and we went to bed subdued and contrite, sure somehow that we had brought about Tom's end, and cried to think of it because he had been kind for all his gruff ways, and he had saved us, we did not know from what, but we knew with the unerring instinct of children that he had saved us from something terrible beyond words.

And late that night, waking from sleep, I crept out and listened at the register to what they were saying below.

"Hoof-marks?" My mother was talking. "But there aren't any animals in that part of the woods. Never were. Or are you pasturing it now, Pa?"

"No." That was my grandfather's voice.

"They were there, all right," said my Uncle Sherwood. "All over."

"My God yes," said my father again. "Cut into his head and his hands and all around that chicken. How did that get there, anyway?"

"You could ask the children," said grandmother.

"Not one word to the children," said Aunt Leonie.

"There'll be an inquest, of course."

"But what kind of animal?"

"They were small hoof-marks, relatively. A sheep perhaps. Is there an old ram loose hereabouts?"

"No."

"Or a goat?"

"No."

"Well, a deer, then."

"Some wild animal, perhaps. A domesticated animal would hardly have killed. I don't see yet how it could have been done, unless, of course, he had really had a heart attack and it was done when he was down .."

That was twenty years ago. And the place in the woods left untouched, undisturbed, so that the brook could murmur through it, as always, and the hushing in the leaves keep on in the absence of the birds, and the mound of earth we had called an altar could catch the roseate light of every setting sun . . .

Until yesterday, when I came upon shocking news in the paper, news about the old Norris farm, still in the family, but being rented now, about a small boy who had been found mysteriously slain in the woods southeast of the farm buildings, with pointed hoof-marks all over his body—a story to jog memory sharply, but no longer the memory of a boy who could not know what he had seen or heard, who could not fully understand.

Perhaps, long ago, old Tom had understood, even if he could not put into words what he know by an intuition common to people close to the earth and the elements. We had no way of knowing.

Grandfather was gone, father gone too, Uncle Sherwood too old to care, Evelyn in Europe. I telephoned Dick, and he met me at once at the railroad station, to go down with me and see to it that the trees at the place of the pool were cut down, and the cedars uprooted, and the pool drained, knowing that there are places on the face of this earth where ancient things die hard, where old Gods linger long past their time, drawing unwitting homage to deities long since embalmed in textbooks, all but forgotten, names like Zeus, Bacchus, and Persephone—and Pan.

Of Kindred Spirits

The Early Years

> . . . A Darling Blessed daughter—Little Zona, to gladden our hearts and make our home O so bright with her glad voice and sweet smiles. Yes, we have a daughter, born on the 26th of August, 1874, and O how we love her, how good that God should send us such a treasure. How I praise Him for it and now may I teach her so to live that it shall be pleasing in His sight.

SO EARLY IN January, 1875, her mother wrote in her *Journal*—that intimate record of the inner life of Eliza Beers Gale, begun in her adolescence, at fourteen—and thereafter exhorted her Creator to assist her in bringing up this child as He would have her do: "possessed to pray for this," as she explained in later years to her daughter. Born in Portage, Zona went soon after with her parents to Delano, Minnesota, and later to St. Paul, before coming back to Portage to spend most of the rest of her life in the picturesque little village at the junction of the Fox and the Wisconsin Rivers, historical arteries of traffic.

She was a grave girl, not staid, but early manifesting that air of withdrawal so characteristic of her, that retreat from horror and violence which was marked in all her life and work and was outstanding in her own memory, for she wrote in 1938 of her early years, ". . . when I went to my first school treat, at nine, in the Portage, Wisconsin 'opera house', I fled at the first sound of applause, and stood outside paradise, with both hands at my throat, and could not return so long as the clapping hands and trampling feet kept on. Not even proffered lemon drops could tempt me. I went away from that place." How strong was her distaste for anything violent is exemplified by her noting in retrospect a single exception, commenting upon the explosion of the Washburn flour Mills near the Gale home in Minneapolis, "It appeared that thunderous detonations a few blocks away did not appall me—as did the heady noise of fireworks and near applause . . ,"

Still Small Voice, 1940

but this may very probably have been because the little girl she was then was that day entranced by having her hair in "frizzes."

In her childhood she began to live in a world of her own, in common with all children, whose consciousness of facet after facet of the physical world around them is a beautiful flowering of actuality becoming not entirely real until the years of maturity. In this she was like all other children; but in one aspect of her consciousness, she differed—at no time in her life did she ever relinquish completely the world of her own which had begun in her childhood; the children of her mind's world in those days became the mature men and women of that world in her later years, peopled her books and the way of her spirit down the long miles before her. "The moment when consciousness arose for me and became continuous was inevitably commonplace. It was on entering the large hall of a strange house in Minneapolis at four years of age, and with my parents. Many objects were on a table. That afternoon to an upstairs front room of the house, my father brought me a box of china birds, especially a duck, in a wooden box without a label, and with a small hole in a knothole of the cover, the whole smelling a little of glue. That afternoon also I had my first molasses candy." So she writes in beginning that autobiography which was never finished.

She gives in that small fragment of autobiography constant evidence of her mother's sense of rightness, of fitness, telling how one afternoon in company, she stole a shell, confident that the owner had not seen her abstract it, only to find her mother's eyes fixed immovably upon her, so that she immediately restored the shell to its shelf. "And then for days and days I heard from my mother of the sacredness of the rights of others. I do not recall her stressing that shell as property—only the fact that every one else had rights like mine." She reveals her great sensitivity and her sentiment, which it took her years to overcome sufficiently to accept some compromise between the world of her mind and hope and the world in which she lived. In every respect she was a normal, healthy child, though she was of such comparatively small proportions that she had the deceptive appearance of threatening to succumb to every illness, great and small, that came along. In her childhood she played with dolls, she played out the tragedy of Little Eva from *Uncle Tom's Cabin* (at the flogging scene of which she wept bitterly), she played "diptheria" after she and her father had had it—an attack which lent credence to the casual impression of her fragility, for it was years before she recovered her health.

If there is in her early years any indication of her later occupation with human misery and sadness, perhaps it lies in her liking for sad stories and poems, and particularly for the melancholy songs of her childhood, in which lay "a delicious heartbreak." *It was whispered one morning in heaven, that the little white angel May, sat ever beside the portal, sorrowing day by day* . . . for her mother left on earth: Mrs. Gale's favorite song in those years was one which never failed to plunge Zona into a deep, pleasurable anguish. She sang with tears about poor *Nelly Gray;* she undoubtedly grieved for *Alice Ben Bolt;* so that when her wise father said years later, "I believe you like to feel bad!" it was not inapropos. She was spellbound by the old ballads of *Robin Adair, The Nut Brown Mayd,* and others; she was mildly pleased with Mother Goose; she disdained utterly the Santa Claus myth, but professed at once and constantly a sneaking belief in fairies which became a part of the essential mysticism that was hers later in life, the mysticism that flashed through so much of her writing. And she held firmly to a faith in immortality, a faith which, if not confined to any orthodox doctrine, nevertheless held to a pattern all the more rigid and precise for having grown from her and with her. But she was indeed, as she writes, "most fortunately conditioned for the convictions" which she had chosen, the source material for deeper convictions supplied by her mother, whose religious beliefs never altered nor faltered, and who was writing in 1920 her last entry in that same *Journal,* for many years abandoned then, writing at a time not long before her death:

> Have had news of Susie's death. So they go. The end for me not far away. Am I afraid? No—for yet I believe the comforter with be with me. O I have tried so hard to be a good wife and mother. I know not if I have been successful, but I do know I love them both with an everlasting love and I know they will not forget me. Help us, Lord, to believe and trust thee, and in order to do that we must have faith to believe.

Still early in Zona's childhood, the Gale family returned to Portage to live there permanently, save for a short time in Milwaukee later on, when Zona was there at work. They settled in a brick cottage on Conant Street, a home blessed with trees and flowers, apple trees, Lombardy poplars, roses, fragrant four-o'clocks, portulacas, balsam. Here her grandmother, Harriet Taylor Beers, came to live with them, and delighted the child's young years with her persence, for she sang (sad songs and ballads to the child's liking), "airs still as present as the old odor of the climbing rose," wrote Zona almost sixty years later. From her Zona learned something of the futility of showing resentment, came to understand by example the dissonance of the will to wound, took from the aging invalid something of her great patience, something of her humor—all these aspects of the older woman permeating the older Zona, who could yet write of her grandmother Beers, "I do not know how to explain her. She must have been what was known as a child of God." From her grandmother, too, came her appreciation of the Bible, from her mother, of Shakespeare, in which Zona took especial delight because so many scenes and lines could be acted out: "Infirm of purpose! Give me the daggers!"—this one done on her way to bed. "That Knight Shakespeare, thin-leaved, in three volumes, bound in morocco and gold, gave me my first reverence for books. The illustrations are steel engravings—portraits of Booth and Keene as Iago and Juliet and Lady Macbeth. In the borders witches leer, there are Tybalt in his tomb, and Hamlet with his skull. These borders were my true fascinations, nearly equal to the burning child who had played with matches, in a gift book, planted forever in my find before it could be snatched away."

In these years Zona was kept from many things she would have liked to do, much playing to which her inclination led her but which her delicate health made difficult. While her mother seldom forbade her to do these things, she nevertheless watched Zona, and often called out, "Don't play too hard!" There was some danger. Edith Rogers, her playmate, used often to coax Zona to play strenuously, to dare her: "Come on, it won't hurt you!" But always something prevented accident; invariably Edith no sooner saw in Zona's willingness to dare her smallness and delicacy, than she would be overcome with fear that something might happen to her playmate, and stop coaxing her, beg her in turn to stop playing strenuously, afraid that Zona might break, so fragile were her arms and legs. There is a typical instance on the occasion that Edith and other girls were enjoying themselves on a large teeter-totter playing Candlestick, and Zona permitted herself to be coaxed to stand in the center as Candlestick, whereupon Edith was appalled at the smallness of her standing there, and flew to urge her down.

Because of the delicacy, this apparent fragility of bone, Zona constructed her own world and lived in it. She did this, made this escape in several ways, and she revealed some of them in her partly autobiographical book, *When I was a Little Girl*, published in 1910. A strong tendency toward mysticism was manifested early in her life, and she was able to invent the most prosaic occurrences with a simple, shining, magic. "When I was on the street with my hand in a grown-up hand," she wrote in *When I Was a Little Girl*,

> the night was invariably bounded by trees, fences, houses, horse-blocks, and the like. But when I stepped to the door alone at night, I always noticed that it stretched endlessly away. So it was now. I could slip out the screen as I had discovered earlier in the season when I had felt the need of feeding a nest of house-wrens in the bird-house below my sill—and I looked out the screen now, and leaned out in the darkness. The stars seemed very near—I am always glad that I did not know how far away they were, for they looked so friendly near. If only, I used to think, the clouds would form behind the stars and leave them all shiny and blurry bright in the rain. What were they? How came they to be in our world's sky?

Her parents, too, tended to interest her in books as if to compensate for her loss in active play.

> On my eighth birthday my father bought me a blue-bound *Paradise Lost* of my own. And that summer my mother read to me *Pilgrim's Progress;* I recall how furious and cheated I was at "And I awoke and behold, it was a dream!" . . . At night I went to sleep dramatizing myself as the whole Swiss Family Robinson . . . An adored friend, Edith Rogers, owned all the *Zig-Zag Journeys in Classic Lands* . . . the mother of another adored friend, Hattie Schenck, read aloud the immortal horror story of the *Gilded Boy;* and we "took" the *Youth's Companion* with which arrived the pens of all New England.

Her love for books grew, and presently Edith introduced her to something new in books; a novel by Ouida, which the two girls read together in Gale's shed until they had the misfortune to hind it under a tin pan in the yard on the approach of Mr. Gale, who subsequently came into the house and announced that he was having a bonfire, "burning up a lot of trash." This was the end of the Ouida, about which no word was spoken.

Always a dreamy child, who never danced, seldom played outside games, did not play the piano or sing, caring for little boys, she evolved almost from the beginning the world of her imagination, into which croquet, tea parties, and dolls seemed to fit very well. Mr. Rogers she told that there was a certain picket fence on the way to town, near the courthouse, which she passed daily and where she met all her friends, because she had named each picket after one of them and, going by, she touched each one lightly with a stick and so met her friends. She always played gravely, seriously. At the house on Conant Street she and Edith played dolls frequently; on one occasion, Zona wished to play dolls asleep at night. So the dolls were undressed, and the two girls lay down also. But Edith, who was chubby and extremely active—a typical little girl who wanted always to be about, doing things—grew restless, rising up to ask, "Morning?" "Oh, no," said Zona gently, "we have to play sleep all night." Edith lay down once more, but in a little while she was up again to ask once again. In this way the "night" was passed, and in later years, whenever Edith suggested doing things when Zona was clearly interested in something else, Zona would say quietly, smilingly, "Morning, Edie?" The two children made a great deal of Zona's sugar lamb, given to her by her father, playing with it, occasionally licking it, but treasuring it until Edith finally nibbled an ear, whereat Zona wept, but was consoled by her share of the candy. Once they fought, pulling their long braids and screaming, whereupon each was punished by being forbidden to see the other; in this they took almost as much delight as if the stricture had not been there at all, for both of them wrote notes to each other and left them in an oak tree, where each could watch for the other.

So close were the two girls that each one kept a toothbrush and a nightgown at the other's home for the nightlong visits which often took place. This friendship continued throughout childhood and school days, girlhood and womanhood.

They shared a dislike for mathematics and studied summers long for fear of failing. They went to see Birdie Wells, who had hurt her spine and lay an invalid for years, going each week on a certain day to visit her, to bring her something, to make her long hours less long, and occupation that was continued through Zona's later years with the same fidelity that characterized the child's intentness. In this period of her first school years, she writes that she learned about "what man can do to man," citing an experience in her first month at public school, when she asked a leading question of a girl who lisped. "That noon I inquired sorrowfully of my mother: 'What kind of people are there in this world? I asked Emma what she stood in Geography, and she told me "None of your buithneth."'"

School, she remember later, was her "first revolution." But something of the halcyon days before and after remained with her, the aspects of living that became for her later in life the portals through which, she came to believe, she might reach that *something more* in living, that indefinable essence of something beyond the immediate time, approached more closely in childhood than at any other time: the intimations of immortality from which she was never freed. She remembered beauty—"The west window of the dining-room from where one could watch the sunset, with implicit belief that beyond that rose and ochre lay heaven. . ..The glory of frost on the windowpanes: tropic leaves, jungle vines, stars, and caramels. . . . The dew on the cobwebs in the Bolting grass, and its long garden beyond the picket fence through which I used to reach for raspberries from Lily Bolting. . . . There was a great corn-field to the west, in which I once was lost. An engaging little door in a high board fence led to this field, and beyond was the home of Bird Wells—and often cookies." She remembered dreams of terror in childhood: ". . . bands of small people, with eyes immovably fixed on my face, bent their knees, pointed at me, jeered at me, and were horribly allied against me. . . . The agony of having gone to bed without caring for the canary, Dick." She remembered "the joy of the mornings when my mother painted. . . . She would raise her easel by the north window of the dining-room, and let me find the tubes in her color box; and I would rejoice in the rattle of the tubes, one against another and in the labels: *Rose Madder* (the best), *Yellow Ochre, Chrome Yellow, Cobalt. . . .*"

She apparently did not possess a great variety of toys, but she did not miss them, for her imagination made up for any lack. Long after her childhood was done, she wrote about the favorite pastimes of these early years.

> My most interesting possessions were an umbrella and a scarf. I sat under one and wrapped myself in the other, and was "lost in the deep woods," and talked with imaginary animals and birds, personated by my mother, who was lost with me. Or I went on long journeys, down short garden paths, or made rooms on the grass separated by walls of autumn leaves, or, if winter came, by rows of buttons—bright buttons for the "parlor," coat buttons for the kitchen. I put my doll in a basket with a string, and let her up and down low heights, and she was Eva in the last tableau, in heaven. I set my toys together in their cupboard and left them for the night—all touching, so that they could talk. No toy that I knew then gave me the thrill that my mother did when she looked into a blossoming apple tree above my swing and said: "I would pick you some, if I knew what ones would not be apples." I had the greatest entertainment in trying to find the blossoms which would never be apples.

From childhood on she was imbued with her mother's convictions, with her father's personality and attitudes. From her mother came religion, moral concepts, principles, but both her parents fed her growing mysticism. She heard about people from her mother, and especially about the Breeses—that family of "peculiar charm and gentle breeding, alien to any frontier," and in church spent her time covertly watching handsome Will, ten years her senior, already at eleven caught by his gentleness, his breeding, a kind of old-world courtliness which he never lost. She was not alone in watching him. "We all did. 'Will Breese is going to sing in the choir,' we would whisper to one another, and listen to his rich young baritone. 'Will Breese is home from college,' we would announce. I remember a doorway in that church where I once met him, and was transfixed by that tall presence." At eleven she fixed upon him, at that early age she looked to him as the man who must some day be her own: no more at first than a childhood fixation, perhaps, but one that strengthened, grew, matured. In that year one winter day she stood near a canal toboggan slide, earnestly hoping to go down, but knowing it was forbidden by parents safeguarding her health. Coming from his father's lumber-yard, Will Breese saw and understood that lonely figure; he came over and asked whether she would like to go down on the toboggan with him. Instantly all prohibitions were forgotten, and she delighted in his company. From that moment she was devoted to him. "By the time I was fourteen I used to state openly, to a limited circle, that I was going to marry Will Breese. . . . That lifelong glamour has never failed me."

No glamour ever failed her.

Her dreamy childhood was succeeded by a dreamy girlhood. It was natural that Zona should seek to transfer the world of her mind to some tangible form in words. At six years, Zona wrote her first poem, which her mother faithfully recorded in the *Journal*:

When I am a lady, a lady,
I'll be a Milliner if I can;
I will make pretty bonnets and hats,
And in my store will be no mice and rats,
When I am a lady.

Soon she wrote many poems, improving her lines slowly. Seven years later she celebrated her Grandmother Beers' seventy-second birthday by writing a six-stanza poem which began,

Just seventy-two years ago today
In an English town that's far away,
In the sweet fresh blush of early morn
A little baby girl was born . . .

And ended,

Grandma now she's called by all—
By Zona, Willie and Daisy small,
And she will always always be
The dearest Grandma in the world to me.

Between the poems, she wrote her first story, which she made up into a handsome little book bound together with amber satin ribbon, its title penciled and boxed with a representation of a sunset on the cover: *The Three Travelers,* by *Z. B. G.*—the *B* to stand for *Bell,* the name Zona chose to compensate her for the lack of the middle name possessed by all her friends. The story was simple, eloquent, and had the additional merit of brevity:

The sun was just sinking below the western horizon when three travelers appeared, walking fast, very fast indeed. One was tall with a beard, one was short with a moustache, and one was middle-sized with a bare face. Suddenly appeared a beautiful maiden. They asked, "Where are you going?" She replied, "I am lost." The tall man loved her right away. So did the short man. But the middle-sized man said, "Will you marry me?" She said, "N—yes." So they were married and lived happily ever afterward.

Of this story she wrote in that autobiographical fragment:

These observable factors of the tale rather touch me: Nightfall—the immemorial time of racial terror. The three travelers belated in the open, about to be overtaken by darkness—the immemorial predicament from which all men shrink. Typal contrast in three heros. The advent of the heroine a bit delayed, as in any real drama. And what! She lost, too: Then events click rapidly: Love, rivalry, surprise, that maidenly hesitation, consummation. There was the old tried formula arising in a state of innocence, as if it were indeed a fundamental of occurrence, and the way in which the world is patterned. Nothing written since by the same author is so tightly knit and so highly formulized. And oh, that glow of achievement, that dream of writing like that all one's life. . . .

In her early attempts, she had the constant encouragement of her mother. But she needed more than this, and she took delight in hearing about the writing visitors at the Rogers' home: George Kennan, whose books on Russia reveal something more than the glitter of the Romanov courts; Ella Wheeler Wilcox, whom she was allowed to go to see because by that time, at eight, she had announced that she intended to enter the writing profession. Ella Wilcox patted her face, called her "Sweetheart," strengthened Zona's determination that nothing must prevent her from becoming a writer "and wearing pink satin and swan's down." She was emboldened to do what later she would never have done, reminding her some years later of that evening so strong and clear still in her memory, and sending her a story ("my only such offense, I swear"), in reply to which Ella Wheeler Wilcox sent her two scrawled and underlined sentences which became for Zona "a second pulse": *"You have talent. Keep on writing."*

She developed a sense for words which was heightened in her mature years. She would go about repeating lines she had read: *I took, oh was it stealing, the bread to give to them . . . I am dying, Egypt, dying, Ebbs the crimson life-blood fast . . .* all with a feeling for the words she quoted rather than for their meaning. In those days, "the creature at the bar of justice, the lost Leonore, the pallid bust, and the prairie fire," held for Zona the secret of effective writing because they could communicate mood, stir emotion, change her world; they entered into her primarily as word-beauty, secondarily as remote, inaccessible individuals in an alien place, as people, as beings against isolated settings. She writes about her devotion to one particular phrase, deriving from the new dark damask curtains her mother had hung in the parlor, which Zona loved to dust—a room with a what-not, a walnut table, a piano—dusting and whispering, *The parlors of hope. The parlors of hope.* "The words made me feel grand, and very happy."

Her mind's growing country began early to express itself in a singular reality of her imagination, a vividness which matured in her later writing. Her assumption that the walls of her home were inhabited by *Theys* is an instance of her strange half-real fantasy. She has chose in her autobiographical fragment to pass this fancy off as a desire to show off, but neither child nor adult shows off when no one is present to see; so that this imagination of hers must be considered as evidence of what it really was—the emergency of her dream world to a point of contact with her physical world. "These *Theys* sat along tidily behind the wall paper, through which they could look out with ease. And they watched me. Affably enough. Always with approbation. . . . I must dust *well* so that the *Theys* would like it. I must order my books and playthings, lay the dining-room table nicely, and be polite..The *Theys* and I understood one another well. I visualized them; their picture is in my mind today. I should know them if I saw them anywhere—lean, dark-haired, slightly smiling, and with most evident eyes." And so, too, the manifestation she has called *animism*: the fancy that her dishes, her playthings must be settled for the night in a way to make conversation among them congenial and easy, that her clothing should be hung so as to avoid any clash of color or personality. These things she confided to her mother, and her mother played at them with her. "The most practical person whom I have ever known, brilliant in her common sense, she was also one of the most imaginative and playful. Who but she would sit with me by the hour, under an opened umbrella, protected by shawls, and surrounded by a family of dolls, and we playing 'Lost' . . . ?"

Her fancy endowed flowers, trees, insects with a kind of mystic existence, so that all her life she found herself unable to destroy any bud or flower, she could not step on an ant or kill an insect, even to the extent of willingly suffering flies if she could not shoo them out of the room by the open windows, through which as many more flies came as fast as she maneuvered the unwelcome occupants into the open. Because she was alone so much, she indulged more and more in such games as a lonely child might play. She would dress herself up, call on her mother, and announce herself some imaginary name, and play out the little farce to its end. She played "Lost," "House," and all those toyless games of which she wrote later. Playmates, in those early years, invariable excited her, unless it were the adored Edith, who was to her what a sister might have been.

If she missed the wilder games of children, there is little evidence of it. She does write that she was anguished because, owing to a fall which had injured the base of her spine, she could not skate on the canal. When later on she did try to skate, both on ice and on rollers, she found herself strangely unable to maintain her balance. She did not dance. Because of her dreamy aloofness, she was not popular with boys; but she did not mind that. She was indifferent to them. On one occasion when Edith Rogers particularly wanted to go to a dance, she persuaded her own escort to take them both, which he did with some reluctance. And on that occasion, Zona danced, not well, but she did take small part. The boys were polite to her, but not enthusiastic. She did not go again, taking her pleasure in hearing about dances from Edith and others. She did not swim; she did not even wade; she carried lifelong antipathy to bodies of water, large or small, though she confessed to a liking for sailboats, and admits that she "could live permanently, or nearly so, on the *Empress of Japan* or the *Lurline* or the *Chichibu Maru*." She did not ride, and she felt this deprivation, which was rather of expense than of health.

Despite her loneliness which she peopled with the characters of her fancy, she was often possessed with a desire to have parties. The relatives who visited the Gale home in Portage caught her fancy, and when her Uncle Alec had his back "cupped" before Zona's eyes, this act seeded in her a distaste for the sick-room, which she avoided all her life. Just as she avoided sickness and pain, she avoided gruesome sights. She did once see two of her relatives skinning a rabbit. "It is a singular thing that down my years, that is the only nauseating sight I have ever seen. I still keep well away when there is a dead chicken in the kitchen." Such was her sensitivity at that early age, and her explaining a simple case of childhood jealousy on the occasion of her hoping her favorite aunt and uncles's new and only baby would die, as evidence of her savagery, does not hold water. She was not savage; she could not have been. The fragility of her body was symbolic of the gentleness of her spirit, of her inner sensitivity, just as the tangible imaginations so often manifested in her childhood afforded a key to that great and beautiful country of the mind which grew so surely to mature in her novels, her stories, her poems and essays.

She was aware all through her childhood of something more and already then she strove dimly, almost unconsciously for it, reaching out to life for the deep mystic experience of what lay beyond the material aspects of that life.

One summer afternoon in her fourteenth year she walked along a street in Portage, looking at the sky, at the light blue sky of summer, filled now with moving clouds, rising from the west and passing rapidly overhead to diminish in the east. She wondered what lay above the sky, beyond the singular cobalt blue, and then suddenly, in the midst of her wondering, realized that there was no sky, there was nothing but distance and somewhere stars: an extension of consciousness, a brief, bright flickering of a sense of infinity, something beyond any sensation she had known before, a moving experience she never forgot. And again, not long after, when she sat on a veranda overlooking the beautiful, slowly-flowing Wisconsin in the cool of a summer evening, she thought of the human face, so small, so inevitable featured, multiple on the earth, ageless on the earth in time past, time still to come, and every face differing from every other; the realization of infinite numbers and their great differences took possession of her, took her outside her self, gave her again that amazing sense of more consciousness—a brief flashing of something more: a mystic experience which was to happen to her again and again, not too often, but enough to spur her ceaseless reaching out to life for new evidence that life is something more than we believe it to be.

And already she was shaping words and sentences toward her inevitable future, all bent in that same great striving, never for one moment forgotten or overlooked: the ceaseless, restless striving of a woman alone, a still small voice against the materialism and blind selfishness of a world she looked upon from the security of her mind's broad, beautiful country.

from Hungarian Count

NOT ALL THE pioneer settlers of the Wisconsin River country were practical men.

Count Agostin Haraszthy had his practical side, but the side of his personality which he nourished was that of the passionate dreamer. When, on a summer day near the middle of July, 1840, the count mounted the moraine ridge east of Sauk Prairie, looked down upon his future home, and shouted, "Eureka! Eureka! Italia!" he already had a distinguished career behind him—a career as a liberal in Hungary which was under the iron rule of Prince Metternich. Born in 1810 in the Comitat of Bacs-Bodrog on the east bank of the Danube, Count Haraszthy was at this time thirty years old. At twenty-two he had made his first trip to America. Already at that age he had taken up the cause of the downtrodden, incurred the anger of the aristocrats, and had found it prudent to take a vacation in America. If he returned to Hungary chastened, he gave no evidence of it' by the end of the decade of the 1830's, he was in trouble again, and it was freely rumored that Prince Metternich admired his leonine head, and would particularly like to see it parted from the rest of him.

This was naturally not a wish that Count Haraszthy could willingly gratify. He took off for the second time when it was apparent that it was either

---

The Wisconsin: River of a Thousand Isles, 1942

his head or his reformation Metternich wanted; since Haraszthy would concede him neither, he found it expedient to look once again to America. But he had no illusions; he knew that Europe was ailing of more woes than he or a hundred like him could cure; he knew he would henceforth look upon America as his home. He had learned of the Sauk Prairie from the account of Captain Marryat; so it was directly to that place that he came in the summer of 1840.

Sauk Prairie was ready for him. It was at that time an incipient settlement little more than two years of age. Early in the spring of 1838, Berry Haney, a stage driver on the Military Road, "received private information from George W. Jones, who was then delegate in congress from Wisconsin Territory, that the treaty with the Winnebago Indians, for their lands north of the Wisconsin River, was ratified." So wrote Charles O. Baxter in recounting his memories of early Sauk City to William H. Canfield many years later. "On learning of the ratification of the treaty, Haney sent Jonathan Taylor to the Wisconsin River, opposite Sauk Prairie, there to await the coming of Solomon Shore, also in his employ, who went with Haney to Fort Winnebago to purchase a skiff to take down the river to Sauk Prairie, in order to get across. They met at that point according to previous arrangement, crossed and proceeded to mark out their claims. The first one marked out by them was for Berry Haney, on what is now Sauk City. Taylor claimed the next above Haney, and Shore the next. Haney, I believe, had the first land broke in Sauk County. In June, 1838, he employed James Ensminger and Thomas Sanser to break ten acres, for which he paid them one hundred dollars. The first place in the shape of a dwelling on Sauk Prairie was built by Ensminger and Sanser. They dug a pit in the ground about four feet deep, twelve by sixteen or eighteen feet square, logged it up and covered the hole with hay and earth, making a sort of root-house. This they did for the purpose of preventing the Indians from burning them out." Thus began Sauk City, and in January of 1839 came the first family in Sauk Country, that of James S. Alban, to settle on the upper prairie and become the first settlers of Sauk City's twin village, Prairie du Sac.

If Sauk City is today typical of the agricultural communities that spring up along the Wisconsin from the mouth to the portage, it was not always so, though it was land that brought its founders and those who came after. Count Haraszthy was the most colorful of the men who came in the village's first decade. When he rode up over the ridge along the east shore of the Wisconsin, and looked down to the valley below, he saw not only that it was a country that reminded him of northern Italy, but also that it was the ideal setting for a town. Forthwith he bought up as much land as he could and employed a courtly Virginian, Charles Baxter, to survey all the land along the river and plat a village to be called Haraszthy, though its name was soon changed to Westfield, and then to Sauk City—in memory of the Sauk who had first occupied the prairie. Characteristically, once the plat was made, the count was in no haste to record it, and it was not until April 26, 1845, "at half past 12 P.M.," that the plat was recorded, bearing this information: "Proprietors' Names: Charles Haraszthy, Robert Bryant, by Charles Haraszthy, agent; Stephen Bates, by Agostin Haraszthy, agent." Charles was Agostin's father; Agostin had returned to Europe in the spring of 1842 and in summer of that year had brought back with him his wife, Eleanora de Dodinsky, their sons Gaza, Attila, and Arpad, and his parents. Robert Bryant was an Englishman of means whom Haraszthy encountered in Milwaukee and induced by his eloquence to become his partner in the proposed town.

The name Haraszthy was soon known far and wide. Frankly, there was no enterprise worthy of attention into which Agostin did not put a finger—and very often capital to a ruinous extent. Throughout that first year, apart from enlisting the interest and capital of Robert Bryant and the surveying services of Charlie Baxter, the count indulged to the full of his desire to hunt and fish. Haraszthy was a commanding figure, as the legends that were to follow his passing from the prairie testify. The only contemporary description of him in his first year on the site of the village he founded was put down by an itinerant preacher, the Reverend T. M. Fullerton, who, under the date of June 23, 1841, wrote in his journal: "There is here an Hungarian Count—so he calls himself—who claims to have quantities of money and is spending it liberally on improvement. There is also an Englishman here (Bryant) who claims to have been a Lord in the old country. He is partnership with the count. They both look like savages, wearing a long beard above as well as below the mouth. And they are the great men of the place, and other adopt their customs, and make themselves as ridiculous as possible."

For all Mr. Fullerton's belief that the count looked like a savage, Haraszthy was precisely the kind of man who would engender legend. He was six feet tall and very dark, with eyes that were as black as his hair. He invariably wore a stovepipe hat and, when on foot, carried a cane. However, he liked best to ride his horse, and as a hunter he was entirely picturesque, wearing a green silk hunting shirt and a wide sash of a crimson color, a garb which did not prevent him from walking or riding through brush and bramble, completely disdainful of damage to his manifestly expensive dress. Decades later, Saterlee Clark said of him: "He was a nobleman in every sense, and he and his wife were among the most refined people I ever knew; and both were exceedingly good looking. I saw them both frequently, both at home and at Madison."

If the count had been comparatively idle until his family reached the prairie, he was so active after that that even today it is impossible to say when he ended one venture and began another. The story is that his ventures were made possible largely through his father's money. Charles Haraszthy, however, was a character in his own right, quickly and lastingly winning the esteem of the settlers who called him either the Old General or the Old Count; he was interested in natural science and contributed his share to the Haraszthy ventures by opening soon after his arrival an apothecary shop, which he conducted until late in 1848, then the Haraszthys left for the West. He worshiped what he himself lacked and what was so manifest in his son: the intrepid daring.

Agostin began by opening a ferry across the Wisconsin River; the date was October 14, 1842, and the earliest record of it appears in a deed of conveyance from Bryant. There had been two ferries established previously—one by Berry Haney and H. F. Crossman, in August, 1839, a second by James S. Alban, in October of that year. But Haney had sold out his interests to Haraszthy and left the prairie; Alban's ferry was presumably still running on the upper prairie. The count operated the ferry for many years, but this was perhaps the least of his enterprises. In that same month, Haraszthy and Bryant opened a brickyard, Bryant filing a mortgage covering all the brick in the yard, "seventeen cows, two yokes of oxen, a span of horses, sofa, and peanna." Shortly after he constructed the first Haraszthy residence; but this was hardly completed before he was about the construction of a second. Sometime in 1842 or 1843, Haraszthy began a retail merchandising store, erecting his own building in which to accommodate it. As if this were not enough, he began a second store in Baraboo, just over the northern rim of the Sauk Prairie, putting up to house the business the first frame structure to be erected in the valley of the Baraboo River near its confluence with the Wisconsin.

Meanwhile, settlers began to flow to the townsite, and Haraszthy did a lively business selling property. A census taken in June, 1842, listed 393 "free inhabitants" for Sauk County, and Sheriff Bird's census included names which were destined to loom large in the history of Wisconsin—Prescott Brigham, Nathan Kellogg, Cyrus Leland, Thomas Kelsey, Abraham Wood; the Haraszthy name did not occur because the count was at the time in Europe arranging to bring his family over. Despite the time the affairs of his commercial enterprises must have taken, Haraszthy managed to indulge in agricultural experiments. The prairie called to him—alluvial soil, most of it within his ownership, and such as was not was owned by no one;

so that he could use it as if it were his own. He began to raise grains; he experimented in growing swine; he raised sheep. He rode up to Fort Winnebago and made a contract to supply the fort with corn; on this memorable occasion, he put in the corn and left it to grow. Unfortunately, that season was a good one for hunting, and Haraszthy had to hunt. When he thought of the corn again, it was long past time for delivery, and also very late in the fall. Nothing daunted, the count summoned his neighbors and friends to a husking, arranged for flatboat transportation, and husked wagonfuls of corn en route to the river, where the corn was loaded into the flatboat and taken up to Fort Winnebago.

Nor did he forget his village. Among the transfers of property in the first volume of Sauk County records, is evidence that ground was set aside for a schoolhouse, and two lots were deeded to the Right Reverend John Martin Henni, Bishop of Milwaukee, for the establishment of the first Catholic church in the county. Moreover, Haraszthy agitated for a permanent parish priest, and not an itinerant. By 1845, the priest had come—Father Adelbert Inama of the Tyrol; on December 12th in that year he wrote to his superior enough to justify Haraszthy's extravagant praise of the country.

". . . by comparison, the climate here in the West is more moderate than in the East, and the seasons run their course more regularly. Since my coming on the twenty-fifth of last month, I made use of the fine weather to ramble through the surrounding country in all directions. I certainly maintain at present that few localities can outdo the environs of Sauk Prairie in fertility, variety, romantic beauty, and healthfulness of climate. Wood, water, freestone, clay, lime and sand—in fact, everything requisite for building—is found here in great plenty. Rich silver-bearing copper mines have been discovered this year only a few miles west of here, and the opening of the mines has already begun; for several years copper and lead mines have been operating twenty-five miles south, stretching out southward through Illinois, Iowa, and Missouri. However, the richest silver and copper mines are near the Menominee River, north of this territory, and were detected first in the vicinity of Lake Superior. About here mineral land is at the same time the most productive soil; thus rich metallic veins run below the most fertile of top-soils.

"At this time I will add a bit about the locality where, if God wills, I contemplate building in the beginning of the year, with the assistance of the parish, my provisional hermitage and chapel. At this point the Wisconsin River, not one-half mile wide, incloses numerous thickly wooded islands, flows majestically and peacefully between scarped banks very like sculpture, which are covered to the water's edge with grass and overgrown with bushes. The hills upon which the chapel will be built, rise precipitously one hundred and ten feet from the river lowland. The side toward the river, a regular triangle, is covered with grass, and the other side with oak trees. Back from the river six or seven miles the land becomes level and has pools where from two mill streams rise. Nearly regular hills from a hundred to two hundred feet rise from this plain, wholly grass-covered or stocked with oaks and birch, . . . from which one enjoys a perspective which can vie with the Rigi. So is the land on the east. The extensive Sauk Prairie stretches to the west, with a semicircular ridge in the distant background, where the mineral region commences. This, the land of my future residence and sphere of activity, for which I ask your blessing, and commend myself to the ever pious remembrances and prayers of my fellow religious and countrymen."

Beside a brook in a low valley among the moraine hills east of Sauk Prairie the Reverend Adelbert Inama erected a chapel, from which he sallied forth to serve several congregations, and subsequently he brought about the building of a church at the hamlet of Roxbury which came into being three miles east of the Sauk Prairie on the road to Madison—the site of Floyd's Folly, an eastern speculator, Charles Floyd, having bought up much of the land for the purpose of speculation and the establishment of Superior City. Like many others, Superior City never grew beyond the paper stage, but ultimately Roxbury sprang up on the abandoned site, and there in 1939 a tablet was unveiled to the memory of the tireless priest who followed the steps of Mazzuchelli.

Finally, Haraszthy invested in a steamboat, the packet *Rock River*, which undertook regular express and passenger service from Sauk City to Prairie du Chien, and north to Fort Winnebago, and even traveled on the Upper Mississippi, between Galena and Fort Snelling. But this venture was short-lived; the *Rock River* was frozen in one winter day at Prairie du Chien, and the ship was abandoned with the casual, almost heroic insouciance with which the firm of Haraszthy and Bryant abandoned any enterprise which seemed no longer profitable. In addition to all this, Haraszthy found time to write in Hungarian a two-volume account of his experience in America; the book was published in Budapest in 1844.

Beyond question, Count Agostin Haraszthy left his mark on the prairie. But destiny did not mean for him to succeed in the town he had founded. One by one his ventures failed, and it developed that he had put comparatively little of his own capital into many of those ventures; the stores failed, the ferry's operation was undertaken by John C. Hawley of near-by Mazomanie for Robert Richards; the brickyard no longer paid for itself; and even his agricultural experiments failed, by no fault of his own, as the incident of his sheep-raising failure illustrates. He had as many as two thousand head of sheep when he engaged to tend them Edmund Juessen, a young Swiss who was destined to become one of early Chicago's leading lawyers; entirely by accident, young Juessen fired the prairie grass, which resulted in the death of almost a fourth of Haraszthy's sheep—an accident that so frightened young Juessen that he ran away and hid among the Baraboo bluffs until the following day, when he was convinced that Haraszthy would not have the loss out of his hide.

Yet it was not the failure of any one of these enterprises which ultimately drove Haraszthy from the prairie; it was the sterility of his dream. For Haraszthy had a dream of great vineyards in America, and he thought that Sauk Prairie would ultimately be host to them. Unfortunately, something was lacking; the grapes did not do well enough to justify his dream; so late in 1848 the Haraszthys—without Agostin's mother, who had died of nostalgia soon after reaching the new home along the Wisconsin—pulled stakes and set out for California. where the count managed to fulfill his dream to such an extent that a little more than a decade later he was selected by President Lincoln to proceed to Europe for the express purposed of obtaining hundreds of grape cuttings, and ultimately found himself put down by the historian, Bancroft, as the father of viticulture in the United States.

He left behind him a flourishing village, whose leading spirits were the men who had come with him or shortly thereafter—most of them the forty-eighters, refugees from the German countries in a turmoil of riot and revolt against oppression, a village which could harbor a group of men who could work together for the best interests of their community despite the variety of their interests. . . .